AUTHORITY AND MEANING IN INDIAN RELIGIONS

Can a text be used either to validate or to invalidate contemporary understandings?
Texts may be deemed 'sacred', but sacred to whom?
Do conflicting understandings matter?
Is it appropriate to try to offer a resolution?

For Hindus and non-Hindus, in India and beyond, Valmiki is the poet-saint who composed the epic *Rāmāyaṇa*. Yet for a vocal community of *dalit*s (once called 'untouchables'), within and outside India, Valmiki is God. How then does one explain the popular story that he started out as an ignorant and violent bandit, attacking and killing travellers for material gain? And what happens when these two accounts, Valmiki as God and Valmiki as villain, are held simultaneously by two different religious groups, both contemporary and both vocal? This situation came to a head with controversial demonstrations by the Valmiki community in Britain in 2000, giving rise to some searching questions which Julia Leslie now seeks to address.

Exploring the relationship between sacred text and religious meaning, Leslie presents a critical, text-historical study of the figure of Valmiki drawing on the sacred texts traditionally attributed to him: the *Vālmīki Rāmāyaṇa* and the *Yogavāsiṣṭha Rāmāyaṇa*, both in Sanskrit. While identifying and examining the various strands of popular stories concerning Valmiki, Leslie disentangles the earliest evidence for him from the narrative threads of passing centuries, and considers the implications of that process.

This ground-breaking analysis, illustrated with paintings of Valmiki, makes a unique contribution to our understanding of the interlocking beliefs of many religious communities, and also provides a greater awareness of the problematic relationship between sacred text and contemporary religious meaning. Invaluable to students of both the study of religions and South Asian studies, this book will also be of interest to Indian communities in the diaspora seeking to understand their roots, including (but not exclusively) the Valmikis.

This book is dedicated to all my students
for asking such good questions

Authority and Meaning in Indian Religions

Hinduism and the Case of Vālmīki

JULIA LESLIE

ASHGATE

Published by
Ashgate Publishing Limited
Gower House
Croft Road
Aldershot
Hants GUl 1 3HR
England

Ashgate Publishing Company
Suite 420
101 Cherry Street
Burlington VT 05401-4405
USA

Ashgate website: http://www.ashgate.com

British Library Cataloguing in Publication Data
Leslie, Julia
Authority and meaning in Indian religions : Hinduism and the case of Valmiki
1. Valmiki 2. Hindu sects 3. Authority – Religious aspects – Hinduism 4. Meaning (Philosophy) – Religious aspects – Hinduism 5. Hinduism – Great Britain
I. Title
294.5'213

Library of Congress Cataloging-in-Publication Data
Leslie, Julia.
Authority and meaning in Indian religions: Hinduism and the case of Valmiki / Julia Leslie.
p. cm.
Includes bibliographical references and index.
ISBN 0-7546-3430-2 – ISBN 0-7546-3431-0 (pbk.)
1. Valmiki. I. Title.

BL1175.V35 A77 2003
294.5'922046–dc21

2002034537

ISBN 0 7546 3431 0 (Pbk)
ISBN 0 7546 3430 2 (Hbk)

Typeset in Times New Roman by Bookcraft Ltd, Stroud, Gloucestershire
Printed and bound in Great Britain by MPG Books Ltd, Bodmin, Cornwall

Contents

List of Illustrations

Frontispiece

Bhagwan Valmik holding the universe
Painting by Kiran Valmiki, reproduced by permission of the Bhagwan Valmik Mandir, Muswell Road, Bedford. Photograph by Julia Leslie, image preparation by Dixie.

Plates

1.1 *The dacoit legend*
From Anant Pai, ed., *Valmiki: the story of the author of the epic, 'Ramayana'*, 1994, pp. 2, 3a, 4a, reprinted by permission from the Amar Chitra Katha title No. 579 'Valmiki' © India Book House Pvt. Ltd.

1.2 *Guru Valmik meditating in the forest*
Painting by Kiran Valmiki, reproduced by permission of the Bhagwan Valmik Mandir, Featherstone Road, Southall. Photograph by Julia Leslie, image preparation by Dixie.

1.3 *Guru Valmik inside the termite mound*
Painting by Kiran Valmiki, reproduced by permission of the Bhagwan Valmik Mandir, Featherstone Road, Southall. Photograph by Julia Leslie, image preparation by Dixie.

1.4 *The killing of the crane*
British Library manuscript of the *Bālakāṇḍa*, ADD.15295, recto 5, reproduced by permission of the British Library.

1.5 *The birth of the śloka*
British Library manuscript of the *Bālakāṇḍa*, ADD.15295, recto 6, reproduced by permission of the British Library.

2.1 *Portrait of Sahib Sri Sri 108 Sat Guru Gian Nath Ji Maharaj*
Painting by Kiran Valmiki, reproduced by permission of the Jagat Guru Valmik Ji Maharaj Mandir Gian Ashram UK, Booth Street, Birmingham. Photograph by Julia Leslie, image preparation by Dixie.

2.2 *Guru Valmik, the amrit, and Amritsar*
Print signed 'Lubhaya', reproduced by permission of the Bhagwan Valmik Temple, Wolverhampton. Photograph by Julia Leslie, image preparation by Dixie.

2.3 *Jiwan Singh carrying the head of Guru Tegh Bahadur*
Reproduced by permission of the Jagat Guru Valmik Ji Maharaj Temple, Coventry. Photograph by Julia Leslie, image preparation by Dixie.

2.4 *Image of Bhagwan Valmik in the prayer hall in Southall*
Reproduced by permission of the Bhagwan Valmik Mandir, Featherstone Road, Southall. Photograph by Julia Leslie, image preparation by Dixie.

3.1 *Rāma beheads Śambūka*
British Library manuscript of the *Uttarakāṇḍa*, ADD.15297, recto 92. Reproduced by permission of the British Library.

5.1 *Guru Valmik as a baby*
Painting by Kiran Valmiki, reproduced by permission of the Bhagwan Valmiki Ashram, Icknield Street, Birmingham. Photograph by Julia Leslie, image preparation by Dixie.

5.2 *Full-length portrait of Guru Valmik*
Painting by Kiran Valmiki, reproduced by permission of the Bhagwan Valmik Mandir, Muswell Road, Bedford. Photograph by Julia Leslie, image preparation by Dixie.

5.3 *Guru Valmik watches Vasiṣṭha teaching Rāma*
Painting by Kiran Valmiki, reproduced by permission of the Bhagwan Valmik Mandir, Muswell Road, Bedford. Photograph by Julia Leslie, image preparation by Dixie.

5.4 *Bhagwan Valmik, the power behind the gods*
Reproduced by permission of the Bhagwan Valmiki Ashram, Icknield Street, Birmingham. Photograph by Julia Leslie, image preparation by Dixie.

Acknowledgements

This book would never have been completed without the interest, enthusiasm and assistance of many different people, all of whom deserve my thanks. Lekh Raj Manjdadria first brought the Birmingham dispute to my attention by asking me to comment on the issues involved. Raina Haig listened to my musings and spotted the potential for a monograph. Apratim Barua served as a cheerful and indefatigable research assistant, locating publications, checking references and photocopying vital material for my use. The Department of the Study of Religions supported my application for research leave, while the School of Oriental and African Studies provided the much-needed funding for replacement teaching so that the project could be completed. And my research students gave me as much space as possible to do my own thing.

Several students and colleagues heard my first presentation on the topic at the Department of the Study of Religions Postgraduate Seminar in late 2000. I am grateful to the following for their responses at what proved to be a critical moment: Apratim Barua, Brian Bocking, Nile Green, Sîan Hawthorne, Shanti Hettiarachchi, Anastasia Karaflogka, Susan Prill, Vena Ramphal, David Tharp and Paul-François Tremlett. Those who kept my interest alive by answering specific queries, suggesting references and serving as sounding boards in their respective areas of interest and expertise include Tim Barrett, Jangam Chinnaiah, Florine Clomegah, Kate Crosby, Peter Flügel, Sean Gaffney, Paul Gifford, Phyllis Granoff, Alexandra Haendel, George Hart, Jerry Losty, Alexander McKay, Asko Parpola, William Radice, Christopher Shackle, Rupert Snell and Richard Widdess.

I owe a particular debt of gratitude to the scholars who shared their own work with me: John Brockington on the Sanskrit epics, Hans Bakker on the *Skanda Purāṇa*, Vidyut Aklujkar on the *Ānanda Rāmāyaṇa* and Walter Slaje on the *Mokṣopāya*; Philip Lutgendorf on Hindi Rāmāyaṇas and William L. Smith on Bengali ones; Sanal P. Mohan, David Mosse and Cosimo Zene on *dalit* communities in South Asia; Eleanor Nesbitt on the Valmikis in Britain; and William Southworth on the culture of Campā.

Very special thanks go to all those who took the time to read an early draft of the book and to send me their comments: Greg Bailey, Apratim Barua, Brian Bocking, John Brockington, Simon Brodbeck, Wendy Doniger, Gavin Flood, Sukhbinder Gill, Nile Green, Jaswinder Kalyan, Lekh Raj Manjdadria, Sanal P. Mohan, Eleanor Nesbitt, Manjula Sahdev, Paul-François Tremlett and Dominik Wujastyk.

Thanks of a different kind must go to the members of the Valmiki community in Britain. Individually and collectively, they welcomed me into their temples, showed me round, talked to me, listened to me, answered my questions, allowed me to take photographs, and even fed me. I should like to take this opportunity to offer my sincere and heartfelt thanks to everyone involved. I am especially grateful to Lekh Raj Manjdadria, Jaswinder Kalyan, Sukhbinder Gill and Joginder Gill (Nahli) for their invaluable assistance.

I am also deeply grateful to the following for permission to reproduce the illustrations used in this book: the Bhagwan Valmik Mandir in Bedford (cover, frontispiece, and Plates 5.2 and 5.3); the Bhagwan Valmik Mandir in Southall (Plates 1.2, 1.3 and 2.4); the Jagat Guru Valmik Ji Maharaj Mandir Gian Ashram UK of Booth Street, Birmingham (Plate 2.1); the Bhagwan Valmik Temple in Wolverhampton (Plate 2.2); the Jagat Guru Valmik Ji Maharaj Temple in Coventry (Plate 2.3); the Bhagwan Valmik Ashram of Icknield Street, Birmingham (Plates 5.1 and 5.4); India Book House Pvt. Ltd. (Plate 1.1); and the British Library (Plates 1.4, 1.5 and 3.1).

Baba Gill (Sri Sri 108 Sat Guru Baba Mahinder Nath Gill) of the Lord Valmik Ji Nirankar Holy Temple Gian Ashram Bhavnashan, Ampthill Road, Bedford, has indicated that he no longer wishes to be associated with this book.

Finally, thanks are due to several people for their part in the production process: Dixie for producing the images from my original photographs, everyone at Ashgate and Bookcraft for their unflagging support, and Simon Brodbeck for stepping into the breach when I became ill. By compiling the glossary, chasing last-minute queries and checking proofs for me, Simon made the completion of this book possible.

All shortcomings are, of course, my own.

Chapter 1

Situating the Problem

1. Introduction

On Monday, 21 February 2000, Central Air Radio Limited (Birmingham, UK), trading as 'Radio XL', broadcast as usual on 1296 medium wave. At 13.45 pm, Vikram Gill was presenting the Panjabi phone-in programme, 'Eck Swal' (*ek svāl,* 'One Question'). Responding to a letter from a listener, Gill referred obliquely to the widely believed story that the great saint Vālmīki was once a 'dacoit'. The Panjabi term he used was *ḍākū*, denoting a 'robber', 'thief' or 'brigand'.[1] While the allocation of this term to Vālmīki is of little consequence to most Panjabis, or indeed to most Hindus, there is a sizeable community in Britain for whom 'Bhagwan Valmik' is God.[2] These are the self-styled 'Valmikis'. The shock wave felt throughout the British Valmiki community was tangible. Representatives made a formal protest to the radio station. They demanded an apology for the disrespect shown to them as worshippers of Valmik, and a public retraction of the dacoit legend in relation to their God. As far as the Valmikis are concerned, the legend is both demeaning and unfounded. This book is an attempt to unravel the complexities of this dispute.

There are four critical issues at the heart of this study. The first is sociological and relates to the implications of caste identity. The distress and anger expressed by the Valmikis throughout the dispute was (and still is) fuelled by a lingering resentment of their so-called 'untouchable' past. Today, in both Britain and India, brahmins (especially men of the older generation) often present themselves as more authoritative than younger, lower-caste men and women. In some ways, the situation in Britain lags behind that in India: visitors from India are frequently struck by the old-fashioned caste-consciousness they find in Hindu and Sikh communities in the UK. In this context, there are some important questions to consider. How much longer must supposedly 'low-caste' communities put up with an identity constructed for them by others? When will their long-standing resistance to such constructions be recorded, let alone taken seriously? When will *their* truth be heard?

The second issue relates to text-historical research, and the complex relationship between sacred text and religious meaning. Is it possible to determine whether or not Vālmīki was a dacoit? As an academic scholar, I certainly believe that one kind of answer lies in the study of early Sanskrit texts. But can texts be used to validate or invalidate contemporary beliefs? Which texts might be

1 For *ḍākū* and *ḍakait*, see Singh, Singh and Kaur (1983: 264, 269).

2 The distinction made between 'Guru Valmik' and 'Bhagwan Valmik' will be explained in chapter 5, section 3.

deemed to count? Some are perceived to be 'sacred', but sacred to whom? Do conflicting understandings matter? Is it appropriate to try to offer a resolution and, if so, who has the right to contribute to the discussion? Is it in fact possible to bridge the gap between textual research and contemporary meaning? Clearly, I believe we should try.

The third issue concerns freedom of speech, what Americans refer to as 'the first amendment'.[3] More precisely, how do we balance the competing freedoms of religion and expression? Regardless of the religion concerned, this is a recurring problem. In relation to Islam, for example, Iran's Ayatollah Khomeini proclaimed a *fatwa* on Salman Rushdie, the author of *The Satanic Verses* (1988). Soon afterwards, Rushdie was persuaded by the British authorities to make a public apology.[4] In my view, Rushdie's capitulation to political pressure was understandable but unfortunate. A Christian example is provided by Martin Scorsese's film, *The Last Temptation of Christ*.[5] Although the film outraged even the Vatican, Scorsese quite rightly refused to apologise. In the Birmingham dispute, the Valmikis demanded both an apology and a retraction of the dacoit legend. Clearly, the apology was important for the self-esteem of the Valmiki community; in the context of their troubled history (see chapter 2), this cannot be ignored. A far more effective response, however, is to provide the evidence necessary for an alternative understanding. That is the purpose of this book.[6]

This brings me to the fourth issue: the role of the scholar and, by extension, his or her relationship to the religious community involved. If academic research can indeed determine whether or not Vālmīki was a dacoit, how would the 'truth' of this assertion matter, and to whom? In different ways and at different levels, many people took part in the dispute in Birmingham. What will they make of this book? Is there some way to grant my right to write the book and, at the same time, their right to object to it? Jeffrey Kripal's scholarly study of the Bengali saint Ramakrishna, *Kālī's Child* (1995), is a sobering case in point. When Kripal wrote of the saint's 'homoerotic' impulses, he was drawing attention to what he perceived to be the truth; and he has been pilloried by Ramakrishna devotees ever since. Was he wrong to write that book? What *are* the politics of scholarship in the study of religions?[7] My position is simple. The scholar's job is to research

3 See also Article 19 of the United Nations Universal Declaration of Human Rights, resolution 217A (iii), 10 December 1948.

4 In the event, his apology was rejected and the death sentence reconfirmed; for further details, see Appignanesi and Maitland (1989).

5 Scorsese directed an adaptation of Nikos Kazantzakis's *The Last Temptation of Christ*, which explores the conflict between the human and divine sides of Jesus' character. Finally released in 1988, the film caused such an uproar among Christian groups that many exhibitors cancelled their plans to screen it (Nowell-Smith 1996: 764).

6 There is also the issue of preventing any further breaches of the peace. As Deborah Tannen puts it, it is easier to find solutions to a problem if one is *making* an argument rather than *having* one (2001: 93).

7 For the author's own reflections on these questions, see Kripal (1998: xi–xxiv and 2000–1).

the evidence, to lay it out in public view as clearly as possible,[8] and to formulate the kinds of arguments that may reasonably be based upon it. Once that job is done and both evidence and arguments are in the public domain, the constructions that are placed upon them by others are beyond the scholar's control. We do the best we can.[9]

These are serious matters. I have chosen to engage with them by exploring one particular situation: the conflict in understandings as they relate to the individual revered in Sanskrit texts as 'Vālmīki'. Before I proceed, however, I must explain my choice of terminology. This choice demonstrates both my stance and my method. Following the conventions of Indological research, the transliterated form using diacritical marks denotes the poet-saint of Sanskrit texts: 'Vālmīki'. Following the conventions of many anthropologists and sociologists of Indian religion, the form without diacritical marks denotes the individuals and communities now known both within and outside India by a range of related names: Valmiki, Valmik, Balmiki, Balmik. My choice here is in line with the preference conveyed to me by my contacts within the communities in Britain: 'Valmiki'. Diacritical marks are also absent from the form used to denote the God who is worshipped by the Valmikis: 'Bhagwan Valmik'. The anglicized title 'Bhagwan' (derived from the Sanskrit term, *bhagavan*, meaning 'Lord') reflects the pronunciation of the prevailing vernacular language, Panjabi. The spelling 'Valmik' is used on the plaques outside all seven places of worship in the UK: 'Bhagwan Valmik Ashram' in Icknield Street, Birmingham; 'Bhagwan Valmik Mandir' in Muswell Road, Bedford, and in Southall; 'Bhagwan Valmik Temple' in Wolverhampton; 'Jagat Guru Valmik Ji Maharaj Mandir Gian Ashram UK' in Booth Street, Birmingham; 'Jagat Guru Valmik Ji Maharaj Temple' in Coventry; and 'Lord Valmik Ji Nirankar Holy Temple Gian Ashram Bhavnashan' in Ampthill Road, Bedford. The question at issue becomes clear with the terminology. What is the link, if any, between the 'Vālmīki' of ancient sacred texts and 'Bhagwan Valmik' as he is worshipped by the 'Valmikis' in Britain today? The juxtaposition of Sanskrit diacritics and vernacular usage here is deliberate. It reflects an important tension within the community: the Valmikis quite rightly want access to the sacred language associated with the higher castes, and to the religious truths it might convey; yet they are justifiably wary of seeming to fall in line with the caste prejudice implied by linguistic hierarchy.[10]

---

8 The need to make one's work transparent – reinforced in this instance by the intense desire on the part of many members of the British Valmiki community to learn about their current situation – has led me to provide perhaps more bibliographical references than might be expected, especially in chapter 2.

9 Several of the Valmikis I have consulted understand this perfectly. For example, Jaswinder Kalyan explained to me most politely that, if my research produces findings he cannot believe, then he will probably discount them. He granted me the right to do my best, and I granted him the right to reject it (personal communication, 4 July 2002).

10 The question of the spelling and pronunciation of the name 'Valmik(i)' was raised in 1991 during a visit to England by Manjula Sahdev, holder of the Maharshi Valmiki Chair in Sanskrit at the Punjabi University in Patiala. As a result of her advice, the letterhead of the Birmingham Sabha was changed from 'Valmik' to 'Valmiki'.

Regardless of one's caste origin, Vālmīki is widely celebrated as the poet who composed the Sanskrit epic, the *Rāmāyaṇa*. Despite his importance for the Indian tradition, however, surprisingly little academic attention has been paid to him as an individual. For example, there is no full-length work on Vālmīki in a European language. The articles that do exist are brief and widely spaced across the decades, including the English-language studies of Bulcke (1958, 1959, 1960), Goldman (1976), Bhargava (1984), Sahdev (1986) and Sahai (1993–4).[11] For most scholars in the broad field of Indian studies, Vālmīki's significance lies not in himself but rather in the work attributed to him. Why waste time speculating on the legends of pre-history when we have the treasure-house of his text? This was my own position until the dispute in Birmingham made me reconsider.

Shortly after the offending radio programme was broadcast, the 'Bhagavan Valmiki Action Committee' was formed. A public protest was held outside the offices of Radio XL in the course of which banners were waved, slogans were yelled and missiles were thrown. The Bhagavan Valmiki Action Committee submitted to the Radio Authority a detailed report on the issue in support of its formal complaint against the programme.[12] In the subsequent dispute, academics were brought in on both sides. In response to the Valmikis' allegations of insensitivity and misrepresentation, the Radio Authority commissioned a report from a colleague of mine (Mandair 2000). The Bhagavan Valmiki Action Committee commissioned their own report from me. At this point, I discovered that the Committee was led by Lekh Raj Manjdadria, one of my MA students at that time. His questions to me on behalf of the Committee were deceptively simple: What do the earliest Sanskrit texts tell us about Vālmīki? And what is the validity of the dacoit legend? I agreed to produce an independent and impartial account of the text-historical evidence for the character of Vālmīki and the relevance of this evidence to the Birmingham dispute (Leslie 2000).[13] The Committee's complaint against Radio XL was eventually upheld by the Radio Authority.[14]

---

11 For studies in Hindi and Panjabi, see Bulcke (1950) and Sahdev (1983) respectively.

12 *Report of the Bhagavan Valmiki Action Committee* (2000). This 191-page report includes 77 pages of signed petitions from individuals and religious communities in both Britain and India.

13 I am indebted to Arvind Mandair for sending me a copy of his report. I was unaware of his involvement in the dispute, and he of mine, until our respective reports had been submitted. Both reports remain unpublished. Mine reached the public domain in the form of evidence placed before the High Court in support of an application for permission to seek judicial review. Copies were later circulated to the Valmiki Sabhas, both in English and in a Panjabi translation.

14 The Radio Authority licenses and regulates independent radio in accordance with the statutory requirements of the Broadcasting Acts 1990 and 1996. All formal complaints and their adjudications are listed in the *Radio Authority Quarterly Programming Bulletin* which is accessible on the Radio Authority website (*www.radioauthority.org.uk*). This particular complaint (Reference P022/38) was published in the *Quarterly Programming Bulletin*, 38 (April–June 2000), with the adjudication 'Partially Upheld'. This was followed by two revised adjudications (2001a and 2001b), both of which upheld the complaint; the second one was published in issue no. 43 (July–September 2001), pp. 52–3.

While I was conducting the research for my report, I became aware of a wealth of unexamined material. Although I was able to reach a provisional conclusion of which I was fairly confident, I was intrigued by the lack of clarity on some of the key points. The significance, even urgency, of the issue for some British Indians sparked my interest further. I was still uncertain about the relevance of text-historical research to a contemporary socio-religious dispute, let alone the appropriateness of an academic wading in with an 'answer'. Since I had been invited to do so, however, I hoped that I might make some useful contribution to the problem. This book constitutes an attempt to bring some of the more significant issues raised in my report into the academic arena of the study of religions.

My goal is a critically nuanced, but essentially text-historical, study of the figure of Vālmīki. The primary sources for this enquiry are the Sanskrit texts that mention Vālmīki, including two which are attributed to him: the *Vālmīki Rāmāyaṇa* and the *Yogavāsiṣṭha Rāmāyaṇa*. In these two texts, according to the tradition of the Valmiki community, Vālmīki narrates his own story. The second level of the enquiry is more complicated but equally important: the identification and examination of the various strands of popular stories concerning Vālmīki. In effect, my plan is to disentangle the earliest evidence for Vālmīki from the narrative threads of passing centuries, and to consider the often disturbing implications of that process. Perhaps this text-historical analysis will contribute in some way to our understanding of the interlocking beliefs of British South Asians and, by extension, to a greater awareness of the problematic relationship between the authority of sacred texts and the meaning of religious lives, hence the title of this book. Like all relationships, that between authority and meaning can never be finally determined: it is (and indeed must always be) one of constant, sometimes painful, renegotiation.

The structure of the book is as follows. Chapter 2 seeks to contextualize the Valmikis. In order to understand the issues of identity and self-representation experienced by this group, which Indian tradition has consistently portrayed as low-caste, it is necessary to draw on several different kinds of material: the terms and implications of untouchability in early Sanskrit texts, ethnographic studies of related castes in northern India, and sociological analyses of British South Asians. I hope to demonstrate that an investigation of the past and present situation, both in India and in the UK, throws significant light on our understanding of the dispute in Birmingham. First, there is no doubt that caste prejudice remains an important issue, even in Britain, even today. Second, even as they embark on the twenty-first century, British Valmikis continue to define themselves to a large extent in terms of their resistance to the 'untouchable' past that is still constructed for them by the higher castes. Third, there are signs that the Valmikis are increasingly able to negotiate a caste-free religious identity, if not so much for their parents, at least for their children.

Chapter 3 begins by considering the references to 'Vālmīki' in the earliest texts of the Sanskritic tradition. In particular, it re-examines Camille Bulcke's assertion that the name refers to 'three and very probably four' different individuals (1959: 348). It then seeks to locate 'our' Vālmīki in three key Sanskrit sources: the *Mahābhārata*, the *Vālmīki Rāmāyaṇa* and the *Yogavāsiṣṭha* (the last two both sacred to the Valmikis). What do these three religious texts tell us about Vālmīki?

What kind of evidence is provided by the epics? What can we learn from the qualitatively different *Yogavāsiṣṭha*? Finally, in what way can these comparisons help us towards a better understanding of the relationship between sacred text and religious meaning? This is the text-historical conundrum referred to earlier.

Chapter 4 considers in turn each of the three motifs that have become associated over the centuries with the figure of Vālmīki: the ascetic in the termite mound, the dacoit turned devotee and the recitation of the *marā-marā* mantra. In each case, my primary sources are Sanskrit texts. My purpose is to demonstrate how the Vālmīki of the *Rāmāyaṇa* apparently becomes enmeshed in, or transformed by, this growing tangle of popular narrative threads. This chapter also considers briefly the significance of the 'untouchable' as the sinner *par excellence*. As will become clear, the textual sources considered contain some of the versions of the emerging dacoit legend that were current at the points in time, and in the particular socio-religious contexts, of their compilation.

Chapter 5 reflects upon the findings of previous chapters, first in relation to vernacular tellings of the dacoit legend, second in relation to the textual and iconographical evidence for his worship, both past and present. The final sections of the chapter address the most important issues of both the Birmingham incident and this book: the tension between caste and salvation and the shifting relationship between sacred text and religious meaning.

The rest of this introduction falls into three sections. Section 2 sketches the events of February 2000 in order to establish at the outset a fuller understanding of the dispute in question. Section 3 provides a brief account of the dacoit legend that lies at the heart of the controversy. Section 4 explores briefly some of the methodological issues that need to be discussed in a study of this kind.

2. The Dispute

The following account is drawn from the transcripts of the programme.[15] The episode begins when the presenter, Vikram Gill, responds on air to a letter written by the listener. Gill summarizes the latter's situation as follows:

> His greatest problem is that some time earlier he served a sentence in jail. He now says he wants to live life from another perspective, on a decent mode, however people do not allow him to. They say that once you've sinned or done wrong … [16] He has also written that he was punished for theft. He says he has served his sentence and accepted his wrongdoing, he has requested forgiveness from his family and outsiders, but even after that our community will not give him employment …

---

15 The extracts are taken from the English translation of the Panjabi transcript of the relevant broadcasts; both are contained in the *Report of the Bhagavan Valmiki Action Committee* (2000: 8–36). The brackets indicate editorial insertions in the printed text; insignificant errors of spelling, punctuation and grammar have been silently corrected.

16 This sentence is incomplete.

Gill advises the listener not to worry about what other people say to or about him. He explains that Asians in particular should refrain from blaming others for their past actions, for they have the evidence of their scriptures to serve as exemplars. It is at this point, and in this context, that he refers on air to Vālmīki:

> When we call someone a thief, when we call someone a sinner, at that time we insult ourselves – because we are Asian people – if we refer to our Shastars and Puranas, if we look at Maharishi Valmik's case. Maharishi Valmiki, who today some communities call Bhagavan Valmiki. This Valmiki before becoming a Rishi (sage), was a daku (dacoit). He couldn't even say 'Ram'. When he said 'Ram', the word 'Mara' came out of his mouth. However with his bhakti, from saying 'Mara, Mara …', he learnt to say 'Ram', and with that he is now known as Maharishi Valmiki, known as Bhagavan Valmiki.

From this, Gill concludes that the persecuted listener should follow Vālmīki's example: he should 'face the world', thinking only of God. The episode is brought to a close with a final snippet of advice: 'Now ignore people, move forward in a happy way with Radio XL's wishes, we Asians are with you' (pp. 8–10).

In context, to a disinterested outsider, the advice is obviously well intentioned. Like so many others before and since, Vālmīki had been able to rise above a wicked past. As a result, he had become the saintly figure revered today by some as God ('Bhagavan'). He achieved this by reciting the name of God ('Ram') as best he could. According to this story, therefore, Vālmīki's religious devotion swept aside his ignorance, his ineptitude and even his past misdeeds. The problem, of course, is that only an outsider would countenance the suggestion that Vālmīki was ever ignorant, inept or wicked. An insider is more likely to be offended. Within the Valmiki community, Vālmīki is revered as the divinized poet-saint who composed two of the most important sacred texts of India: the *Vālmīki Rāmāyaṇa* and the *Yogavāsiṣṭha Rāmāyaṇa*, both in classical Sanskrit. Unfortunately but understandably, Gill's radio broadcast mentioned none of this. It dwelled only on the well-known story that Vālmīki was once an uneducated dacoit (that is, a robber and a murderer) who was unable even to pronounce the name of God. The revered Bhagwan of the Valmikis had suddenly been reduced in the public discourse of the air-waves to an uneducated and simple-minded bandit. How could such a man have invented the epic verse-form, the Sanskrit *śloka*, as Vālmīki is believed to have done? How could he have fashioned the elevated language of the gods into the divine form of the *Rāmāyaṇa*? How could he have attained the spiritual heights necessary to convey the deep insights of the *Yogavāsiṣṭha*? In this context, clearly, the dacoit story is inherently impossible.

Representatives of the Valmiki community in Britain made their protest to the radio station. On Tuesday, 22 February, two formal apologies were offered on air by Vikram Gill: one in Panjabi, the other in English. In the Panjabi version, Gill requested 'forgiveness' from the 'followers of Maharishi Valmiki Ji, whose feelings were hurt' by the broadcast. 'If I hurt anyone's feelings,' he added, 'I request forgiveness from the world.' In the English version, he offered his 'deepest apologies to all of Valmiki Society and followers'. He pointed out that 'a great prophet was mentioned', and said: 'I did not mean to hurt anybody's feelings'. This formula went some way towards mollifying the Valmikis. However, it was noted that both apologies related only to the distress caused to the community. No apology had been offered with regard to the accuracy of the information broadcast. Even if no further comment had been made, therefore, it would have been surprising if the matter had ended there.[17]

Unfortunately, Vikram Gill added further fuel to the fire in his broadcast on Thursday, 24 February. In response to a sympathetic caller, he began to speak more freely:

> I have read the four Vedas, the Koran, the Mahabharat, the Gita. I have read everything. Why? So that today my parents' and my management's faces could be blackened by those who we've spoken well of.
>
> When all these things happened, who stood by us? Whether it's a Gurudwara, or a Mandir's story, or any religion's story, we all come and stand by everyone. However, today when lies have conquered truth, and I had to request forgiveness from everyone for speaking the truth, nobody came to ask me then.
>
> This is why over and over again I cry that today we people are not alive. Today if people say that we are in the truth era (*sat yug*), and that we receive wholesome food ...[18] Has this food intoxicated us? Is this the result, that I had to clasp my hands and ask for forgiveness from all communities for saying the truth? Did anyone ask me?

The diatribe continues. If what Gill has said on air is wrong, then:

> Today the Mahabharat is wrong, the Guru Granth Sahib is wrong, and today all stories are wrong.

He concludes:

> This is religion's story – in the name of religion they [the Valmikis] have come and got promises that no story of their religions or any other religions should be spoken (p. 14).

This last assertion appears to be unfounded. According to the *Report of the Bhagavan Valmiki Action Committee*, the representatives of the Wolverhampton and Birmingham committees asked only that the radio station's comments in relation to the Valmiki religion should be better informed (2000: 14 n. 13).

The broadcast continued in this way for some time. Rather than document the twists and turns of its content, however, I shall draw everything together under six points. All six are already apparent in the above outburst. All six reappear as persistent, powerful themes during the rest of the programme that day. I shall take each in turn.

---

17 For the widespread phenomenon of an apology that manages to avoid any admission of wrongdoing and therefore fails to mollify its recipient, see Tannen (2001: 95–123). While one may question the need for an apology in the first place (on the grounds of the right to free speech, as mentioned on p. 2), the fact remains that the whole dispute could have been avoided by a sincere apology early on. As it was, the opposing factions became caught up in 'a mutually aggravating spiral', which Tannen calls 'complementary schismogenesis'.

18 This sentence is incomplete.

First, Gill believes that he has done nothing wrong. In simple terms, of course, this is true. He invariably refers to Vālmīki in terms of respect ('Shri', 'Ji'), calling him a great sage ('Maharishi'), divine ('Bhagavan'), a man of devotion ('bhakti') and courage, a 'great prophet' (p. 11). These are not the words of someone intending to insult the religious beliefs of others. Indeed, Gill insists that his broadcasts have always been respectful towards both the Valmiki religion and their revered *Rāmāyaṇa* (p. 21). He talks about the important service he and his programme offer to the South Asian community, including the Valmikis (p. 17).[19] 'Radio XL is your Radio XL,' he claims, '... where your entertainment is catered for all the time, your prayers, all manner of discussions, blessings ...' (pp. 25–6). Gill is evidently dismayed that the 'very community' he has dedicated himself to serve with songs and prayers should accuse him in this way (p. 27). As he explains, he told the dacoit story in order 'to give strength to a troubled person'. His intention was entirely without malice. 'Learn from our seniors, our elders, our great seers and our prophets', he tells his listeners. 'If they have worked at moving forward, look at them' (p. 20). 'Don't be troubled', he exhorts them. 'Learn from Maharishi Valmiki' (p. 22). But Gill's tone is at times despairing: 'There seems to be no route of friendship', he says. 'We have never damaged anything of anyone's, we have only sought to elevate. We've done nothing' (p. 24).

Second, Gill is convinced that he has spoken the truth. At the heart of his distress is his belief that the apology he has been forced to offer is inappropriate. The point is explicit and repeated several times. 'I request forgiveness from everyone for telling the truth', he says without a hint of humour (p. 16). In one passage, he describes 'the voice of truth' as being 'suppressed by the beating of sticks, the throwing of eggs, and the telling of various lies', and then adds, 'At this time I will request forgiveness from you clasping my hands' (p. 18). Later, he declares, 'I requested forgiveness for telling the truth, that I was wrong for wanting the truth' (p. 28). When a caller suggests that he let slip the dacoit story by mistake, Gill's response is again quite explicit: 'The story did not slip out of my mouth; there are recordings of it. If it offended the sentiments of some communities, I have asked forgiveness for that' (p. 29). Later, he refers to the 'accusations, bones of contention' arising from 'all these stories', and suggests that these problems might be solved by talking things over 'as brother and sister'. But then, again, he adds: 'Even still there is a lot of difference between truth and falsity. In today's times, the time of 'Kal Yug' (the Dark Era), one has to stay underground even for speaking the truth' (p. 30). Throughout the discussion, Gill seems certain that he has spoken only the truth: it is that truth which has offended the Valmikis.

Third, Gill believes that the evidence for the dacoit story that he told on air can be found in the sacred texts of all religions. His conclusion is explicit: if the Valmikis' claim is upheld, then all those texts and traditions must be declared false. As Gill puts it,

19 This point is picked up on by at least one of his callers (see, for example, p. 34).

> ... [the Valmikis] have come to those of thamam religions,[20] the communities of thamam faith, and said that they are false, and if anyone is truthful only they were. Today the Guru Granth Sahib has become false, today the Gita has become false also, and the Ramayana has become false. Today the truth that has been written in books has today all become false, and only they have remained truthful (p. 17).

This devastating idea recurs a few minutes later:

> I had to request forgiveness and because of my request for forgiveness the Guru Granth Sahib is rendered false, the Mahabharat is rendered false. Due to my action, all the names of all my elders have been sunk, today the faces of my mother and father, my education and qualifications have been blackened (p. 19).

This version of events may have arisen naturally from Gill's distress, but its effect is to polarize the situation. He builds his own defence by insisting that the 'peoples of the Gurudwaras, the Churches and the Mandirs' (that is, the Sikhs, the Christians, and the Hindus) have been 'disrespected': they have not been consulted (p. 24). When a caller offers to go to the Valmikis to beg forgiveness on Gill's behalf, she is told: 'You ask them for forgiveness, because my faith, which is the faith of the Guru Granth Sahib, is false. Also [ask them] for forgiveness that the Mahabharat is false' (p. 28). Gill is clearly implying here that the evidence to support the dacoit story may be found in the texts he mentions. He therefore berates himself for his enforced part in besmirching these sacred texts, these great traditions. 'Because of my request for forgiveness,' he says, 'all and every religion has become false' (p. 28).

Fourth, by placing himself at the centre of the drama, Gill cannot help taking everything personally. For example, he declares at one point, 'If there is anyone who is the greatest falsifier in the world, then it is I!' (pp. 17–18). At one level, he feels isolated, exposed as the presenter of the programme. He is disturbed that no representatives of other faiths have come to his defence, and asks: 'Where are these communities now? Where were these communities at the time my life was likened to that of a mouse in a cage? What was the story then? At that time no one came in front of me' (p. 13). He describes how 'small, small children' threw eggs at the radio station's windows, and protesters made threats on his life. He asks plaintively: 'Who will stand with me? Today the voices of everyone are silent, today no Mandir will take a stand, no Gurudwara will take a stand, today no people from Mosques will stand with me' (p. 16). Again and again, Gill asks this same question: 'Where have these people gone, who today should be supporting me?' (p. 17); 'Who comes and makes a stand?' (p. 18). He feels abandoned: 'For my faith, the faith of others, I have made a stand, and yet today I am verily alone' (p. 17). Later, he asks rather sadly, 'What can I do by myself?' (p. 23), and again,

---

20 The term 'thamam' (*tamām*, Arabic) means 'complete'. In Panjabi, Urdu etc., the term usually means 'all' or 'total'; 'thamam religions' would thus mean 'all religions'. However, a member of the Valmiki community explained to me that only mainstream religions were included. Whichever interpretation one places on the term, the context indicates a perceived opposition between the Valmikis and everyone else.

'Who is so great that [they] would make a stand for a weak person such as me?' (p. 25). Under Gill's direction, callers to the programme pick up the idea. They suggest that everyone should write to the management to support their presenter (p. 34), to insist that he has been wronged (p. 35). But Gill also feels deeply hurt. He explains that he has not touched any food since the Monday broadcast yet no one has sought him out to commiserate with him: 'Has anyone asked me? No one has. … No one came once to ask the state of my feelings' (p. 15). He believes that he has supported the Valmikis and received only abuse in return: 'Those communities threw eggs at us, tomatoes at us, swore at us, held banners' (p. 17). His refusal to eat reflects the depth of his pain: 'Rather than live in notoriety it is better to die at one's own doorstep' (p. 22). 'Today,' he asks rhetorically, 'doesn't my heart feel pain? Am I not troubled?' But then he is not really troubled, he explains, because his cause is just, yet the hurt feelings remain (p. 18). Despite all his efforts on behalf of others, he is unappreciated: 'I live for the world, I say all the time that my body, my soul, is the property of the public. … I am hurt then, hurt for a lie' (p. 19). There is no doubting the strength of these feelings. Finally, judging by Gill's choice of words, his experience is primarily one of anger and shame: he feels humiliated by being made to apologize. This becomes a complex but dominant theme. For example, he takes personally the alleged assertion that 'all stories are wrong', proclaiming: 'Have I today become false?' Then he continues: 'I take pride that I am Sikh, take pride that I am a Hindu, that people of my faiths are my people. What should I do? Change my religion? What if I change my religion?' (p. 15). This notion recurs: 'I've never been ashamed of saying I'm a Sikh, I'm a Hindu. … You tell me, should I change my religion today and become a Muslim or a Christian?' (p. 26). We should note that there is no suggestion here of a Sikh versus Hindu dispute. In common with many British Asians, Gill lays claim to both religious traditions.[21] For Gill, this is a personal issue.

Fifth, by personalizing the issue in this way, he is both expressing his discomfort and instinctively trying to gain sympathy from his non-Valmiki listeners. Unfortunately, this natural instinct to gain sympathy for an unsolicited problem – when combined with the accusation that the Valmikis have declared all religions false – soon turns into something far more alarming. In effect, Gill's outburst becomes a demand that his non-Valmiki listeners – the Panjabi-speaking Hindus, Sikhs and Muslims – should come out in his defence. Since he is defending their religions, they should now come forward to defend him. There is a clear suggestion here that opposing sides are being drawn up: 'them' (the Valmikis) versus 'us' (Gill, supported by listeners belonging to 'all' faiths). This theme reappears in various forms. For example, when banners are waved bearing Gill's name with the exhortation 'Murdabad' (literally, 'May he die!'),[22] and

21 For further discussion of some of the problems involved in using these religious categories, see Nesbitt (1990b and 1991).

22 The cry of 'Murdabad!' (*murdābād*, Persian) is the opposite of 'Zindabad' ('May s/he/they live!'). Both are protest rally clichés, along the lines of 'Down with Blair!' and 'Long live the Pope!'. A more serious death threat is implied by the phrase 'Marg bar ...' ('Death to ...'), as in 'Marg bar Shah!' or 'Marg bar Bush!'.

some of the protesters curse him, Gill insists that the hostility is aimed not at him as an individual but at 'all the religions, and all the great books' (p. 13). A little later, he claims that 'the number of eggs that fell here have fallen on the faces of the public' rather than on himself as the presenter (p. 15). Gill's anger has shifted the goalposts significantly. What began as an enforced formal apology to a minority religious group (the Valmikis) has now become a heartfelt apology to everyone else: 'From our *thamam* listeners once again I request forgiveness' (p. 30). Blame is laid squarely on 'those who have brought the situation to this', that is, on the Valmikis (p. 32). Gill's confrontational approach seems designed to transform his community of British South Asian listeners into two opposing sides, with potentially serious consequences for the larger community of South Asians in Britain.

Sixth, as the broadcast continues, a further accusation is made against the Valmikis: that they are ignorant of their own tradition. While this idea is always implicit in what Gill has been saying, it becomes explicit in the responses he elicits from his callers. One caller in particular spells out the implications: 'What Valmiki was, everyone knows. Who doesn't know? ... What these communities are saying, they don't know. ... They say that they are Valmikis, they don't even have any knowledge about him' (pp. 21–2). Another caller concludes that an 'injustice' has been done to Gill by the Valmikis, describing their behaviour as 'really, really unfair', 'totally absurd', and 'not civilized at all' (p. 34). This conclusion is derived directly from the suggestion that the Valmikis are ignorant of their own tradition as it is embedded in the sacred texts of India.

The outcome of this series of broadcasts is unfortunate. Gill's formal apology to the Valmikis has been slowly but inexorably demolished. Moreover, the portrayal of the Valmikis as ignorant, belligerent and uncivilized seems set to damage their relationship with other South Asian communities in Britain. Finally, the point at issue – the accuracy or otherwise of the dacoit story in relation to Vālmīki – has not been addressed at all. It is this story that I shall turn to now.

3. The Legend

At the heart of the problem is the notion that Vālmīki was once an ignorant and brutish dacoit. This idea will be familiar to anyone who has read any of the widely distributed comic-book accounts of the poet's life. An excellent example is provided by the Amar Chitra Katha series, edited by Anant Pai and subtitled 'The Glorious Heritage of India'.[23] This extraordinarily popular comic-book series, available in many Indian languages as well as in English, is read and re-read by millions of adults as well as children all over the world. Indeed, the message printed on the inside front cover of every issue reads: 'AMAR CHITRA KATHA means good reading. Over 78 million copies sold so far'. The English edition of issue no. 579 is entitled *Valmiki: the story of the author of the epic,*

23 For discussions of the comic-book genre with particular reference to the Amar Chitra Katha series, see Pritchett (1995) and Hawley (1995).

'Ramayana' (Pai 1994). This issue was first published in 1973 but, after Valmikis burned an effigy of Anant Pai in the streets of Jalandhar and Patiala, the title was officially dropped from the publisher's list and replaced by a new no. 579 entitled *Madhvacharya*.[24] Even so, the popularity of this comic-book series surely bears some responsibility for the spread of the legend and thus for the continued attribution of a wicked past to the divinized poet-saint, Vālmīki.

Let us look more closely at the Amar Chitra Katha version of the story. The preamble, printed on the inside front cover, is suitably reverential:

> To Valmiki, we Indians owe a deeper debt of gratitude than to any other poet. He gave us the Ramayana, one of the most fascinating stories of all time. No words can describe the hold the Ramayana has had on the people of India from ancient times to the present day. It has affected the life and thought of our people and played an important role in shaping Indian culture. Valmiki was the Adikavi, the first poet, and his Ramayana the Adikavya, the first poem.

But the preamble does not stop there. 'While remembering the man's work,' it continues, 'we must not forget the man. How he wrote the Ramayana, and under what conditions, is itself an absorbing story.' We are then informed that this comic-book version is 'based on Valmiki Ramayana and Vallathol's Malayalam translation'. Finally, we are presented with a series of sayings attributed to the great man:

> The mind is the cause for the direction of all senses leading to good and evil acts.
> Honour the wives of others and protect them, O Ravana, as you will your own. Set an example by loving your own wife.
> Kindness is a supreme virtue.
> Great men when they undertake to do a great deed, are never upset.
> They are the blessed, who by their wisdom, can control their anger, even as water subdues a conflagration.
> Whoever does anything with enthusiasm rarely fails to achieve his object.

We may note in passing that none of these sayings is to be found in the critical edition of the *Vālmīki Rāmāyaṇa*. More important is the fact that there is evidently no intention to demean Vālmīki. None the less, the urge to focus on the stories that have circulated about the man rather than on his work inevitably leads us to the controversy in question.

Both the illustration on the cover and the first frame of the comic format portray the key moment of Vālmīki's life: an ascetic-looking figure with long

24 On 25 June 2002, I received the following email with the signature line 'Anant Pai (editor)': 'Title No. 579 was on "Valmiki", but since a few devotees of Valmiki objected to Valmiki being referred to as a dacoit in his early life (confirmed by many ancient texts), we dropped this title from our active list and replaced it with "Madhvacharya".' On further enquiry, a second email explained that the new title no. 579 (*Madhvacharya*) was first published in 1978, and the old one (*Valmiki*) was withdrawn from the 'regular list' in May 2000 (16 July 2002). This explains how, in Bangalore in 1995, I was able to buy a copy of the *Valmiki* comic carrying the publication date of 1994 and still listed as no. 579.

white hair and a long white beard sits on a deerskin in what appears to be a deer-inhabited hermitage, writing the *Rāmāyaṇa* on palm-leaves. In the cover illustration, we can clearly make out the *nāgarī* script in which he is writing and the feather-tipped quill he is holding.[25] He is wearing a necklace and bracelets made from *rudrākṣa* beads, while his long hair is caught up in the *rudrākṣa*-bead top-knot of the sage. In the first frame of the story, and in the rest of the comic, Vālmīki's skin is markedly darker than that of most of the people he encounters: this is a pointed allusion to his presumed tribal (and therefore, according to the brahmin perspective, low-status) origins.

The second frame of the comic takes us to Vālmīki's life as a young man. Here he is depicted as young and muscular, with dark hair and beard, and a hard expression on his face. He is wearing the animal-skin loin-cloth of the forest-dwelling tribal. Slung across his back is a quiver of arrows, in his hands a bow. The caption reads: 'Strangely, Valmiki was a hunter and robber in his early life.' The next few frames show him 'roaming the jungle', shooting down 'harmless birds', killing 'gentle animals' (he is pictured stalking deer) and bringing home the 'carcasses' for food (p. 2). We are then told that he 'also waylaid and robbed lone travellers in the jungle', threatening to kill them if they refused to hand over their goods (p. 3). This preliminary scene is set with the words: 'Thus he lived a life of violence and crime' (p. 4).[26]

The following pages narrate the story of the young bandit's meeting with the so-called 'Seven Sages' (*sapta-ṛṣi*). Throughout the exchange, there are striking differences between the bandit and the sages. The former's dark skin, blue-black hair and muscled body contrasts sharply with the pink skin,[27] white top-knots and ascetic build of the sages. Their clothing and body decorations are quite different: animal-skin loin-cloth as opposed to saffron robes and *rudrākṣa* beads. The hunter's bow and arrows and the robber's curved and brandished knife are thrown into relief by the sages' total lack of weaponry. The harsh expression on the attacker's face is met by the untroubled gaze of holy men.

The sages enquire gently why the young man wants to rob them. The answer is simple. 'I have to maintain my wife and children,' replies the young man. 'Robbery is my livelihood' (p. 5). The leader of the sages requests permission to ask one more question: 'Your family lives on the fruits of your sin. Will they partake of your sins as well?' (p. 6). The robber insists that they will. However, his face betrays a hint of uncertainty, and he agrees to go home to check. The sages promise to wait for his return.

---

25 This charming picture is, of course, a misrepresentation of the (probably) preliterate and (certainly) oral traditions of India. As Richard Salomon explains in his review article on recent publications on this topic, there are 'no securely datable specimens of writing' before the Ashokan rock inscriptions of around 250 BCE (1995: 271). For a comprehensive study of the key issues relating to early writing in India, see Falk (1993).

26 Several frames from this sequence are reproduced in Plate 1.1.

27 In the context of the Amar Chitra Katha, pink skin can be an indicator of race, caste and/or beauty. In this example, the contrast between the sages and the tribal hunter suggests a distinction of caste, while the pink skins allocated to the hunter's wife and child (see p. 15) are more likely to indicate beauty.

Back in his hut in the forest, the robber's conversation with his pretty, pink-skinned wife is short and shocking:

> 'Dear wife, you benefit from my sinful life. Don't you?'
> 'Of course, I do. What of that?'
> 'You will share my sins, won't you?'
> 'Certainly not! You are the sinner. Why should I share your sin?'

He turns to his equally pink-skinned son:

> 'Won't you at least share my sin, my darling?'
> 'No father, I will not.'
> 'Oh, my God!'

The robber stands 'stunned and dazed', unable to believe what he has heard. He is shown returning to the sages, bent and staggering under 'the weight of sorrow', his face distraught. As he approaches them, he bursts into tears. Throwing himself at their feet and 'weeping bitterly', he begs their understanding and help. 'My soul is lost', he declares. 'Redeem it, O compassionate ones' (pp. 7–9).

The sages take pity on the young man. They tell him to sit down and recite the sounds *ma-rā*. 'Put your heart and soul into it', they say. 'Don't stop for a moment till we return.' The young man, still described as 'the robber', obeys. He is depicted sitting cross-legged on the ground, his eyes closed, 'forgetting himself'. The caption tells us that the sounds *ma-rā* are in fact the name Rāma 'inverted'. This means that the continued repetition of the apparently fake mantra (the sounds *ma-rā*) will culminate in the recitation of a real mantra: *ma-[rā ma]-[rā ma]-rā*, and so on. The implication is that the ignorant fellow is unwittingly reciting the name of God. He sits there meditating like this for weeks, months, years. Time passes. Slowly, a termite mound begins to take shape around him, growing up inch by inch until it has covered him completely.[28]

When the sages return at last, years later, to the spot where they had left him, they find only a large, man-shaped termite mound. They summon the meditator forth. The caption reads: 'The anthill burst open and out stepped a person different in every respect'. This striking individual pays homage to Rāma and to the sages for the miracle of his transformation while the latter acclaim him as 'among the greatest rishis' with yet 'greater glory' ahead of him. The caption explains: 'He came out of "Valmik" meaning anthill, and so the rishis called him by the new name of "Valmiki" ' (pp. 10–11). This is the legend at issue in the Birmingham dispute, the legend rejected absolutely by the Valmiki community.[29]

---

28 Like the Sanskrit terms *pipīlika* and *valmī*, the English terms 'ant' and 'termite' are often used interchangeably, despite the differences between the creatures concerned. Termites, for example, are often called 'white ants'. However, termite mounds can grow considerably larger than anthills; indeed, only termite mounds can grow tall enough to conceal a seated ascetic, let alone one who is standing upright. For further distinctions between ants and termites, see König (1984: 4–34).

29 The Valmikis reject both the dacoit aspect of the legend and the idea that Bhagwan Valmik's name (*vālmīki*) is derived from any incident involving termites (*valmī*) or termite mounds (*valmīka*). It is important to be clear here. Three of the paintings in

The rest of the comic-book story of Vālmīki's life may be summarized more briefly. News of his 'spiritual power and knowledge' spreads. He meets the great sage Nārada, who narrates the story of Rāma, the perfect man. One day, while Vālmīki is watching a pair of birds, 'husband and wife, billing and cooing', the male is killed by a dark-skinned hunter. Vālmīki curses the hunter, his curse emerging in the Sanskrit verse form called *śloka*.[30] The god Brahmā then appears. He instructs Vālmīki to compose the story of Rāma, including both what he already knows and what will be revealed to him. Vālmīki composes the *Rāmāyaṇa* (pp. 12–19). Years later, Rāma's queen, Sītā, is abandoned in the forest, where she is rescued by Vālmīki, who brings her to his hermitage. There she gives birth to twin sons, who are later taught by Vālmīki to recite the *Rāmāyaṇa*. Later still, he sends the boys to Rāma's court to perform a formal recitation. When Rāma realizes who they are, he sends a message to Vālmīki: if Sītā will swear in public that she is pure, he will take her back. Vālmīki accompanies her to the royal court where he swears publicly on her behalf. But Rāma insists that Sītā speaks for herself. Instead, the earth opens up and the Earth Goddess takes her away. Rāma is grief-stricken. Vālmīki returns to his ascetic life (pp. 20–31).

This is the so-called 'popular' tradition. While it is necessary to concede this point, it is also important to recognize that the key elements of the story – clearly unproblematic for many[31] – are controversial for some. In 1968, for example, when the Hindi film *Lav Kuś* depicted Vālmīki as a robber, the Valmikis in India organized a mass agitation against this portrayal, and the film was withdrawn. I have already mentioned the burning of an effigy of the editor Anant Pai when the Amar Chitra Katha comic on Vālmīki was first published in 1975.[32] More

---

the Bhagwan Valmik Mandir in Southall are devoted to the termite-mound sequence (for the first two, see Plates 1.2 and 1.3). None the less, as was repeatedly explained to me, especially in Southall, the presence of these paintings should *not* be taken as evidence of the acceptance by Valmikis of the termite-mound story.

30 In this version of the story, Vālmīki's legendary transformation is further emphasized by the reversal of roles: the previously 'low-caste' hunter (presumably ignorant of Sanskrit) now uses Sanskrit to curse another hunter for doing what he himself used to do. With or without the legendary accretions, however, this is a moving episode usually known in Sanskrit as 'the killing of the crane' (*krauñca-vadha*) and in English as 'the birth of the *śloka*'. The Sanskrit title stresses Vālmīki's compassion, the English one his poetic prowess; in this study, in order to reflect the characteristically Indian emphasis, I use the Sanskrit term. The episode has proved extremely popular with artists and illustrators (see, for example, Plates 1.4 and 1.5). Contemporary examples may be found in the Bhagwan Valmik Ashram in Icknield Street, Birmingham, in the Bhagwan Valmik Mandir in Southall, and in the Jagat Guru Valmik Ji Maharaj Temple in Coventry. For an exploration of the significance of this moment in the *Vālmīki Rāmāyaṇa*, including the identification of the birds as a pair of Indian Sarus Cranes, the implications of their symbolism and details of further illustrations, see Leslie 1998b. For the *śloka* as a new verse form, and for the different cultures of hunting, see the relevant sections of chapter 3.

31 For example, Shastri (1962: xv) and Ayyangar (1991: 48–53).

32 Sukhbinder Gill relates an incident from his childhood at around the same time. He was eight years old when he found a comic-book version of the Rāmāyaṇa story.

recently, when the serial *Jai Hanumān* was broadcast on India's national television network, Doordarshan, the Valmikis in India undertook protest marches in several towns, forced shopkeepers to close down, and burnt an effigy of the producer, who promptly apologized.[33] In each case, two related issues were at stake: respect for Vālmīki, and respect for his namesakes in a caste-driven world. So we should not be surprised that a similar incident in Birmingham has led to a protest in this country too. An interesting development is the formal request from the Bhagavan Valmiki Action Committee for the 'historical facts' of the Vālmīki story.

4. Fact, Text and Religious Meaning

An outsider might wonder why the Valmikis do not simply accept the widely understood model of sinner-to-saint, and revere Vālmīki as popularly portrayed. There are plenty of parallel examples which appear to be unproblematic, both in the Indic context and beyond. Buddhism, for example, has the famous robber brigand Aṅgulimāla. After meeting the Buddha, Aṅgulimāla gave up his wicked ways, took the vows of a monk, and is now revered. In the Christian tradition, Saul of Tarsus persecuted believers until he saw the light on the road to Damascus and became 'Saint' Paul. The first story demonstrates the power of the Buddha, the second the power of the Christian God. Vālmīki's supposed transformation from dacoit to poet-saint could simply be regarded as a demonstration of the power of Rāma.

But Vālmīki's case is different. While both Aṅgulimāla and Saul are transformed from sinners to saints, there is no suggestion that either is himself divine. Perhaps a closer analogy can be made with the Scorsese film mentioned on p. 2. Jesus is portrayed here as a flesh-and-blood male in his relationship with Mary Magdalene. The traditional Indic parallel is another example of God in human form. In this case, it is Rāma who succumbs to human frailty: he sheds real tears at the loss of his beloved Sītā and uses treacherous methods to defeat Vālin (also called 'Bali' or 'Vali'). There are two main responses to a scenario of this kind. We can take the story (Rāma's weakness, the worldliness of Jesus, or Vālmīki's supposedly wicked past) as evidence of a God who has himself experienced the human predicament, and who therefore really understands the depth of human weakness. Or we can take offence and call it blasphemy. My point here is that the issue is not peculiar to South Asians, in Britain or elsewhere, and the stance taken by the Valmikis is both not without precedent and not the only one possible.

Using his own pocket money, he bought a copy to show his father, expecting him to be pleased. But his father was angry: he ripped out the offending pages and admonished his son. Sukhbinder still remembers how taken aback he was by the strength of his father's feelings (personal communication, 14 July 2002).

33 On this occasion, protests occurred in a number of towns including Patiala, Kapurthala, Bhagwara, Jalandhar, Amritsar, Ferozepore, Ludhiana and Chandigarh; see, for example, reports in *The Sunday Tribune* (10 May 1998) and *The Tribune* (13 May 1998).

In all these examples, there lurks the possibility, if not the likelihood, of researching the 'truth' behind the stories. What can we find out about Jesus, about Aṅgulimāla, about Vālmīki, if we study the texts at our disposal? My original title for this study, *Disentangling Vālmīki*, certainly implied that such a project was feasible. But there is another problem here. In what sense has 'Vālmīki' (or Aṅgulimāla or Jesus) become 'entangled'? Is there a suggestion here of a real, 'original' Vālmīki? Is there a factual core at the heart of the story? Do we need to know, or believe, that there is? Finally, what is implicit in the creative gap between the 'facts' of sacred text and the 'meanings' of this or that religious community?

There seem to be several important assumptions here. First, there is the assumption that sacred texts are more authoritative than contemporary belief and practice; hence the request to seek the truth by researching the texts. Second, there is the belief that the most sacred text, the most authoritative scripture, will provide the closest approximation of that truth, the nearest thing to the 'facts' of the Vālmīki story; hence the discomfort in Birmingham regarding whose scripture takes precedence – the *Gurū Granth Sāhib* of the Sikhs or the *Vālmīki Rāmāyaṇa* of the Valmikis. Third, there is the assumption that the more ancient a text is, the more authoritative it must be; hence the significance of the earlier date for the *Vālmīki Rāmāyaṇa*. Fourth, there is the belief that Sanskrit texts are both more ancient and inherently more authoritative than texts in vernacular languages; on these grounds alone the *Vālmīki Rāmāyaṇa* outranks the Sikh texts.[34] In this context, my brief was to research the earliest Sanskrit texts in order to ascertain the truth about Vālmīki.

This brings me to another uncomfortable question. The idea that an academic can tell any religious community what it has got wrong or right smacks of cultural imperialism. It is true that I was asked for my opinion, but what is the status of that opinion in the context of the religious beliefs of the individuals concerned? This raises a sobering question for all scholars and teachers engaged in the academic study of religions. How much does the 'ordinary believer' (assuming there is such a person) want to know about the 'facts' of research once the scholars start? A parallel example is provided by Mettanando Bhikkhu's research into the retrievable facts relating to the death of the Buddha. Drawing on his own medical training and basing his work on a careful study of the relevant Pali texts, Mettanando Bhikkhu argues convincingly that the Buddha did not 'choose' the moment of his death, as the tradition maintains; nor did he die of food poisoning, as some scholars have suggested. Instead, the evidence points to death by mesenteric infarction, a condition caused by obstruction of the blood to

34 What is the evidence for the idea that vernacular traditions are later than Sanskrit traditions? Questions of chronology and influence are notoriously hard to pin down in cultures such as those of India in which oral transmission dominates and textual records disintegrate. The views recorded in Sanskrit texts would surely have been affected by the vernacular contexts in which they arose. This is obviously so in the case of late Sanskrit texts that have incorporated stories/motifs found in existing vernacular materials; in principle, similar processes must have been in place with regard to earlier texts too. For a discussion of 'vernacularization' in India during the period 1000–1500, see Pollock (1998).

the bowel, common among the elderly. The texts suggest that the Buddha had his first attack some months earlier; the second one, brought on by a large meal, was fatal. The conclusion of this careful study is that the Buddha died of 'septic shock due to bacterial toxins and the infiltration of contaminated intestinal contents into the blood stream'.[35] His illness was thus brought on by natural causes combined with advanced age. But, we might ask, who is this information for? What exactly is at stake here?

Finally, in a postmodern world, is there such a thing as a 'fact' in the realm of religious truth? Surely, all we have is text, meaning and the creative space between the two. So what do we do when, as in the case of the Birmingham dispute, we are faced with two (or three, or a dozen) different sacred texts expressing radically different views? Within one religious tradition, there will be multiple texts, a myriad 'facts' and a corresponding array of meanings. How do we deal with this problem? There are several possible responses.

We might argue that religious truth transcends human understanding. In Buddhism, for example, the *bodhisattva* or Buddha-to-be must be able to hold in mind two conflicting propositions at once: 'There are no beings' and 'I shall save all beings'.[36] Clearly, one needs to be enlightened to assert both propositions together. Or we might take a leaf out of Jain philosophy and argue that there is an infinite variety of perspectives, not only one (*anekāntavāda*). Or we might fall back on the unanswerable question: Who speaks for 'Hinduism'?[37] There are so many forces, factions, voices that contribute to the formulation of a tradition that it is virtually impossible for an outsider to give priority to one over another. The politically correct (and safe) decision is not to choose, not to become involved in the dispute in the first place.

However, I am reluctant to withdraw simply because the issue is a tough one. To conclude this sub-section, therefore, I shall consider in turn the relevance to this discussion of three quite different approaches: Stephen Jay Gould's principle of Non-Overlapping Magisteria (NOMA), Carrette and Keller's notion of 'orientation' and Bakhtin's ideas on dialogue.

In *Rocks of Ages*, Gould proposes the NOMA principle as what he calls 'an irenic solution' to an ancient dispute: science versus religion, the two 'rocks' of his title. He defines 'irenic' as applying to persons or proposals that 'tend to promote peace, especially in relation to theological and ecclesiastical differences'

---

35 Mettanando Bhikkhu and von Hinüber (2000: 111). Mettanando Bhikkhu provides the medical diagnosis while von Hinüber summarizes the food-poisoning debate surrounding the Buddha's last meal of *sūkaramaddava*. Von Hinüber concludes that the Buddha probably did eat a local dish of pork (*sūkara*, 'boar', 'pig') but that this contributed only indirectly to his death. The question of who cares relates partly to the fact that later sources insist that the Buddha could not have eaten meat. I am grateful to Brian Bocking for drawing my attention to this material.

36 This is a reference to the Buddha's sermon on the *bodhisattva*'s vow from the *Diamond Sūtra*; the relevant section is translated from the Chinese in Conze (1973: 132). I am grateful to Brian Bocking for alerting me to this conundrum, and to Youxuan Wang for helping me to locate it.

37 An entire issue of the *Journal of the American Academy of Religion* (68.4, December 2000) is devoted to asking, and attempting to answer, this question.

(1999: 208–9). In Gould's view, the dispute arises out of a 'false conflict'. He explains that science focuses on 'the factual character of the natural world', developing theories that make sense within that narrow context. By contrast, religion 'operates in the equally important, but utterly different, realm of human purposes, meanings, and values – subjects that the factual domain of science might illuminate, but can never resolve'. The NOMA principle is therefore based on 'respectful noninterference' between the two 'magisteria' or domains of discourse, together with an ongoing 'intense dialogue' between the two (1999: 4–6). According to Gould, rejecting 'the siren song of false sources' frees us 'to seek solutions to questions of morals and meanings in the proper place – within ourselves' (1999: 197).

There is a parallel here with my own concerns. The two 'rocks' of my research are those of text-historical study and contemporary religious belief. Textual study provides information that can lead to conclusions of a certain kind: a summary of the medical symptoms displayed by the person known as 'the Buddha'; the possible meanings of the term *sūkaramaddava*; perhaps even the version of the Vālmīki story in circulation at a given time. But as a guide to contemporary religious meaning, textual study is of little use: that is to be found within.[38] Yet a complete separation between science and religion (or, in this case, textual study and religious experience) is in my view not the answer. While there is a strong temptation to refuse to engage – after all, neither side seems hugely interested in the findings of the other – that would seem to me to be a mistake. As Gould remarks, if we refuse to talk to each other, these 'tough but resolvable issues will continue to fester and haunt us'. He concludes that we should have more confidence in our ability to think and in our 'intrinsic good will' (1999: 221).

Unfortunately, the solution Gould proposes is not entirely clear to me. In what sense are these issues 'resolvable' if the relationship between the two domains is one of 'noninterference'? Furthermore, the goal of 'respectful' noninterference is, quite frankly, impossible to achieve. A perfect example of what I mean may be found in the striking failure of non-resident Indians (NRIs) and professional Indologists to communicate meaningfully on the original Indology discussion list on the internet. Despite frequent attempts by the moderator to separate the two domains – in this case, academic study and issues of personal, religious or political identity – 'flaming' was endemic. Eventually, when 'respectful noninterference' proved unworkable in practice, the discussion list was formally and reluctantly closed down.[39] I shall continue to put my faith in human intelligence and good will, along the lines suggested by Gould, but my expectations are considerably more modest.

Jeremy Carrette and Mary Keller adopt a different approach. They propose the notion of 'orientation' as a way of understanding 'the interrelated forces

---

38 Religious meaning resonates within. This is not to say that it is the result of isolated introspection; indeed meaning emerges in dialogue and through social interaction. See my comments on 'dialogics', on pp. 22–3.

39 The old Indology discussion list, founded in 1990 by Dominik Wujastyk, was closed down on 18 April 2001. The online archives may be consulted at *www.indology.org.uk*.

involved in the localized struggles of religious lives' (1999: 21). Their aim is to reveal the extraordinary complexity of such struggles. After reviewing the use of the term 'orientation' in the history of religions, they conclude that there are 'four principles of orientation'. First, orientations are 'embodied knowledges'; that is, we attain religious knowledge as embodied beings. Second, orientations exist 'within systems of power relations'; that is, both religions and individuals orient themselves within the discourses of power (race, class, gender, sexuality). Third, orientations enable one to come to terms with 'the ultimate significance of one's location in the world'. Fourth, orientations 'interconnect knowledges'; that is, knowledge 'is never neutral' but continues to serve particular interests (1999: 27–31).

Within this theoretical framework, Carrette and Keller focus on the much publicized confrontation at the 1998 Lambeth Conference on the issue of gay sexuality. On the one hand, Reverend Richard Kirker represents the Lesbian and Gay Christian Movement; on the other, in stark opposition, stands Bishop Emmanual Chukwuma of Enugu, Nigeria. For Kirker, homosexuality is God's will for him; for Chukwuma, it is evidence of demonic power. The tension between these two subjectivities is difficult to resolve. The incident raises important issues: notions of masculinity (and the insight that 'nationalist politics is a major venue for "accomplishing" masculinity'),[40] the impact of colonial power with its implicit or explicit forms of racism, and the meaning of exorcism in the post-colonial West. Rather than trying to prioritize any one over the others, Carrette and Keller argue that we need to identify the overlapping 'orientations' and the strategies in force to maintain them. We need to ask how religious orientations shape cultural realities, how they may collude with forms of oppression, how and where the different power systems meet. In the context of the Lambeth Conference incident, how and where does 'the Enlightenment background espoused by the Anglican church' and 'the indigenous tradition of spirit possession' meet (1999: 38)? As Foucault might say, any attempt to find 'religious truth' in such a context means exploring the power relations involved.

Power is at the heart of the Birmingham dispute too. What appears at first glance to be a minor wrangle over scripture turns out to be a major power struggle between competing diaspora discourses: the mainstream religions led by a self-designated 'Sikh/Hindu' spokesman versus the Valmiki community with its so-called 'untouchable' past. As Carrette and Keller remark in the context of the Lambeth Conference incident, 'this is not to reduce religion to politics but grounds religion in politics' (1999: 40). The religious dispute – whether at Lambeth or in Birmingham – is embedded in the politics of identity.[41] I shall return to this complex topic in chapter 2.

---

40 The quotation is taken from Joane Nagel, 'Masculinity and nationalism: gender and sexuality in the making of nations', *Ethnic and Racial Studies*, 21 (2) (1998), p. 251; cited in Carrette and Keller (1999: 32 n. 20).

41 Further consideration of the constant 'flaming' on the old Indology discussion list might be helpful here. All too often what appeared to some to be matters of scholarly evidence and counter-evidence became for others a bitter dispute combining religious belief, nationalist politics and notions of personal identity. See, for example, the heated exchanges relating to the 'Aryan invasion theory' or the 'Harappan horse'.

The third approach that I would like to consider is derived from Mikhail Bakhtin's influential ideas on 'dialogics', or culture as dialogue. Gardiner and Bell provide a useful starting-point. According to Bakhtin, all 'sociocultural phenomena' are formed by means of an 'ongoing, dialogical relationship between individuals and groups, involving a multiplicity of different languages, discourses and symbolizing practices' (Gardiner and Bell 1998: 4). In this context, there can be no such thing as objective truth; on the contrary, truth is constituted through dialogue and between subjectivities. The rationale behind this stance is the belief that we should challenge 'structures of domination' in order to create 'more just and equitable relations of power'. 'If this is postmodernism,' Gardiner and Bell declare, 'then it is *practical* postmodernism – postmodernism we can do something with' (1998: 7, italics in the original). For those of us uncomfortable with the 'ivory tower' concept of scholarship, this is an attractive approach.

In the same volume, Bell's essay on 'culture as dialogue' takes this idea further. Seeing culture as dialogue places the focus on creativity. Culture is a kind of conversation: unpredictable, full of surprises, open to change, yet not random. While the monologue so typical of much scholarly work (especially in the realm of textual studies) takes little or no account of non-scholarly others, a dialogue requires interaction. In Bell's words, 'we negotiate, we discuss, we mistake, we mislead, and we otherwise stumble to a jointly creative response to the conditions of our understandings and misunderstandings'. In this kind of creative dialogue, we discover our boundaries and transcend them in our search for 'collective agency'. The main obstacle in our path is what Bell terms 'the problem of monologue' (1998: 53–4).[42] A brief consideration of the Birmingham dispute reveals at least two such monologues; it is important that this study does not become a third.

So what impedes dialogue? Bell identifies three obstructive positions: objectivism, subjectivism and what he terms 'subjectivo-objectivism'. Objectivism denies difference: the assertion that 'X is the case' is proved by external criterion Y (whether according to science or scripture), and is therefore unassailably true; what you say may be discounted. Subjectivism sees only difference: everyone has his or her opinion, so my view or experience is as valid as yours; what you say may be ignored. The 'subjectivo-objectivist' position draws on the other two to create a third type of monologue. In this case, difference itself is irrelevant: my view or experience emboldens me to say that mine is right and yours is wrong. All three positions make dialogue virtually impossible (1998: 54–5).

While it is tempting to draw parallels between these conversational positions and the stances taken by the protagonists in the Birmingham dispute, I shall not do so. In my view, the more important task is to apply these insights into the study of culture to the culture of study. 'Let us study dialogue with dialogue', recommends Bell (p. 56). Ideally, the research process itself should be a dialogue,

---

42 There is, of course, in Bakhtin's view (and Bell's), no pure monologue. All statements imply a speaker and, therefore, a listener too. Hence what Bell terms 'the ultimate inescapability of dialogue' (1998: 54).

an ongoing conversation allowing for mutual surprises, mistakes and criticism. Bell lists five 'guidelines' for dialogic research: care (precision in the collection and analysis of data), consideration (openness to others, although not uncritical), honesty, straightforwardness, and a sense of responsibility. If we as researchers take these as our professional guidelines, he maintains, 'we open up the conversational space for a sixth feature of dialogic talk: the collective agency represented by dialogic criticism' (p. 58). The alternative is to study dialogue with monologue, a prospect that is both unedifying and ineffective.

But what might this mean in the context of the Birmingham dispute? One obvious example is that there are serious issues of status, class and caste here. On the one hand, scriptural authority is used to legitimize the caste hierarchy; on the other, subaltern groups appropriate or 're-employ' sacred texts in order to advance their interests as they see them. In both cases, sacred texts are used in the processes by which a group becomes conscious of itself *as* a group. While the ideals of scholarship require that the academic writer adopts a position of scrupulous neutrality, the notion of responsibility demands something more. The first step is to acknowledge that caste prejudice is deeply embedded both in the dispute in Birmingham and in the sacred texts under discussion in this study. The second is to wonder how the concept of 'Hinduism', with its pronounced bias towards brahminical sources, can possibly make adequate space for so-called 'untouchables', including those who now present themselves as 'Valmikis'.

Chapter 2

Contextualizing the Person

1. Introduction

Who are the Valmikis? This apparently straightforward question has an apparently straightforward answer. As explained in chapter 1, the term 'Valmiki' denotes a devotee of the poet-saint Vālmīki, that is, one who worships Bhagwan Valmik as God. At this point, my definition is intentionally simplistic. As anyone familiar with the Valmiki community in Britain today will know, this statement conceals a broad spectrum of often overlapping attitudes: respect for the teachings of Vālmīki as for the teachings of a saint or guru; devotional worship of Bhagwan Valmik as the manifest form of God; and a monistic understanding that he represents the unmanifest source of all things.[1] However, even this answer conceals a cluster of ideas, each of which needs to be explored further. This chapter attempts to clarify some of these ideas by asking a number of more focused questions.[2]

The first step is an examination of terms. For example, we know that the Valmikis are considered by other South Asians to be low caste; that is, they are perceived as belonging to the category of person once formally designated 'untouchable'. The Sanskrit word, *aspṛśya* (literally, 'one who is not to be touched'), is first found as a generic term in the later *dharma* texts, dated somewhere between the fourth and sixth centuries CE (Aktor 1997: 82). Today, the English and vernacular equivalents are not only politically incorrect but legally invalid. The original historic resolution, passed prior to independence in 1932 and ratified by the Indian Government in 1950, declares:

> ... that, henceforth, amongst Hindus no one shall be regarded as an untouchable by reason of his birth and that those who have been so regarded hitherto will have the same right as other Hindus in regard to the use of public wells, public schools, public roads and all other public institutions.[3]

In 1955, Article 17 of the Abolition of Untouchability in the Untouchability (Offences) Act XXII replaced all earlier provisions, and applied across the whole of India (M. P. Sharma 1983: 138–79). As we shall see, 'untouchable' is not the

---

1 I return to these issues in my discussion of the UK community in chapter 5, section 3.

2 I am especially grateful to Apratim Barua, Simon Brodbeck and Nile Green for their thoughtful comments on this chapter.

3 Cited in Mukherjee (1988: 11). As it stands, the resolution continues to allow for untouchability on grounds other than birth. We may also note the assumption that 'Hinduism' includes 'untouchables', an assumption that is rejected by many of those to whom the term was once routinely allocated.

only term for this uncomfortable category, either in the past or today. In the discourse of the Indian constitution, for example, the preferred term is 'Scheduled Caste', a designation first used by the British in 1935. Implicit in this terminology is the idea of a list (or 'schedule') of castes that were deemed to be in particular need of help from the state, giving rise to the paradox of special provisions being allocated to a group that had been officially abolished. One consequence of this paradox is that the term 'untouchable' has never really gone away; it is still in use today, hence my continued use of the term in the following discussion when nothing else quite fits.[4] In the discourse of subaltern strategies and identity politics, however, the self-selected and generally (if not unanimously) preferred term today is *dalit*. Popular since the so-called 'untouchable protests' in the 1970s, this term is redolent with political, even militant, implications.[5] The starting point of this discourse is injustice: a passionate rejection of traditional Hindu culture with its divisive notions of pollution, *karma* and caste hierarchy; and a demand for change. Each term – *asprśya*, 'Scheduled Caste', *dalit* – derives from and reinforces a different discourse on the dynamics of caste identity: two from outside, only one from inside. In section 2 of this chapter, I shall explore some of these discourses.

Section 3 looks more closely at how *dalit* communities view themselves. Several scholars have written about the 'false consciousness' that makes a person internalize the evaluations of the dominant group. According to this scenario, *dalit*s submit not because they have no choice (although that may also be true) but because, at some level, they agree with that dominant group.[6] While there may be some truth in this idea, there are also positive forms of self-representation. In fact, there is a significant counter-rhetoric that is especially relevant for our understanding of the Valmiki position in the Birmingham dispute: the myth of origin.

Section 4 narrows the focus to the north of India, and to the names and terms applied to the groups identified there as 'Valmiki'. A perusal of late nineteenth-century colonial sources gives us a glimpse of the religious beliefs and practices of some of these groups. The marked influence of both Islam and Sikhism in this material is important.

Section 5 takes us to the Panjab. How do the people who now call themselves 'Valmikis' fit into the 'untouchable' or *dalit* politics of the Panjab in the twentieth and twenty-first centuries? A consideration of the separatist Ad Dharm movement led by Mangoo Ram is instructive here.

Section 6 shifts the focus to Britain. What do we know about Panjabi-

4 In order to force the reader to distance him- or herself from the outsider terminology constantly imposed on people whose self-definitions have not been recorded, I shall continue to place the word 'untouchable' in inverted commas.

5 The word is derived from the Marathi *daḷṇĕ*, 'to grind', which is in turn derived from the Sanskrit *dal*, 'to split open, burst asunder, grind into fragments' (Turner 1966: 355). According to Molesworth's classic Marathi dictionary, this emotive term means: 'ground', 'broken or reduced to pieces generally' (1857: 404). It thus denotes someone who has been deliberately and inexorably downtrodden over a long period of time by those with the status and power to do so.

6 See, for example, Freeman (1979: 383–4), Moffatt (1979: 290–304), and Deliège's discussion of Weber, Dumont *et al.* (1997: 105ff.).

speaking immigrants in the UK? How far have the traditional divisions along caste and religious lines persisted outside the Indian context? And what does this tell us about the position of the Valmiki community in Britain today?

The concluding section reflects on the material discussed in this chapter. How does all this help us to understand the dispute in Birmingham? What does it tell us about the underlying issue of religious authority and meaning?

2. Untouchability: Terms and Meanings

There is no evidence for untouchability in the oldest layers of textual evidence, that is, in the earliest Ṛgvedic hymns usually dated to 1200 (or 1500 or 1900) BCE. The earliest reference to a social hierarchy is that found in the late Ṛgvedic hymn, 'The Hymn of Man' (*puruṣa-sūkta*, *Ṛgveda* 10.90), that is, in approximately 900 BCE.[7] This hymn describes the primal sacrifice in which the cosmic 'Man' was dismembered, and by which all the elements of the universe were generated. According to verse 12, his mouth became the brahmin (*brāhmaṇa*), his arms the warrior (later known as *kṣatriya*), his thighs the people (later known as *vaiśya*), and from his feet the servants or *śūdra*s were born. This verse is often used to give Ṛgvedic authority to the *varṇa* system, but it almost certainly represents a deliberate post-Vedic reworking of an ancient theme for later political purposes. None the less, the verse constitutes the first mention of a society divided into four religiously ordained orders in what may reasonably be termed an ideological as well as a social and economic system (*varṇa*). As we move on to the texts of classical Hinduism, we often find the term *dvija* ('twice-born') applied to males of the three higher *varṇa*s: it signifies one who has undergone Vedic initiation (*upanayana*) and a period of religious education, and who is therefore eligible to wear the sacred thread. By the time of the Dharmasūtra texts (that is, somewhere between the beginning of the third century BCE and the end of the second), the function of the *śūdra* has become service to the twice-born *varṇa*s.[8] It is not until the later stratum of the *Viṣṇusmṛti* (that is, no earlier than the fourth century CE) that we find the term *aspṛśya* used in an explicitly generic sense. This is not to say that the groups later defined as 'untouchable' did not exist. For example, the terms *niṣāda*, *caṇḍāla* and *śvapaca* are already recorded, and the groups so named were evidently already pegged low on the socio-religious scale.[9] The point

7 Generally speaking, Indian scholars tend to promote much earlier dates (sometimes as much as two thousand years earlier), largely based on what may be referred to as the 'astronomical method'. Western-trained Indologists with their focus on linguistic evidence are likely to prefer the more conservative dates given here. For a useful account of both views, see Bryant (2001: 238–66).

8 See, for example, *Āpastamba Dharmasūtra* 1.1.7, *Gautama Dharmasūtra* 4.56, *Vasiṣṭha Dharmasūtra* 2.20. For the dating of these texts, see Olivelle (1999: xxviii–xxxiv).

9 The term *niṣāda*, originally the name of a tribe, came to denote any tribal person. In particular, the term was often used to refer to the tribal hunter or fisherman (see, for example, the *niṣāda* cursed by Vālmīki for killing the crane) and, by extension, to any 'wild' tribal considered likely to attack and rob the unwary. The term *caṇḍāla*

I am making is that the word *asprśya* ('untouchable') was not yet applied to them as a generic term.

Once it comes into effect, the notion of untouchability seems to exist within a timeless, ideally harmonious, hierarchy encapsulated by traditional Sanskrit terminology. The word *asprśya* refers both to temporary states of pollution (such as menstruation, death and childbirth) and to the permanent untouchability of low-caste status.[10] In the latter case, the word makes sense only when used by someone who believes that they belong to a 'purer' category, to a 'higher' caste (*jāti*), someone who believes that they will be polluted by contact. Strictly speaking, this means any member of the four *varṇa*s.[11] The term *avarṇa* (literally, 'without *varṇa*' or 'one for whom there is no *varṇa*') denotes a person deemed permanently 'untouchable': such a person is pegged even below the *śūdra* in the classical Hindu hierarchy.

However, this clear distinction between *śūdra* and 'untouchable' is an even

---

(also *cāṇḍāla*) may also be derived from the name of an early tribe. However, this term is more often linked with the Sanskrit word *caṇḍa*, meaning 'violent', 'cruel', 'fierce'; hence the tendency to use *caṇḍāla* to denote what are perceived to be the lowest of 'untouchable' groups. The term *śvapaca* is usually translated 'dog-cooker' (from *śvan*, 'dog', and *pac*, 'to cook'; see Doniger and Smith 1991: 242 and Hiltebeitel 2001: 198) and, by extension, 'dog-eater'; the term is clearly intended to denote a despised category of barbaric tribals. But the word in question is almost certainly the result of popular etymology. An alternative spelling, *śvapaka*, suggests a more likely source of meaning: the tribal custom of keeping dogs. According to this version of the term, *śvapa-ka* means 'a person who is involved in keeping dogs' (*pa*, 'keeping', from *pā*, 'to protect or keep'). Unfortunately, the popular etymology combined with the spelling *śvapāka* (understood as *śva-pāka*) brings us back to the 'dog-cooking' idea (from *pāk*, 'cooking'). I am grateful to Clifford Wright for helping me to think through these ideas. To summarize, whatever their original meanings, all three words – *niṣāda*, *caṇḍāla* and *śvapaca* – became highly derogatory terms used to convey the brahminical view of those who lived beyond the village boundaries.

10 For a careful account of untouchable persons and categories in the Dharmasūtras, with a particular focus on the distinction between temporary and permanent untouchability, see Aktor (1997: 85–90). For a discussion of the range of attitudes towards menstruation expressed in different discourses – in medical texts (*āyurveda*), in the ascetic discourses of early Buddhism and Jainism, and in the discipline of religious law (*dharmaśāstra*) – see Leslie (1994). For the perceived link between menstruation, childbirth and caste, the idea that 'only certain castes experience a second, sacred birth which cleanses them of the first, bloody birth', see Prashad (2000: xvi).

11 In order to avoid the common confusion between *varṇa* and *jāti*, both of which are often translated by the English word 'caste', I shall retain the Sanskrit terms. Where I do use the English terms, 'caste' denotes *jāti*, 'high caste' refers in general terms to *jāti*s within the twice-born (*dvija*) *varṇa*s, while 'low caste' refers equally generally to non-*dvija* groups. As Nicholas Dirks has established, however, 'caste' is neither an unchanged survival of ancient India nor a single system reflecting a notional 'core culture'; it is a relatively modern phenomenon arising from the British presence in India. While the British certainly did not invent caste, it was under British domination that 'caste' became a single term capable of defining the diverse forms of social identity and organization to be found in India (2001).

later development. The issue of a possible fifth grouping (*pañca, pañcama*) is raised in a number of late texts, and there was evidently some difference of opinion. While some authors explicitly placed a particular group (*niṣāda*, perhaps, or *caṇḍāla*) below the *śūdra varṇa*, others dismissed the idea of a fifth category altogether.[12] The *Manusmṛti*, for example, roundly declares that 'there is no fifth' (*nāsti tu pañcamaḥ*, 10.4).[13] However, this refusal to accept a fifth *varṇa* cannot be taken as a rejection of untouchability. It seems that individuals and groups that were already – for a variety of reasons – regarded as 'untouchable' were increasingly allocated to the fourth *varṇa* as inferior *śūdra*s. All *śūdra*s were deemed to have one birth (*ekajāti*, *Manusmṛti* 10.4); but while some were held to be ritually pure (*sat*), others were considered ritually impure (*asat*) and therefore polluting. At some point, the latter group became defined as separate from, and definitively lower than, the *śūdra*, that is, as both 'untouchable' (*aspṛśya*) and without a place in the four-*varṇa* system (*avarṇa*). Both terms carry powerful associations of ritual pollution and social exclusion.

But who were these people? The question of why a person or persons might have become regarded as 'untouchable' – whether as part of the *śūdra varṇa* or not – has been addressed by many scholars. I shall mention only some of the more pertinent suggestions here. The individuals and groups considered 'untouchable' probably included the following: members of the *varṇa* system who were deemed to have transgressed society's rules (the so-called '*vrātya* theory'); tribal groups which had failed to assimilate, or who were deemed to be lacking in culture; the offspring of inappropriate (that is, *pratiloma*, 'against the grain') marriages (a traditional explanation much favoured by the *Manusmṛti*, but inadequate to explain the great proliferation of 'untouchable' *jāti*s); and those who followed professions that were considered unclean and inauspicious, professions such as refuse collection, human waste removal and dealing with corpses. The answer probably lies in a combination of these and other explanations.[14] The end result of this ancient classificatory process is that an individual became 'untouchable' not because of what he or she had done, or was engaged in doing, but by birth. Mikael Aktor concludes his doctoral thesis on the subject with the following words (1997: 224):

---

12 For further discussions of the terms *pañca* and *pañcama* in this context, see Kane (1968–77: II.i, 167–8) and Mukherjee (1988: 26, 101–2, 106 n. 8).

13 The *Manusmṛti* (also known under the title *Mānavadharmaśāstra*, both usually translated into English as *The laws of Manu*) is the work of several authors over a considerable length of time. Popularly known as *Manu*, the text served as the standard source of authority regarding the social and religious duties of orthodox Hinduism (*dharma*, including *varṇadharma*) from the early centuries CE onwards. For an excellent introduction to this text, see Doniger and Smith (1991: xv ff.).

14 For brief accounts of the origins of untouchability, see Michael (1999a: 13–16) and Mukherjee (1988: 12–13). For the *vrātya* theory in particular and the proliferation of 'servile and peasant castes' in general, see R. S. Sharma (1990: 332–45). For a more recent analysis of 'stereotypes and proliferations', see Aktor (1997: 94–112). For a discussion of the auspicious/inauspicious paradigm in relation to both impurity and untouchability, see Aktor (1997: 22–8, 216–20).

> By making untouchability an inborn quality of particular people this segregation is professionalized and utilized. The removal and handling of inauspiciousness is assigned to specific groups which are set off by these very tasks and the avoidances they imply. They are prevented from any upward mobility and make up a controllable labour force at the disposal of more powerful masters.

Whatever justifications may be found in the doctrine of *karma* and rebirth,[15] the economic and political implications are obvious. The two essential poles of untouchability are the supposedly degraded state of those concerned and their economic indispensability. The link between the two is powerfully made.

The writings on untouchability and related issues reveal a wealth of further terms. Most (like *aspṛśya* and *avarṇa*) derive from and continue to reinforce the blatantly one-sided, brahminical framework of the construct. For example, Aktor's glossary of Sanskrit terms gives us the following synonyms: *abhojyānna* ('one whose food should not be eaten'), *adṛśya* ('one who should not be looked at'), *agamya* ('one who should not be approached for sex'), *apapātra* ('one with whom one should not exchange food vessels'), *apratigṛhya* ('one from whom nothing should be received', including gifts and material goods), *asaṃbhāṣya* ('one with whom conversation should be avoided'), *aśrāvya* ('one who should not be heard'), and *bāhya* ('one who is segregated', that is, one who lives outside the village boundary). Several terms reinforce the idea that the individuals concerned are placed at the 'end', that is, that they belong to the lowest castes of all: *anta*, *antya*, *antyaja*, and *antyāvasāyin*. According to some late *smṛti* texts, the term *antyaja* denotes a standard list of seven groups including washermen, fishermen, leather-workers, dancers/actors and workers in reeds. Below *antyaja* in the hierarchy of 'untouchable' terms stands *antyāvasāyin*, a word which denotes an even lower set of seven groups, this time including the *caṇḍāla* and the *śvapaca* (Aktor 1997: 225–6). The last two terms appear in *Manusmṛti* 10.51–2:

> But the dwellings of *caṇḍāla*s and *śvapaca*s should be outside the village. They should use discarded vessels, and their [only] wealth should be dogs and donkeys. They should wear the clothing of the dead, and eat their food from broken dishes. Their [only] ornaments should be made of black iron, and they should wander constantly.[16]

Clearly, this grim passage does not reflect any particular social reality; it is a construction that demonizes the 'untouchable' as other, a construction that tells us more about the fears of its authors than about the people they claim to describe. That said, the texts of Dharmaśāstra place *caṇḍāla*s and *śvapaca*s at the very bottom of the socio-religious hierarchy, even below other so-called 'untouchables'.

But not all terms for these people were derogatory. For example, during his 1933–34 campaign against untouchability, Mahatma (Mohandas Karamchand)

15 For a discussion of the implications of the physical body in which one is born, with special reference to the doctrine of *karma*, see Leslie (1999).

16 This translation is adapted from Doniger and Smith (1991: 242). The notion of constant wandering may suggest a link with early gypsies (Simon Brodbeck, personal communication, 8 June 2002).

Gandhi famously proposed the vernacular term *harijan* (literally, 'born of God') as a positive substitute. His professed aim was to improve the conditions of 'untouchables' by reintegrating them into the Hindu fold. Today, however, while the word *harijan* is still used by some,[17] it has been abandoned as patronizing and manipulative by many of those it was intended to uplift. Indeed, the great 'untouchable' leader, Dr B. R. Ambedkar (1892–1956), himself a Mahar from what is now Maharashtra, resisted from the start both Gandhi's terminology and his general philosophy regarding 'untouchables' (see Zelliot 1996: 150–83). Vasant Moon (also a Mahar) was a schoolboy at the time, and he recalls how his own refusal to accept the name 'Harijan' cost him a scholarship (2001: 37). More recently, a study of 200 Harijan leaders in Bihar revealed that the term was widely understood as 'a term of abuse meaning a person whose father is unknown' (Sachchidananda 1977: 3). Rajshekar's dismissal of the term (1995: 53n.) is particularly outspoken:

> Prostitution of young Black Untouchable girls is sanctioned by Hindu religion, under their appelation Devadasi, meaning maid-servant of God. These girls, coming from impoverished Dalit (Black Untouchable) families, live around Hindu temples, work as dancers and singers, but remain unmarried, to be enjoyed by the priests and other upper caste Hindus. The children born to these 'maid-servants of God' are called 'Harijans' (children of God), which is the new name that the 'Mahatma' gave to our people. In reality, 'Harijan' means bastard.[18]

Clearly, as far as his target audience was concerned, Gandhi's plan backfired.[19]

The British also sought positive terminology. For example, they introduced the terms 'Scheduled Castes' and 'Scheduled Tribes' (both adopted by the Indian Constitution) to replace the more negative (and also British) appellation, 'Depressed Classes'. Unfortunately, while 'Scheduled Castes/Tribes' seems to be an improvement on 'Depressed Classes', the suggestion of top-down charity made it an unwelcome label. An additional problem here remains the lack of clarity surrounding the lists and definitions relating to the terms 'Scheduled Castes' and 'Scheduled Tribes', and the relationship between the two groups. In the 1991 Census, 67.76 million people were considered to belong to the category of Scheduled Tribes. In their four-volume *Encyclopaedic profile of Indian tribes* (1996), Sachchidananda and Prasad present a catalogue of these tribes, together with descriptions of their socio-cultural lives and illustrations of representative individuals. As the editors explain, the closest indigenous term to the English

---

17 For example, the Harijans of Rateyur in Karnataka prefer the term to either 'Scheduled Caste' or 'Adi Karnataka' (signifying an original inhabitant of the Karnataka region), both of which may be used in official contexts (Charsley 1998b). Similarly, Deliège writes that almost all the Paṟaiyars he met in Tamilnadu referred to themselves by the term 'Harijan' (1997: 125). For an excellent overview of names and terms, see Deliège (1999: 9–18).

18 Rajshekar (1995: 53n.). The phrase 'Black Untouchable', suggesting the darker skin colour of many so-called 'untouchables', is intended to link all Indian *dalit*s with the slave history of Black Americans.

19 For the Dalit Panther Manifesto on 'that man Gandhi', see Joshi (1986: 143).

word 'tribe' is the Sanskrit *jana*, meaning 'community', understood in this context to denote an 'agglomeration of individuals with specific territorial, kinship and cultural patterns'.[20] Official designations in English ranged over a period of time from 'forest tribe' to 'primitive tribe' (1931), 'backward tribe' (1935), 'Adivasi' (*ādivāsī*; literally, 'original settler' or 'aboriginal'; 1948), and 'Scheduled Tribe'. Today, few tribes in India fit the anthropologist's schema: they are viewed instead as 'tribes in transition'; that is, the decision to call a particular community a 'tribe' rather than a 'caste' depends not on its current status but on its earlier history (1996: xviii). As Deliège points out, the passage from tribe to caste is a significant one, involving hierarchy, caste divisions, an acceptance of 'Hindu values', and the practice of 'untouchability' (1985: 106–12).[21] Apratim Barua prefers a distinction that takes the insider's point of view: most 'tribals' take pride in their tribal identity whereas there is little pride in belonging to a Scheduled Caste (personal communication, 27 May 2002). Perhaps this distinction underlies K. S. Singh's two volumes, one allocated to India's 'Scheduled Castes' (1993), the other to her 'Scheduled Tribes' (1994). From the outsider point of view so often expressed in brahminical texts, however, the distinction between the two categories is minimal.[22]

The missing insider view is supplied by the term preferred by many 'untouchables' today: *dalit*. The *dalit* discourse constitutes an explicit rejection of traditional Hindu culture. This has led to resentment on the part of the higher castes and to frequent anti-'untouchable' violence. For example, in their detailed analysis of 'Harijan atrocity', Mendelsohn and Vicziany distinguish between what they call 'traditional violence' (that is, violence which stems from traditional social hierarchies) and the increasingly dominant form of violence which arises from the combination of 'untouchable' resistance to those hierarchies and caste-Hindu responses to that resistance (1998: 44–76). The worst recorded cases consist of 'large numbers of caste Hindus – sometimes many hundreds – pursuing Untouchables in vengeful retribution' (p. 53). It is no surprise that this kind of hostility has resulted in a fiercely politicized *dalit* identity, not to mention *dalit* resistance and counter-violence.[23]

There are other, more specific terms too. Some are simply tribal or *jāti* names (such as *caṇḍāla* and *niṣāda*, discussed above). 'Untouchable' *jāti*s today include

---

20 Both *jana* ('community') and *jāti* ('caste') are derived from the Sanskrit root *jan*, 'to be born'.

21 For further discussion of terms, and for lists of tribes, see Roy Burman (1994) and K. S. Singh (1994). For the transitional status of tribes in India, see Vyas and Mann (1980). For a study of Indian tribes in general from 1940 to 1980, see the now classic work by von Führer-Haimendorf (1982); for a specific focus on the Bhils of western India, see Deliège (1985). For a more recent discussion of the concept 'tribe', and the notion of tribal identity, see Béteille (1992: 57–78).

22 For a discussion of the distinction between tribe and caste in the context of the dacoit motif, see the final section of chapter 4.

23 For examples, see Pantawane (1986: 79–87) and Michael (1999a, 1999b). For a field report of the riots in Gujarat in 1981, when hostility towards 'untouchable' medical students led to three months of violence against 'untouchables', see Joshi (1986: 71–6).

the 'Chamars' (*camār*),[24] the 'Chuhras' (*cuhḍā*)[25] and 'Bhangis' (*bhaṅgī*)[26] of north India, the Mahars (*mahār*) of central India, the Paṟaiyars of Tamilnadu,[27] the Pullayas of Kerala, and so on. Not surprisingly, there is widespread resistance to many of these terms. In particular, Valmikis today reject absolutely the appellations 'Chuhra' and 'Bhangi', while the Ravidasis similarly reject the term 'Chamar'. In order to maintain the necessary critical distance, therefore, these terms are placed within inverted commas throughout this study.

Then there are the 'untouchable' groups who have adopted the more prestigious-sounding names of titles and chiefs to reflect their ambitions, names such as 'Konar' ('king') and 'Nadar' (*nāḍār*, 'lord'). Still others have deliberately chosen a name to indicate not their status with regard to the brahminical world, but their preferred devotional (*bhakti*) orientation. The Valmikis may be placed in this category, as may the Ravidasis (*ravidāsī*), worshippers of the poet-saint (*sant*) Ravidās, also called 'Raidās'. Other examples include Chandals (*caṇḍāla*) who call themselves 'Namasudra' (*nāmaśūdra*, *śūdra*s who worship the 'Divine Name'), Julahas who prefer the name 'Kabirpanthi' (following the path of the saint Kabīr), and 'Chamars' converted to Sikhism who call themselves 'Ramdasi' (*rāmdāsī*, 'servant of Rām'). The most spectacular change of status by means of religious name remains the mass conversion to Buddhism in 1956 of many thousands of Mahars in Maharashtra and their adoption of the name 'neo-Buddhist'. The principle is widespread. As Deliège puts it, 'at each census-taking, hundreds of castes change their name in this way, hoping to gain in status' (1997: 123–4); I would prefer to say that they are hoping to disassociate themselves from the identities contructed for them by others. Clearly, *jāti* names are significant, a point to which I shall return below. For the moment, I shall note only this: while a shared identity lies at the core of all these terms – and nowadays a shared resistance to the definitions of others – their overlapping meanings are both complex and disturbing.

But what is meant by 'a shared identity'? What did being 'untouchable' mean in the past? According to Sanskrit *dharma* texts, the prohibitions understood by

---

24 The word *camār* is derived from the Sanskrit term *carman* ('hide, skin'), hence *carmakāra* or 'leather-worker' (Turner 1966: 255). For an account of the tanning process and the making of leather articles including shoes, see Briggs (1920: 256–60).

25 The Panjabi word *cuhḍā* is usually translated as 'sweeper' or 'scavenger'. In the Indian context, the term 'scavenging' is understood to cover the removal of rubbish, including dead animals, from within the village boundaries, and the carrying of headloads of human excrement, commonly referred to as 'nightsoil'.

26 The Panjabi word *bhaṅgī*, also translated as 'sweeper', is derived from the Sanskrit word for 'hemp', *bhaṅga*; today the vernacular term denotes a marijuana drink. Turner's dictionary of Indo-Aryan languages offers two primary meanings for the Sanskrit headword *bhaṅga* (1966: 531). The first, derived from the root *bhañj*, means 'to break'; this supports the Assamese derivation of 'Bhangi' from their traditional occupation of splitting bamboo for basket-making, as reported by K. S. Singh (1993: 239). The second meaning given by Turner, the one more commonly understood, is 'hemp'; his translation of the derivative term *bhaṅgī* as 'hemp addict' is unfortunate.

27 The Tamil term 'Paṟaiyar' has given rise to the English word 'pariah'; both mean 'outcaste'.

the term 'untouchability' (*aspṛśyatva*) are wide ranging. For example, there is the requirement for a high-caste person not to have sexual relations (*agamyatva*) with an 'untouchable'. As one would expect from the power dynamics involved, the penalty incurred depends upon 'whose' woman is involved, whether she becomes pregnant, and so on. We should remind ourselves here that the point of view represented in Dharmaśāstra literature is invariably that of the twice-born male householder. In this context, the control of 'his' woman – whether mother, wife, sister or daughter – is crucial. Not touching may be understood in several ways: avoiding direct contact with an 'untouchable', avoiding indirect contact such as touching something previously touched by an 'untouchable', and avoiding being too close to an 'untouchable'. Being 'too close' to an 'untouchable' is understood as being within the stipulated distance from him or her or, for some texts, being touched by his or her shadow.[28] Another important component of the untouchability complex is the requirement not to eat the food made or given by an 'untouchable' (*abhojyānnatva*). In the world of traditional *dharma*, feeding others is the responsibility and privilege of the twice-born male householder, and thus a mark of his moral superiority. The prohibition on accepting water from an 'untouchable' is even more restrictive since it extends to not drinking water from a well or tank that has been dug by 'untouchables'. In this context, it makes sense that the vessels in which 'untouchables' have taken food or drink are impure, and should be discarded (*apapātratva*). But there is more. One should not associate in any way with 'untouchables': one should not converse with them or use their language (*asaṃbhāṣyatva*); one should not look at them or allow their glance to fall on one's food (*adṛśyatva*); and one should not allow their noise to disturb ritual recitation (*aśrāvyatva*). The last prohibition is taken to grotesque lengths: if *śūdra*s (including *asat-śūdra*s, the 'impure' or 'untouchable' *śūdra*s) deliberately listen to Vedic recitation, molten tin or lac should be poured into their ears; if they recite from the Veda themselves, their tongues should be cut off; and if they learn Vedic passages by heart, their bodies should be cut in two.[29] Two points should be noted here: first, we have no evidence that these threats were ever carried out; and second, these and other similar rulings have been contested at least since the nineteenth century, often by *dalit*s themselves. But the implications are clear. These prohibitions (or, to use Aktor's more precise term, 'avoidances') derive from and relate to the ritual

28 Might shadow be regarded as in some sense a substance – that is, as another form of the person concerned – rather than simply an effect of the absence of light? In Jain philosophy, certainly, shadows are substances, just as darkness is a substance rather than the absence of light; hence the ruling that one should not step over the guru's shadow and the Buddhist stories of artists painting in the Buddha's shadow on a given surface (Phyllis Granoff, email communications, 26 April and 2 May 2002). In the context of myth, the shadow is substantial enough to be taken for a real person, as when Sītā's shadow (*chāyā*) serves as a substitute or 'illusory' Sītā (*māyāsītā*; Doniger 1999: 12ff.). Cf. Slaje's insightful discussions of salt as another form of water in the context of Yājñavalkya's teaching in the Upaniṣads (2001b, 2001c).

29 *Gautama Dharmasūtra* 2.3.4 (12.4–6 in Olivelle 1999: 98). For detailed textual accounts of each of the avoidances listed, see Aktor (1997: 122–60). For the standard account of untouchability in *dharma* texts, see Kane (1968–77: II.i.165–79).

context of brahminical ideology. Because of their supposed association with polluting substances, including dead bodies, 'untouchables' were deemed ritually impure. As the representatives of (as well as a primary source of) pollution, they had to be excluded from the religious arena. All other rulings stem from this one requirement: that 'untouchables', by definition, have no place in auspicious forms of brahminical religion.

Despite resistance on the part of the so-called 'untouchables', many of these textual prohibitions were reflected in social practice, from the ban on their entry into high-caste temples to that on them taking water from high-caste wells. All over India there was the widespread refusal of higher castes to accept food or water from 'untouchables'. In her classic book, *Caste today* (1962), Taya Zinkin emphasizes two criteria: water and daughters. Who will drink the water you offer? Who will accept your daughter in marriage? In a more recent overview of untouchability (1999), Deliège arranges what he considers the most common restrictions into seven categories: religious taboos, the use of public facilities, residential segregation, professional services, commensality taboos, 'languages and attitudes', and a final section on physical appearance ('dress, adornments and status symbols'). While the specifics often seem secular in provision and effect, the momentum behind them is evidently religious. For example, the ban on temple entry included a ban on walking in high-caste areas adjoining or leading to the temple, invariably extended to the village as a whole. The result was that 'untouchables' could only enter the main village if they had a caste-specific task to take care of, such as collecting refuse or removing a corpse. The primary concern of the higher castes was to keep the 'untouchable' person at a distance from their (auspicious and highly valued) religious centre while taking full advantage of his or her (inauspicious and devalued) labour. One result was that the 'untouchable' hamlet sat precariously on the edge of the human world, marked out as barely human. In Tamilnadu, for example, 'untouchables' still refer to the village proper as *ūr*, while their own separate hamlet is called *cêri*; this suggests that the inhabitants of the latter do not really belong to the village. Similarly, 'untouchables' in that region call the inhabitants of the *ūr* 'Tamils', a term they do not apply to themselves; the social exclusion that defines untouchability is thus reflected in the language that they use themselves (Viramma *et al.* 1997: 282 n. 3, 296, 300). According to Charsley and Karanth, the situation in Karnataka is more nuanced. They maintain that the admittedly 'separate localities' of older 'untouchable' communities are 'in no clear sense' defined as outside the village; yet twentieth-century developments have produced 'the most clearly segregated Untouchable housing to be found'. They add that, while not impossible, it is still extremely difficult for 'untouchables' to build houses outside the areas designated for them (1998b: 272–3). Another result of the upper-caste determination to separate themselves from 'untouchables' was that the latter were expected to demonstrate their inferiority and submission in their language, their deportment and their dress. This included bans on smart or new clothes, on footwear and jewellery (including flowers in the hair), on umbrellas for men and breast-coverings for women, and so on (Deliège 1999: 91–110). Hence, no doubt, the determination of some 'untouchable' groups to wear garments or colours traditionally forbidden to them. A striking example is provided by the decision of Mangoo Ram, founder of the Ad Dharm movement (see p. 55ff.), that his mainly 'untouchable' followers should wear red (Juergensmeyer 1982: 53–4). While the religious origin of many of the restrictions listed may no longer be obvious, they served to mark 'untouchables' in ways that made their exclusion from the religious domain easy to enforce.

But what is the situation today? One influential analysis, based on a range of micro-studies, concludes that traditional caste-based prejudice against 'untouchables' persists throughout India (Joshi 1982: 25, 166). A more recent survey of Rajasthan argues that, while there has been some decline in the extent of discrimination in public places such as schools, shops and hospitals, the private sphere has not been affected in a major way. As one might expect, the level of change has been greater in metropolitan than in rural areas, and the perception of change is more pronounced among older and wealthier individuals than among the younger and poorer. The authors of this study conclude that caste still exerts a 'stranglehold' over the rural population of Rajasthan where the Scheduled Castes remain largely unaware of the provisions of the Untouchability Offences Act (Lal and Nahar 1990: 124–9). Again, the survey of Karnataka is more optimistic. The extent of discrimination, and the effects on the 'untouchables' concerned, seems to vary enormously: in some areas, change is 'minimal'; in others, there is reason for hope. The authors conclude that 'there is no longer any question of such discrimination entering the very identity of those suffering from it' (Charsley and Karanth 1998b: 287). For the scholars represented by this volume, 'humiliation is ... in retreat'. 'Untouchables' are increasingly able to stand at the centre of their own worlds, rather than perch on the periphery of someone else's (pp. 295–6). Writing in 1997, Deliège is less upbeat. His research among the Paṟaiyars of Tamilnadu indicates a marked improvement in the lives of 'untouchables', but discrimination continues to exist. For example, 'untouchables' are permitted by law to enter temples and attend schools but the reaction is such that few will take the risk (1997: 146–61). As Deliège puts it (p. 161),

> The struggle of the untouchables will be long and hard since the high castes are not ready to accept dealing with the untouchables as equals. Their feeling of superiority towards the untouchables is still deeply ingrained, and it is surprising to see to what extent the traditional values are embedded in the collective consciousness of the high castes.

Similarly, Mendelsohn and Vicziany conclude that, while the situation for 'untouchables' in India has changed radically during the twentieth century, 'what remains of the *ancien régime* is far from merely residual' (1998: 260). 'Untouchables' are still sharply divided from the rest of society in many ways. Continuing anti-'untouchable' violence is a measure of the strength of caste-Hindu resistance as also of *dalit* determination; and poverty remains a major additional factor (pp. 258–71).

From the perspective of the twenty-first century, it is obvious that untouchability is no longer what it was. The old questions of ritual pollution are now superseded by a range of economic and political changes.[30] New *dalit* strategies have transformed Indian politics. Nothing will ever be the same again. None the less, traditional values continue to subvert the ideals of the Indian legal system: segregation wherever possible, an assumed (if unspoken) superiority on the part of the higher castes reinforced by threats of violence, and 'untouchables' caught between fear and revolt.

For those wishing to explore further the complexities of past and present untouchability in India, there is much to read, especially in recent years. Historians continue to wrestle with the origins of the concept, the development of the cluster of brahminical ideas, colonial and post-colonial responses, and so on.[31] Text specialists in a variety of languages engage with the implications of recorded rhetoric.[32] Anthropologists provide critical analyses of the phenomenon of untouchability in general,[33] and detailed ethnographies of its practice in particular places or regions.[34] Increasingly, they also provide gender-sensitive studies with a

30 For a summary of the impact of economic and political change on the relationship between brahmins and 'untouchables' (mainly cobblers) in a Hindu village in western Nepal, for example, see Caplan (1972: 85–96).

31 For the classic study of *śūdras* (including 'untouchables') in India up to *c.* 600 CE, see R. S. Sharma (1990). For a brief history of Indian 'untouchables', see Mukherjee (1988). For a detailed exposition of the ideas of Mahatma Jotirao Phule, the most influential theoretician of the low-caste protest movement in nineteenth-century Maharashtra, see O'Hanlon (1985). For the history of the Ambedkar movement, also in Maharashtra, see the collection of papers by Zelliot (1996), including the bibliographical essay fronting the revised edition and the addenda to Parts II, III and IV.

32 For a detailed analysis of the discourse on untouchability in Sanskrit texts, see Aktor's discussion of the *Parāśarasmṛti* and its medieval commentary, the *Parāśaramādhavīya* (1997, 2000). As for early Tamil sources, George Hart (2001) discusses the emergence of marginal and low-status groups (*kuṭi*, a term which can be translated as 'caste'), the members of which functioned as controllers of dangerous sacred power; in effect, they became the 'untouchables'. According to Hart, the modern form of the caste system in south India is the result of changes introduced at a later stage by the kings and brahmins of (Aryan) Hindu orthodoxy.

33 For critical studies, see especially Dumont (1970), Mahar (1972), Moffatt (1979), Quigley (1991), Deliège (1992, 1999) and Mosse (1994a, 1994c). For a useful summary of theories of caste in relation to the academic understanding of untouchability, including a detailed critique of Moffatt's study, see Deliège (1997: 102–20).

34 With regard to Tamilnadu, see Hardgrave's work on the Nadars, or toddy-tappers, including the life histories of five individuals (1969); Moffat's analysis of the structure of rural untouchability (1979); Mosse (1986, 1994b); Kapadia (1995); and Deliège (1997). For Kerala, see the work of Mohan (1999, 2002 and forthcoming). With regard to Karnataka, see the volume edited by Charsley and Karanth, detailing the patterns of experience for particular 'untouchable' castes in seven different towns and villages (1998a). With regard to western India, see Deliège's study of the Bhils (1985). For Maharashtra, see Jogdand (1991) on the *dalit*, mainly Mahar, protest movement; Murugkar (1991) on the militant 'Dalit Panther' movement; as well as Zelliot and Berntsen (1988), Gokhale (1993), Omvedt (1994), and Pillai-Vetschera (1999). For the 'Chamars' of north India, see Briggs's classic account, including black-and-white photographs of 'representative' individuals, all

focus on 'untouchable' women. These include Kapadia's account of Pallar women in Tamilnadu (1995), Pillai-Vetschera's article on Mahar women in the Ahmednagar district (1999), and Searle-Chatterjee's analysis of women 'sweepers' in Benares (1981). There is also an invaluable account of life as a Paṟaiyar woman in Tamilnadu between 1980 and 1990, based on recorded conversations in Tamil (Viramma *et al.* 1997). It transpires that, in many contexts, 'untouchable' women experience a greater freedom in their daily lives than their higher-caste sisters. In Benares, for example, the lives of 'sweeper' women are hard, but they do the same work as men and are paid the same, and they tend to control the family finances. In the home, domestic tasks are usually interchangeable, with men and women working together to care for the family. In Searle-Chatterjee's words, the women 'walk boldly and with confidence' (1981: 2). In Tamilnadu, however, the emulation of upper-caste practices seems to have resulted in a 'drastic fall' in the status of low-caste women, accompanied by a loss of their earlier freedoms (Kapadia 1995: 66–7). In other contexts, the perceived boldness of 'untouchable' women, when combined with their low status and lack of protection outside their own community, often leads to sexual harassment and exploitation. For example, Contursi's informants in Maharashtra speak of 'numerous incidents of abuse, rape and kidnap[p]ing by police and outsiders', and women activists are 'special targets of police harassment' (1993: 329–30).[35] Matters are complicated by the fact that Indian women's organizations tend to ignore caste while low-caste associations are usually dominated by men (Omvedt 1990: 41); this is evidently a topic that would benefit from further research.[36]

There are other approaches too. Political theorists study the effects of the recent creation of quota opportunities for *dalit*s and the dangerous backlash against them on the part of the higher castes, as well as the emergence of *dalit*-led movements.[37] There are personal narratives. For example, Vasant Moon has written a vivid memoir of his own childhood spent in the Mahar slums of Nagpur in Maharashtra, against the backcloth of the independence movement and the

male (1920); Khare's discussion of the 'Chamars' of Lucknow (1984, 2000); and Lynch's study of the Jatav caste (a sub-group of the 'Chamars') in Agra, Uttar Pradesh (1969). For the Panjab, see Juergensmeyer (1982, 1988) and Saberwal (1990). For an account of the Harijans of the Kumaun Hills in the Himalaya, see Upadhyay (1990). For the Rishis of Bangladesh, traditionally leather-workers and musicians, see Zene (2000, 2002).

35 For the widespread rape of *dalit* women by caste Hindu men in the Panjab, and the contempt shown for the resulting offspring, see Prashad (2000: 34).

36 I support Omvedt's assertion that the work of feminist scholars has much to offer the study of the *dalit* contestation of 'Hinduism'. The themes of caste domination, exploitation and patriarchy need to be examined together in relation to the brahminical Hindu system and the resistance to it of both women and *dalit*s (Omvedt 1995: 100–3).

37 For a study of the Indian policy of protective discrimination for 'untouchables' and the resulting patterns of social change, see Joshi (1982). For a collection of essays on the link between occupation and inherited low status, and discussions of *dalit* and labour movements from the eighteenth century to the recent past, see Robb (1993). For studies of *dalit* movements, see Jognand (1991), Murugkar (1991), Contursi (1993), Gokhale (1993) and Omvedt (1994).

growing influence of Ambedkar (2001). Freeman has compiled a constructive and insightful biography for Muli, an 'untouchable' man from the Bauri community in Orissa, based on the latter's narrations in Oriya over a period of six months (1979). The Racines worked in a similar way with Viramma, the Tamil Paṟaiyar woman mentioned earlier (Viramma *et al.* 1997).[38] Fictionalized portrayals can be equally instructive. Mulk Raj Anand's controversial novel gives a moment-by-moment account of a day in the life of Bakha, a 'sweeper' and latrine-cleaner ('outcaste', 'Bhangi', 'Chandal') in the English-language classic, *Untouchable* (1935). Equally controversial at the time of its publication (1947) was Thakazhi Sivasankara Pillai's Malayalam novel, *Scavenger's son*, also set in Kerala. It chronicles the life of Chudalamuttu, a 'scavenger' desperate to save his own son from a life of cleaning latrines.[39] Finally, there are hard-hitting documents written by activists.[40] We can now say, with some real justification, that the 'untouchable' experience is at last on its way to being usefully documented.

Perhaps the most important conclusion to be drawn from all this evidence is that there is no such thing as one 'untouchable experience'. It would be impossible, or at least highly misleading, to treat the many 'untouchable' groups across India, perhaps 15 per cent of the population of the country, as a monolithic

38 For the autobiography of an 'untouchable' born during the British era in what is now Uttar Pradesh, see Hazari (1969). He gained employment as 'head-bearer' in a British household, converted to Islam, and eventually travelled to England. The Muslim name may be a pseudonym to conceal the author's identity. For a more recent account of being a 'Chamar' in India and the UK, see Shukra (1994). The name 'A. Shukra' is acknowledged as a pseudonym. This author stresses two important points: that the high-caste view of lower castes is *not* internalized by the latter, especially those who have been influenced by the *dalit* movement; and that most South Asian organizations in Britain are caste-based.

39 Despite the similarity of its English title, Matampu Kunjukuttan's *Outcaste* (1996), also set in Kerala, is a rather different kind of novel. The Malayalam title, *Bhrushtu* (*bhṛṣṭe*), is a technical term denoting the social excommunication of someone who has broken the strict caste laws of the orthodox Nambudiri brahmins; there is no reference here to the communities often called 'outcaste' or 'untouchable'. For two Hindi short stories relating to the experience of 'untouchables', see Premchand (1988): 'The price of milk' (*Dūdh kā dām*, 1934) tells of a woman who acts as the midwife and wet-nurse for the village zamindar, while 'Deliverance' (*Sadgati*, 1931) describes the death of an 'untouchable' 'Chamar' overworked by the local *paṇḍit*. For a study of seven short stories about being a Mahar, written in Marathi, see Miller and Kale (1972). For a brief summary of *dalit* writing in Marathi, see Zelliot (1996: 273–80).

40 For a popular book by a *dalit* activist, linking the experience of *dalit*s in India to African slaves in America, apartheid in South Africa, Nazism and colonialism, see Rajshekar (1995). For a provocative account of the differences between the 'dalit majority' – the self-styled 'Dalitbahujan' – and the socially and culturally dominant Hindus, see Ilaiah (1996). See also the publications of Voice of Dalit International, an organization formed in 1999 to bring together *dalit*s in India and abroad: Voice of Dalit International (2000); *Voice of Dalit International Newsletter* (ed., R. Eugene Culas), launched in the UK in January 2001; and the related website *www.vodi.org.uk* announced in issue no. 2 (December 2001). There is also a *Dalit International Newsletter* (ed., John C. B. Webster) published from the United States.

group. The issue of numbers is important. As Zelliot put it in 1996, 'every seventh human being is an Indian; every seventh Indian is an ex-Untouchable' (p. 314). According to both Deliège (1999: ix) and Mendelsohn and Vicziany (1998: 1), there are approximately 150 million people in this category.[41] How could so many people be treated as one? Furthermore, the defining features of segregation and exclusion that mark the *varṇa-jāti* system as a whole are in evidence within 'untouchable' groups too. As K. S. Singh (1993: 11) explains,

> Scheduled castes in every region and area in the country have their own hierarchy which prohibits the acceptance and exchange of water and food. For a Mala, a Madiga is an untouchable, and for both of them a Thoti is an untouchable. For a Meghwal, a Regar and a Bhangi are untouchables, whereas among the latter two the Bhangi is an untouchable.

Similarly, in Viramma's south Indian community, Paṟaiyars will not touch food cooked by members of the launderer and cobbler *jātis*; as she says, 'they're lower than us' (Viramma *et al.* 1997: 106).[42] A conservative herself, she continues to refer to her own community as 'Paṟaiyar'. She does this despite the fact that activists have denounced the term as demeaning, and have rejected it in favour of the emancipationist *dalit*. There are indeed many names and many voices here.

It is within this complicated and troubled context – the authorized oppression of 'untouchables' in India's past, the current resentment amongst high-caste groups regarding the opportunities being offered to Scheduled Castes, and the potential for *dalit*-led unrest in the future – that the Valmiki community must be placed. But before narrowing our focus to the Valmikis themselves, whether in India or in Britain, we need to shift our stance from outsider to insider. The terms applied to 'untouchable' persons and the meanings imposed upon them by others are clear enough. But how do they view themselves? What do they see when they stand at the centre of their own universe?

3. Self-Representation: Myths and Politics

To return briefly to February 2000, it is clear from the events outlined in chapter 1 that self-representation was a key issue in the Birmingham dispute. The British

---

41 The figures for the Panjab are particularly interesting for our purposes. According to the National Commission on Scheduled Castes and Scheduled Tribes, the Panjab (one of the richest states in India) has the highest percentage of *dalits* (23 per cent). However, only 2.54 per cent of the land is owned by *dalits*, while 53.8 per cent of all *dalit* families live below the poverty line (figures cited from *Dalit International Newsletter*, February 2001); by contrast, in India as a whole, 80 per cent of those living below the poverty line in India are *dalits* (*Voice of Dalit International Newsletter*, 2, December 2001, 6–7).

42 For further examples, see Moffatt (1979: 99–153), Deliège (1997: 3–8, 161–5) and Moon (2001: 6–7); for the Panjab, see Juergensmeyer (1982: 16). For a dramatic treatment of this issue in twelfth-century Karnataka, see Karnad (1993) and Leslie (1998a: 253–4).

Valmikis rejected outright the way they and their guru-God had been portrayed on public radio: that is, as ignorant, uneducated and belonging to the lowest of the low. They felt it was imperative to put the record straight.[43] The battle fought over this issue, both on air and in court, is a measure of the strength of feeling on both sides. But while the details of this particular dispute are new, in general terms the story goes back a long way.

Given the history of 'untouchables' in India, it is not surprising that a great deal of energy has been devoted to 'putting the record straight'. The higher castes may focus on the demonstrable inferiority of the 'untouchables', on the validations of *karma* and rebirth, on charitable top-down giving (or refusal to give). Scholars tend to concentrate on analyzing the position of 'untouchables' as it is defined in the structure of the caste 'system', or on providing further ethnographic details. But for the so-called 'untouchables' themselves, the focus is elsewhere: on their innate humanity, on their perceived prior claims to the land they live in, on their superior origins in the distant or mythical past, or on their own direct line to religious or political truth. From their point of view, these approaches give rise to far more satisfying explanations for the low status of 'untouchables' than those proposed or assumed by Indian society in general.

At its simplest, and if one can generalize at all, the core demand of the 'untouchable' is to be regarded as human, as an integral part of humanity. Thus the heartfelt cry of the Rishis of Bangladesh is: 'We too are humans (*manus*)!' (Zene 2000). Ambedkar understood both plea and problem well. In a speech given in 1930 as part of the temple entry campaign, he declared:

> Our problem ... extends into the political, social, religious and economic spheres. Today's satyagraha is a challenge to the Hindu mind. From this true satyagraha we shall see whether Hindu society is ready to treat us as human beings.[44]

A similar sentiment may be found in the earliest documented evidence of the Mahar movement. In 1890, in his petition for the readmission of Mahars into the army, the early *dalit* leader Gopal Baba Walangkar wrote: 'God made man the highest of beings and does not make man high or low by differences in eating or outward cleanliness. ... We have begun to realise our proper rights of humanity'.[45] More than a century later, Khare describes the 'untouchable' women he meets

---

43 It is important to be clear here: at no point during the dispute were the Valmikis looking for sympathy or charity; they were asking for the same respect that is accorded to all other religious faiths, beliefs and traditions in Britain.

44 The Sanskrit term, *satyāgraha* (literally, 'holding on to truth'), was invented by M. K. Gandhi to denote the power of truth to effect political change without physical violence; see also the Gandhian concept of 'non-violence' (the usual English translation of the Sanskrit term, *ahiṃsā*, literally, 'the absence of the desire to harm'). The quotation is taken from Ambedkar's speech at the Kalaran Mandir, Nasik, in 1930; cited in Zene (2000: 94 n. 32).

45 A retired soldier from Ratnagiri, Walangkar started the first Mahar newspaper. His petition to the British protesting against the closure of army service to 'untouchables' constitutes the first documentary evidence of the Mahar movement (Zelliot 1996: 36, 57; for further details of the petition, see pp. 198–201).

during his fieldwork in Lucknow as 'twice subaltern' (2000: 200). In the words of one of his informants, 'untouchable' women are 'birds in a cage': 'facing more hardship than all other [Indian] women', they 'long to be free as humans' (p. 198). Caste details vanish beneath this single need. Thus some of Deliège's 'untouchable' informants refuse to divulge their caste names: 'What does it matter? After all we are human beings like you' (1999: 13–14). But this, of course, is the problem. Few see past their supposed 'untouchability', not the other members of the village they 'share', nor the scholars who depend upon their data. An unseeing gaze objectifies them as 'untouchable'. Transfixed by the scrutiny of others, these people are rendered powerless in the negotiation of their own humanity.[46]

The first step towards understanding must therefore be to shift the focus of our gaze. Instead of being abandoned forever on the periphery of another's universe, 'untouchables' must be viewed where they truly stand: at the centre of their own. Do they have traditional ways of defining themselves? How have these processes of self-definition changed in recent decades?

The most striking evidence of the basic human need for self-definition is provided by the widespread existence of origin myths. What do these stories tell us? Was Weber right when he maintained that 'untouchables' have simply internalized the ideology of brahminical texts (1958: 18)? More recently, was Moffatt right when he talked of 'consensus' (1979: 290–304)? According to this view, there is little or no resistance on the part of 'untouchables' to the brahminical concepts of *dharma*, *karma* and rebirth. By accepting the ideology, they accept that their present condition (as individuals and as a group) is the karmic result of their behaviour in a previous life. This would mean that their only hope is to accept their lot in this life in order to bring improvement in the next. Deliège's response to this idea is to comment rather crisply that Weber obviously never asked an 'untouchable' for his or her opinion on the matter (1999: 31). Most Valmikis in Britain today would agree.

I turn now to Deliège's findings.[47] On the basis of his own enquiries in the field, and of the work of others, Deliège concludes that 'untouchables' today suffer from none of the illusions supposed by Weber. While not all 'untouchables' engage in emancipation movements, even those unwilling to do so for one reason or another resist the idea that their miserable lot is in any karmic sense deserved. Similarly, Kathleen Gough's informants 'collapsed in merriment' at the very idea: 'Brahmans say anything,' scoffed an elder. 'Their heads go round and round!' (1973: 234). These Adi Dravidas denied absolutely the explanatory link, so popular with the so-called 'higher' castes, that actions in a previous life are responsible for wealth and status in this one. A similar disbelief in *karma* may be found among the 'lower' castes in the Panjab (Juergensmeyer 1982: 97–9). What, then, is the 'untouchable' version of events? One answer to this question lies in an analysis of 'untouchable' origin myths.

46 As Apratim Barua points out, *dalit*s are aware of this objectification but their awareness does not always inform the resulting text (personal communication, 27 May 2002).

47 While I realise that Deliège has his own critics, I base the following account on his 1993 article, and its reworkings in later books (1997: 127ff.; 1999: chapter 4).

Before we look at some particular stories, however, several general points should be made. First, the absence of texts should not blind us to the significance of oral traditions. Second, the fact that some of these myths are already reported in nineteenth-century accounts suggests that they are part of an established tradition and not simply the result of recent political change. Third, I agree with Deliège that, behind the idiosyncracies of each telling, in whichever region or community, there lies a common structure that allows us to draw overarching conclusions about the nature of 'untouchable' self-representation that are of relevance today.

Deliège's study includes origin stories told by a range of 'untouchables' across India: the Paṟaiyars of Tamilnadu, the 'Chamars' of north India, the 'Bhangis' of north India, the Mahars of Maharashtra, the Doms (*ḍom*) of the Panjab, and the 'Chamars' of Senapur. I shall gloss over the details here. The classic formula underlying all these stories runs as follows.

- Step 1: At the beginning of time, before caste divisions came into existence, there were two (or more) brothers. The point of this beginning is the idea that all castes are descended from an original set of brothers who were essentially of equal status (that is, apart from age order).
- Step 2: A cow dies, or a dead cow is found, and God (or the king, or the boys' father) asks the brothers to remove the carcass. (In some versions, this step involves the cooking of beef by one brother to be consumed by them all.)[48] The point here is the introduction of a source of pollution which needs to be dealt with. We may note the assumption that a dead cow is polluting, the requirement that the source of pollution be removed, and the fact that no inherent fault is attached to any brother at this point.
- Step 3: The elder brother says that the younger sibling will do it, but God (or some other authority) understands him to say that the younger brother is a brahmin. On the basis of this misunderstanding, the younger brother is declared a brahmin and the elder brother an 'untouchable'. The point of this step is that the irrevocable division between the sibling lines of descent (brahmins and 'untouchables') is accidental. Deliège stresses that this has nothing to do with inherent worth or previous conduct: the brother who becomes an 'untouchable' has done nothing wrong. We may also note that, in this story as in many others, the 'untouchables' are the descendants of the elder (and therefore, in traditional terms, superior) brother.[49] The initial higher status of the 'untouchable' brother is an important aspect in some versions of the myth.

---

48 The Paṟaiyar myth of Tamilnadu, that untouchables were once temple priests whose task was to officiate at cow sacrifices, is found also amongst the Rishis of Bangladesh. According to one set of myths, the Rishis were originally the compilers of the Vedas, ritual specialists in cow sacrifice, and capable by virtue of their ascetic powers of restoring the sacrificial animals to life. When one of their ancestors stole some meat, that moment of greed (here, at least, we find a clear statement of blame) robbed his descendants of their ritual status if not of their name. For further details, see Zene (2000: 77–8; 2002: Appendix 2a).

49 This idea is retained today. Thus a Paṟaiyar song declares: 'I am the first-born / I first wore the sacred thread'. For further examples, see Deliège (1997: 131).

Following Deliège, we may draw several conclusions from this basic storyline. The introduction of a source of pollution serves to divide the brothers into opposing castes. There is no attempt to deny that the activities concerned are polluting, nor even that those who engage in them are degraded thereby. But the allocation of the task to 'untouchables' is viewed either as arbitrary or as the consequence of deliberate trickery.[50] According to this view, the 'untouchable' brother does not deserve his low status; he is not, nor has he ever been, at fault. The low status of today's 'untouchables' is, therefore, a dreadful mistake in the sense that it has been allocated to a community which does not deserve it. But the concept of 'untouchability' remains intact.

While I find Deliège's comments highly instructive, it seems unwise to generalize too freely. Judging by the work of Moffatt and Mosse, there are certain elements of 'consensus' on the part of 'untouchables': caste hierarchy is replicated between 'untouchable' groups; there is general agreement on their degraded meanings; some origin stories imply blame; and (like most human beings) 'untouchable' groups are usually ready to improve their own status even at the expense of another's. The question of how much choice an individual or group has in such matters remains an issue for debate.[51] There is another reason for caution too: the three key scholars concerned in this discussion – Deliège, Moffatt and Mosse – all draw their conclusions from fieldwork conducted in rural Tamilnadu. Until we have the results of similar fieldwork relating to origin myths among a range of other 'untouchable' communities across India, it is as well to be careful.

That said, and bearing in mind the need for further research, an 'untouchable' origin myth like those described serves several functions. At an ideological level, it removes or distances blame, re-establishes status, and thus reconfers the lost humanity of 'untouchables'. Blame is either removed altogether or pushed way back to the beginning of time where it need not be taken seriously. The restored status may be one of equality or superiority. As we have seen, the 'elder brother' scenario portrays the 'untouchable' ancestor-brother as originally superior to the ancestor-brother of the brahmins. Other superiority scenarios include the 'former *kṣatriya*' myth shared by the Mahars (Zelliot 1996: 57), the Jatavs of Agra (Lynch 1969: 68–75) and the Kolis of Kangra (Parry 1979: 118–20); and the legend of the Rishis of Bangladesh that they were once Vedic specialists (Zene 2000: 77–8). The claim to former *kṣatriya* status demonstrates the flexibility of the *varṇa* categories in contrast to the rigidity of *jāti* distinctions. For example,

50 A variation on this theme is provided by a common Mahar myth of origin. A cow had four human sons. She asked them how they would remember her after her death. Three sons promised to worship her, but the fourth said he would carry her inside his body as she had him. This child-like innocence makes him the ancestor of the meat-eating, 'untouchable' Mahars. For this and other Mahar origin myths, see Zelliot (1996: 54). For a version of the myth that includes a set of brothers and a clear statement of blame, but this time to explain the hierarchy between three 'untouchable' caste groups in Karnataka, see Neil Armstrong (1998: 175–6).

51 For useful summaries of the contested issues of 'replication', 'consensus' and 'coercion', with particular reference to the work of Moffatt, Deliège and Mosse, see Charsley (1998a: 54–8, 61–2) and Zene (2000: 72–3, including endnotes).

the Jatavs do not claim to belong to a specific higher *jāti*. Drawing on a popular high-caste legend, they claim to be the remnants of the *kṣatriya varṇa* destroyed by the anger-crazed brahmin, Paraśurāma;[52] having once disguised themselves as lowly shoemakers in order to escape Paraśurāma's anger, they now find themselves trapped in their own disguise. These are essentially uplifting stories of origin. At the level of contemporary politics, however, these myths become an essential part of the process of social mobility. A community that wishes to move up the ladder of caste status needs, at the very least, a new name and a positive myth of origin.[53]

The most significant myth of more recent decades, perhaps of the twentieth century as a whole, is the simple but powerful claim of primacy. The 'untouchables' are the 'Adivasis', the original inhabitants of India, the first claimants to the land. To understand the full implications of this claim, we need to place it within the much larger context of the 'Indo-European homeland' debate. After the discovery of Sanskrit by western European intellectuals, the search for the geographical source of the Indo-European language families, including Sanskrit, was on. By the nineteenth century, Western scholars had decided that that source was not India. While the primary focus of the debate was on Europe, the implications for India were compelling. What had begun as a theory relating to the spread of language now became widely (mis)understood as a theory relating to the physical migration of people, known as 'the Aryan invasion theory'. According to this view, and in its most simplistic form, a group of people speaking an 'Aryan' language came into the Panjab from the west and conquered the indigenous inhabitants (termed *dāsa* or *dasyu*). The interaction between the two groups (that is, between the 'invaders' on the one hand and the indigenous people on the other) was said to have given rise to what is now known as 'Indian' civilization. There are many problems with this theory, not least the fact that the 'invasion' form of the theory has not been espoused by Western scholars for years.[54] But the problem that concerns us here is that a *linguistic* theory (that is, a theory relating to the movement of languages, not people)[55] has been turned into a clash of *races*: the Vedic *dāsa*s (now identified with modern

---

52 Paraśurāma is also known as Rāma Jāmadagnya ('Jamadagni's son Rāma') and 'Rāma Bhārgava'; the name Paraśurāma does not appear in the *Mahābhārata*. Recent studies of this ambiguous figure include those by Lynn Thomas (1991, 1996) and Fitzgerald (2002); see also John Brockington's summary (1998: 140–1).

53 We may note here that, in common with many *dalit*s today, the Valmikis in Britain reject both the hierarchy of caste and the supposed link between caste and *karma*; their concern is not to climb up the caste ladder but to kick it away altogether.

54 On this point, Greg Bailey writes that 'very few European or American Indologists in the last fifty years have argued for the idea of an Aryan invasion', and refers to the Aryan invasion theory as 'long-abandoned'. He concludes that what he calls the 'Indo-American historians' have set up a straw man against which to argue (2002: 173, 183).

55 Simon Brodbeck's comparison of the spread of Sanskrit with the spread of English in modern times is helpful: 'More and more foreign academics publish in English, and future archaeologists will possibly think that it was their mother tongue' (personal communication, 8 June 2002).

dalits) are widely believed to have been subjugated by a Sanskrit-speaking, culturally and racially distinct people called 'Aryans'. This is a myth, and it has all the power of a myth. In the Indian context, it is not hard to see why the idea of an 'Aryan' invasion (or even migration) into India – bringing with it the twice-born *varṇas*, the earliest religious texts, and the seeds of brahminical Hinduism – should appeal so thrillingly to *dalits* while irrevocably antagonizing the higher castes.[56]

The Mahars of Maharashtra were probably the first to take up the idea, in the form of 'lords of the earth', the so-called 'pre-Aryan' inhabitants of India. While the idea faded in time for the Mahars, it served to link them with similar 'untouchable' movements in the north and south of India. Today, several *dalit* names, many of them also generic terms, stem from this idea: 'Adi Dravida' ('original Dravidian' or speaker of the Tamil language), 'Adi Andhra' ('original' settler of Andhra Pradesh), 'Adi Karnataka', and so on, all denote localized *dalit* groups. The term 'Adivasi' or 'Adibasi', more common in north India, tends to denote those believed to be of tribal origin. 'Adi Karnataka' was formally adopted by the Mysore State to replace the earlier term, 'Panchama' (see p. 29). 'Adi Dravida' continues to be used in Tamil-speaking areas, despite the breaking away of several sub-groups under their own preferred terminology.[57] As Charsley explains, this is 'a characteristically modern myth, historical in form and challenging the rights of current rulers' (1998a: 62). Using this general argument, Indians challenge the British, Hindus challenge the Muslims, southern 'Dravidians' challenge the so-called 'Aryans' of the north, and now the *dalits* challenge everyone else: they were in India first.

A parallel notion of primary claim, but this time with regard to religion, may be found in the nomenclature 'Ad Dharm' ('first' or 'original religion') which appeared in the Panjab in the 1920s. As will become clear in section 4 of this chapter, the Ad Dharm movement played a significant part in the 'untouchable' protests in the Panjab. First, it helped to mobilize a high percentage of 'untouchables' in the area with immediate and persistent effect. Second, the daring claim to primacy in religion provoked great hostility among caste Hindus, a hostility which increasingly found expression in outbreaks of anti-'untouchable' violence. But the most important point to understand here is the appeal of religion as a means of positive self-representation.

Before turning our attention to the strategies of 'untouchable' and *dalit*

---

56 For a comprehensive analysis of the whole issue of Indo-Aryan origins, including the rise of the 'Indigenous Aryan school' which promotes the opposite idea (that Indian civilization began on Indian soil) for equally political reasons, see Bryant (2001). For discussions of the proposed locations of the Indo-European 'homeland', ranging from the Baltic to Anatolia, see Mallory (1989: 143–85) and Bryant (2001: 13–45).

57 For a study of the Adi Karnatakas of Mahepura, previously known as 'Madigas', see Neil Armstrong (1998); for the confusing usage of the terms 'Adi Karnataka' and 'Scheduled Caste' in Karnataka, see Charsley and Karanth (1998b: 265–6). According to Singh's *Survey of Scheduled Castes*, Malas and Madigas call themselves 'Adi Andhra', Pallans and Parayans use 'Adi Dravida', while the Holeyes of Karnataka prefer 'Adi Karnataka' (1993: 13).

groups in the Panjab, it is important to understand the link between religious identity and the affirmation of humanity. Zene confronts this issue in his discussion of the Rishis in Bangladesh. His hypothesis runs as follows. Since 'untouchables' have been denied human status largely through religion, 'it is through the same idiom that they wish to affirm their identity as humans'. Furthermore, since they have been excluded from both religion and humanity on the basis of religious norms, it makes sense that the 'arena' they choose for their struggle is that of religion. It also makes sense that 'religion' is understood in terms of what distinguishes humans from other species (2000: 70). In this context, then, the 'untouchable' focus on religion and religious identity – the Rishis' negotiations either to be classified as Hindus or to convert to Christianity, the Ambedkarites' mass conversion to Buddhism in 1956, the frequent adoption of religious caste names such as 'Valmiki' – constitutes a powerful force for change. As Zene puts it, it all makes sense 'only if taken as part of a more general framework which includes the struggle to achieve self-consciousness and affirm self-identity' (p. 70). As we move on to consider the Valmiki movement in northern India, these are important points to keep in mind: while the dehumanizing of 'untouchables' is justified by one religious discourse, the search for a new *dalit* humanity is sought within another.

4. The Valmikis of North India

This section requires a further consideration of a range of names that the Valmikis in both Britain and India reject: 'Chuhra', 'Bhangi', and so on. As indicated on p. 33, the most unacceptable of these is 'Chuhra'. In the following account, I shall use such terms for two reasons: either because they are employed in the source I am discussing, or because it is necessary to distinguish between specific *jāti*s prior to the formal adoption of the name 'Valmiki'. In both cases, the power to name did not lie with the groups being named. Today, the Valmikis have that power and they use it to reject outright the allocation of such degrading terms.

A search for Valmikis in India leads to a confusing collection of names and candidates. K. S. Singh's survey of Scheduled Castes provides two separate entries. Under 'Balmiki/Balmik/Valmiki', he includes 'some sections of a cluster of communities like the Bhangi, Mehtar, Lalbegi and other castes who were associated with scavenging in the past'. These groups, now treated as one community, 'claim a common descent from the legendary saint Balmiki' (1993: 105). They are distributed across Uttar Pradesh, Haryana, the Panjab, Delhi and Chandigarh. In Uttar Pradesh, many serve as 'sweepers' in the public or private sector, while others work as agricultural labourers and cultivators. They consider themselves Hindus and are mainly Hindi-speakers. Those in Haryana – where they may also be termed 'Valmiki', 'Chuhra', 'Lalbegi' and 'Khakrobe' – speak Haryanvi locally and Hindi with outsiders. The Balmikis in the Panjab are usually called 'Chuhra' in rural areas and 'Bhangi' in urban districts. They speak Panjabi and Hindi; their primary occupation tends to be refuse collection ('scavenging') in urban areas and agricultural labouring elsewhere. The Balmikis in Delhi are often referred to as 'Chohra', 'Chuhra', 'Bhangi', 'Mehtar' and 'Jamadar' (p. 109). Those in Chandigarh (also known as 'Bhangi' and 'Chuhra') are immigrants from the Panjab and Haryana. These people are mainly 'sweepers', but some work in agriculture, industry and the government sector. In Madhya Pradesh too, the Valmikis usually work as 'sweepers'. They speak Hindi, worship the major Hindu gods, and observe the usual Hindu festivals (1993: 105–12). Under 'Valamiki/Valmiki', Singh distinguishes two further subgroups in Orissa: 'Valmiki' and 'Dom'. Both subgroups speak Telugu, use the Telugu script, and communicate with others in Oriya. These people work as cultivators and agricultural labourers, as well as providing other services for the community. Again, they are deemed to be Hindus: they observe the relevant festivals while the name 'Valmiki' marks their claim to be descended from the saint in question (pp. 1281–3).

The name 'Valmiki' may also be found among the catalogues of Indian tribes. For example, K. S. Singh locates a tribal community of Christian Valmikis among the coastal villages of Andhra Pradesh. While they too claim descent from the saint Vālmīki, they converted to Christianity under a variety of denominations either during British rule or after independence. There seems to be no great difference in traditions between Hindu and Christian Valmikis in Andhra Pradesh; for example, they observe both Christian and Hindu festivals. Despite conversion, however, the Valmikis are still ranked at the bottom of the list of tribes in that area (1994: 1172–3). As Christians, they are also denied constitutional protection as members of Scheduled Castes. A more detailed account of this Telugu-speaking Andhra Pradesh 'tribe' of Valmikis is provided by Saheb (1996) who offers the following derivation of their name:

> According to tradition, the name of the tribe is derived from the sage of Ramayana epic, Valmiki, who did penance in one spot for such a long period that a white ant hill (putta/valmiki) grew up round him.

Saheb also informs us that the Valmiki 'tribe' stands at the bottom of the social hierarchy, that 'untouchability' is still in evidence, and that their religion is 'full of superstitious beliefs and practices'. Their celebration of the local harvest festival is said to reflect their hunting skills, described as 'a unique feature of the tribes' (1996: 1030–3). This volume also contains a selection of black-and-white photographs of individuals or couples from the designated tribes. One of these portrays a smiling man and woman above the caption 'Valmiki couple' (Sachchidananda and Prasad 1996: 954–5).

We may conclude that the holders of the name 'Valmiki' stem from what are perceived by others to be the lowest rungs of society. These are people who, in their various regions, are still treated as 'untouchable' even by other 'untouchable' groups. In the tribal context, they are hunters; in the caste hierarchy, they are traditionally 'sweepers' or 'scavengers'. According to both sets of terminology (tribe and caste), the Valmikis are deemed by others to be the lowest of the low.

Since the Valmikis in Britain are mainly Panjabi-speakers, it makes sense to narrow our focus to the Panjab. The two largest *jāti*s considered 'untouchable' –

the Panjabi word is 'achut' (*achūt*) – are the 'Chamars' and the so-called 'Chuhras'.[58] The primary occupation of both groups in most rural areas of the Panjab is agricultural labour. Both belong to what Ibbetson famously called 'the vagrant, menial and artisan castes' of the Panjab (1916: 266–338). In caste terms, the 'Chamars' are traditionally leather-workers, which means that they were deemed collectively responsible for the tanning and preparation of animal skins. In a similar way, 'Chuhras' are often called 'Bhangi', especially in urban areas. For example, this was the term Gandhi used when he lived among the Delhi 'sweepers' for a few months in 1946, but he was severely criticized for using it.[59] The term is highly derogatory. As K. S. Singh puts it, the 'Bhangi' is the representative *par excellence* of the *Manusmṛti*'s *caṇḍāla*, the classic 'untouchable' (1993: 235). 'Bhangis' are traditionally associated with the lowest level of service tasks: sweeping and 'scavenging'. As a result, to use the words of Mendelsohn and Vicziany, they are 'uniquely despised' throughout north India; that is, they are despised even by other 'untouchable' *jāti*s (1998: 38). In the colonial period, many 'Bhangis' moved out of their villages into urban areas in response to the British need for 'sweepers' in towns and cities. Others found work in the building trade, in stone quarries and brickworks, and on plantations. According to Singh's account, 'Bhangis' are usually Hindus, and many of them worship Valmik as the god of their community.[60] Today, although not all 'Bhangis' worship Bhagwan Valmik, and by no means all Valmikis were originally called 'Bhangi', the two terms are often used interchangeably. For example, Mendelsohn and Vicziany gloss 'Bhangi' as 'Untouchable sweeper caste of northern India; see *Valmiki*', while 'Valmiki' is explained as 'the now usually preferred name for the Bhangi or community which follows the teachings of the saint Valmiki' (1998: xii, xvi). By contrast, Juergensmeyer explains 'Balmiki (*bālmīki*, *vālmīki*)' as 'a designation of the Chuhra caste using the name of Rishi Valmiki', while 'bhangi (*bhaṅgī*)' is 'a term used in some areas for the Chuhra caste' (1982: 315). We may note here the persistent tendency on the part of

58 Griswold distinguishes between the 'Chuhras' of north and west Panjab and the 'Bhaṇgis of the United Provinces' (1934: 229). For an account of the 'Chuhra' caste/tribe in general, see K. S. Singh (1993: 380–4 and 1998: 724–5); see also Youngson (1906, 1907). For a study of change amongst 'Chuhras'/Valmikis in a village of north-western Uttar Pradesh during the 1950s, see Pauline Moller Mahar (1960). For a historical study of the 'Chuhras' in Delhi, see Prashad (2000: 25ff.).

59 See Prashad (2000: 112; for a brief account of the resentment caused by Gandhi's stay among the *dalit*s, especially by his inability to accept their offers of food, see pp. 139–40). Today, the lodgings used by Gandhi in Delhi are attached to the new Valmiki Temple, situated at the junction (now called 'Valmiki Chowk') of Mandir Marg and Panchkunian Road. As a result of large-scale works to remove the surrounding buildings and landscape the grounds, this temple has been attracting more and more attention. It is the object of regular high-profile visits by eminent Indian politicians and other dignitaries, including the Prime Minister (himself a *dalit*). It is increasingly common for Valmikis visiting India from Britain to pay their respects there too (Jaswinder Kalyan, personal communication, 2 July 2002).

60 For a fuller account of the different 'Bhangi' communities all over India, see K. S. Singh (1993: 235–43; 1998: 380–3).

scholars as well as of higher castes to equate scavenging with the 'Chuhra' caste, and therefore with the Valmikis. A prime example is Saberwal's comment that the 'scavengers' ('Chuhras') are 'now known as "Balmikis" ' (1990: x, 51–85). This is a common and long-standing oversimplification.

Vijay Prashad's historical study of *dalit*s in the Delhi area (2000) demonstrates how important it is to understand the implications of such caste-related terms. For example, in the late eighteenth and early nineteenth centuries, the refuse collectors of the Delhi area were known collectively by the term 'Mehtar' ('prince'). They were 'more a community of sweepers than a discrete caste community', and consisted of 'the dregs of all caste communities', including 'Chuhras' (p. 21). Between the 1850s and the 1930s, the Delhi Mehtars lost their relative control of refuse collection: the British circumvented Mehtar strike action by seeking outside 'sweepers' while, at much the same time, large numbers of 'Chuhras' migrated to the city from the Panjab to escape famine and to look for work. As a result, 'Chuhras' became indelibly associated with that function in Delhi as well as in other urban areas; in time, they were considered ineligible for any other kind of work (p. 45). These 'sweepers' were increasingly viewed as a caste which, as Prashad puts it, 'far from being a feudal relic, was the backbone of an unequally structured municipal system' (p. 64). In this way, the 'Chuhras' became the largest 'untouchable' group to join the Mehtars in Delhi and elsewhere, and thus to become identified with what was called the 'sweeper caste'. We may note that this development strongly supports the idea of caste as construction rather than as the result of religious injunction. In the 1930s, it was these so-called 'sweepers' who became Balmikis. Today, the term preferred by most of the individuals concerned indicates religious allegiance rather than caste status or the occupation implied: 'Balmiki' or 'Valmiki'. This is the case both in Delhi and in the Panjab.

In the context of this study, my preference for the Sanskritic form ('Valmiki') over the Panjabi pronunciation ('Balmiki', 'Balmik') is in line with the preference indicated to me by my contacts within the Valmiki community in Britain. When it is necessary to refer to *jāti* origins rather than religious allegiance, I use the term 'Chuhra' but without endorsement. The Valmiki preference for religious rather than *jāti* names is explicit.

The choice of the name 'Valmiki' is significant in other ways too. In the context of 'Chuhra' beliefs and practices, there are at least two other names that might have been selected: Lāl Beg and Bāla Shāh. The confusion surrounding all three is long-standing. In the 1881 Census report, for example, Ibbetson notes that 'Chuhra' shrines are dedicated to Lāl Beg or Bāla Shāh, 'the high priests of the caste', and the latter is identified with Bālmīk, 'the traditional author of the Ramayana'. Ibbetson writes that Bāla Shāh is 'another name for Bal Mik, a hunter of the Karnal district who was converted by a holy Rishi, and eventually wrote the *Ramayana*'. He also reports that the 'Chuhras' worship 'one supreme deity without form or habitation', but then apparently disagrees with this finding with the remark that most 'Chuhras' worship Lāl Beg or Bāla Shāh 'directly ... as divine' (1883: 154). Apart from folk or village memory, our main source of information on such questions is the material gathered on the religious beliefs and practices of the 'Chuhras' during the British period. Examples include the songs and 'genealogies' (*kursīnāma*) of Lāl Beg recorded by Richard Temple (1884), and those of Bāla Shāh compiled by J. W. Youngson from 1891 onwards (1906, 1907).[61]

Temple's focus is Lāl Beg. He lists a number of alternative names for this figure[62] before suggesting that the name must originally have been 'Lâl Bhekh', that is, a mendicant priest (*bhikṣu*) clothed in red or saffron (*lāl*), the personified priest of the 'scavengers'.[63] Temple concludes that Lāl Beg is the 'tutelary saint of the scavenger castes of the Eastern Panjâb, and the pivot on which all their notions of religion turn'. He then identifies Bāla Shāh with Vālmīki:

> Bâlmik, Wâlmîk, Bâlnîk, Bâlmîg, Bâlâ Shâh and Nûrî Shâh Bâlâ are the variations of the name of a sacred personage in the scavengers' hagiology who occupies the place next to Lâl Beg, and who is very frequently mixed up with him. He is without difficulty and beyond all doubt to be identified with Vâlmîki, the low-caste author of the Sanskrit *Râmâyaṇa*.

In addition, Temple's summary makes three important assertions. First, the worship of Lāl Beg constitutes a religion in its own right, with its own priesthood and rituals. Second, it contains elements of the Hindu, Muslim and Sikh religions 'thrown together in the most hopeless fashion'. Third, 'the monotheism taught by the medieval reformers underlies all their superstitions' (1884: 529). Temple's language is typically judgmental. But there is a more important point here. The evidence is 'late' in two senses: first, it is a nineteenth-century colonial record; second, the material recorded is already heavily influenced by the *bhakti* tradition generally and by Sikhism in particular. It is therefore impossible to reconstitute the 'original' beliefs and practices of the 'Chuhras' from this account, or indeed from any extant colonial record.

A more extensive collection of 'Chuhra' beliefs and practices is that compiled by the Rev. J. W. Youngson of the Church of Scotland Mission at Sialkot (1906, 1907). His 'Chuhra' contacts, 'priests and genealogists among them' (1906: 82), provided him with several possible genealogies for what he calls their 'tribe', as well as a complete set of songs sung at 'Chuhra' rituals. Youngson's primary focus is Bāla Shāh. For example, his account includes the dedication of a temple to Bāla Shāh, the 'litany' of Bāla Shāh, two genealogies of Bāla Shāh and several songs (1906: 340ff.). According to Youngson's contacts, the religious leaders (*pīr*) of this religion – whose own names include 'Bāla Shāh', 'Lāl Beg' and 'Bālmīk' – are considered to be incarnations of the original Bāla Shāh. In this monotheistic religious system, Bāla Shāh is the mediator between God and his devotees. Rituals include animal sacrifice (usually a chicken or a goat), and the

61 I have been unable to locate a copy of Richard Greeven's classic work (1894).

62 Lāl Guru, Lāl Khān, Samali Beg, Lāl Shāh, Miran Shāh, Lāl-o-lāl, and 'many other honorific titles' (1884: 529).

63 Prashad (2000: 72) traces the name 'Lāl Beg' to a story told of Vālmīki. God gave Vālmīki a coat. Later, when asked to fetch it, Vālmīki found a boy in the coat. He called fondly to the boy to come out quickly and thus the name was born: Lāl ('loved one') Beg ('quickly'). Unlike Temple's analysis, Prashad's story subordinates Lāl Beg to Vālmīki; in neither case is Vālmīki deified.

worship of both ancestors and the spirits of the dead. For Youngson, the overlapping names suggest a saint of many names and forms, rather than what Temple sees as 'hopeless' confusion. According to one song, for example, Bāla 'became' Lāl Beg, and subsequent verses call him both 'Bāla' and 'Bālmīk' (1907: 114–15). Similarly, we are told that village shrines are named after Bāla Shāh, but newborn babies are dedicated to Bālmīk and named after him (1906: 354–5). For Youngson's contacts, the primary name of this 'Chuhra' saint (or priest or prophet) is Bāla Shāh. God once conversed with him directly (1907: 27ff.), exalting him above both Muhammad and Nānak (p. 30). Indeed, God struck an astonishing bargain within him long ago. According to this account of the 'Chuhra' myth of origin, Bāla was the eldest of Brahmā's four sons, all of whom took human form as brahmin priests. When a cow died unexpectedly in their midst, the four brothers argued about who should remove the corpse. To solve the problem, God made a deal. If Bāla (here also called 'Jhaumpra') agreed to take on this task, then he and his followers would be guaranteed access to heaven, unlike the Hindus and Muslims. We may note here the explicit assumption that the 'Chuhras' belong to neither Hinduism nor Islam. Youngson's verse translation reads as follows:

> ... God said,
> 'O Bâlâ, understand: be wise and know
> That on the resurrection day their deeds
> Will bring to these despairing grief. I'll make
> Of Hindu and of Muslim faiths a sea,
> Beyond it I will make a heaven that they
> Shall see but enter not. The burning sun
> Will come within a spear and a quarter's length,
> The dread alarms of hell will compass them.
> The worshippers of Râm, and of Rahîm,
> Will hide themselves in fear and dark despair,
> But thine will cross themselves secure, in safety they
> Will enter heaven at last.

The convenant made, Bāla removed his sacred thread and 'caste marks all', and threw the corpse beyond the sacred precincts. The myth explains: 'Hence rose the Chuhra sect and worship, one and separate'.[64] In the context of 'untouchable' origin myths generally, we may note that Bāla is the eldest and therefore superior son, that he starts out as a brahmin priest, that the story attaches no blame to him personally, but that the mark of permanent untouchability remains.

But it is the link with Bālmīk that concerns us here. If Bāla and Bālmīk are the same individual, then Bālmīk is the first ancestor of the 'Chuhra' myth of origin, a brahmin priest until he agreed to remove his sacred thread for the sake of the community. This Bālmīk is repeatedly identified with what Temple calls the 'low-

64 For the full story, and the original text, see Youngson (1907: 26–30). Other versions of the myth of 'Chuhra' origin are similar: a cow falls dead, one man saves the day, he is called unclean and made to sit apart, and 'thus a nation separate arose' (see Youngson 1906: 345, 350ff.).

caste' author of the *Rāmāyaṇa*. The result is extraordinarily powerful. As the first 'Chuhra', Vālmīki himself becomes an 'untouchable', both ancestor and representative of his *dalit* descendants. However, as the eldest son of Brahmā, a brahmin priest, and the author of the Sanskrit *Rāmāyaṇa*, he simultaneously represents the highest levels of the Hindu scriptural tradition. The name thus symbolizes both low-caste solidarity and an inclusive Hinduism. Only the story of the robber strikes an uncomfortable note. We may note that Youngson's contacts relate a version of this story too: that Bālmīk was a robber who preyed upon travellers in the forest, until Nānak and Mardana made him see the error of his ways (1906: 349–50).[65] Before trying to unravel the threads of meaning woven together in these colonial records, however, it is necessary to explore the peculiar combination of *dalit* religion and politics as it emerged in the Panjab.

5. Religion and Politics in Twentieth-Century Panjab

For a vivid portrait of the role of religion in the politics of social reform, particularly with regard to 'untouchables', we need only consider twentieth-century Panjab. This heady mixture of religion and politics is, of course, an essential part of modern India generally. Efforts towards self-improvement amongst the lower castes took many forms. At one level, there is evidence of what M. N. Srinivas has called 'Sanskritization': the abandoning of low-caste habits and occupations in emulation of the higher castes, as a means of following them up the rungs of the caste hierarchy (1952: 30).[66] At another level, self-improvement took a distinctly religious turn. From the late nineteenth century, for example, south Indian 'untouchables' seeking to improve their lot converted *en masse* to Christianity. In the 1920s, both Gandhi and Ambedkar viewed the problem of untouchability as soluble only through religion. Gandhi's mission was to reform Hinduism in such a way that even those traditionally perceived to be on the bottom rung of the caste ladder would find a valued and respected place within the religious paradigm; but he called in vain for a change of heart among caste Hindus. Ambedkar contemplated several solutions, all of them religious. First, like Gandhi, he resolved to 'improve' Hinduism: in particular, he campaigned for 'untouchables' to be allowed to enter, and worship in, high-caste temples.[67] The hostility aroused by this demand eventually made him reject Hinduism altogether as inherently unable to offer religious sanctuary to 'untouchables'. The first, and perhaps most striking, demonstration of Ambedkar's rejection of Hinduism was the ceremonial burning of the *Manusmṛti* in 1927, an action still calculated to shock the caste Hindu today. The second occurred in 1936 when –

65 Nānak's dates (1469–1539) make this version particularly incongruous.

66 For examples of such emulation in the Mahar movement, with an emphasis on 'social rather than ritualistic' changes, see Zelliot (1996: 205). For the Sanskritization and social mobility of the Kolis in Kangra, see Parry (1979: 115–28).

67 For a summary of what Ambedkar understood by an 'improved' Hinduism, one that offered religious equality even to those considered 'untouchable' by the rest of society, see Zelliot (1996: 207).

as the *Manusmṛti* burned once more – Ambedkar declared: 'I will not die a Hindu!'. The third was the mass conversion of Mahars to Buddhism in 1956.[68] During his search for alternatives, Ambedkar had considered both Sikhism and Marxism before opting for the Buddhist path. In the Panjab too, Marxism was an option that failed to appeal to early twentieth-century 'untouchable' leaders. Although the 'untouchable problem' was seen to emanate from religion, it was generally believed that a new religious movement would be more effective than a secular one. For most 'untouchable' reformers, the political message had to be located in a religious framework.[69]

What becomes clear even in this brief analysis is that there are two distinct approaches to the 'untouchable problem' in the context of religious discourse. The first, epitomized by Gandhi, is to include the 'untouchable' within Hinduism; this solution is fuelled by a desire on the part of its adherents to find a respectable place within the mother religion. The second approach, epitomized by Ambedkar, is to thrust the 'untouchable' irrevocably outside Hinduism, usually by means of conversion.[70] We may note that there have been mass conversions of 'untouchables' from Hinduism to Buddhism (primarily in Maharashtra), to Christianity (mainly in south India but also in the Panjab) and, to a lesser extent, to Islam (for example, in south India). Underlying all these conversions, there lies an explicit rejection of Hinduism. For example, in his address to the Mahar conference in Bombay in 1936 (Zelliot 1996: 192), Ambedkar declares:

> Religion is for man; not man for religion. If you want to gain self-respect, change your religion. If you want to create a cooperating society, change your religion. If you want power, change your religion. If you want equality, change your religion. If you want independence, change your religion. If you want to make the world in which you live, happy, change your religion.

Similarly, the aspirations of the *dalit* movement today tend to take two distinct forms: on the one hand, a desire to redefine 'Hinduism' along more egalitarian lines; on the other, a defiant resistance to the *dharma* hierarchy that high-caste Hinduism implies. Ilaiah's diatribe against the Hindutva discourse in his pamphlet, *Why I am not a Hindu* (1996) belongs to the second group. The growing cult of Bhagwan Valmik – as evidenced, for example, by the huge temple in Delhi – seems to belong to the first.[71] To understand this distinction fully, however, we need to explore the religio-political mix peculiar to early twentieth-century Panjab.

68 Conversion to Buddhism, unlike conversion to Christianity, does not deny *dalit*s their constitutional protection.

69 For an account of some of the more obviously political initiatives to improve the status and conditions of untouchables, see Mendelsohn and Vicziany (1998: 118ff.).

70 For further reading on this issue, see Mendelsohn and Vicziany (1998: 86–8) and Nagaraj (1992). Mass conversions still take place today. On 4 November 2001, for example, thousands of *dalit*s converted to Buddhism in New Delhi (Harrison 2001); unconfirmed reports spoke of over 3,000 converts (*www.dalitstan.org/journal/buddhism*), others of one million (*www.indiatogether.org.dalit/events*).

71 The question of how the Valmikis position themselves in relation to 'Hinduism' will be discussed in chapter 5.

Juergensmeyer's classic study of religious and social change in modern Panjab begins by problematizing the English word 'religion'. As he explains, the Panjabi language provides three possible equivalents: *qaum*, *panth* and *dharm*. The Urdu term, *qaum*, denotes 'a large religious community', as exemplified by the Muslims who were in the majority in pre-partition Panjab. The term *panth* ('path') denotes a religious group that professes devotion (*bhakti*) to a lineage of gurus or spiritual teachers, as exemplified by early Sikhism. The term *dharm* denotes the codes of behaviour, social grouping and ritual practices implied by a caste society, as exemplified by traditional Hindu *dharma*. As Juergensmeyer demonstrates, however, these three terms cannot easily be aligned with the three main religions in the Panjab. The typically *qaum* form of Islam is complicated by the widespread worship of Muslim saints (a *panth* quality). As a result of the reformist Singh Sabha, the typically *panth* form of Sikhism now has many of the elements of a unified *qaum*. In theory, caste is part of neither Islam nor Sikhism, and yet status divisions along caste lines (the key component of *dharm*) are evident in both, as they are in Christianity, a minority religion in the Panjab. Hinduism is equally untidy. In the Panjab in particular, the efforts of the Hindu reform movement, the Arya Samaj, to create a monolithic belief system favour the *qaum* definition of 'religion', while the proliferation of *bhakti* saints has resulted in the vertical lineages of the *panth* format. Most important, when *dalit*s declare that they are 'not Hindu', it is the social divisions of Hinduism (the *dharm* aspect) that they are rejecting (1982: 1–7).

If we now reconsider the two-fold response to Hinduism described earlier in relation to Gandhi and Ambedkar, the choice facing the 'untouchable' is clear. As Juergensmeyer puts it, 'the *dharmik* end of the spectrum holds no appeal' (1982: 5). It is not surprising that 'untouchables' have shown a marked preference either for *bhakti* movements or for conversion out of Hinduism altogether. The '*panthik* end of the spectrum' is exemplified by *bhakti* paths generally. For example, as I have discussed elsewhere, the Vīraśaiva form of *bhakti* expounded by Basava in twelfth-century Karnataka appealed to great numbers of low-caste groups including 'untouchables' (Leslie 1998a: 243). But Basava was born a brahmin. In the Panjab, the most popular movements were those associated with low-caste saints such as Ravidās (an 'untouchable' 'Chamar' or leather-worker), Kabīr and Dādū (both low-caste weavers).[72]

In the Panjab, a major solution to the 'untouchable problem' was initiated by a 'Chamar' named Mangoo Ram. Like both Ambedkar and Gandhi, Mangoo Ram spent a crucial period abroad, in his case partly in the United States and primarily as a revolutionary for the Indian national cause.[73] When he returned to India in 1925, he found the Panjab in the midst of political and religious turmoil,

72 For Ravidās, see Callewaert and Friedlander (1992); for Kabīr, see Hess (1983) and Vaudeville (1993); for Dādū, see Thiel-Horstmann (1983: 5–11, 63–105) and Callewaert (1988). For a wide range of movements within the *sant* tradition in general, see Gold (1987) and Schomer and McLeod (1987).

73 For an account of the early life of Mangoo Ram, including his association with the militant 'Gadar' movement of expatriate Panjabis in California, see Juergensmeyer (1982: 283–9).

ready for change. Because of their numbers, 'untouchables' were being courted by both political and religious groups: by the Congress movement, for example, as well as by Christians, Sikhs, the Muslim Ahmadiyya movement, and the Arya Samaj. The Arya Samaj had been particularly effective. Founded in 1875 by the brahmin reformist Dayananda Sarasvati, the movement sought to return Hinduism to its Vedic form by, among other things, rejecting the distinctions of caste. The movement became extremely popular in the Panjab, especially among the lower castes. A radical part of its religious programme was the ritual purification (*śuddhi*) of 'untouchable' converts to other faiths in order to restore them as 'clean-caste' members of Hinduism; but the problem of what to do with them after their 'purification' remained.[74] By means of this campaign, the Arya Samaj had reconverted to Hinduism large numbers of 'untouchables' who had previously been persuaded to become Christians, Sikhs or Muslims. All these tensions and rivalries combined to create a new self-consciousness on the part of 'untouchables' and a growing realization of the importance of a unified movement. It was at this point that Mangoo Ram returned to India, primed by his experience as a militant nationalist, but now determined to focus on improving the lot of 'untouchables'. His solution was simple but ambitious: a new religious movement entitled 'Ad Dharm', the 'original' religion of India.

This new religion was also a separatist movement. 'We are not Hindus,' declares the fifteenth resolution of the Ad Dharm Mandal. 'We are not a part of Hinduism, and Hindus are not a part of us.'[75] In view of this explicit statement, it seems inappropriate to categorize the Ad Dharm as a religious movement 'within Hinduism', as Deliège does (1999: 164–8). In line with the 'Adi' movements in the south, Mangoo Ram's 'first religion' was based on the idea that 'untouchables' are the descendants of the 'original' inhabitants of the country. The same idea lay behind the 'Adi Hindu' movement, subsequently introduced by Swami Achutanand into what is now Uttar Pradesh. However, despite attempts to unify the various 'Adi' movements, each remained essentially distinct and autonomous (Juergensmeyer 1982: 24–6). None the less, for all of them, reconstructing their lost identity meant rediscovering their primacy, their nationhood and their religion. Particularly instructive is Mangoo Ram's use of the term *qaum* to denote the unity of 'untouchables' as distinct from that of 'Hinduism'. For example, the posters for the first Ad Dharm conference in Jalandhar in 1927 read:

> We are the original people of this country, and our religion is Ad Dharm. The Hindu qaum came from outside and enslaved us. ... Brothers, there are seventy million of us listed as Hindus, separate us, and make us free. We trusted the Hindus, but they turned out to be traitors. Brothers, the time has come. ... Centuries have passed, but we were asleep, brothers. ... There was a time when we ruled India, brothers, and the land used to be ours. The Hindus came from Iran and destroyed our qaum. They became the owners, and then called us foreigners, disinheriting seventy million people. ... The Hindus rewrote our history, brothers.

74 Jones (1976: 129ff., 202ff.); for Dayananda Saraswati, see Jordens (1978).
75 For the full text of the twenty-five resolutions passed at Mugowal, see the 1931 Report of the Ad Dharm Mandal (Juergensmeyer 1982: 299–302).

This powerful declaration of both primacy and implied racial difference culminates in the exhortation that 'untouchables' should flock to the Ad Dharm movement to 'start the *qaum* anew' (Juergensmeyer 1982: 45–6). We may note that it is precisely this kind of racial theory that Ambedkar sought to avoid with his own explanation of the origins of untouchability. According to him, modern 'untouchables' are the descendants of 'Broken Men', remnants of defeated tribes who attached themselves to stable communities as watchmen. In time, these peripheral groups were formally excluded from the rest by the notion of untouchability, a deliberate construction to secure the labour of these dispossessed people. At no point, however, did Ambedkar admit of racial difference (Ambedkar 1948: 32–4, 64).[76] Mangoo Ram and the Ad Dharm did.

It is now possible to place the Ad Dharm manifesto within the context of the 'untouchable' myths of origin outlined in section 3. While the myths considered by Deliège are defined by their pre-nineteenth-century antiquity, the Ad Dharm mythology is the direct result of recent political change. But the major contrast is the lack of a narrative moment in which the 'untouchable' ancestor is first defined as polluted, polluting and eternally inferior. Instead, we find a tale of brutish ignorance on the part of others, followed by centuries of war and, eventually, deliberate but unjustified subjugation. A comparison with the Deliège schema produces the following pattern:

- Step 1: At the beginning of time, long before the advent of caste distinctions, there existed one harmonious community, the Adi or original inhabitants of India. According to the more popular, exclusive version of the myth, these were the ancestors of the later 'untouchables' alone. According to the less popular, inclusivist version, they were the ancestors of all later castes. The second version recalls both Deliège's classic pattern of an original set of brothers to which all castes can be traced, and the 'Chuhra' myth outlined on p. 52.
- Step 2: At some point in the distant past, the so-called 'Aryans' migrated into India. According to the exclusivist version of the myth, the 'Aryans' were simply outsiders intent on self-aggrandisement; according to the inclusivist version, they were part of the Adi community who had earlier migrated out of India. Either way, the Aryans are depicted as ignorant, lacking in both spiritual awareness and community feeling, and bent on war. They invaded India from the west, killed or enslaved most of the Adi people, and pushed the rest from the plains into the remoter areas of mountain and jungle.
- Step 3 brings us to the modern era. After centuries of oppression, the Adi people have forgotten their glorious origins. Through no fault of their own, they are classed by their oppressors as 'untouchable', whether as

76 For a list of Ambedkar's 'guiding principles', including his insistence on 'no racial difference' between 'untouchables' and caste Hindus, see Zelliot (1996: 61–2). The issue of the racial origins of caste is an old chestnut, as Risley demonstrates as early as 1908 in his summary of the views of yet earlier scholars (1908: 247–66); for a more recent discussion of racial interpretations of caste, see Trautmann (1997).

castes or tribes. Worst of all, their inferiority is now enshrined in a self-justifying but false 'Aryan' mythology: 'traditional' Hindu *dharma*.

Not surprisingly, the proponents of Ad Dharm saw the Arya Samaj as merely the latest in a long line of 'Aryan' lies. They therefore dismissed the purification and social uplift programmes of the Arya Samaj as further attempts to keep the 'untouchables' in their place. In fact, the persistent antagonism between the Arya Samaj and the Ad Dharm mirrors the conflict between Gandhi and Ambedkar: in each case the former sought to create a modified Hinduism that would include 'untouchables', while the latter insisted that the only certain solution was separatism.[77]

Mangoo Ram's origin myth provides the two key elements of the Ad Dharm religion: the idea of an original people (*ādi*), and the notion of a unified and potentially universal religious identity (*qaum*). Other important components of the new religious movement included: the rejection of all social and religious hierarchies in favour of an innate equality; the worship of an impersonal (*nirguṇ*) notion of God along the lines of the *sant* tradition; and the veneration of low-caste saints, including devotion to living low-caste gurus. Of particular significance for this predominantly 'Chamar' community was the 'Chamar' saint, Ravidās. When the Ad Dharm movement sought to compile their own scriptures, for example, it was to Ravidās that they turned. Many of the hymns attributed to Ravidās are included in the *Gurū Granth Sāhib*, the scripture honoured as 'Guru' by the Sikhs. Strictly speaking, however, Ravidās is a *bhagat*, a mystic among many, not one of the Sikh Gurus. For the Ad Dharm movement, by contrast, Ravidās was not only their primary guru; he was also the guru of Nānak, the first Guru of the Sikhs.[78]

But the new religion considered other saints and heroes within its low-caste remit too, figures such as Lāl Beg, Bāla Shāh and Vālmīki. Indeed, Vālmīki is listed first among the four 'founders' of the Ad Dharm religion in the Ad Dharm Mandal report of 1931, the other three being Ravidās, Kabīr and Nāmdev.[79] This constant stress on the significance of Vālmīki suggests that Mangoo Ram expected Vālmīki devotees to become an integral part of the Ad Dharm. Why did this not happen?

Clearly, Mangoo Ram's aim had been to establish a self-contained 'religious nation' (*qaum*) of 'untouchables'. The 1931 Report of the Ad Dharm Mandal makes this explicit: 'The Ad Dharm Mandal ... was founded in 1925 as a collective organization of all Untouchables in the Panjab'.[80] While other caste groups were

77 For a more detailed analysis of Mangoo Ram's position *vis-à-vis* Gandhi and Ambedkar, and of the Ad Dharm refusal to support Indian independence as long as it implied government by high-caste Hindus, see Juergensmeyer (1982: 124–31).

78 For an account of how the Ad Dharm movement appropriated the symbolism and mythology surrounding Ravidās, simultaneously reclaiming and reviving his appeal for untouchables, see Juergensmeyer (1982: 83–91).

79 For an English translation of the sections of the report outlining the myth of origins and the main components of the faith, see Juergensmeyer (1982: 291–308; for the four 'founders', see pp. 298–9, 304).

80 Cited in Juergensmeyer (1982: 293).

welcomed, 'untouchables' – all 'untouchables' – would represent the core constituency. But there were several major problems. First, the gap between the progressive urban élite responsible for the running of the movement and the more traditional village 'untouchables' proved insurmountable. Second, the professed unity of the organization was fractured by disagreements between the leaders of the three main factions associated with Jalandhar, Hoshiapur and Lyallpur. Third, it was (and still is) not at all clear what might be meant by 'an untouchable religion'. Writing about the 'Chuhras', for example, Griswold explains that they are called 'Hindu' only 'by courtesy'; the term 'covers by a process of elimination all who have not become Sikhs, Musalmans or Christians' (1934: 227). Juergensmeyer questions the application of the term 'Hindu' to any 'untouchable', but an alternative characterization proves elusive. The elements he considers typical of 'untouchable religion' in rural areas include: resistance to upper-caste notions of Hindu *dharma* and to the traditional implications of *karma* and rebirth; respect for the spirit world inhabited by the souls of the dead, including the souls of saints and ancestors; the replacing of the divinities of pan-Indian Hinduism by legendary figures associated with the lower castes; and the overarching notion of a formless God (1982: 92–106). In addition, the urban manifestation of Ad Dharm constructed a new set of egalitarian values couched in religious terms: advancement by merit as a result of hard work, self-discipline, and education, ideals that fitted less well in rural contexts (1982: 119–23). But perhaps the main reason that the Ad Dharm failed to unite all 'untouchable' castes under the one banner was the continuing caste-consciousness of the 'untouchables' themselves. The Ad Dharm became increasingly identified with the 'Chamars'. The other large 'untouchable' *jāti* in the Panjab, the 'Chuhras', gradually turned away to form their own religious movement.

None the less, the Ad Dharm movement reached a peak in 1931. Thanks to Mangoo Ram's petition to the British government, Ad Dharm was listed as a separate religion in the 1931 census, on a par with Hinduism, Islam, and Sikhism.[81] Apart from the formal petition to the British government, Mangoo Ram instigated a major campaign to persuade as many Panjabi 'untouchables' as possible to register their religion as Ad Dharm.[82] If Mangoo Ram's hopes had been realized – that is, if all the 'untouchables' in the Panjab had registered as Ad Dharmis – then they would have been as numerous, and as powerful politically, as the other three major communities. As it was – partly because of the violence inflicted on them by their rivals, especially the Sikhs, partly because of their failure to attract the 'Chuhras' – the number registered was only half a million, roughly the same number as that registered for Christianity, the other significant minority community in the Panjab. We may note in passing that most of the

81 For details of the 1931 Census of India in relation to the Panjab, see K. A. H. Khan (1933: 310–11, 333–5).

82 A frivolous comparison may be made with the recent campaign in Britain, prior to the 2001 Census, to persuade as many people as possible to register their religion as 'Jedi Knight' in honour of the *Star Wars* films directed by George Lucas. So many people complied (including my own fifteen-year-old daughter) 'that the Office of National Statistics has given the creed an official numerical code, denoting it as a religion within the "other" category' (Gray 2001).

converts to Christianity were drawn from the 'Chuhra' *jāti*, with the result that Panjabi Christianity has been seen by some scholars as a 'sweepers' revolt'.[83] For those concerned, however, Christianity was simply another 'untouchable' religious movement, an instrument of change on a par with (and to some extent in competition with) the Valmiki religion and the Ad Dharm.[84]

From the high point of the 1931 Census, the Ad Dharm movement went into decline. For a while, Mangoo Ram flirted with the notion of a separate land or state for 'untouchables' ('Achutistan'), a reflection of contemporary demands for a 'Pakistan' for Muslims, a 'Sikhistan' for Sikhs, and even a 'Jatistan' for members of the powerful Jat caste. More successful was the issue of legislative representation. The Ad Dharmis competed for the eight seats now reserved for the Scheduled Castes, winning seven of them in 1936. Significantly, the 1931 Report of the Ad Dharm Mandal recommends that the date of that deputation to the Governor of Panjab which resulted in eight seats in the legislative assembly (12 October 1929) should be marked as 'the birthday of "Untouchables" as a people, for we were then recognized as human beings'.[85] Winning seven seats was a political victory; having eight seats formally reserved for 'untouchables' was a recognition of their humanity. But this move towards a more political orientation, with the consequent need to form alliances with overtly political groups, necessitated a move away from the earlier focus on religion. For example, Mangoo Ram's support of the low-caste, but largely Muslim, Unionist party concentrated on their shared political agenda. In the resulting coalition, Ad Dharm as a religious movement virtually disappeared. 'Ad Dharm' became the preferred caste name for many 'Chamars' and, in 1946, the name of the movement was changed from 'Ad Dharm Mandal' to 'Ravi Das Mandal' (Juergensmeyer 1982: 152–3). For our purposes, however, the decline of the Ad Dharm movement meant that the fundamental *jāti* division within it – that between the 'Chamars' and the supposedly even lower *jāti* of 'Chuhras' – was transformed into a distinction between two separate religious groups. While the 'Chamars' mainly revered the 'Chamar' *sant*, Ravidās, and so became 'Ravidasis', the 'Chuhras' tended towards Vālmīki and became 'Valmikis'. In both cases, caste names were obliterated by emerging religious identities.

In fact, while the activities of the two movements were often intertwined, the Valmiki Sabha both predated and survived the Ad Dharm. For example, the first meeting of the Valmiki Sabha was held in Jalandhar in 1910, fifteen years before Mangoo Ram returned to India. In the context of my earlier discussion of the two main responses to the 'untouchable problem' – Gandhi versus Ambedkar, the Arya Samaj versus the Ad Dharm – the name 'Valmiki' places them on the same side as Gandhi and the Arya Samaj, that is, in favour of reforming

83 For an account of 'Chuhra' conversions to Christianity in nineteenth-century Panjab, see Prashad (2000: 40–2).

84 For further discussion, see Juergensmeyer (1982: 181–92). For studies of Christianity in relation to other *dalit* groups, see Mosse's research on a mixed Hindu–Catholic village in Tamilnadu (1986), Zene's on the Rishis of south-west Bangladesh (2002), and Mohan's work in Kerala (1999, 2002 and forthcoming).

85 Cited in Juergensmeyer (1982: 293–4).

Hinduism. As a result, the Arya Samaj allied themselves with the Valmiki movement amongst urban 'Chuhras'. The largely political alliance between the Valmiki Sabha and the Ad Dharm movement was short-lived. Despite Mangoo Ram's intention that the Ad Dharm should represent the entire 'untouchable' *qaum*, it had in fact always catered primarily for the mainly rural 'Chamars'. In 1932, the 'Chuhras' left the Ad Dharm. Before that, they had regularly sided with the Ad Dharmis against the Arya Samaj; afterwards, they kept their distance. Thus Saberwal, drawing on fieldwork conducted in 1969 and 1989, is able to treat the two as quite separate groups: the 'Ad Dharmis', combining 'Chamars' and Julahas (weavers), and the 'Balmikis', consisting of 'Chuhras' (1990: 68–85, 51–67). As the 'untouchable' *jāti* deemed lowest of all in the Panjab, the 'Chuhras' had evidently decided to pursue their unique political and cultural interests in their own religious movement, the Valmiki Sabha.

The role of the Arya Samaj in this venture is important, as is clearly demonstrated by Prashad's summary (2000: 91ff.). In 1933, an Arya Samaj activist by the name of Ami Chand volunteered to live and work amongst the 'Chuhras' in Lahore. At first, he was shunned; only after joining the 'sweepers' strike' in 1935, and enduring imprisonment with the rest, was he accepted. In 1936, Chand wrote the pamphlet, *Vālmīki Prakāś*, that served to focus the Valmiki community in India. The basic principles contained in the first half of this work are presented in the form of a dialogue; the rest consists largely of devotional songs (*bhajan*). The message is quite explicit. First, no Adi movement, including the so-called Ad Dharm 'religion', can constitute a separate religious community; if Ad Dharmis were not Hindus (as they claimed not to be), then they were Muslims or Christians. Second, Vālmīki was never a *dalit*. The dialogue on this point reads as follows (pp. 93–4):

> 'Maharaj,' asks the Balmiki, 'tell us if Valmiki was our ancestor [*pita guru*] or our teacher [*shiksha guru*]?' The Ram Sevak replies, 'Shri Valmikiji is your teacher not your ancestor.'

The implications are clear. If Vālmīki is their ancestor, then either he is also a *dalit* (in which case Hindus revere a book written by a *dalit*) or the Valmikis are not in fact *dalit*s (in which case they should be treated accordingly). For the Arya Samaj neither option was acceptable. Ami Chand explains Vālmīki's link with *dalit*s as 'a statement of alliance with the low castes rather than a statement about bloodlines' (p. 94). Third, since everyone needs a guru, *dalit*s chose Vālmīki to serve as their guru on the grounds that he had composed a sacred text accessible to all caste groups. The possibility of alternative guru figures such as Bāla Shāh and Lāl Beg is curtly dismissed (pp. 95–6). Fourth, if the Valmikis reject their 'Muslim' customs (such as burying their dead) and adopt Hindu customs instead, then their untouchability (deemed to be the result of such evil practices) will cease. The anti-Muslim rhetoric is marked. Chand concludes that Valmikis are Hindus, their holy books are the Vedas and their God is Rām (p. 97). Not everyone agreed with this scenario, of course. A major point of contention was the Hindu idea that 'untouchability' was the result of *karma* arising from bad actions in the past. Others concerned the figure of Vālmīki. Was he a *dalit* ancestor? Was he divine, God in human form, or merely a saint? There was also a lingering preference for other *dalit* hero figures such as Bāla Shāh and Lāl Beg. Gradually, however, the old traditions were superseded, at least in part, by the new. Shrines to Bāla Shāh and Lāl Beg were transferred to Vālmīki. Temples to Bhagwan Valmik began to be built, first in Jalandhar, then all over north India: in Shimla in 1931, in Delhi in 1937, then Hoshiarpur, Patiala, Allahabad, Meerut, Dehradun and Lahore (pp. 103–7). As Prashad puts it, 'Bala Shah Nuri was on the way to his death, and Valmiki was on the way to his birth' (p. 107).

We may note here that the name 'Bāla Shāh' continues to be remembered by the older generation of Valmikis in Britain, but in a rather different way from that suggested by Prashad and earlier sources. According to Joginder Gill (Nahli), for example, many villages in the Panjab (including Nahal village, near Lohian in Jalandhar district) maintain, or in the recent past have maintained, solidly constructed mud or brick shrines known locally as 'Bāla Shāh'. The name invariably denotes a site for the worship of Bhagwan Valmik; indeed, it usually displays pictures of Bhagwan Valmik, Lav and Kuś, and Sītā. Whether or not the shrine holds such pictures, however, it always supports five 'little towers' (*burjiān*).[86] These carefully shaped stone or clay objects, rounded in the middle and pointed on top, represent the five *ṛṣi*s on whom Bhagwan Valmik is believed to have bestowed his greatest knowledge: Gautam, Janak, Agast, Vasiṣṭh and Mataṅg. According to Valmiki tradition, the idea of Bhagwan Valmik having five great disciples is ancient: it was later imported into both the Sikh faith (as the five *pīyārai*) and the Muslim tradition (as the five *pīr*), not the other way round; it is also believed to be the source of the term used to denote the village council (*pañcāit*). The question of the relationship between the names 'Bālmīk' and 'Bāla Shāh' remains unclear to most Valmikis in Britain today. The general feeling is that the link with a Muslim saint, and thus with Islam, is simply a mistake. A more acceptable explanation is that the worship of 'Bālmīk' was camouflaged as Muslim for political reasons during the Islamic period: 'Bāla' is close enough to 'Bāl' and 'Shāh' means 'king', making the resulting combination a 'not unattractive pseudonym'.[87] As Nile Green points out, however, names are perhaps *the* most significant statement of personal identity; a name change of this kind would therefore indicate a considerable degree of Muslim influence in one form or another.[88] Today, there is certainly a marked resistance to any suggestion of past or present Muslim identity.[89] Moreover, the Bāla Shāh in Nahal has now been

86 For the term *burji* (plural, *burjiān*), see Singh, Singh and Kaur (1983: 417).

87 I am grateful to Joginder Gill (Nahli) and Sukhbinder Gill for discussing these shrines with me (personal communication, 13 July 2002).

88 Personal communication, 5 July 2002. For the interdependence of Sufism, sainthood and shrines, the role of Muslim sainthood in religious oral narratives, and the mixed Hindu–Muslim clientele of some shrines, see Green (2002).

89 For example, it was pointed out to me that Valmiki temples in East Africa were referred to by the host community and by non-Valmiki South Asians as 'Maskitiya Chura' (literally, 'the mosque of the Chuhras'), but that this was only because there is no alternative word in the Swahili language to denote a place of worship (Sukhbinder Gill, personal communication, 14 July 2002).

replaced by a two-storey, brick-and-mortar temple to Bhagwan Valmik, following the pattern outlined by Prashad for the 1930s onwards.[90]

By 1950, when the waves of immigration from the Panjab to Britain began, the two large *dalit* groups – the 'Chamars', mainly Ravidasis, and the 'Chuhras', mainly Valmikis – were quite distinct. However, they were in agreement on several key points: that untouchability was invalid; that it had arisen from a religious concept preached for selfish ends; that religion and society are inextricably entwined; and thus that freedom from social oppression can be attained only by means of a new religious movement or, at the very least, by a reconstituted religion. This belief explains the plethora of religious movements to which the *dalit*s flocked. What is interesting about many of these movements is the constant tension between separatist and assimilationist approaches. In the case of the Valmiki religion, worshipping a saint in the place of caste-Hindu deities is at one level a mark of separatism. At another level, the choice of Vālmīki as the focus of that worship links the community with the high-caste or Sanskritic tradition of India. But the link is established in such a way that the traditional patterns of hierarchy and dominance are reversed: by association with Vālmīki, his followers are elevated to his level; by association with the 'Adi' myth of origin, all 'untouchables' move from the margins to the centre, from the bottom of the hierarchy to the top.

In the Panjab as elsewhere, 'untouchables' sought advancement through religion as well as politics. For example, while matters relating to the social and economic advancement of the Panjabi 'Chuhras' were being taken care of by the overtly political Sweepers' Union, the Sabha concentrated on the veneration of Vālmīki. As temples sprang up in major cities, each contained representations of him in the form of pictures or icons. Sometimes, he is depicted as a human being: usually as the historical author of the epic, often (despite the efforts of Ami Chand) as the real-life ancestor of his 'untouchable' devotees. Sometimes, he is treated as a divinity in his own right, placed alongside other gods to receive the offerings due to him. Central to the worship of, or reverence for, Vālmīki is the propagation of stories that both add to his reputation and link him – and, therefore, his illustrious reputation – to the 'Chuhra' *jāti*. Much of the energy of the Valmiki Sabha goes into this activity. The significance of the dacoit myth outlined in chapter 1 – the key element in the Birmingham incident – is now clear. Any slur on Vālmīki's name is a slur on the religious identity and personal dignity of every member of the Valmiki community.

Before moving on to consider the Valmikis in Britain, a brief comment should be made concerning nationalist politics in India today.[91] We have already seen how the Valmiki religion allows its adherents to contextualize themselves both within and outside Hinduism. The scriptural context encourages an assimilationist or inclusivist approach at the same time as the 'untouchable' focus gives rise to an

90 I am told that the Bāla Shāh might have been retained in a single-storey building; it was considered disrespectful for it to occupy the lower level of a two-storey construction (Joginder Gill (Nahli), personal communication, 16 July 2002).

91 For further information on 'religious nationalism', see the work of van der Veer (1994) and Hansen (1999).

alternative, separatist strategy. While this tension persists today, the tide seems to have turned towards inclusivism. Of particular interest is the link between the Valmikis and the Hindutva ('Hindu-ness') movement. The anti-Muslim sentiments pressed upon Valmikis by earlier Hindu militants enabled them to respond positively to the emergence of the Bharatiya Janata Party (BJP) in the 1980s. By the end of the decade, a number of Valmikis were working with (or for) the BJP, first in anti-Muslim activities in Delhi and Khurja, then as part of the attack on the Babri Masjid mosque in Ayodhya in 1992. The latter action was no doubt fuelled by the promise made to them by the Hindu nationalist movement, the Vishwa Hindu Parishad (VHP), to build a temple to Bhagwan Valmik on that spot (Prashad 2000: x–xi). In the margins of these activities, the BJP has sought to reconstruct the Valmikis, along with other *dalit* communities, within their brand of Hinduism. Despite the inherent conflict between the two camps – the BJP pledged to defend orthodox Hinduism, the *dalit*s determined to dismantle it – there has been some success in this venture. In Uttar Pradesh, for example, the one Valmiki elected to the Lok Sabha in 1991, Mangal Ram Premi, represented the BJP. In the 1993 Assembly elections, the Valmikis voted *en masse* for the BJP.[92] Like Gandhi and the Arya Samaj before them, the BJP offers an inclusivist solution to the 'untouchable problem'. Unlike the Ad Dharm movement, which remained openly hostile to Hinduism, the Panjabi Valmikis seem to be allowing themselves to be welcomed back into the Hindu fold. Vikram Gill's polarization of the Birmingham incident can thus be linked to this larger Hindutva discourse and its recurrent theme of reconversion. According to this view, Muslims, Sikhs, Christians and Buddhists are simply converted low-caste or 'untouchable' Hindus; it is therefore necessary to bring them back to Hinduism. By contrast, it could be argued that the Valmikis never really left.

6. The Valmikis in Britain

Immigration to Britain has a long history, from the early invasions of Celts, Anglo-Saxons and Normans to the more recent influxes from Ireland and Europe. Since the Second World War, however, there has been migration of a different kind and on a different scale from South Asia and the Caribbean. By the early 1990s, according to Roger Ballard's estimate, Britain included 2.7 million people of non-European ancestry, thus creating for the first time a visibly multiracial and polyethnic society. Ballard concludes that the impact on British culture may yet prove to be 'almost as great as that precipitated by the arrival of William of Normandy in 1066' (1994b: 1–2). What is now apparent is that each of these minorities has reconstructed on British soil a multiplicity of cultural and religious groups. In the context of South Asian communities in Britain, the

92 For further information on 'untouchable politics' in north India (with particular reference to Kanshi Ram, a Panjabi 'Chamar' converted to Sikhism), and for a brief biography of Mangal Ram Premi, see Mendelsohn and Vicziany (1998: 218–37, 248–9).

defining factor is neither national nor regional origin, but the 'much narrower loyalties of caste, sect and descent-group' (p. 4). While the host community tends to focus on distinctions of skin colour, British South Asians are constructing identities derived from their own understandings of religious authority and cultural meaning.

South Asians began to arrive in Britain in the seventeenth century. The nineteenth century saw the gradual development of South Asian settlements, consisting mainly of Indian seamen, in all the major ports. These were the 'pioneers', constituting the first of the so-called 'four stages' of South Asian settlement in Britain (Ballard and Ballard 1977: 21–2). After the Second World War until the 1970s,[93] large numbers of workers were recruited to combat labour shortages in Britain's industrial regions. For most South Asian migrants, work in Britain provided an opportunity for economic advancement, both for the individual and his immediate family as well as for the caste group concerned. Initially, immigrants from South Asia were mainly men, intent on maximizing their earnings for the benefit of those back home. Sending money home and sponsoring male relatives was an effective way of raising the community's status in the ancestral hierarchy. From an approximate estimate of under 7,000 Indians living in Britain in 1945 (before Partition the figures included Sikhs, Muslims and Hindus), the number leapt to about 70,000 in the late 1950s, not all of them Hindus (Burghart 1987b: 6–7). This was the second stage.

The third stage represents the formation of family units. Following the 1962 Immigration Act, wives and children began to join their menfolk. Male-only households were transformed into predominantly ethnic, residential settlements ripe for the construction of religious and cultural communities (Ballard 1994b: 12–18). The mid-1960s and early 1970s saw the arrival, often in complete family units, of what Parminder Bhachu has termed the 'twice migrants' from East Africa.[94] Most were Gujarati-speakers. By 1977, approximately 307,000 Hindus (as opposed to Indians) lived in Britain, of which 70 per cent were Gujaratis and 15 per cent Panjabis (Burghart 1987b: 8). It was during this third phase that regular rituals began to be performed, and religious associations began to function. This was partly the effect of increased numbers, and partly due to the arrival in Britain of Hindu women, who traditionally take the active role in the pursuit of lay religion. Temple trusts were formed with a view to establishing temple-centred worship. The first Hindu temple was constructed in Leicester in 1969. Religious activities continued and intensified in the fourth stage, that of the emerging second generation, from the early 1970s onwards.

The formation of these communities is instructive. As Ballard so neatly puts it, most migrants arrived not as 'unconnected individuals, but in cascading chains along increasingly well-worn paths of kinship and friendship' (1994b: 11). Each of these 'cascading chains' delivered migrants from a specific community (encompassing caste, language and region) into an equally specific community in Britain. The result has been the creation in Britain of close-knit and tightly

---

93 Much stricter immigration rules came into force in the 1980s.

94 Like the more recent influx of Tamils from Sri Lanka, the East African Indians came as refugees. For the East African diaspora, see Bhachu (1985, 1991).

structured groups that to a large extent reflect the networks of ethnicity, caste and language in the source country. For example, most South Asian migrants came from one of three regions: the Panjab, Gujarat and the Sylhet District in Bangladesh. The largest group consisted of Panjabi-speakers, originating from both sides of the Indo-Pakistan border; more than half came from the Pakistan side. Most Panjabis from the Indian side were Sikhs, with perhaps a quarter classed as Hindus. The Hindus in Britain were divided by ethnicity, caste, sect and, especially, language: Gujarati-speakers were in the majority, with Panjabi-speakers forming a vocal minority.[95] David Bowen's study of the Gujarati community in Bradford offers one solution to the conflicting set of allegiances. The initial organization there included Gujarati Muslims but excluded Panjabi Hindus, thereby defining itself in linguistic and cultural rather than religious terms (1987: 15–31).

If we now focus on the Panjabi contingent, we find that caste is equally important. Perhaps 10 per cent of Panjabi immigrants were *dalits*, predominantly 'Chamars', while the rest were mainly Jat Sikhs. Juergensmeyer traces this unexpectedly large number of immigrant 'Chamars' to the appointment in the Panjab of the first Scheduled Caste officer in charge of passports (1982: 245–6). The Panjabi immigrants came mainly from the Jalandhar area, specifically from the Jalandhar doab,[96] the thickly populated region between the Sutlej and Beas rivers in eastern Panjab. In Britain, they settled in the industrial areas of London, Birmingham and the Midlands. Despite the lack of interest in caste in Britain, perhaps because of it, the old caste divisions persisted in the new locations. As Juergensmeyer described the situation in 1982, 'the Jat Sikhs do not hesitate to remind the Chamars that they are still Chamars, even in England' (p. 246).[97] The 'Chamars' responded by using the name and ideology of the Ad Dharm movement in order to establish their equality as a separate religious community (*qaum*). Beginning in 1956, the Ad Dharm 'Chamars' organized Ravi Das Sabhas that functioned both as caste-based societies and as the key components of a religious movement. It was from this British base that the campaign to revive the Ad Dharm movement in the Panjab began. In 1970, the first issue of *Ravidās Patrikā* was published; in 1971, the Ad Dharm Federation of the United Kingdom was established. Again, efforts were made to include other 'untouchable' religious groups, especially the Valmikis, in this endeavour. For example, articles in praise of Vālmīki as guru and saint were published in the *Ravidās Patrikā* to counter the general impression that the term 'Ad Dharm' was merely a caste name for Panjabi 'Chamars' (Juergensmeyer 1982: 253–68). However, the distinction between the two communities – the predominantly 'Chamar' devotees of Ravidās versus the largely 'Chuhra' followers of Vālmīki – remained.

95 These figures are taken from Ballard (1994b: 19–21). For studies of some of the Gujarati communities in Britain, see Bowen (1987), Dwyer (1994), Knott (1994) and Warrier (1994); for a study of the smaller community of British Bengalis, see Gardner and Shukur (1994).

96 For the Panjabi terms, *duābā* and *doābā*, see Singh, Singh and Kaur (1983: 372, 377).

97 Anjali Purewal (1976) argues that it is the fact that 'Chamars' and Jats have the same jobs and educational opportunities in Bedford which rankles with the Jats, who then emphasize their caste superiority (cited in Nesbitt 1997: 204).

The Panjabi 'Chuhras' emigrated to Britain in smaller numbers than the 'Chamars', but they have been equally determined to preserve their identity. Some came via East Africa, some via Singapore.[98] Nairobi saw the establishment of the Shree Valmiki Dharam Sabha in 1908, the Shree Valmiki Gurdwara in 1910[99] and a new temple in 1936. A temple was constructed in Singapore too. Other migrants came direct from the Panjab. In the earliest years of migration, attempts were made to work and even worship together, hence the marked Sikh influence in the religious practices of both Valmikis and Ravidasis. As the numbers rose, however, caste tensions increased (Nesbitt 1994: 128). It was soon necessary for the *dalit* groups, including the Valmikis, to establish their own centres of community and worship. The shift away from the Sikh gurdwaras was marked initially by the organization of worship in temporarily hired halls, and subsequently by the building of their own temples. With their legacy of poverty, it took a while for the Valmikis to begin their own temple-building programme. Although a small organized group had been promoting the idea of a Valmiki temple since 1963, it was not until 1972 that action was taken. This coincided with the first visit to the UK of the charismatic religious leader Sahib Sri Sri 108 Sat Guru Gian Nath Ji Maharaj (see Plate 2.1). Although only two Valmiki temples today maintain an explicit affiliation with Sat Guru Gian Nath Ji, all continue to honour him.[100]

Wherever there was numerical support, Valmiki Sabhas were established: today, Southall, Birmingham, Bedford and Coventry are the largest,[101] followed by Wolverhampton and Oxford. These associations function on at least two levels. At the social and practical level, they afford their caste members a sense of solidarity and economically useful kinship networks. At the level of religion, they promote and facilitate both the worship of Bhagwan Valmik and the socio-cultural ideas associated with him. The result is a powerful combination: a religious ideology for what were once perceived to be the lowest 'untouchables' of India, now living among caste-conscious South Asian communities in an otherwise disinterested Britain. As Nesbitt puts it,

98 Several contacts have suggested that the Valmikis who came to Britain via Africa are more forthcoming regarding their caste identity, and less likely to hide it, than those who came directly from India.

99 The Panjabi term is *gurdwārā* (in Gurmukhi script; *gurudvārā* in Devanāgarī), meaning 'doorway to the Guru'. For the implications of the Hindu/Sikh nomenclature, 'Valmiki Gurdwara', see pp. 69–71.

100 The two temples with explicit affiliations are the Lord Valmik Ji Nirankar Holy Temple Gian Ashram Bhavnashan (led by Sat Guru Gian Nath Ji's successor, Sri Sri 108 Sat Guru Baba Mahinder Nath Gill) in Ampthill Road, Bedford, and the Jagat Guru Valmik Ji Mandir Gian Ashram in Booth Street, Birmingham. Portraits of Sat Guru Gian Nath Ji are also prominently displayed in the Bhagwan Valmik Mandir in Southall, in the Bhagwan Valmik Temple in Wolverhampton, and in the Jagat Guru Valmik Ji Maharaj Temple in Coventry.

101 For studies of the Valmiki community in Coventry, see Nesbitt (1990a, 1994). For brief life stories of two key individuals – Mr Mattu, the first Valmiki to settle in Coventry, and Rattan Chand, one of the founders of the Valmiki community in England – see Nesbitt (1990a: 263 and 1994: 125–7).

'only a distinctive Valmiki religious organisation and temple could enable group self-esteem to grow and Valmikis' image vis-à-vis other (higher-caste) Panjabi communities to improve' (1990a: 264). The Valmiki temple-building initiative may be seen as a 'step towards separatism' (Nesbitt 1994: 128),[102] a clear parallel to the separatist movement of the Ad Dharm in the Panjab. Just as Mangoo Ram found it necessary to differentiate his 'untouchable' *qaum* from the mainstream (largely upper-caste) Hindu *qaum*, so the Valmikis in Britain have felt the need to establish a religious community along caste lines, one that is quite separate from mainstream Hindus and Sikhs.

The importance of caste loyalties in the diaspora cannot be overstressed. While the traditional foundations of caste may have been eroded in the British context, intercaste tussles for status seem to have increased. In the 1980s, for example, as Ballard's volume of studies demonstrates, the so-called 'higher' castes seemed ever more preoccupied with preserving their rank, while 'lower' castes seemed ever more determined to work their way up. More to the point, the old high-caste attitudes towards those once termed 'untouchable' persist. As Nesbitt notes, the higher castes normally try to disguise their instinctive reactions, if not always with complete success. But when they lose their tempers, 'caution is thrown to the winds' and 'abuse ... becomes overt' (1994: 119). Something along these lines seems to have happened in Birmingham in February 2000: as the veneer fell away, the insults returned with a vengeance.

In fact, intercaste rivalry affects all South Asian communities in Britain, not only those which class themselves as 'Hindu'. British Sikhs and Muslims are internally divided by caste while British Jains and Parsis function as separate castes themselves.[103] Each group that can command caste or caste-like loyalties forms its own community, constructs its own identity, and strives for its own advancement. As Ballard puts it, 'to talk of an "Asian" community – or even of "Indian", "Pakistani" or "Bangladeshi" ones – is often to reinforce a fiction' (1994b: 29). I would include 'Panjabi' in this list of fictional communities. As

---

102 The first Valmiki temple was opened in 1972 in Ampthill Road, Bedford, followed by those in Coventry (1978), Bedford again (this time in Muswell Road), Birmingham (Booth Street and Icknield Street) and Wolverhampton. The Southall temple originally opened in Hamborough Road in 1978, the much larger site now occupied in Featherstone Road in 1982. The Oxford Sabha does not have its own temple yet; still in the process of developing one, they hire premises on a regular basis. There are also Sabhas in Glasgow and London but these are smaller and more loosely organized, and they have no temples.

103 For caste among Sikhs, including detailed studies of two Sikh castes in Britain, the Ramgarhia (artisan) Sikhs in Leeds and the Ravidasi Sikhs in Bradford, see Kalsi (1992: 16–59, 103–24, 125–47; 1999), and Ballard (1994c); for Bhāṭrā Sikhs in Cardiff and Nottingham, see Thomas and Ghuman (1976), Ghuman (1980), and Nesbitt (1980: 56–7). The Bhāṭrās are perhaps the least-known of the Sikh sub-groups, largely because they have no written history. Currently accorded low-caste status by others, Bhāṭrās claim brahmin descent, tracing their origins to a brahmin sage, singer and poet who fell in love with a dancing girl. For Muslims in Britain, see Saifullah Khan (1977), Anwar (1979), Shaw (1991, 1994) and Lewis (1994); for Jains in Britain, see Banks (1994); for Parsis in Britain, see Hinnells (1994).

dalit groups from the Panjab, both Ravidasis and Valmikis define themselves primarily in contrast to the supposedly higher-caste Panjabi communities, in particular in contrast to the Jat Sikhs. For *dalit*s in particular, whether they are Sikhs or Hindus (or Christians) is less important than their shared caste origins.[104] Again, this is significant in the context of the Birmingham incident.

There is an element of fiction in the application of religious labels too. This is particularly clear in the case of *dalit* castes. In the Panjab, for example, religious labels such as 'Hindu' or 'Sikh' are almost always understood to denote members of the 'higher' castes. As a result, whatever their chosen religion, Panjabi *dalit*s are invariably defined by caste: either they are grouped together as 'untouchable' (or by a similarly demeaning label, such as 'Chuhra-Chamar') or they are marginalized as a sub-category of the religious tradition in question, such as 'Achut' ('untouchable') Hindu or 'Mazhabi' Sikh.[105] In fact, as Juergensmeyer points out, Panjabi *dalit*s rarely describe themselves as members of the wider religious tradition (whether as Hindu, Sikh, Muslim or Christian) 'except when political or social reasons make it expeditious to do so' (1982: 92). This helps to explain the solidarity experienced by *dalit*s in Britain, both *en bloc* and in separate caste groups, even across the apparent boundaries of religious tradition.

It also explains the tendency among Panjabi 'Chuhras' to blur the distinction between Hinduism and Sikhism when applied to themselves; that is, they blur the distinction between Valmiki 'Chuhras' (Achut Hindus) and Sikh 'Chuhras' (Mazhabi Sikhs). Blurring the Hindu/Sikh distinction reinforces the solidarity of the 'Chuhra' *jāti*. It is no surprise, therefore, that one of the first actions of the group in Britain was to abandon stigmatic *jāti* names such as 'Chuhra' and 'Bhangi' in favour of the religious name 'Valmiki'. Indeed, once 'Valmiki' was viewed as a caste name rather than (or as well as) a religious one, it became possible to find both Hindu and Sikh elements within that community. It was this kind of discourse that facilitated the construction of the 'Shree Valmiki Gurdwara' in Nairobi in 1910.

There is a similar discourse in Britain today. For example, several Valmiki temples display pictures relating to Sikh history, especially when the story in question is shared with the Valmiki past as well.[106] In the Jagat Guru Valmik Ji

104 For a study of Panjabi Christians in the UK in relation to both other Christians and other Panjabis, especially their Valmiki relatives, see Nesbitt (1993: 162–4).

105 The term *mazhabī*, literally 'religious', denotes members of the 'Chuhra' caste who have converted to Sikhism.

106 Two stories are especially popular. First, Valmiki's role in the foundation of the Sikh Golden Temple in Amritsar is commemorated by pictures of him burying the pot of healing amrit (*amṛta*) that would give rise to the holy lake on which the Golden Temple would be built. Second, the death of the ninth Sikh Guru, Tegh Bahadur, is commemorated by pictures of Bhai Jiwan Singh carrying the Guru's severed head to safety when no one else dared. Jiwan Singh, previously called 'Bhai Jaita', was given his new name by Guru Tegh Bahadur after the creation of the Khalsa. Venerated today as an 'untouchable' ancestor of the Valmikis, Jiwan Singh is believed to have been killed in the battle of Chamkaur Sahib in 1704 (Karam Chand Thapar, personal communication, 12 July 2002). Pictures of the amrit story may be found in the Bhagwan Valmik Temple in Wolverhampton (see Plate 2.2), in the Bhagwan Valmik Ashram in Birmingham, and in the Bhagwan Valmik Mandir

Maharaj Temple in Coventry, for example, the prayer hall resembles a Sikh gurdwara rather than a Hindu temple (*mandir*), and the behaviour of worshippers conforms to Sikh rather than Hindu practice (for example, the requirement that worshippers cover their heads). Moreover, while the other Valmiki temples and ashrams in Britain give the central place of honour to the *Vālmīki Rāmāyaṇa*, in the Coventry temple that place is shared with the *Gurū Granth Sāhib*.[107] However, the focus of worship in Coventry as elsewhere remains Bhagwan Valmik. Thus Nesbitt's rendering of the opening lines of the *āratī* or 'hymn of praise' runs:

> Praise to Valmik, praise to God Valmik, praise to
> Valmik, the true Guru.
> You are Lord of the whole creation, sustainer of the
> whole creation, giver of liberation.
> Praise to Guru Valmik, praise to Lord Valmik, praise to
> Valmik, the true Guru.[108]

Nesbitt suggests that the marked Sikh influence amongst Valmikis in Coventry can be explained by the fact that the first family to settle there, together with its subsequent chain of settlers, were Mazhabis (1990a: 265–7). It may also be seen simply as an example of what Sukhbinder Gill referred to as the 'Bedouin effect': that is, the tendency for 'feuding tribes' to combine forces to defend themselves

---

in Bedford. Several pictures of the Jiwan Singh story may be found in the Jagat Guru Valmik Ji Maharaj Temple in Coventry (for example, see Plate 2.3), and one in the Wolverhampton temple. Other narrative links between Sikh and Valmiki pasts include the following: the Sodhi and Vedhi lineages of the Sikh Gurus are traced to Sītā's sons, Kuś and Lav; Sangat Singh, also a Valmiki ancestor, was made eleventh Guru of the Sikhs by his 'look-alike' (*ham-śakal*), Guru Gobind Singh, but was martyred during his rescue of the Guru; and Guru Gobind Singh wrote a vernacular version of the Rāmāyaṇa story known as the *Gobind Rāmāyaṇ*, part of the *Dasam Granth* (Sukhbinder Gill, personal communication, 13 July 2002). For a study of the *Dasam Granth* from the perspective of Sikh Khalsa identity, see Deol (2001b).

107 For a photograph of the two volumes in the Coventry temple, see Nesbitt (1991: 13); the *Rāmāyaṇa* volume on display contains a Panjabi translation of the Sanskrit *Vālmīki Rāmāyaṇa*, printed in the Gurmukhi script. We may note here that, at the official opening in 1978, the sole text in the Coventry temple was the *Rāmāyaṇa*; the *Gurū Granth Sāhib* was introduced later to facilitate some of the Sikh modes of worship. In fact, the word 'Temple' was included in the name of the building at the suggestion of Joginder Gill (Nahli), and with the agreement of the original committee, precisely to differentiate it from both a Sikh gurdwara and a Hindu *mandir* (Joginder Gill (Nahli) and Sukhbinder Gill, personal communication, 13 July 2002). Both Birmingham temples and the one in Wolverhampton keep the *Rāmāyaṇa* in the central place, with a copy of the *Yogavāsiṣṭha* nearby. In the Bhagwan Valmik Mandir in Bedford, the central place goes to a Hindi version of the *Yogavāsiṣṭha*. For the splendid statue of Bhagwan Valmik which dominates the temple in Southall, see Plate 2.4.

108 These words are sung to the tune of a popular Hindu *āratī* but there is no circling of a lighted lamp around the focus of worship as one would expect in a typically Hindu context (Eleanor Nesbitt, personal communication, 11 July 2002).

against a common enemy.[109] In the context of a caste-conscious South Asian diaspora, it makes sense for *dalit* groups to join forces in shared worship even across religious boundaries. The history of the Coventry temple makes this clear: when the UK Central Sabha was first formed (informally in 1963, and under a written constitution in 1964), the Coventry temple was included; when the Central Sabha decided that all Valmiki temples should focus on the teachings of Bhagwan Valmik, Coventry withdrew.[110] Today, while there is a growing desire on the part of the wider Valmiki community to distinguish themselves from both Sikhs and Hindus, those in Coventry continue to defend their primary emphasis on caste solidarity.[111]

The point I wish to make here, however, is a more general one. Both in the Panjab and in Britain, religious distinctions – Sikh, Hindu, Muslim, Christian – are superseded by the significance of caste solidarity. Returning to the Birmingham incident, therefore, what appears at one level to be a clash between the members of two religions (Sikhs and Valmikis) turns out to be part of the ongoing conflict between 'higher' castes (in this case, Sikhs) and 'untouchables' (in this case, Valmikis). The fact that the Bhagavan Valmiki Action Committee received letters of support from both Mazhabi (Sikh) and Valmiki (Hindu) communities demonstrates that the conflict was one of caste rather than religion.[112]

Like almost all South Asian groups, therefore, the Valmiki community is overtly caste-based.[113] Because of the stigma surrounding 'untouchability', however, this is a sensitive issue in the British context, particularly among first-generation migrants. Older Valmikis are more likely to profess their supposedly 'untouchable' origins, continuing to use caste to construct a sense of community; but they find the word 'untouchable' offensive and tend to avoid using it with regard to themselves.[114] As Nesbitt notes in relation to her research in Coventry,

---

109 The term seems to have been coined by Paul Harrison to refer to British soccer hooliganism: 'people from different housing estates who are "deadly enemies" all week can be allies on Saturdays in the face of outsiders from another town' (cited in Haley and Johnston, p. 5; *www.thesportjournal.org/vol1no1/menaces.htm*, consulted 16 July 2002).

110 The Coventry temple remained unrepresented in the Central Sabha for many years until 2000, when it was again represented for a short while. In early 2002, rumours that they would be required to remove the *Gurū Granth Sāhib* from its place of honour persuaded the newly elected Coventry committee to withdraw once more (Joginder Gill (Nahli) and Sukhbinder Gill, personal communication, 13 July 2002).

111 For a detailed study of how far children in the Ravidasi and Valmiki communities of Coventry view themselves as Sikhs or Hindus, see Nesbitt (1991). Her research findings demonstrate the inadequacy of Western terminology: 'secular' versus 'religious', 'Hindu' versus 'Sikh', and so on. In particular, Nesbitt raises questions about how teachers in British schools (and, I would add, universities) might critique their presentations of Indic traditions in the classroom.

112 For letters of support from a range of religious communities in India and the UK, see *Report of the Bhagavan Valmiki Action Committee* (2000: 70–88).

113 The Indo-Caribbean migrants from Guyana and Trinidad prove an exception to this rule; see Vertovec (1994).

114 For the Valmiki dislike of the use of the term 'untouchable' by the British press, see

first-generation Valmikis tend to transmit to the next generation 'not the memories of discrimination but an assurance of self-worth second to none' (1990a: 264). Younger Valmikis avoid the term 'untouchable' for a different reason. They are more likely to engage with, and therefore be influenced by, the wider British culture in which caste is irrelevant. But even second-generation Valmikis consider their caste origins and past history in India a crucial part of their current socio-religious identity. For both generations, whether in India or in Britain, religion is perceived as a significant means of challenging and resisting caste prejudice and exclusion. For the Valmikis, the search for a religious identity in Britain is merely the latest development in a long-standing social and cultural protest.

The issue of generational differences among British-born South Asians recalls both James Watson's notion that they have to struggle to cope with 'two cultures' and Roger Ballard's more upbeat description of those same individuals as 'skilled cultural navigators'.[115] A major shift has taken place between first-generation migrants and those who were born in Britain. The former were content to establish clear boundaries between their own world and the alien host. The latter move easily in and between both worlds. But both insist on creating their own identities on their own terms.

The geographical shift to Britain has undoubtedly instigated change, and will probably continue to do so. Kim Knott identifies five major factors at work here: 'home traditions', relating to the migrants' own sense of cultural and religious identity; 'host traditions'; the nature of the migration process; the nature of the migrant group; and the nature of the host response to those migrants (1991: 87–8). With regard to the 'host reponse', most migrants have to deal at some level with exclusion on the grounds of race. *Dalit* groups such as the Valmikis, who face caste prejudice from fellow migrants as well, are excluded twice. As Nesbitt explains, 'casteist insults are the more hurtful because they emanate from those whom they might have expected to be their allies in battles against racism'. She concludes that 'nothing is more likely to sustain the Valmikis' vitality and solidarity than their bitter experience of double exclusion' (1994: 138). There should be no surprise that the impact of these factors on a transplanted religion have produced change, but the precise nature of that change, both now and in the future, remains unclear. As Knott points out, these communities are to a large extent still being led by first-generation migrants, those who arrived in the 1950s and 1960s. As cultural and religious leadership passes to the second and third generation, there will inevitably be further change. Knott concludes her article by reflecting on what she believes are key issues for future research: the use of native languages, the transmission of cultures, the identity of the individual, the identity of the group, the question of leadership, universalization, and the impact of Western religious ideas (1991: 100–4). I believe that some of the questions she

---

Nesbitt (1990a: 272 n. 6). For a similar position taken by the Ravi Das Sabha, in this case in relation to the press headline marking Jagjivan Ram's presidency of the Congress party ('India Makes Untouchable President'), see Juergensmeyer (1982: 252).

115 The first phrase is taken from the title of Watson's volume of papers on British minorities (1977), the second from Ballard (1994b: 31).

asks can be usefully adapted for a better understanding of the British Valmiki community. In particular, I shall consider the issues of language, the transmission of culture and the pursuit of a coherent socio-religious identity.

First, how important is the preservation of Indian languages for the consolidation of the Valmiki community? For example, Panjabi is the language of ethnic origin and therefore significant for the preservation of their ethnicity. What efforts have been, and are being, made to preserve Panjabi among its members? On this point, I merely note the existence of Panjabi-language publications and broadcasts, including the radio programme described in chapter 1. The speed with which the Birmingham incident swelled to riot proportions is evidence of the significance of the vernacular channel of communication. Similarly, what importance is given to Sanskrit as the sacred language of the *Vālmīki Rāmāyaṇa*? Here, I can point to a number of key elements: the intensity of the debate surrounding the character and past history of its author; the explicit desire to learn precisely how he is depicted, not only in Panjabi translations, but in the Sanskrit *Rāmāyaṇa* and *Yogavāsiṣṭha*; and the fact that some members of the Valmiki community have embarked on their own research into ancient India and Sanskrit texts.[116] Clearly, both languages remain important in the construction of the religious identity of Valmikis in Britain, and therefore in the ongoing negotiations relating to authority and meaning.[117]

Second, how is the transmission of culture changing in the British context? Generally speaking, traditional methods of transmission within the family are increasingly being undermined by the British lifestyle (smaller family units, for example, and longer working hours). Moreover, all South Asian children in Britain now study 'religion' in school, but with a particular focus on the universalizing elements of the so-called 'great traditions'. The danger here is that the minority Valmiki tradition is unlikely to be taught (or perhaps even mentioned) in British schools and universities. A further factor in this debate is the transmission of culture through film and video. Most Valmiki children will be familiar with the Hindi movies produced in Bombay, and will therefore be influenced by the increasing universalization of 'Hinduism'.[118] Will this contribute to the removal of differences between the Valmiki tradition and the overarching template of Hinduism within which its meaning is embedded? Or will the Valmikis be able to maintain their semi-separatist stance? For example, from their point of view, the most important film/video event in recent history was the broadcasting, first in India (1988) and subsequently in Britain (1991, 1992), of the *Rāmāyaṇa* in one hundred episodes. When it was suggested that the episode portraying Vālmīki with Rāma's sons might be omitted, the community in India

116 For example, Lekh Raj Manjdadria, the convenor of the Bhagavan Valmiki Action Committee and a pharmacist by training and occupation, recently gained an MA in Indian Religions, including the study of Sanskrit, at the School of Oriental and African Studies at the University of London.

117 By contrast, Panjabi Christians are less concerned to perpetuate the Panjabi language in the UK since they perceive English as a prior language for their sacred text (Nesbitt 1995: 228).

118 For a discussion of the importance of visual images and video presentations in Valmiki and Ravidasi communities in Coventry, see Nesbitt (1991: 27–30).

threatened to come out on strike. The episode was reinstated.[119] Clearly, the poet-saint's role at the end of the epic is of fundamental importance for the self-representation of the Valmiki community.

This brings us to the third issue: socio-religious identity, whether in relation to the individual or the community as a whole. In the matter of religious allegiance, will individuals opt for the broad labels understood by the host culture such as 'Hindu' or 'Sikh'? Or will they continue to identify with traditional sectarian and caste-based communities as the Ravidasis and Valmikis do? If, as seems likely, the latter proves the case, then will those communities be able to include within their numbers individuals from other caste and ethnic groups? How essential will the currently defining elements of caste and ethnicity prove in the future? The British location may in time serve to dislocate both. If it does, the effect will be to destroy the source of its past and current identity. For there is no doubt whatsoever that the Valmiki community in Britain today draws both strength and meaning from the ancient imposition of 'untouchability' in the Panjab.

7. Making Meaning

I shall bring this chapter to a close by drawing somewhat tentatively on the writings of Viktor Frankl. This renowned psychiatrist endured years of horror and hardship in Nazi concentration camps during the Second World War. Partly as a result of that experience, Frankl developed a new approach to psychotherapy now known as 'logotherapy'. He defines the term as follows (1984: 125–6):

> Logotherapy deviates from psychoanalysis insofar as it considers man a being whose main concern consists in fulfilling a meaning, rather than in the mere gratification and satisfaction of drives and instincts, or in merely reconciling the conflicting claims of id, ego and superego, or in the mere adaptation and adjustment to society and environment.

Central to his theory is the belief that the primary motivational force of all human beings is the search for meaning. According to Frankl, the deepest human need is not so much Freud's 'will to pleasure', nor even Adler's much-vaunted 'will to power'; it is the 'will to meaning'. Frankl believed that there are three ways to discover meaning in life: by creating or doing something, that is, through achievement; by experiencing a profound emotion such as love; and by suffering. Perhaps the most powerful, if also the most elusive, way to discover meaning is through suffering. At some level, of course, as the Buddha well knew, all life is suffering. Indeed, this is the message of existentialism: 'to live is to suffer, to survive is to find meaning in the suffering'.[120] But Frankl is trying to make sense of suffering in particularly desperate circumstances: his own suffering, and that of other prisoners, struggling to survive in concentration camps designed to exploit them to and past the point of death. Frankl is fond of quoting Nietzsche's

119 For an account of this incident, see Jain (1988).
120 Gordon Allport, cited in Frankl (1984: 11).

maxim: 'He who has a *why* to live for can bear almost any *how*' (1984: 126, Frankl's italics). But how does one find the 'why' in suffering of this nature and on this scale? At one point in his reflections, Frankl remembers how often his fellow prisoners fell to discussing politics and religion. Politics was discussed endlessly, every rumour and possibility dissected for meaning. But it was religion that brought out the sincerest feelings: improvised prayers muttered in corners, beliefs shared in the dark. As Frankl remarks, 'the depth and vigor of religious belief often surprised and moved a new arrival' (pp. 53–4). Frankl's focus throughout his concentration camp reflections is on the power of the individual to construct his or her own meaning. I believe that his ideas can be extended usefully to embrace the collective meaning of 'untouchable' religious ideology.

There are obvious parallels with the inmates of Frankl's concentration camps. In the context of Indian society, those deemed 'untouchable' endured (and, to some extent, still endure) lives of hardship and humiliation. In both cases, there is little that the individual or group – whether concentration camp inmates or the aggregate of 'untouchables' – can do in the face of unbearable stigma and suffering. The only freedom available is the freedom to take a stand, to choose an attitude, to find a meaning. In this sense, human beings are ultimately self-determining.

Richard Burghart suggests that it is only in Western secularism that meaning is 'fundamental to the experience which modern man imputes to his humanity'. In the West, he maintains, 'life is expected to hold some meaning; and more often than not that meaning is seen to lie in the extension or development of one's self as remembered or anticipated in one's personal history'; but he does not apply this to Hinduism. According to Burghart, the experience of the Hindu devotee 'refers to the inkling of his divine proto-consciousness awakened by spiritual discipline, not the construction of his personal history' (1987c: 238). I have to disagree. It seems obvious to me that the Valmiki religion is the response of one supposedly 'untouchable' caste to the essentially human need for a religious meaning that makes sense of its past collective history of suffering.

Let us now summarize the origin myth of the Valmikis that provides that meaning.[121] A comparison with the Deliège and Ad Dharm schemas used earlier produces the following three-step pattern:

- Step 1: At the beginning of time, the Panjab was the birthplace of (Hindu) civilization. The original inhabitants (*ādivāsī*) were the Nags (*nāga*) who lived noble and civilized lives. Vālmīki was the tenth son of the Nag king, Pracheta (*pracetas*). He was also a contemporary of both Rāma and Kṛṣṇa.
- Step 2: The invasion of the Aryans spelled the end of the original great civilization. The Nags were enslaved by the invaders, who forced them to take care of the most demeaning tasks in society and banished them to live beyond its boundaries.

121 I am dependent here on the account of Pandit Bakshi Ram's history of the Valmikis, *Bālmīki jāti da sankhep itihās* (1969), as it is presented by Nesbitt (1994: 120–1); see also Saberwal (1990: 52).

- Step 3: Centuries later, the descendants of those original inhabitants (Adivasis, Nags) are ranked at the bottom of the 'Hindu' (read 'Aryan') hierarchy. Stigmatized by the caste names imposed on them by their oppressors, they are now permanently excluded from the religious and social lives of the dominant group. Only the caste memory of their ancestor, Vālmīki, provides relief and dignity. This is why the most important festival in the community's religious calendar is the celebration of Vālmīki's birth.[122]

As we saw in the case of the Ad Dharm movement, 'untouchables' generally feel both ennobled and politically empowered by the religious vision of the 'Adi' people, the original owners of the land, essentially the equals of their current overlords, sometimes their superiors. In addition, Valmikis feel celebrated, even sanctified, by the worship of their deified and saintly ancestor. Bhagwan Valmik is the community's God and guru, its *jagat guru* or 'World Teacher'. He also represents everything that they have lost: earthly power, religious authority, personal honour and pride.

122 For an account of the celebration of 'Valmik Jayanti' in Coventry, celebrated at the end of a week during which the Panjabi *Rāmāyaṇa* has been read aloud each day in the temple, see Nesbitt (1991: 22–3).

Chapter 3

Identifying 'Vālmīki' in Early Sanskrit Texts

1. The Text-Historical Approach

There is a sad irony here. The religious tradition of the Valmikis, a people once classified by other castes as 'untouchable', now appears to depend for its validation on upper-caste – largely Sanskritic – Hinduism. Apart from the element of caste or folk memory, the primary strategy of resistance employed by the Valmikis today rests upon Sanskrit sources. Hence the Birmingham incident; hence too this monograph. Even a cursory examination of the evidence suggests that the figure of Vālmīki has attracted a number of legendary elements over the centuries.[1] The text-historical approach requires that we search for references to him, and stories about him, at the earliest level of ancient texts. But how relevant is the text-historical approach to this kind of dispute?[2]

Historians of Indian religion are familiar with the way ancient material is progressively reinterpreted by later traditions. John Brockington's classic study of the *Rāmāyaṇa* offers a perfect example. In *Righteous Rāma* (1984), Brockington reveals how a hero poem, an oral epic of bardic origins, was progressively reworked: first, according to brahminical concerns with *dharma*; second, through the complex understandings of *bhakti*. The notion of a definitive *Rāmāyaṇa* text – fixed, original, eternally true – is strikingly absent in Brockington's study. Instead he demonstrates what is required of the 'textual archaeologist': the painstaking attention to detail, the slow sifting of the accumulated evidence of the centuries to reveal patterns of historical change. A second example is provided by Noel Sheth's work, *The Divinity of Kṛṣṇa* (1984). Sheth too is in pursuit of change (history), not truth (religion). Again, painstaking textual analysis clarifies the shift in perception. In Sheth's case, a close study of the *Harivaṃśa*, the *Viṣṇu Purāṇa* and the *Bhāgavata Purāṇa* reveals the transformation of Kṛṣṇa as fallible hero to Kṛṣṇa as God, the divine recipient of devotional worship. Once more, the process of change illustrates the growing tension between the demands of *dharma* and the liberating complexities of *bhakti*. In a more recent study, Freda Matchett examines the same three texts in order to understand the emergence of the *avatāra* myth and, in consequence, the evolving relationship between Kṛṣṇa and Viṣṇu (2000). While the *avatāra* framework identifies Kṛṣṇa with Viṣṇu, it also allows the mythology of Kṛṣṇa to

---

1 See, for example, my preliminary foray into this area (Leslie, in press).

2 I am especially grateful to Apratim Barua and Simon Brodbeck for helping me to think through some of the issues in this chapter.

develop in its own way. Von Stietencron's work on the Goddess will serve as a final example of the text-historical project. As in the previous examples, von Stietencron compares and explores textual versions of a religious story – in this case, the Purāṇa versions of the *mahiṣāsuramardinī* myth – to reveal the impact of the emerging *bhakti* tradition (1983: 123–7). Again, the primary concern is with the evidence of historical change and not with the religious story at its heart, let alone with the impact of that story on its devotees.

Clearly, the text-historical approach produces results. Perhaps something similar can be achieved with regard to the figure of Vālmīki. But first, a word of caution. Historians often forget that the believer is usually neither trained in the historical method nor necessarily interested in its conclusions. For the devotee, for example, Rāma is both man (the ideal representative of human *dharma*) and deity (the proper object of human worship). While scholars and commentators may struggle with the concept of a man who does not realize his divinity, or of a god who laments his humanity, believers embrace and draw strength from the paradox. This complex issue is addressed in an article by Pollock (1984a).[3] Both he and the text he is studying – the *Dharmākūtam*, an eighteenth-century commentary on the *Vālmīki Rāmāyaṇa* by Tryambakarāyamakhī – tackle the question of whether it is possible for God not to know that he is God. Tryambaka argues that Rāma is indeed God (that is, Viṣṇu); however, to achieve his purpose of killing Rāvaṇa, he must become truly human, which means not knowing that he is God, at least until after Rāvaṇa's death. For Pollock, this interpretation fits perfectly within the logic of the narrative. He concludes that it is no longer possible to argue – as, for example, John Brockington does (1984: 323–6) – that the theme of Rāma as a human hero belongs to the earlier stratum of the poem while indications of his divinity must be later additions. Following Pollock, Hiltebeitel also rejects the idea of Rāma and Kṛṣṇa as 'divinized heroes'; for him, their divinity is 'fully structured into the plans of the original composition' (1999a: 156). In my view, each approach is valid in its context: tracing the shift from human hero to divine figure is an inescapable part of the text-historical project; the embedding of divinity within a temporarily human mind makes perfect sense in the hermeneutics of religious understanding. Similarly, devotees of Kṛṣṇa are more likely to see the historical shift from hero to deity in terms of the gradual awakening of human consciousness than as evidence of change in the object of their affection. For practising Hindus, *bhakti* is a given not a phase. Furthermore, the religious story is viewed as a whole, not as a synthesis. Thus Rāma is God; his apparent humanity arises from the paradox of the avatar. Kṛṣṇa too is God; his mischievous and amorous antics arise from the paradox of his *līlā*. As a Sikh teacher in Britain remarked recently, 'It's not a matter of head knowledge but bhakti' (Nesbitt, in press). In this context, text-historical precision is less important than faith.

The situation is even more difficult when the deity in question is portrayed not merely as human but as ignorant and evil. This is the problem for the Valmikis. For the devotee, Bhagwan Valmik is God. How then does one explain the popular story of his brutish early life as narrated both in later texts and in

3 For another approach to the 'problem of Rāma's divinity', see Pollock (1984b).

modern retellings of the tale? The historian will want to examine the earliest evidence for the story, primarily textual. Differences between this evidence and later versions of the story will then give rise to discussions of historical change and the possible explanations for it. But we must not forget that these discussions may be of little interest to the devotee; they may in fact be 'academic' in both senses of the term.[4]

That said, I begin this chapter by examining the references to the name 'Vālmīki' in the earliest available sources. I follow in the footsteps of Camille Bulcke, whose classic 1958 article opens with two indisputable assertions: that 'tradition' proclaims Vālmīki to be the author of the *Rāmāyaṇa*; and that 'his life is hidden in obscurity' (p. 121). Bulcke continues:

> There is no reason for us to challenge the unanimous voice of tradition, there is no other poet whom we may set up as the possible rival to Vālmīki in his right to be called the author of the Rāmāyana. Indeed, the problem that faces a biographer of Vālmīki is not that of defending his title of 'Ādikavi', but, that of finding out who he was, and the Everest which the same biographer has to conquer is the sad lack of reliable biographical data, and the mass of legend, myth and romance that surrounds the figure of our hero. All that the biographer can do is to gather traditions which deal with Vālmīki, sift them, and study the evolution of his life-story as it becomes revealed in them. He must delve into the literature of the past in order to bring his hero, Vālmīki, to stand before our eyes here in the present.

This remains a worthy goal. My intention, therefore, is to start where Bulcke finished. This means following the leads that he discovered, but also taking into account scholarly research since 1958, as well as weighing up the implications of caste-led political and religious movements today. The major difference between Bulcke's stance and mine is that I place my discussion squarely within the contemporary context of religious meaning. As the Birmingham incident demonstrated only too well, the key issue today is not merely text-historical accuracy but also – perhaps primarily – the contesting of authority and meaning by the faith communities concerned, and by those who wish to understand them.

The rest of this chapter falls into four unequal parts. Section 2 offers a brief discussion of the earliest occurrence of the name 'Vālmīki', in the *Taittirīya Prātiśākhya*. Section 3 considers several rather different occurrences of the name in the great epic of India, the *Mahābhārata*, and teases out some of the implications. Section 4 examines the references to, and information concerning, Vālmīki to be found in the earliest Sanskrit *Rāmāyaṇa*, the text deemed most sacred to the Valmiki community. Section 5 discusses the references to Vālmīki in the text known as the *Yogavāsiṣṭha*, and contextualizes those references in terms of recent research into its textual transmission. None of the key motifs at the centre of what I have called the Vālmīki 'legend' – the ascetic in the termite mound, the dacoit story and the *marā-marā* mantra – appear in these sources. These motifs are therefore not considered in this chapter. The focus here is on what these early

4 We should also note that two crucial assumptions underpin the text-historical project: that historical time is linear and that narrative time is teleological; both need further examination.

– and therefore, in the context of scriptural authority, especially important – texts tell us about Vālmīki. The motifs of the legend emerge in the later Sanskrit texts discussed in chapter 4.

2. The Taittirīya Prātiśākhya

The name 'Vālmīki' is not always linked explicitly to the poet-saint of the *Rāmāyaṇa*, especially in the earliest references. This explains Bulcke's assertion that the name suggests several different individuals in India's rich past: an ancient grammarian, a famous ascetic or *muni*, a mythological 'Suparṇa bird', and the poet-saint who composed the *Rāmāyaṇa* (1958: 348). Two points should be noted here. First, the word *muni* is probably the Sanskrit epithet most frequently applied to Vālmīki, if not in the *Taittirīya Prātiśākhya*, certainly in most of the other passages under discussion in this chapter. While the term has been translated in a variety of ways – saint, sage, seer, ascetic, monk, devotee, hermit, and so on – the important element to keep in mind is the ascetic's vow of silence (*maunavrata*).[5] In order to take advantage of the full range of potential meanings and associations, including the strong suggestion of the ascetic practice of silence, I have chosen to retain the Sanskrit term in this study; any one English alternative is inadequate. Second, the idea that three or four different contexts for the name 'Vālmīki' indicate three or four different individuals requires further examination. It seems to me unnecessary to challenge what Bulcke calls 'the unanimous voice of tradition' without good reason, and tradition tells us without any doubt that the name 'Vālmīki' was only ever applied to one person: the poet-saint of the *Rāmāyaṇa*. While there is no concrete evidence to support this claim, there is also none to disprove it. Until such evidence emerges (in support of either position), I shall proceed on the tentative assumption that we are dealing with one 'Vālmīki'. I shall now examine the evidence for the grammarian.

Bulcke seems to have been the first to investigate the question in any depth (1958, 1959), and his conclusions have been largely supported by later scholars (John Brockington 1998: 24–5). According to Bulcke, the earliest mention of the name 'Vālmīki' is in the *Taittirīya Prātiśākhya* of the Black Yajur Veda school (*śākhā*), one of the ancient pronunciation manuals for students of the Veda (1958: 121). This is a very different genre of text from the epics which we will consider next. Scharfe's definition (1977: 127) is as follows:

> To attain their goal of perfect preservation of the sacred texts, the Veda students required also a sound knowledge of pronunciation techniques. This was a concern for every school (*pariṣad/parṣad*) or branch (*śākhā*) of the Vedic tradition and hence the manuals devoted to this task are called *pārṣada* or *prātiśākhya*.

As is usually the case with early Sanskrit texts, the precise date of this manual is impossible to pinpoint. Even the relative chronology within the *prātiśākhya* genre

---

5 For the etymological context, see Mayrhofer (1994: 362); for textual examples, see Shee (1986: 331–3).

is hard to trace. That said, Scharfe posits a date at some point after Pāṇini but before Patañjali – that is, between *c.* 350 and *c.* 150 BCE[6] – and a possible regional home in central India.[7]

The *Taittirīya Prātiśākhya* contains three references to someone called 'Vālmīki'.[8] All three concern minutiae of Vedic pronunciation. For example, 5.34 provides the rule: 'The sound *ś* preceded by an unvoiced consonant (*sparśa*) becomes *ch*'. Verse 35 gives a qualifying rule: 'But not when it is preceded by the sound *m*'. Verse 36 adds another qualifier, this time on the authority of a named expert in the field: 'Nor when it is preceded by the sound *p*, according to Vālmīki'. The other two references are similar. At 9.4, the text cites a qualifying rule attributed to two authorities: Āgniveśya and Vālmīki. The commentary, *Tribhāṣyaratna*, describes these two as 'teachers belonging to a Vedic school' (*śākhinor ācāryor*; Whitney 1871: 207). Finally, in a section concerning the correct pronunciation of the auspicious syllable *oṃ*, one more qualifying rule is attributed to 'Vālmīki' (18.6). Altogether, the *Taittirīya Prātiśākhya* cites by name three schools (the Mīmāṃsakas, the Āhvārakas, and the Taittirīyas) and twenty-one names that are usually taken to denote individuals, including 'Vālmīki', as well as several vague references to acknowledged authorities (*ācārya*).[9]

There is some intriguing evidence here. First, while we must acknowledge the traditional belief that the name 'Vālmīki' denotes a single individual, it is quite possible that it refers here to what Simon Brodbeck calls 'a bunch of speakers, representing a distinctive school or community or locality' (personal communication, 8 June 2002). After all, the issue being discussed relates to differences in pronunciation; such differences may well reflect a mother-tongue different from speakers belonging to other communities or schools. Even if the name denotes a single individual, the same considerations apply. Second, this possibility of a different (that is, non-Sanskrit) mother-tongue speaker (or school of speakers) can be linked to the 'birth of the *śloka*' (*krauñca-vadha*) episode in the *Rāmāyaṇa*. Perhaps Vālmīki was able to invent a new Sanskrit metre precisely because he came from a different linguistic community. Third, these ideas are of particular interest when linked to the contemporary claim that Vālmīki belonged to the aboriginal (*ādi*) inhabitants of India, whatever that means. These are exciting possibilities. However, no explicit connection is made with the Rāma story in the *Taittirīya Prātiśākhya*. Of course, our poet must have had a past, and that past could easily have been an orthodox one; that is, he may well have belonged to a Vedic school. If he had been an expert in pronunciation, this could explain how it

6 In fact, Scharfe offers an approximate date of *c.* 250 BCE for Pāṇini while Cardona, in his classic survey of research on grammatical literature, argues for *c.* 350 BCE. I have followed Cardona here. For a discussion of the evidence for the relative dates of the key figures concerned – that is, Pāṇini, Kātyāyana and Patañjali – see Cardona (1976: 260–8).

7 For further information on the Vedic *prātiśākhya* texts, and suggestions for further reading, see Scharfe (1977: 127–34).

8 In the following, the Sanskrit text references are from Whitney (1871), while the English translations are mine.

9 Whitney (1971: 427, 430). See also Albrecht Weber (1858: 77–9).

was he spoke such beautiful Sanskrit that Brahmā himself invited him to compose the Rāma story. In real terms, certainly, it is unlikely that our poet burst on to the scene without some kind of prior training. But we have no concrete evidence to this effect. We do have some negative evidence: an electronic search of the Sanskrit text of the *Vālmīki Rāmāyaṇa* reveals neither *pś* nor *pch*; but that is all.

From the material we have here, we may draw only one certain conclusion: that the name 'Vālmīki' was in use in orthodox and highly specialized Vedic circles at that time (*c.* 350–150 BCE). From this we may deduce that the name existed in its own right long before popular etymology gave rise to the termite-mound legend to explain it. Finally, the pronunciation differences indicated in the *Taittirīya Prātiśākhya* (together with the invention of a new verse-form as it is recounted in the *Vālmīki Rāmāyaṇa*, and the traditional view that the two names denote the same single individual) allow us to speculate further on the implied *ādi* origins of the holder of the name 'Vālmīki'.

3. The Mahābhārata

I turn now to India's great epic, the *Mahābhārata.*[10] It is generally agreed that the text of the Sanskrit epic reached its extant form by at least the seventh century CE, probably earlier still. The best-known version is that compiled by Nīlakaṇṭha in the late seventeenth century, and printed in Bombay in 1862–63.[11] Frequently referred to as the 'Vulgate' or the 'Bombay edition', Nīlakaṇṭha's version is usually identified with the northern recension of the text. The southern recension, which is somewhat longer, was first published in Kumbakonam in 1906–10. In order to reach some understanding of the relative chronology of the passages relating to Vālmīki, one needs on the one hand to be aware of the tensions between these two main recensions, and on the other to appreciate the process by which the text(s) developed over time. This is no easy task.

The first question, one that it is impossible to answer definitively, relates to the date of the great war at the heart of the epic. In John Brockington's words, 'probably the war, if it actually occurred, took place early in the 9th century [BCE]' (1998: 133).[12] Despite a range of alternative suppositions, I shall assume the more conservative date of accumulated scholarship presented here.

The second question concerns the emergence of the epic. This development process was first outlined by Hopkins as probably taking place in five stages (1901: 397–8), a provisional analysis on which many later scholars have built. The first stage (before 400 BCE) has none of the features one expects of an epic poem. Instead, we have bardic narratives, what Hopkins calls 'Bhārata (Kuru)

---

10 Unless otherwise specified, the Sanskrit extracts are from the Poona critical edition, while the English translations are mine. For a summary of research into the dating of the text, its growth and development, see John Brockington (1998: 130–58).

11 The first printed edition of the *Mahābhārata* was the Calcutta edition (1834–39).

12 For a summary of the archaeological evidence discussed in relation to the *Mahābhārata*, see John Brockington (1998: 159–62).

lays, perhaps combined into one' (p. 397). Regarding this phase, van Buitenen comments that, while the origins of the *Mahābhārata* probably 'fall somewhere in the eighth or ninth century [BCE]', it is widely agreed that 'the oldest portions preserved are hardly older than 400 BC[E]' (1973: xxiv–v). In the second stage (400–200 BCE), what Hopkins calls the 'Mahābhārata story' is constructed around the Pāṇḍava brothers, together with the bardic narratives and numerous legends, but without the divinity of Kṛṣṇa. During the third stage (between 200 BCE and 100–200 CE), the poem is reworked with Kṛṣṇa as the supreme deity, together with the frequent interpolation of elements associated with the Purāṇas, and the addition of lengthy passages of didactic material. It is worth noting here that van Buitenen resists the temptation to revive what he calls the 'antibrahmanism' of nineteenth-century Western scholarship. He talks instead of 'a necessary symbiosis of brahmin and baron'. Perhaps, he suggests, 'the baronial-bardic tradition, out of which the epic grew, was ... absorbed into another tradition of wandering reciters of brahmin-type lore'. According to this view, the *kṣatriya* bards were 'succeeded, reinterpreted, in the end preserved, by ... prototypes of the Paurāṇikas, reciters of Purāṇas ... in which all traditions are mixed' (1973: xxvi). During the fourth stage (200–400 CE), the last books (Sanskrit, *parvan*) are added (much of book 1, for example, and the three short final books), and the *Anuśāsanaparvan* becomes separated from the *Śāntiparvan*. According to Hopkins, 400 CE marks the beginning of the last of the five stages, in which all further changes, additions and interpolations were made; according to van Buitenen, it is 'the approximate date after which no more substantial additions were made' (1973: xxv). The text of the critical edition is an attempt to reconstitute the text of approximately the sixth century CE. John Brockington revisits these issues in his summary of research into the growth and development of the *Mahābhārata*. While allowing that the divisions suggested by Hopkins remain a useful starting-point and overview, Brockington concludes that a careful analysis of language, style and metre in specific passages and sections (as well as in individual books) reveals a considerably more complex process (1998: 132–4, 158).

There is one point on which everyone seems to agree: the transformation of the *Mahābhārata* was directly related to the transfer of authorial control away from the traditional reciters of martial poems – the itinerant bards or *sūta*s associated with the *kṣatriya*s – to the brahmins with their strong didactic streak. It was V. S. Sukthankar who first drew attention to what he saw as the deliberate role played by the Bhārgavas in this 'brahminization' process – what he called the 'bhṛguization' – of the epic (1936–37). Put very simply, Sukthankar argued that, at a formative stage in the development of the *Mahābhārata*, a powerful 'Bhārgava influence' was involved in a deliberate reshaping of the epic to its own advantage. Certainly, the earlier books of the *Mahābhārata*, such as the *Sabhāparvan*, contain little evidence of Bhārgava influence while later ones, such as the *Anuśāsanaparvan*, contain considerably more. For Sukthankar, however, the term 'Bhārgava' ('descendant of Bhṛgu') denotes a member of a particular group or clan of brahmins whose editorial concern was to demonstrate the superiority of brahmins over *kṣatriya*s, with particular emphasis on the Bhārgavas themselves and on what might be called 'Bhārgava themes'. According to Shende (1943a), the transformation of the *Mahābhārata* was wrought jointly by the Bhārgavas together with the Aṅgirases.[13] Several scholars have taken Sukthankar's theory further. For example, Bhattacharji (1991) provides a list of ideas that were probably not part of the epic before the brahminical reshaping process but which then became systematically embedded in it. These include: sectarian theology, the deliberate appropriation of the notion of past *karma* to justify a current situation, the idea of God as saviour, a strict application of *varṇadharma* and a resistance to caste mobility, the condemnation and control of women, the importance of giving gifts to brahmins, and the merits of pilgrimage, fasting, and *tapas*. Several of these ideas have serious implications for *dalit* history, in particular the new emphasis on the supposed link between caste and *karma* and the impossibility of escaping from the implied restrictions of one's birth.

Goldman's study (1977) is another extension of the 'bhṛguization' theory: a detailed examination of what he calls the major 'Bhārgava myths' in the *Mahābhārata*. But while many scholars have embraced Sukthankar's analysis of the Bhṛgus, in recent years others have taken to criticizing it. For example, Minkowski recommends a greater focus on what is now known of 'the dynamics of traditional oral narrative' and a rejection of 'what amounts to a conspiracy theory' (1991: 400). Criticism has come from Hiltebeitel too. Influenced by Robert Alter's work in Biblical scholarship (1981) and by Pollock's 1984a article, Hiltebeitel takes issue with the prevalent view of the epics as 'byproducts of an historical period of synthesis'. For him, 'the largest inadequacy in *Mahābhārata* scholarship', including his own up to 1991, is 'simply the failure to appreciate the epic as a work of literature' (1999a: 155–6). The result of such criticisms is that the earlier 'conspiracy theory' has been largely replaced either by more complex accounts of textual evolution or by a more unified approach. None the less, Bhārgava names and themes remain prominent. Top of the list of Bhārgavas, second only to Bhṛgu himself, is Rāma Jāmadagnya, the militant brahmin hero responsible for the destruction of the *kṣatriya*s, whether this story is intended as a military or a literary victory.[14] But there are other famous names to which the epithet 'Bhārgava' has been applied as well: Aurva and Cyavana, for example, and occasionally (but, as we shall see, inappropriately) Vālmīki. I return to this point below and in chapter 4.

This brings me to the difficulty of dating specific passages. It is impossible to allocate the epic as a whole to one era; this means that the dating of each part of that whole has to be assessed in its own right. In addition, scholars now recognize that, in van Buitenen's words, so-called 'later accretions' may have been 'hoary' to begin with (1973: xvii). This uncertainty makes our task extremely difficult. Even when the (relative) dating of particular books or episodes seems secure, there is no guarantee that the details within them necessarily abide by the same (relative) chronology. With these *caveat*s in mind, I now return to the references to 'Vālmīki' in the *Mahābhārata*, beginning with the passage least likely to be relevant to our purpose.

---

13 For the Bhārgavas and Aṅgirases in the *Rāmāyaṇa*, see Shende (1943b).

14 As mentioned in chapter 2, Rāma Jāmadagnya is known outside the *Mahābhārata* as 'Paraśurāma'.

The identification of the name 'Vālmīki' with a 'Suparṇa bird' is brought to Bulcke's attention by Sandesara (1959: 305; cf. Bulcke 1959: 348). The episode under discussion (chapter 99) is part of the myth of Mātali (chapters 95–103) in book 5, the *Udyogaparvan* or 'The book of the effort'.[15] As a result of the work of the editors of the critical edition, it is now generally agreed that book 5 as a whole contains fewer large-scale insertions than many of the others, and that the northern and southern recensions seem to be in greater agreement; both discoveries point to a comparatively early date (De 1940: xxvff.). According to Agrawala (1956), however, the Mātali episode is one of these additions, probably dating to the Gupta period. For van Buitenen, the Mātali story is a perfect example of what he calls the 'new myth', by which he means 'a myth with no discoverable Vedic provenance and with a distinctively new outlook' (1978: 166), not so much an epic myth as one more appropriate to the Purāṇas. In the main storyline of the epic, the Pāṇḍavas have returned from their thirteen-year exile, expecting to be given back their kingdom, but the Kauravas have reneged on the agreement. Kṛṣṇa now seeks an honourable settlement at Dhṛtarāṣṭra's court. It is at this point that the *ṛṣi* Kaṇva intervenes.[16] He narrates the story of Mātali in order to persuade Duryodhana of the futility of fighting the Pāṇḍavas: just as Mātali has Viṣṇu's support against Garuḍa, so the Pāṇḍavas have Kṛṣṇa's support against the Kauravas. The story runs as follows. Indra's charioteer, Mātali, with Nārada as his travelling companion,[17] journeys to the world of supernatural snake-beings[18] where he will eventually select a husband for his daughter. On their way, Mātali and Nārada stop to consider possible suitors in the world of the *suparṇa*s, the supernatural birds that kill and eat snakes. Generally speaking, the term *suparṇa* (literally, 'fine-winged') describes any large bird of prey with an impressive wing-span, such as the eagle or vulture. In this context, the term denotes the descendants of Garuḍa, the supernatural bird-

15 For a complete English translation of the Mātali story, and an analysis of the story as myth, see van Buitenen (1978: 384–95 and 166–8). For a summary of research on the *Udyogaparvan* in general and the Mātali episode in particular, see John Brockington (1998: 143–5).

16 The term *ṛṣi* is commonly used to describe Vālmīki too. According to Mayrhofer, a *ṛṣi* is first a poet, a singer of hymns and seer of visions; later the term includes the ascetic and the holy sage or saint (1988: 261). Thus the term may denote a visionary poet of Vedic hymns, a saintly individual, a semi-divine being who is neither god nor human, or a patriarchal sage of the ancient past (see also Monier-Williams 1899: 226–7 and Mitchiner 1982). No single English word captures this potential breadth of meaning. In this study, therefore, in order to exploit the full range of implications – in Vālmīki's case, with particular emphasis on the notions of poetic inspiration and the visionary power to 'see' – I have chosen to retain the Sanskrit term.

17 We may note in passing Agrawala's view that the mention of Nārada is evidence that this episode is a later addition to book 5 (1956: 3).

18 The term one might expect to be applied to this world (*nāgaloka*) here designates the world of elephants (also *nāga*; Mbh. 5.97.1). The world of snakes (*nāga*, *pannāga*) is described as 'the city of Bhogavatī', the term *bhoga* denoting the coils of the snake inhabitants (Mbh. 5.101.1). Van Buitenen's 'Bhogāvatī' is a misprint.

being, son of Vinatā.[19] Because of the long-standing enmity between Vinatā and her sister Kadrū, their respective descendants – the supernatural bird-beings and the supernatural snake-beings – are eternally opposed, but the birds have divine licence to kill and eat the snakes. While Garuḍa is sometimes regarded as a brahmin *ṛṣi*, in this context Nārada describes him and his descendants as *kṣatriya*s: their pitiless killing of their snake cousins disqualifies them from brahminhood. The implications of this comment for the main story of the epic – where cousins stand poised for battle – are obvious. Finally, after praising the *suparṇa*s as devoted followers of Viṣṇu, Nārada lists the chief birds by name, one of which is 'Vālmīki' (5.99.11). No link is made with the Rāma story. This Vālmīki is neither a *ṛṣi* nor a brahmin. Despite the label *kṣatriya*, and along with all the other characters in the story, he is not even human. As van Buitenen puts it, the main protagonists are 'second-rank', 'somewhat divine' beings, while the rest – semi-divine elephant, bird and snake beings, *daitya*s and *dānava*s – are 'denizens of a celestial *demimonde*' (1978: 167).

In the context of our search for the author of the *Rāmāyaṇa*, this passage seems unhelpful. Again, the only firm conclusion that we can draw is that the name 'Vālmīki' existed independently of the popular etymology of the termite-mound legend; but that is important. The rest is considerably more speculative.[20] For example, it seems likely that the two groups marked by animal names represent tribal peoples engaged in a long-standing feud.[21] Brodbeck refers to them rather neatly as the '*suparṇa*-folk' and the '*nāga*-folk'. When Mātali gives his daughter in marriage to one of the *nāga*s, his own people (Brodbeck calls them the 'Indra-folk') become embroiled in the feud on the *nāga* side. There are some intriguing ideas here. First, the tribal origin of the *suparṇa*-folk, including the *suparṇa* named 'Vālmīki', may be linked with the contemporary claim that the poet-saint of the *Rāmāyaṇa* was an 'aboriginal' (*ādi*). Second, the relative supremacy of the Indra-folk is indicated by the fact that they are the ones who apply the brahmin/*kṣatriya* distinction to the other two. But their supremacy is counterbalanced by an element of equality: Mātali considers suitors from both tribal groups before he chooses a son-in-law. We may conclude that a *varṇa*-type hierarchy is in place, and that it is not yet fixed. The *Taittirīya Prātiśākhya* material certainly suggests that it was once possible for non-Sanskrit-mother-tongue speakers to participate in Vedic learning, so some movement was evidently possible. Third, the *suparṇa*-folk (including the *suparṇa* called 'Vālmīki') are categorized as *kṣatriya*s rather than brahmins on the grounds that they are killers, the killers of the *nāga*-folk. Is it possible that what began as a stereotypical slur against a tribal community re-emerged much later as a personal slur against Vālmīki? In my view, none of this is out of the question.

---

19 In this episode, see 'sons of Vinatā' (*vainateyasutaiḥ*, v. 2) and 'descendants of Garuḍa (*garuḍātmajāḥ*, v. 15); hence van Buitenen's translation of the first *pada* of verse 1 ('This is the World of the Garuḍas').

20 I am grateful to Simon Brodbeck for his reflections on this episode (personal communication, 8 June 2002).

21 For a discussion of *nāga*s and *suparṇa*s as mutually hostile, early tribes, see Mishra (1987: 217–30).

I shall now examine the evidence for what Bulcke thought was a possible third individual named 'Vālmīki'. The key theme in all four references is asceticism. I shall consider each one in narrative order.

In book 1, the *Ādiparvan* or 'The book of the beginning',[22] the brahmin Āstika is intent on rescuing the supernatural snake-beings from King Janamejaya's great sacrifice. In order to be allowed to enter the sacrificial enclosure, he praises the sacrifice, the assembled brahmins and the king. His praise of the king includes comparisons with the acknowledged greatness of others. These include Yama and Indra, Kṛṣṇa and Rāma, Vālmīki and Vasiṣṭha. 'Like Vālmīki,' he declares, 'your great firmness is gentle; like Vasiṣṭha, your anger is restrained' (Mbh. 1.50. 14). Van Buitenen has no difficulty identifying this Vālmīki with the 'sage and author of the *Rāmāyaṇa*' (1973: 445). But what is the evidence? All we have is a statement of 'gentle firmness', and the proximity of Vasiṣṭha. But perhaps these carry enough weight to make the connection: invoking the author of one epic at the start of another is appropriate; and the linking of Vasiṣṭha with the poet of the *Rāmāyaṇa* is standard, not least in the famous *Yogavāsiṣṭha*. True, there is no explicit mention of the defining characteristic of Vālmīki – the composition of the Sanskrit *Rāmāyaṇa*, or at least a link with the Rāma story – but perhaps there need not be. The epic story is implied.

The second reference in this group occurs during Nārada's visit to Yudhiṣṭhira's magnificent assembly hall (*sabhā*) in book 2, the *Sabhāparvan* or 'The book of the assembly hall'. The book as a whole, but not necessarily in all its parts, is described by John Brockington as 'part of the oldest core of the *Mahābhārata*' (1998: 139). Of all the eighteen books of the epic, van Buitenen calls this the 'pivotal one': it foreshadows the events of all the rest (1975: 3, 6). After the building of the assembly hall, Nārada arrives to honour Yudhiṣṭhira. He praises the hall as the finest he has ever seen on earth. When Yudhiṣṭhira asks about the halls of heaven, Nārada first describes the splendid hall of Indra (chapter 7). Much of his description is taken up with two long lists of the eminent *ṛṣi*s who attend upon Indra there, including 'the great ascetic Vālmīki' (*vālmīkiś ca mahātapāḥ*, 2.7.14).[23] This is all we are told specifically about Vālmīki. But the list of qualities attributed to the gathering as a whole is instructive: all the brahmin, royal and divine *ṛṣi*s are there (*brahmarājarṣayaḥ sarve sarve devarṣayas tathā*, 2.7.23), including the so-called 'Seven Sages' (*saptarṣayas tathā*, 2.7.25);

---

22 For a summary of research concerning the dating of the *Ādiparvan*, much of which is perceived as a later addition, see John Brockington (1998: 135–9).

23 The first list reads: Parāśara, Parvata, Sāvarṇi, Gālava, Śaṅkha, Likhita, the *muni* Gauraśiras, Durvāsas, Dīrghatapas, Yājñavalkya, Bhāluki, Uddālaka, Śvetaketu, the powerful (*prabhu*) Śāṭyāyana, Haviṣmat, Gaviṣṭha, King Haviścandra [van Buitenen reads 'Hariścandra'], Hṛdya, Udaraśāṇḍilya, Pārāśarya, Kṛṣīhvala, Vātaskandha, Viśākha, Vidhātṛ, Kāla, Anantadanta, Tvaṣṭṛ, Viśvakarman and Tumbura (vv. 9–12). The second list reads: Sahadeva, Sunītha, the great ascetic (*mahātapas*) Vālmīki, Samīka, Satyavat, the reliable (*satyasaṃgara*) Pracetas, Medhātithi, Vāmadeva, Pulastya, Pulaha, Kratu, Maruta (van Buitenen reads 'Marutta'), Marīci, Sthāṇu, the great ascetic (*mahātapas*) Atri, Kakṣīvat, Gautama, Tārkṣya, the *muni* Vaiśvānara, the *muni* Kālakavṛkṣīya, Āśrāvya, Hiraṇyada, Saṃvarta, Devahavya, and heroic (*vīryavat*) Viṣvaksena (vv. 14–16).

both those who are human born and those who are not (*ayonijā yonijāś ca*), those who live on air and on sacrificial offerings (*vāyubhakṣā hutāśinaḥ*, 2.7.13); all are without blemish, their sins destroyed by ascetic practice (*amalā dhūtapāpmāno*), their bodies blazing like fire (*dīpyamānā ivāgneyaḥ*), and so on (2.7.8). The division of the category of *ṛṣi* into three types is typical of the epics and Purāṇas: 'royal', 'brahmin' and 'divine' (*rāja*, *brahma*, *deva*).[24] Even in this exalted company, Vālmīki is important enough to be given his own epithet within a list of largely unqualified names, but the epithet conveys only his ascetic prowess. There is no mention here of the *Vālmīki Rāmāyaṇa*; again, within the tradition, that context is implied.

The third example is from book 3, the *Vanaparvan* or 'The book of the forest', also known as the *Āraṇyakaparvan* or 'The book of the forest teachings'.[25] As a result of several detailed studies on individual episodes, it is clear that this book incorporates a variety of unrelated materials. The history of the *Tīrthayātrāparvan* (3.80–93), in which the Vālmīki reference occurs, is especially complex.[26] In the main storyline of the epic, Arjuna is away, paying a five-year visit to Indra. His brothers, together with Draupadī, are living disconsolately in the forest when Nārada drops in once more. When Yudhiṣṭhira asks him about the rewards of pilgrimage, Nārada responds by telling him about a pilgrimage once made by Bhīṣma on the advice of the *ṛṣi* Pulastya. While the topic of pilgrimage appears to be a late addition to epic discourse, its occurrence here seems to constitute the earliest evidence available for what was almost certainly a more ancient practice. Furthermore, it has been shown that this whole section (3.80–83), which contains one set of *tīrtha*s or pilgrimage sites, is a later insertion into an already late passage describing another set of *tīrthas*.[27] Nārada concludes his account by urging Yudhiṣṭhira to undertake such a journey himself, in the company of the most distinguished *ṛṣi*s and ascetics (3.83.102–5). The first name on Nārada's list is 'Vālmīki'.[28] While there are certainly references to the Rāma story later in the

24 A less frequent division into seven includes these three and a further four: *maharṣi*, *paramarṣi*, *śrutarṣi* and *kāṇḍarṣi* (Monier-Williams 1899: 227; see also Mitchiner 1982).

25 On the evidence of the manuscripts consulted, the editors of the critical edition opted for *Āraṇyakaparvan*; for the English translation, van Buitenen preferred the shorter *Vanaparvan* 'with the understanding that it implied the other' (1975: 174).

26 For a summary of research relating to book 3 – including studies on the Nala, Ṛśyaśṛṅga, Rāma Jāmadagnya, Yavakrī, and Sāvitrī episodes, as well as work on the *Tīrthayātrāparvan* in question – see John Brockington (1998: 140–2). See also van Buitenen (1975: 173–215; for the *Tīrthayātrāparvan*, 185–7).

27 For the lateness of pilgrimage generally, see Shende (1943a: 75) and Bhattacharji (1991: 473). For a detailed analysis of the structure of the *Tīrthayātrāparvan*, see Oberlies (1995).

28 The complete list is as follows: Vālmīki, Kāśyapa, Ātreya, Kauṇḍinya, Viśvāmitra, Gautama, Asita Devala, Mārkaṇḍeya, Gālava, Bharadvāja, Vasiṣṭha, the *muni* Uddālaka, Śaunaka and his son, Vyāsa (described as 'most excellent murmurer of mantras', *japatāṃ varaḥ*), Durvāsas (described as 'best of hermits', *muniśreṣṭha*), and the great ascetic (*mahātapas*) Gālava (3.83.102–4). Gālava's double appearance is unexplained: van Buitenen (1975: 397) silently replaces the second 'Gālava' with 'Jābāli'. The divine *ṛṣi* Lomaśa, described as 'of infinite radiance' (*amitadyuti*), is

book (3.147.11–12, 23–38), no explicit link is made here with the poet Vālmīki. The most important thing about Vālmīki in this context is that he is a powerful and revered ascetic; the rest is implied.

For the fourth *Mahābhārata* reference to ascetic qualities of Vālmīki, I return to book 5, the *Udyogaparvan* or 'The book of the effort'. In the main story of the epic, we are once again at the point when the Kauravas have reneged on their agreement to hand back the kingdom to the Pāṇḍavas. Before Kṛṣṇa leaves for Dhṛtarāṣṭra's court, he is honoured by a large number of illustrious holy men and great *ṛṣi*s. The list of named *ṛṣi*s – both brahmins and divine – includes 'Vālmīka', alongside Vasiṣṭha, Nārada and Bhṛgu.[29] The unusual form of 'Vālmīka', and the lack of detail linking this name to the Rāma story, throws some small doubt on the individual concerned. However, just as Vasiṣṭha, Nārada and Bhṛgu are ascetic *ṛṣi*s first and participants in specific stories second, so perhaps Vālmīki (or, in this case, 'Vālmīka') was then associated primarily with ancient ascetic practice, and only secondarily (perhaps subsequently) with the *Vālmīki Rāmāyaṇa*. I draw two conclusions here: first, there is nothing to prove that this 'Vālmīka' is not the epic poet; second, the frequent stress on his asceticism is significant. The second point will be developed further in chapter 4.

This brings us to four *Mahābhārata* references to Vālmīki that evoke his poetic achievements rather than his ascetic prowess. The clearest example occurs in the midst of the great battle in book 7, the *Droṇaparvan* or 'The book of Droṇa', where Vālmīki is mentioned both by name and explicitly as a poet. Of the four so-called 'battle books' (books 6–9), the *Droṇaparvan* seems to have absorbed the most interpolations, while the style of language suggests a later rather than an earlier date.[30] When the great warrior Bhuriśravas seems on the point of killing the youthful Sātyaki, Arjuna saves his protegé by cutting off the older man's sword arm. Sātyaki promptly kills Bhuriśravas, to the unanimous disapproval of the assembled warriors. Sātyaki defends himself by insisting that Bhuriśravas' death was ordained. To absolve himself from any wrongdoing, Sātyaki cites a verse (*śloka*) sung (*gīta*) by Vālmīki long ago: 'Whatever damage can be inflicted on one's enemies should indeed be done'.[31] We can be fairly certain that this is 'our' Vālmīki. First, he is described as a poet who 'sings in *śloka*s'. Second, the half-*śloka* quoted can in fact be identified as the second half of 6.68.27 in the critical edition of the *Vālmīki Rāmāyaṇa*. In Goldman's view, this is the only certain reference to Vālmīki in the whole of the *Mahābhārata* (1976: 99). I would add that the violent sentiment expressed in the half-*śloka* could be taken to reinforce

---

mentioned separately in verse 106. Brodbeck observes that the parallels between Vālmīki and Vyāsa, both 'murmurers of mantras', are intriguing: both composed epics in a new kind of verse, and neither are Vedic characters (personal communication, 8 June 2002). Is Vyāsa perhaps associated with another *ādi* community?

29 The complete list reads as follows: Vasiṣṭha, Vāmadeva, Bhūridyumna, Gaya and Kratha; Śukra, Nārada and Vālmīka (listed as a triad); Maruta, Kuśika and Bhṛgu (5.81.27–9). For further references to Vālmīki as an ascetic amongst other ascetics, see Tagare (1983: 676).

30 For a summary of these issues, see John Brockington (1998: 148–9).

31 *api cāyaṃ purā gītaḥ śloko vālmīkinā bhuvi / pīḍākaram amitrāṇāṃ yat syāt kartavyam eva tat //* Mbh. 7.118.48.

the notion of an intertribal feud between *suparṇa*s and *nāga*s, as discussed above. Finally, we should note that there is no mention of ascetic practice here. This Vālmīki is quite simply the famous poet.

The second example is rather less clear-cut. It occurs in book 12, the *Śāntiparvan* or 'The book of the peace', in the long subsection entitled *Mokṣadharmaparvan* (12. 168–353). Considered as a whole, book 12 consists of a series of passages and episodes loosely grouped together into three large units, with an overall chronological progression from the first (the *Rājadharmaparvan*, chapters 1–128), through the second (the *Āpaddharmaparvan*, chapters 129–167), to the third, the *Mokṣadharmaparvan* (John Brockington 1998: 151–2). According to this scenario, the Vālmīki reference under discussion cannot by any accounts be early. In the main story, Bhīṣma has been mortally wounded in the great battle. He lies on his bed of arrows, postponing death, receiving homage and answering questions. Encouraged first by Nārada and then by Kṛṣṇa, Yudhiṣṭhira takes a seat beside the dying warrior and asks him about *dharma*. One of his questions concerns Lord Viṣṇu, about whom Yudhiṣṭhira wishes to learn more. Bhīṣma begins by telling the Pāṇḍava about the excellent sources of his information. He has heard about Viṣṇu in conversation (*jalpataḥ*) with Rāma Jāmadagnya, with Nārada and Vyāsa (here called 'Kṛṣṇa Dvaipāyana'), while Asita Devala, Vālmīki and Mārkaṇḍeya have each recounted at length (*kathayati*) the great marvel of Viṣṇu (12.200.3–4). The explicit *bhakti* context is another clear marker of late material. The difference between the verbs *jalp* and *kath* is that between general conversation and more sustained narration. It makes sense, therefore, that the latter term is used for Vālmīki and Mārkaṇḍeya to whom are attributed an epic and a Purāṇa respectively. Perhaps Asita Devala (also known as either 'Asita' or 'Devala') is included in this category because he is believed to be the composer of several Ṛgvedic hymns. But perhaps no great distinction between the two terms is intended; after all, the composition of the *Mahābhārata* is attributed to Vyāsa. Either way, it is interesting that Vālmīki the poet is also described here as a 'great ascetic' (*mahātapas*), evidence that the two associations (ascetic and poet) are being applied to the same person simultaneously. In this context, however, the reason for the list of names is not asceticism but the ability to speak about Viṣṇu. We may conclude one of two things: either there were originally two separate individuals who were subsequently merged by tradition into one, or the poet Vālmīki was also a renowned ascetic. The second alternative is supported by tradition.

The third passage in this category that I wish to consider does not mention the name 'Vālmīki', but it has been much discussed in that connection (see Goldman 1976: 99). Like the previous example but at an earlier point in the *Mokṣadharmaparvan*, this extract occurs in the long discussion between Yudhiṣṭhira and Bhīṣma while the latter languishes on his bed of arrows. In fact, the passage is part of Bhīṣma's answer to Yudhiṣṭhira's very first question, on the duties of a king. Bhīṣma's response is to quote 'a verse about kingship sung long ago by the great-souled Bhārgava in his narration of the life of Rāma' (12.57.40).[32] The verse runs as follows: 'A man should first find a king, then (choose) a wife, then (earn) some

32 *ślokaś cāyaṃ purā gīto bhārgaveṇa mahātmanā / ākhyāte rāmacarite nṛpatiṃ prati bhārata //* Mbh. 12.57.40.

wealth. Without a king (to offer protection) in the world, what is the point of wife or wealth?'[33] Bulcke identifies the verse as '*Rāmāyaṇa* 2.67.11', but fails to provide either the Sanskrit verse in question or details of the edition he is using (1958: 125 n. 26). According to Hopkins, the *Mahābhārata* verse agrees closely enough with this '*Rāmāyaṇa* 2.67.11' to suggest that the author of one was aware of the other (1901: 61); more important, he supplies the evidence to support his assertion.[34] Goldman is more concerned with the fact that the *Mahābhārata* verse is not to be found in 'any known' manuscript of the *Vālmīki Rāmāyaṇa* (1976: 99). His focus is the identity of the 'Bhārgava' mentioned in that verse. In his article on this issue, Goldman summarizes the evidence against attributing the epithet to the author of the *Vālmīki Rāmāyaṇa*: the absence in the *Rāmāyaṇa* text of the precise verse quoted; the vagueness of the term *rāmacarita*, which might apply equally well to the *Mahābhārata*'s own *Rāmopākhyāna* (Mbh. 3.258–75) or to yet another version of the Rāma story; and the equally vague term, 'Bhārgava', which (as we have seen) can be applied to a number of other figures in the course of both epics, including Mārkaṇḍeya, the narrator of the *Rāmopākhyāna*. Goldman concludes (1976: 99):

> It seems impossible, on the basis of this verse or any other that I have so far seen in the *Mahābhārata*, to assert unequivocally that the great epic knows Vālmīki as a Bhārgava. In fact the absence of such a clear reference is, in the light of the theory of Bhṛguisation, strong evidence that it did not.

In chapter 4, where I examine the theme of asceticism, I shall return to the vexed question of what it may mean to say that Vālmīki was a 'Bhārgava', that is, to claim that he belonged to the famous Bhṛgu clan.

The last *Mahābhārata* passage in this series is perhaps the least persuasive of the four. Indeed, it is dismissed by Purushottam Lal Bhargava as 'spurious' and 'full of absurdities' (1984: 77). The reference occurs in book 13, the *Anuśāsanaparvan* or 'The book of the instructions'. This *parvan* appears to have been separated from the *Śāntiparvan* at a late date, the bulk of it (that is, the *Dānadharmaparvan*, chapters 1–152) constituting a fourth large unit along the lines of the previous three (John Brockington 1998: 152–3). Bhīṣma is still lying on his bed of arrows, still being questioned by Yudhiṣṭhira. When he is asked for a comprehensive account of the virtues of Lord Śiva, Bhīṣma turns to Kṛṣṇa for an authoritative response (Mbh. 13.14.1ff.). There follows a long discourse on Śiva, including a recitation of the many names of God. When Kṛṣṇa has finished speaking, the assembled *ṛṣi*s rise one after the other to speak about the benefits attained by Śiva's grace, either as a result of asceticism practised in remote places or through reciting his name (Mbh. 13.18.1ff.). We may note in passing the conflation here of the ideals of asceticism and *bhakti*.[35] In the critical edition, the

---

33 *rājānaṃ prathamaṃ vindet tato bhāryāṃ tato dhanam / rājani asati lokasya kuto bhāryā kuto dhanam //* Mbh. 12.57.41.

34 The verse cited by both Bulcke and Hopkins as '*Rāmāyaṇa* 2.67.11', and quoted in full by Hopkins, appears in the critical edition at 2.61.10: *arājake dhanaṃ nā 'sti nā 'sti bhāryā 'py arājake / idam atyāhitaṃ cā 'nyat kuto satyam arājake //*

35 Studies of *tapas* show that asceticism was originally a form of power, a means of attaining the desired goal (Hara 1979, Shee 1986, and John Brockington 2000).

name 'Vālmīki' stands second in the list.[36] While some of these individuals are given the specific title of *ṛṣi*, they are all described as *muni*s (Mbh. 13.18.46). Vālmīki and Gṛtsamada are also allocated the honorific 'Lord' (*bhagavān*, Mbh. 13.18.7, 15). The term *bhagavat* (*bhagavān* in the masculine nominative singular) is another epithet frequently applied to Vālmīki, both in the early texts and in contemporary discourse. While the literal meaning of the word is 'possessor of fortune' or 'fortunate', it is more usually translated as 'blessed', 'holy', 'illustrious'. Depending on the context, its meaning can be either descriptive (as in 'holy man' or 'divine being') or honorific (as in 'Lord Vālmīki' or 'Blessed One'). In this study, I vary my English translations accordingly.

Vālmīki's contribution to the discussion is a curious one, so I shall reproduce it here in full:

> And Lord Vālmīki also spoke to Yudhiṣṭhira. 'In a dispute relating to a *sāma* ritual, some ascetics called me a brahmin-killer. Once they had said this, I was immediately possessed by that *dharma* (of being a brahmin-killer), O Bhārata. I took refuge in Śiva (*īśāna*) who is without sin, and I praised him. I was released, free from sin. Then that destroyer of unhappiness, he who demolished the triple city, said to me, "Your fame will be supreme indeed!".'[37]

There are several interesting points about this passage. First, Vālmīki is mentioned as one ascetic among many; his asceticism is the reason for his inclusion. Second, as is the case with several other *muni*s who speak up, Vālmīki's story begins with an apparently adharmic act on his part. While the narrative strongly suggests that he is not guilty, Vālmīki is accused of killing brahmins; since the accusation is levelled by brahmins, it is enough to imbue him with that sin. By contrast, Rāma Jāmadagnya freely admits the crime of brahmin-murder. Gṛtsamada's sin is different: by mispronouncing the words of the *sāma* recitation, he endangered Indra's sacrifice; cursed to become a deer, he is finally rescued by Śiva. Like Vālmīki, Māṇḍavya is wrongly accused, in his case of being a thief; impaled on a stake for the supposed crime, he too is saved by Śiva. I shall return to this intriguing combination of apparent sin and false accusation in my consideration of the dacoit motif in chapter 4. A third point lies in Śiva's final blessing, when he prophesies that Vālmīki's fame will be great. This is usually taken as an allusion to Vālmīki's subsequent composition of the *Rāmāyaṇa*. As we shall

---

Thus *tapas* has no necessary religious connection, either as part of a soteriological path or as an instrument of *bhakti*. The religious context of the asceticism practised in this passage is therefore another mark of lateness. I shall return to this issue in chapter 4, where I deal with the conflation of motifs in the development of the legend surrounding Vālmīki.

36 The other ascetics who speak are listed as: Catuḥśīrṣa, Rāma Jāmadagnya, Asita Devala, Gṛtsamada, Jaigīśavya, Gārga, Parāśara, Māṇḍavya and Gālava.

37 *vālmīkiś cāpi bhagavān yudhiṣṭhiram abhāṣata / vivāde sāmni munibhir brahmaghno vai bhavān iti / uktaḥ kṣaṇena cāviṣṭas tenādharmeṇa bhārata //* Mbh. 13.18.7. *so 'ham īśānam anagham astauṣaṃ śaraṇaṃ gataḥ / muktaś cāsmy avaśaḥ pāpāt tato duḥkhavināśanaḥ / āha māṃ tripuraghno vai yaśas te 'gryaṃ bhaviṣyati //* Mbh. 13. 18.8.

see in chapter 4, the vignette of a divine figure prophesying future greatness for Vālmīki is frequently met with in later works, where the fame referred to relates specifically to his great poem; but here no overt link with the Rāma story has been made. Fourth, like all the other ascetics, Vālmīki takes refuge with Śiva and not, as we might expect in view of later developments, with Viṣṇu; but then, in this episode, even Kṛṣṇa does that. Finally, there are two possible links to passages discussed above. Might the 'dispute relating to a *sāma* ritual' have arisen from a difference of opinion concerning pronunciation, as in Gṛtsamada's case, thus linking this episode with the *Taittirīya Prātiśākhya* passage? And might the epithet 'brahmin-killer' be a link with the murderous reputation of the *suparṇa*-folk, as a result of which they were classified as *kṣatriya*s not brahmins? Both connections are tenuous perhaps, but neither is impossible.

There is one last passage to consider before we move on to examine the *Vālmīki Rāmāyaṇa*. Rather than being evidence for the presence of the poet Vālmīki in the *Mahābhārata*, this one constitutes a clear demonstration of his absence. The episode in question is the *Rāmopākhyāna*. In the main story, the Pāṇḍavas are relaxing in the forest after their spirited rescue of Draupadī from her abductor, Jayadratha. Reflecting upon the abduction of his (and his brothers') wife, Yudhiṣṭhira asks Mārkaṇḍeya if the latter has ever seen or heard of a man who has suffered greater misfortune (Mbh. 3.257.10). The word 'man' (*nara*) in Yudhiṣṭhira's question, coupled with Mārkaṇḍeya's response, stresses the human as opposed to divine dimension of the Rāma story at the time of the composition of the *Rāmopākhyāna*. The *ṛṣi* responds by narrating an abbreviated version of the Rāma story. Much has been written about the relationship between this episode and Vālmīki's poem, and I shall summarize the main points here.[38] First, the closeness of the two texts is established by John Brockington's realization that one in seven *pāda*s of the *Rāmopākhyāna* has precise parallels in the *Vālmīki Rāmāyaṇa* (1978). Second, the former is more closely linked with the latter's northern recension than its southern one, and more closely still with the north-eastern recension. Third, broadly speaking, the *Rāmopākhyāna* must be the later of the two. As Brockington notes, however, a careful examination of parallels with the different recensions indicates that the relationship is more complicated than this simple statement suggests (1978: 292; 1998: 475). Fourth, while the *Rāmopākhyāna* was essentially derived from the central core of the *Vālmīki Rāmāyaṇa* (that is, books 2–6), the *Bālakāṇḍa* and *Uttarakāṇḍa* (books 1 and 7) are subsequent to, and partly derived from, the *Rāmopākhyāna*. In section 4, I shall relate this pattern of mutual influence to the stages of development outlined by John Brockington in his classic study of the *Vālmīki Rāmāyaṇa* (1984). For now, I need only emphasize that the *Rāmopākhyāna*, the longest and most complete version of the Rāma story contained in the *Mahābhārata*, fails even to mention the name 'Vālmīki'. Similarly, the references to the Rāma story found

38 For detailed references to, and discussions of, the arguments put forward since Weber first raised the subject in 1807, see Raghavan (1973: 11–25), van Buitenen (1975: 207–14), Goldman (1984: 33–9) and John Brockington (1998: 473–7). For discussions of other passages relating to the Rāma story, and the broader question of the relationship between the two epics, see John Brockington (1998: 477–84).

in the *Harivaṃśa*, traditionally viewed as an appendix to the *Mahābhārata*, also fail to mention Vālmīki.

To summarize this section, there are several early references to the name 'Vālmīki' outside the *Rāmāyaṇa*.[39] The two isolated allusions – one, to an expert in Vedic pronunciation; the other, to a mythological *suparṇa* bird – may constitute evidence of Vālmīki's non-Sanskritic, tribal origins, which may in turn be linked with the *ādi* discourse of contemporary *dalits*. In most of the remaining passages, the key element is not the composition of the *Vālmīki Rāmāyaṇa* but extensive ascetic practice.

4. The Vālmīki Rāmāyaṇa

Before considering what the *Vālmīki Rāmāyaṇa* tells us, a closer look at the relative chronology of the two epics is necessary. As is generally agreed, both epics began as bardic narratives. Elements of these early tales formed the core of each work. With the increasing authorial power of the brahmins, both epics were then reworked: treatises on *dharma* were inserted and the original tales were retold from the brahminical point of view. In the *dharma* literature generally, the tension between the more orthodox ritualists and the more autonomous ascetics became increasingly evident, a tension that spilled over into all the literature of that extended but indefinite period. Overlapping with this development, the advent of *bhakti* began to take effect, reworking the epic material yet again.

This overall pattern can be linked with the stages of development outlined by John Brockington in 1984 in relation to the *Vālmīki Rāmāyaṇa*. After a series of detailed articles in which he revisited the work of earlier scholars in the light of the new data provided by the Baroda critical edition, Brockington applied his discoveries to the *Vālmīki Rāmāyaṇa* text. As he explains in a subsequent work (1998: 348, parentheses added),

> This took the form of a classification into five overlapping stages: the first stage is the reasonably homogeneous core of the *Ayodhyā* to *Yuddha kāṇḍas*, the second stage comprises the material within those books showing evidence of later reworking or addition, the third stage consists of the *Bāla* and *Uttara kāṇḍas*, and the fourth and fifth stages comprise the * passages and Appendix 1 passages with good or poor manuscript support respectively. The first and second stages each comprise about 37–38 per cent of the [critical] text and the third almost 25 per cent, with the fourth and fifth stages together roughly equal in length to the [critical] text or somewhat longer.

Dating is necessarily approximate. Thus the first stage includes both the composition of books 2–6 some time in the fifth century BCE, and their oral transmission (with all the embellishments that that implies) up to and including the fourth century BCE. The presentation of Rāma as a martial and essentially human hero,

39 There is also a mention of Vālmīki in the *Harivaṃśa*, although only in a passage relegated to an Appendix in the critical edition (Appendix 1.28.29), as Mary Brockington points out in a forthcoming paper (personal communication, 17 June 2002).

and the generally heroic basis of the Rāma narrative, are most evident here. The second stage extends from the third century BCE to the first century CE, during which time those five books were reworked and expanded. This period brings greater status for the king, greater control of women, and more frequent mention of ascetics. For most of this period, Rāma is viewed as an ethical, human hero; by the end, he is divine. The third stage extends from the first to the third century CE, bringing with it the addition of book 1 ('The book of childhood') and the somewhat later book 7 ('The last book' or 'Epilogue'). This stage is marked by the presentation of Rāma as an avatar of Viṣṇu, by a shift away from the Vedic pantheon to that associated with the Purāṇas (with special prominence given to Brahmā), and by a further decline in the position of women. More important for our purposes, this stage also produced a pronounced emphasis on *varṇa-dharma*: Śambūka, the *śūdra* ascetic, is killed by Rāma in order to bring a brahmin boy back to life (see Plate 3.1); and the so-called 'untouchables' (such as the tribal *niṣādas*) are increasingly despised. There is also a marked emphasis on the practice of *tapas* and on the powers accruing thereby to the ascetic. Finally, Bhārgava names and themes become more prominent in this period, a reflection perhaps of the editorial process of 'bhṛguization' described earlier in the context of the *Mahābhārata*. The fourth stage extends from the fourth to the twelfth centuries CE, incorporating further additions and changes to the text. This period is marked by popular religious practices such as image and temple worship, and pilgrimage; and by an even more pronounced decline in the position of *śūdras*, 'untouchables' and women. The fifth stage includes the changes made from the twelfth century onwards. Both these last stages demonstrate the incorporation of the Rāma narrative into the increasingly popular *bhakti* tradition.[40]

We have already noted that the *Mahābhārata*'s *Rāmopākhyāna* was composed at some point prior to the third stage, and that it formed the basis for books 1 and 7 of the *Rāmāyaṇa*. While there are many allusions to the Rāma story in the *Mahābhārata*, however, there is, according to Brockington, 'no direct mention in the *Rāmāyaṇa* of any central character or incident from the *Mahābhārata*' (1998: 481). Yet, especially in the later phases of the development of the *Rāmāyaṇa*, there are plenty of indications of both mutual influences and borrowings, and similar patterns of development and transmission. Brockington concludes that, 'at least in their later phases of evolution, the two epics developed in parallel, and possibly in the same locality' (1998: 484). Despite the reservations that inevitably arise from this kind of discussion, there remains little doubt within the pan-Indian tradition generally that Vālmīki composed the first Sanskrit *Rāmāyaṇa*. There is no external evidence to support this attribution, but the internal evidence is clear. So, what does this text, supremely sacred to the Valmiki community, reveal about its author, the 'first poet' (*ādikavi*) and their guru-God?[41]

Perhaps the most important point to note is that there are no references to Vālmīki in books 2–6 of the critical edition. My focus on the critical edition is

40 For the main features of these five stages, and a tabular presentation of the material assigned to each one, see John Brockington (1984: 307–27, 329).

41 Unless otherwise specified, extracts from the Sanskrit text of the *Vālmīki Rāmāyaṇa* are taken from the Baroda critical edition, while the English translations are mine.

not unproblematic, of course. In most manuscripts of the text, for example, the *Bālakāṇḍa* opens with verses in praise of Rāma, Hanumān or (a particular favourite) Vālmīki. Goldman takes issue with the editors of the critical edition for omitting these passages. While he accepts that the verses 'certainly do not belong to the oldest stratum of the text', he suggests that they probably belong to 'an early version of the poem' and, 'judging by their popularity, are seen as an important part of it'. Some commentators incorporate the verses into their own work; one commentary (the *Rāmāyaṇa Śiromaṇi* of Vaṃśīdhara Śivasahāya) attributes them to Kuśa and Lava, the first reciters of the poem. To give a flavour of what is missing, I include here three verses in praise of Vālmīki taken from the critical apparatus at the beginning of the critical edition of the *Bālakāṇḍa*, all three translated by Goldman:

> I praise the cuckoo, Vālmīki, who sits upon the highest branch of the tree of poetry, sweetly warbling the sweet syllables, 'Rāma, Rāma'.
>
> For who, upon hearing the droning tale of Rāma told by that bee among sages, Vālmīki, a wanderer in the woodlands of poetry, would not attain the highest bliss?
>
> Thus I praise that sage, Pracetas' equal in might, who, though he drinks forever the nectar of the tale of Rāma in this world, is never sated with it.[42]

In the following, I shall note some of the other occasions when traditional references to Vālmīki have been dropped from the critical edition.

The frame story of the poet's involvement in the narrative was added in stage 3 in the development of the epic: that is, somewhere between the first and the third century CE. The phrase 'frame story' is not used here in the way that many scholars have used it in discussions of the embedding of stories, frame within frame, in the *Mahābhārata*.[43] The nearest frame story in that sense in the *Rāmāyaṇa* is the recitation of the Rāma story by Rāma's sons at the start of the epic (1.4). The story of Vālmīki displays more of a 'book-end effect', with books 1 and 7 providing the two book-ends, than a true 'frame story'. This does not mean that the *Mahābhārata* passages referring to 'Vālmīki' are equally late. In my view, it is far more likely that the *Mahābhārata* references stressing the asceticism of Vālmīki belong to an earlier period than those focusing on the poet. If this is indeed the case, then these 'ascetic Vālmīki' passages probably also predate the *Rāmāyaṇa* passages I shall be looking at next.

In the critical edition, then, all the information about Vālmīki is found in books 1 (*Bālakāṇḍa*) and 7 (*Uttarakāṇḍa*). More important for our purposes, every reference to him is couched in entirely complimentary terms. There are no accusations of brahmin-murder in the distant past, whether these are understood as true or false. Nor is there even a hint of the dacoit motif of the future. This Vālmīki is cast in the mould of supreme – indeed, potentially divine – virtue.

42 Goldman (1984: 273–4). For the Sanskrit text, see the Baroda critical edition, vol. 1, p. 3, nos. 3*, 4* and 5*. See also Shastri (1962: 441).

43 For the early ritual context of frame stories, and the technique of embedding, see Witzel (1987) and Minkowski (1989).

In book 1, the first four chapters describe Vālmīki in some detail. The first chapter begins by describing him as an 'ascetic' (*tapasvin*, Rām. 1.1.1), adding later that he is a 'great *muni*', in fact the 'most potent of *munis*' (*mahāmuni*, vv. 1, 4; *munipuṃgava*, vv. 16, 22, 29; see also *muni*, vv. 19, 37, 41). The Sanskrit epithet *munipuṃgava*, meaning literally 'bull among *munis*', is frequently applied to Vālmīki and others as a superlative. My attempt at an English equivalent – 'most potent of *munis*' – goes some way towards capturing the two poles of meaning implied: the virility of a bull amidst a herd of cows, and the fact that greater ascetic power is conveyed by greater virility. As we shall see, this notion of Vālmīki as one who is seriously engaged in ascetic practice becomes a constant theme in the *Rāmāyaṇa*. In my view, this is significant.

In the second chapter, we are told that Vālmīki is an 'eloquent speaker' (*vākyaviśārada*), a 'saintly' man (*dharmātman*),[44] one who is sufficiently learned and charismatic to attract his own disciples (Rām. 1.2.1). He is also described as 'great-souled' (*mahātman*, v. 7).[45] Finally, this 'holy' (*bhagavat*, v. 9) man, this 'saintly *ṛṣi*' (*ṛṣer dharmātmanas tasya*, v. 12), is also classed as a 'twice-born' (*dvija*, v. 13). The term *dvija* can be taken to denote anyone who has undergone Vedic education, or a member of any of the three *varṇa*s eligible to do so. In the epics, however, the term is usually understood to denote a brahmin.[46] In addition, Vālmīki is explicitly called 'brahmin' in the *Rāmāyaṇa* (see, for example, v. 30), and many terms normally associated with the brahmin *varṇa* (such as *muni*, *ṛṣi*, *tapasvin*, and so on) are applied to him. In the epic context of the *Rāmāyaṇa*, therefore, there is little doubt about his *varṇa* status.

As an 'extremely wise' individual (*mahāprājña*, v. 16), Vālmīki is so moved with compassion at the death of an Indian Sarus Crane at the hands of a tribal hunter (*niṣāda*) that he unthinkingly utters a curse (which is also a lament) in the *śloka*-form:

> May you find no peace, Niṣāda, for all eternity – because you killed the male of this loving *krauñca* pair when he was intoxicated by desire! (Rām. 1.2.14)[47]

---

44 The epithet *dharmātman* has been translated as 'pious', 'religious' or 'religious-minded', 'virtuous', 'dutiful', and so on. My choice of 'saintly' is intended to convey both the gentleness of innate goodness and the more aggressive and prescriptive notion of 'knowing what is right'.

45 Most of the English equivalents offered for the epithet *mahātman* are inadequate in some way: 'great-souled' (clumsy), 'high-minded' (suggesting an unintended link with the Sanskrit *manas*), 'noble' or 'having a noble nature' (suggesting an unintended link with the Sanskrit *ārya*), 'magnanimous' (surprisingly unsatisfactory considering its etymology), while 'eminent', 'mighty', 'distinguished', and so on, fail to carry the important resonances of *ātman*. As a result, I have alternated between 'great-souled' and 'high-minded', according to the context.

46 Of course, anything deemed to be subject to a 'second birth' may be termed *dvija*. This includes birds and reptiles, both of whom are born once as an egg and a second time from that egg; for an epic passage that deliberately plays on this connection, implying that the magnificent Indian Sarus Crane holds the status of a brahmin, see Leslie (1998b: 478 n. 20). In medical literature, the term also denotes teeth, since they too are 'born' twice.

47 *mā niṣāda pratiṣṭhāṃ tvam agamaḥ śāśvatīḥ samāḥ / yat krauñcamithunād ekam avadhīḥ kāmamohitam // Vālmīki Rāmāyaṇa* 1.2.14. For the rationale behind my

So inspiring is that moment of poetic creation that Vālmīki's delighted disciple promptly commits the verse to memory (v. 18). Soon afterwards, the god Brahmā comes in person to speak with this man who 'knows what is right' (*dharmavid*, v. 21), this 'great *ṛṣi*' (*maharṣi*, vv. 25, 39). He addresses Vālmīki as 'brahmin' (*brahman*) and 'best of *ṛṣi*s' (*ṛṣisattama*, v. 30). Brahmā is impressed by Vālmīki's eloquence (*sarasvatī*, v. 30), evidence of the depth of the latter's compassion, and asks him to compose the story of Rāma in the form of *śloka*s. Furthermore, Brahmā promises Vālmīki that he will 'see' for himself what has happened: everything will be revealed to him, both what has been kept secret and what is public knowledge (v. 32); even what he does not know will now become known to him (v. 33);[48] and, like that first astonishing *śloka*, every word of his poem will be true (v. 34). The final references to Vālmīki in this chapter are in a similar vein: he is described as being 'serene' (*bhāvitātman*, v. 40),[49] 'celebrated' (*kīrtimat*) and 'highly intelligent' (*udāradhī*, v. 41), a poet whose great work will add to the glory of Rāma.

In the third chapter, Vālmīki is again described as 'saintly' (*dharmātman*, Rām. 1.3.1), as a *muni* (v. 2), as 'holy' (*bhagavat*) and a *ṛṣi* (v. 29). Sitting with appropriate ritual and due reverence, he meditates in order to 'see' the story he has to tell. We are told that he first performs the *ācamana* ritual, sipping water from the palm of his hand in the proper way. After arranging the sacred *darbha* grass so that the ends point to the east, he sits down on this ritual seat, his hands placed together reverently in the *añjali* gesture. Then, according to established law and custom, he seeks his goal (v. 2).[50] As Brahmā promised, the entire Rāmāyaṇa narrative, in all its detail, enters his consciousness (vv. 3–28). Next, Vālmīki transforms his vision into poetry (*kāvya*); even those events that have not yet taken place are included in the final (*uttara*) part (v. 29). As we learn at the start of the next chapter, Vālmīki composes his great poem after Rāma has returned from exile and regained his kingdom, that is, before the events recorded in the *Uttarakāṇḍa*. As a result of the visionary powers granted to him by Brahmā, however, Vālmīki is able to incorporate even those future events into his finished work (Rām. 1.4.1–2).

---

translation of this passage, see Leslie (1998b). The *śloka* verse form is described by Brahmā as a new invention (vv. 29–36). Brodbeck comments that the *śloka* is to a large extent a 'non-brāhmanical metre' associated with the participation in Sanskrit culture by new sections of society, such as local chiefs elevated to the level of *kṣatriya*s (personal communication, 8 June 2002).

48 As Brodbeck observes, it is no coincidence that 'what Vālmīki already knew' is the epic up to and including Brockington's second stage of growth, and that 'what was revealed to him by Brahmā' is the additional material of the third stage. Parallels may be drawn with Vyāsa's composition of the *Mahābhārata*, although he is not clairvoyant to the same degree (personal communication, 8 June 2002).

49 Translations of the epithet *bhāvitātman* range from the low-key (e.g. 'contemplative'; Goldman 1984: 129, v. 40) to the awkward (e.g. 'one whose soul is purified by meditating on the universal soul'; Monier-Williams 1899: 755). My choice of 'serene' is intended to convey a sense of equanimity, of self-cultivation and personal transformation effected by ascetic practice.

50 *upaspṛśyodakaṃ samyaṅ muniḥ sthitvā kṛtāñjaliḥ / prācīnāgreṣu darbheṣu dharmeṇ-ānveṣate gatim // Vālmīki Rāmāyaṇa* 1.3.2.

In that fourth chapter, Vālmīki is described again as 'holy' (*bhagavat*, v. 1), as a 'great *ṛṣi*' (*ṛṣi*, v. 1; *maharṣi*, v. 3), as 'extremely wise' (*mahāprājña*, v. 2) and as 'serene' (*bhāvitātman*, v. 3). In addition, he is called 'self-possessed' (*ātmavat*, v. 1), 'powerful' (*prabhu*, v. 2), and 'a man who always keeps his vows' (*caritavrata*, v. 6). We are told that Vālmīki then teaches the *Rāmāyaṇa* poem he has just composed to Kuśa and Lava, Rāma's sons. As many scholars have pointed out, these names are derived from the term for an itinerant singer or balladeer (*kuśīlava*), what Goldman describes as 'a loose-living, wandering rhapsodist' (1984: 286). This suggests that an earlier version of this story may have involved, not Rāma's sons, but one or more traditional reciters or unrelated travelling bards. This in turn has led to the suggestion that Vālmīki himself may have belonged to this professional group. As John Brockington points out, however, this idea is to some extent contradicted by the portrayal of Vālmīki's poetic training: the future poet gains access to the story of Rāma by means of a vision attained in meditation rather than by the usual method of learning through recitation. According to Hara, Vālmīki's ability to put the story into verse so effectively is evidence that he was a gifted 'singer of tales' in a tradition comparable to that of Homer (1972; cf. Lord 1960). Both scholars agree that the first reciters proper of the *Rāmāyaṇa* are Kuśa and Lava, not Vālmīki.[51]

These scene-setting chapters portray Vālmīki as an exemplary individual: *muni*, *ṛṣi* and ascetic (*tapasvin*); high-minded, innately wise, trained in religious ritual, and learned in matters of *dharma*; a 'seer' to whom the highest truths are revealed in mystical vision; and a poet with a perfect command of the Sanskrit language. In short, he is a great man worthy of the company of gods, if not yet deemed a god himself.

If we restrict our analysis to the text of the Baroda critical edition, we now find no further mention of Vālmīki until book 7 (*Uttarakāṇḍa*). Of course, as I have already pointed out, most people's knowledge of the *Vālmīki Rāmāyaṇa* is not restricted to the critical edition. In Britain, for example, the best-known English translation is that by Hari Prasad Shastri. While Shastri's textual sources are unclear, his translation was certainly completed before the publication of the critical edition. Shastri's translation thus contains several references to Vālmīki towards the end of book 6: first, that 'this renowned and sacred epic ... was composed by the Rishi Valmiki'; second, that 'one who ... listens to this epic, formerly composed by Valmiki, overcomes all obstacles and those who hear this story set forth by Valmiki will ...' and so on; and finally, that 'those who, in devotion, transcribe this history of Rama, composed by the Rishi Valmiki, attain to the region of Brahma' (1976: 371–2).

Returning to the critical edition, by the end of book 6 (*Yuddhakāṇḍa*) Rāma has won victory on the battlefield, Sītā has survived the fire ordeal,[52] and the royal

---

51 For discussions of the implications of the term *kuśīlava*, see Goldman (1984: 73, 286) and John Brockington (1998: 394–5).

52 Interestingly, Sītā's ordeal by fire is not part of the *Rāmopākhyāna*. In the *Mahābhārata* episode, instead of entering the fire to prove her innocence, Sītā declares that the elements of which her body is made will leave her if she is guilty. When Vāyu (wind, breath), Agni (the fire within), Varuṇa (the juices of the body), Brahmā, and her (now immortal) father-in-law Daśaratha respond that she is innocent, Rāma takes Sītā back (Mbh. 3.275.22–38). It is highly likely, therefore, that

couple has returned to Ayodhyā in triumph. As Rāma is installed once more as the rightful king, we reach the end of the core chapters of the epic. Much of book 7 is taken up with mythological tales relating to characters we have already met in the epic: for example, flashbacks into the past history of Rāvaṇa and Hanumān. But we also return to the frame story provided by Vālmīki's involvement in the epic narrative: at the start of book 1, we learned that the epic was composed after the main events described in it had already occurred; now, at the end of book 7, we find its resolution.

In chapter 44 of book 7, as a result of rumours circulating in the city, Rāma reluctantly banishes Sītā for the second time. He commands Lakṣmaṇa to take Sītā into the forest and abandon her there. His instructions are precise:

> The ashram of the extremely high-minded Vālmīki is a heavenly place, situated far away on the other side of the Ganges, on the bank of the Tamasā river. Abandon her there in a solitary spot, [O Lakṣmaṇa]! Come back quickly, [Lakṣmaṇa]! Obey my command!'[53]

The choice of Vālmīki's ashram is no accident. As Lakṣmaṇa explains in chapter 47, this ashram has been chosen partly because, as a sacred place, it offers safety to an abandoned woman, and partly because it is in itself an enchanting spot. But the main reason is that Vālmīki – described here as 'the most potent of *munis*' (*munipuṃgava*), 'the most excellent (*paramaka*) of inspired seers (*vipra*)', 'high-minded' (*mahātman*) and 'of very great renown' (*sumahāyaśas*) – was a very close friend[54] of King Daśaratha, Rāma's late father (Rām. 7.46.16–17). After his travels, Rāma would have been familiar with many ashrams and many sages. We may conclude that his choice of Vālmīki demonstrates the esteem in which this particular *muni* was held, by Rāma as well as by his father. It is evidently Rāma's hope that Vālmīki will take the best possible care of his beloved wife, despite his own apparent doubts about her innocence. Is there a link here between the falsely accused Sītā and the false accusations laid against Vālmīki in the *Mahābhārata* passage discussed above? I return to this question at the end of this chapter.

Chapter 48 of the critical edition describes the meeting between Sītā and Vālmīki. His disciples see her first, sobbing and distraught on the bank of the river. Running to inform their teacher – described here as 'blessed' or 'holy' (*bhagavat*), 'supremely wise' (v. 1),[55] and 'great *ṛṣi*' (*maharṣi*, v. 2) – they address him formally as 'Lord' or 'Blessed One' (*bhagavat*, vv. 3, 4). Vālmīki, that 'great *muni*' (v. 6) who 'always knows what is right' (*dharmavid*, v. 5), realizes at once

---

the (in)famous fire ordeal was not part of the Rāma story until at least the third phase in the development of the *Vālmīki Rāmāyaṇa*.

53 *gaṅgāyās tu pare pāre vālmīkeḥ sumahātmanaḥ l āśramo divyasaṃkāśas tamasātīram āśritaḥ ll tatrainām vijane kakṣe visṛjya raghunandana l śīghram āgaccha saumitre kuruṣva vacanaṃ mama ll Vālmīki Rāmāyaṇa* 7.44.16–17.

54 It is unclear to me whether *paramako* qualifies *sakhā* or *vipro*, or both; I have assumed both.

55 Where the critical edition reads *agryadhīḥ* (7.48.1), Hara prefers the manuscript variant *ugradhīḥ* (1972: 120).

that what his disciples are telling him is true: because of his ascetic powers (*tapas*, v. 5), he is instantly aware of what has happened. That 'most potent of *muni*s' (v. 7) approaches Sītā and speaks to her gently. Gladdening her heart with his fiery ascetic energy (*tejas*), he offers her the water of ritual hospitality (v. 12). He explains that, as a result of the visionary power he has attained through ascetic practice (v. 10), he knows exactly what has happened to her. Realizing that she is innocent of the charges laid against her, Vālmīki appoints himself Sītā's guardian (v. 18). In addition to the epithets cited above, Vālmīki is also described in this chapter as: *muni* (vv. 13, 14), 'best of *muni*s' (*muniśreṣṭha*, v. 16), 'of great renown' (*mahāyaśas*) and 'great ascetic' (*mahātapas*, v. 20). Clearly, several important aspects of Vālmīki's character and abilities are confirmed in this episode: his reputation as a saintly man is of the highest; his charismatic powers as a spiritual leader have brought him many disciples; his ascetic practices have given him visionary powers that enable him to see into past, present and future. Like all the *Rāmāyaṇa* passages under consideration, however, there is no hint whatever of criminal, or even suspect, behaviour.

In chapter 57, Śatrughna visits Vālmīki's ashram on his way to fight the *asura* Lavaṇa. Here Vālmīki is described as 'great-souled' (*mahātman*), 'best of *muni*s' (*munisattama*, v. 3), 'most potent of *muni*s' (v. 5), and 'great *ṛṣi*' (vv. 8, 35), and he is addressed by Śatrughna as 'Lord' (v. 4). In chapter 58, Sītā gives birth that same night to Rāma's two sons, and Vālmīki ritually names them Kuśa and Lava. He is addressed by his disciples as the 'possessor of great ascetic energy' (*mahātejas*, v. 2). He is also described three times as *muni* (vv. 3, 8, 12) and once as 'twice-born' (*dvija*, v. 4).

In the critical edition, there are no further references to Vālmīki until the denouement of the *Uttarakāṇḍa* which finally brings the frame story to a close. This means that Vālmīki does not appear in chapter 63 of the Baroda text: after defeating Lavaṇa, Śatrughna goes straight back to Ayodhyā to inform Rāma of his success. However, according to six of the forty-one manuscripts collated for the critical edition of book 7, Śatrughna spends one night at Vālmīki's ashram on his journey home. That evening, he and his companions are treated to a performance of the story of Rāma in song, the poem so moving that it reduces Śatrughna to tears. Despite his own amazement, and the overt curiosity of his men, however, Śatrughna decides that it is inappropriate to question a great ascetic like Vālmīki about the poem. This popular passage is often found in English translations of the text, including those by Shastri (1976: 576–7) and Sen (1965: 698–9).[56]

At the start of chapter 84 of the critical edition, Rāma's performance of the *aśvamedha* sacrifice has been underway for a year. Sītā's two sons, Kuśa and Lava, are now old enough to have been trained, as Vālmīki's disciples, in the recitation of the *Rāmāyaṇa* poem. It is at this point that the poet-saint instructs the boys to enter the gathering for the sacrifice and to sing the poem in full wherever they can, even in front of Rāma. The epithets applied to Vālmīki in this

56 For the Sanskrit text, see vol. 7 of the Baroda critical edition: Appendix I, No. 9, pp. 625–9, lines 1–52. For a discussion of the episode in the context of the tradition of musical recitation, see Hara (1972: 123–5).

chapter are: 'most potent of *muni*s' (v. 1; and *muni*, v. 15), 'descendant of Pracetas' (*prācetasa*), 'of noble birth' (*paramodara*), 'of great renown' (*mahāyaśas*), and 'descendant of Bhṛgu' (*bhārgava*, v. 16). In addition to some of the usual compliments indicating both high status and extreme asceticism, we have here what appears to be the attribution of two quite different lineages to Vālmīki. I shall return to these patronymic epithets, *prācetasa* and *bhārgava*, at the end of this chapter.

Chapter 85 of the critical edition contains the extraordinary moment when the two boys recite the *Rāmāyaṇa* in front of their father for the first time. When Rāma first hears the poem, he is consumed with curiosity (v. 3). His response is to gather everyone of any standing for a command performance: great *muni*s and kings, paṇḍits and elderly brahmins, specialists in Veda and Purāṇa, in short, all the experts in the realm (vv. 4–5). The entire assembly is transfixed with amazement and delight. Once he has heard the first twenty chapters or cantos, Rāma asks the two boys about the source of the poem and the identity of its author (v. 28). As instructed by their teacher, the boys inform him that this poem which miraculously tells Rāma's own life story was composed by the holy Vālmīki (*vālmīkir bhagavān*, v. 17). The other epithets applied to Vālmīki in this chapter are all familiar: *ṛṣi* (v. 1), *muni* (vv. 9, 17, 19) and 'most potent of *muni*s' (v. 22).

In chapter 86, Rāma continues to listen as the boys recite the rest of the poem. The implications sink in. He realizes that Kuśa and Lava are his own sons. He understands that Sītā is still living in Vālmīki's ashram, and he recalls – for at some level he always knew – that she is innocent. He reaches a decision. If she wishes, and if Vālmīki gives his approval (v. 5), Sītā may swear an oath before the assembled company that she is pure. Rāma's message is delivered to Vālmīki, and the event is set for the following day. The other epithets applied to Vālmīki in this chapter are: 'holy' or 'Lord' (*bhagavat*, v. 3), 'most potent of *muni*s' (v. 7; see also *muni*, vv. 9, 11a, 11b), 'great-souled/high-minded' (vv. 8, 12), 'blazing with radiance' (*jvalanta*), 'of immeasurable splendour' (*amitaprabha*, v. 8), and 'of very great ascetic energy' (*sumahātejas*, v. 9). The repeated stress on Vālmīki's demonstrably brilliant ascetic power is evidently intended to indicate the consequences of long-term austerities. According to these epithets, his powers – as both *muni* and poet – are derived from his asceticism.

Chapter 87 brings us to the dramatic climax both of the epic and of the frame story of Vālmīki's involvement. The following day, in the midst of the crowds now reassembled in the sacrifical enclosure, Vālmīki testifies to Sītā's innocence. The eminent *ṛṣi*s gathered there, all described as 'great ascetics', are named in a way reminiscent of the *Mahābhārata* lists discussed on pp. 87–9.[57] The assembled

57 On this occasion, the named *ṛṣi* are listed as follows: Vasiṣṭha, Vāmadeva, Jābāli, Kāśyapa, Viśvāmitra, Dīrghatapas, Durvāsa, Agastya, Śakti, the *bhārgava* Vāmana, Mārkaṇḍeya, Dīrghāyus, Maudgalya, the *bhārgava* Cyavana, Śatānanda, Bharadvāja, Agniputra (vv. 2–4). I have understood the two occurrences of the term *bhārgava* as epithets qualifying the names that follow, Vāmana and Cyavana respectively. However, while Cyavana is traditionally associated with the lineage of Bhṛgu (see chapter 4), Vāmana is not.

multitude stands motionless, as if turned to stone (v. 8). When Vālmīki enters the public arena, followed by Sītā fighting back her tears, he is likened to Brahmā followed by the goddess Śrī (v. 10). Then Vālmīki ('best of *muni*s', v. 8; 'most potent of *muni*s', v. 13) makes his famous declaration (vv. 13–20). The relevant verses are reproduced here:

> These two sons of [Sītā], these twins, these are indeed your invincible sons. I am telling you the truth. (v. 16)
>
> I am the tenth son of Pracetas, [O Rāma]. I do not remember ever telling a lie. These two are therefore your sons. (v. 17)
>
> I have performed austerities for many thousands of years. May I never obtain the rewards accruing to those [austerities], if [Sītā] is not innocent! (v. 18)
>
> When, with my five senses and my mind as the sixth, I was meditating on Sītā amidst forest waterfalls, she was revealed to me as pure. (v. 19)

It is worth noting here that the words so often placed in Vālmīki's mouth at this point – variations on 'I have never sinned in thought, word or deed' – have been relegated to the critical apparatus of the Baroda edition.[58] At one level, Vālmīki's public insistence on his truthfulness merely demonstrates his determination to prove Sītā innocent. At another level, his words confirm what the tradition tells us: that Vālmīki is of noble birth, an immensely powerful ascetic, and a man of the highest moral principles. Moreover, if he can 'see' the story of Rāma, then he can 'see' Sītā's innocence too. The emphasis here is on his virtue, his lineage and his renowned ascetic powers.

The remaining references to Vālmīki are few. In chapter 88, Rāma addresses Vālmīki as 'brahmin' (vv. 2, 3), 'a man of great good fortune' (*mahābhāga*), and 'one who knows what is right' (*dharmavid*, v. 2). He also announces that the ascetic's words are 'without blemish' (*akalmaṣa*, v. 2). After this public vindication, Sītā steps forward to prove her innocence. To the astonishment of the assembled company, and to Rāma's evident distress, she descends into the earth, her innocence and dignity intact.

Vālmīki does not appear again in the critical edition. In several manuscript versions, however, an intriguing episode is inserted between chapters 88 and 89.[59] After Sītā's disappearance, Rāma is on the verge of collapse with anger and grief (line 6). In order to prevent him from thoughtlessly destroying the world, Brahmā reappears (line 22). Reminding Rāma that he too is divine, Brahmā points out that he will be reunited with Sītā in heaven in due course. He then draws Rāma's attention back to Vālmīki's poem, praising it as divine in origin,

58 *manasā karmaṇā vācā bhūtapūrvaṃ na kilbiṣam* (critical edition, vol. 7: 477, 1359*). See, for example, Shastri (1976: 616), Bulcke (1960: 54), and *Report of the Bhagavan Valmiki Action Committee* (2000: 90).

59 For the Sanskrit passage, see vol. 7 of the critical edition, Appendix I, No. 13, pp. 639–44, lines 1–56. For English translations of this episode, see Shastri (1976: 618–19, chapter 98) and Sen (1965: 709).

extraordinarily beautiful in form, truthful in content, and a means of removing ignorance (line 34). Finally, he informs Rāma that the poem contains the whole story of the king's life, even what has not yet happened. If Rāma wishes to know how everything turns out, therefore, he has only to listen to the rest of the poem, that is, the part called *uttara* (line 37). Rāma gives in. Together with his sons, he spends the night with Vālmīki in the ascetic's forest hut. The next morning, the two boys recite the final chapters of the epic tale and Rāma learns what Vālmīki already knows will happen. In that creative space between narrative and reality, it is Vālmīki not Rāma who holds the key of knowledge.

5. The Yogavāsiṣṭha

There is one more text to consider in this chapter. I include it here partly because of the significance it holds for the Vālmīki community, partly because of the popular misconception that the text as we now have it is as old as, or even older than, the two epics. In its current form, the *Yogavāsiṣṭha* ('Vasiṣṭha's treatise on yoga') presents Vālmīki's account of the teachings given by Vasiṣṭha to Rāma when Rāma was a fifteen-year-old boy. Other names by which this text is known include: *Yogavāsiṣṭha-Rāmāyaṇa*, *Vāsiṣṭha-Rāmāyaṇa*, *Ārṣa-Rāmāyaṇa* ('Rāmāyaṇa of the *ṛṣi*s'), *Jñānavāsiṣṭha* ('Vasiṣṭha's teaching on spiritual knowledge') and 'Great' or *Mahā-Rāmāyaṇa* (Aiyer 1975: vii). As we shall see in chapter 5, however, the term *Mahā-Rāmāyaṇa* is understood by the Valmiki community to denote a much larger text that incorporates both the *Vālmīki Rāmāyaṇa* and the *Yogavāsiṣṭha*; that is, together these complementary works constitute the 'Great' Rāmāyaṇa. Although the teaching contained in the *Yogavāsiṣṭha* is presented as being delivered by Vasiṣṭha, credit for the composition of the text is given to Vālmīki. For the Valmiki community, therefore, this means that the *Yogavāsiṣṭha* is second only to the *Vālmīki Rāmāyaṇa* in terms of both sanctity and authority. While the *Vālmīki Rāmāyaṇa* takes the form of an epic narrative, however, the *Yogavāsiṣṭha* is essentially a philosophical work.[60] In the current form of the text, Vasiṣṭha's teaching is imparted to Rāma in the assembly hall at Daśaratha's court: that is, within the larger structure of the Rāma narrative. Within this epic setting, and by means of an interconnected series of folkloric tales, Vasiṣṭha presents the kind of monistic message usually associated with Advaita Vedānta: that the manifest world is an illusion. At one level, Rāma is assumed to be the object of devotional worship, even if the fifteen-year-old is not yet aware of his own divinity. At another level, prompted by the inner turmoil of his shared humanity, and under Vasiṣṭha's instruction, he is engaged in the process of becoming a *jīvanmukta*, that is, an enlightened but still embodied being.[61] The primary teaching is thus the path of knowledge (*jñāna*).

---

60 For a brief analysis of some of the narrative and philosophical links between the *Vālmīki Rāmāyaṇa* and the *Yogavāsiṣṭha* (and other texts), see John Brockington (1995).

61 For discussions of the term *jīvanmukta* in this context, and for the historical development of the concept *jīvanmukti*, see Slaje (2000a and 2000b).

As in the *Bhagavadgītā*, this is a non-ascetic path that facilitates liberation for those still actively engaged in day-to-day living. Wendy Doniger puts it well:

> ... to know that a course of action is intrinsically unreal is an argument to *do* it, not an argument *not* to do it. When Arjuna realizes that he is not really killing his cousins, he can go and kill them; when Rāma realizes that he is not really a king, he can go on and rule.[62]

Beneath all this lurks the path of devotion (*bhakti*) traditionally implied by the figure of Rāma.

This complex and voluminous text has been popular for centuries.[63] It has been cited in Indian writings since at least the thirteenth century. During the Moghul period, it was translated into Persian several times at the behest of Akbar, Jahangir and Darah Shikuh, a fact that no doubt reflects the popularity of the work among the Hindu population of the time. The attention of Western scholars was first brought to the text by Helmuth von Glasenapp's studies in the early 1950s, together with his judgement that the *Yogavāsiṣṭha* was one of the most comprehensive philosophical works of all time. Many scholars today consider its influence on Indian thought comparable to that of the *Bhagavadgītā*. The Sanskrit text is widely available. Generally speaking, there are two printed versions, neither available in critical editions: the full vulgate text, sometimes known as the *Bṛhad* or 'Great' *Yogavāsiṣṭha*, in approximately 32,000 verses; and a much shorter version in 6,000 verses, abridged by Abhinanda of Kashmir and known as the *Laghu* or 'Little' *Yogavāsiṣṭha*.[64] In India today, translations are available in most vernacular languages and the stories are still relayed to children in a variety of formats. The best-known English translations are probably those by B. L. Atreya (1936), Hari Prasad Shastri (1937), Vihari-Lala Mitra (1976–78) and, most recently, Swami Venkatesananda (1984, 1993).[65] The *Yogavāsiṣṭha* seems to be as popular as ever.

Before considering the text's portrayal of Vālmīki, however, it is necessary to outline the origins and historical development of what proves to be a comparatively late text. Thanks to the work of the scholars involved in the Mokṣopāya Project at the Martin-Luther Universität in Halle-Wittenberg, it is now possible to distinguish between two main strands of textual transmission. The first strand is

---

62 O'Flaherty (1984: 141). The emphases are in the original.

63 For a useful summary, see Slaje (2001a) and the website of the Mokṣopāya Project (*www.indologie.uni-halle.de/forschung/Moksopaya*), consulted 11 March 2002. See also Slaje (1996b).

64 For further information on the *Laghu-Yogavāsiṣṭha*, if from the perspective of a long-standing member of Madame Blavatsky's Theosophical Society, see the 1896 introduction by Aiyer to his free English translation of the text (1975: ix–xxxiii).

65 Swami Venkatesananda, born into a Tamil brahmin family, was a disciple of Swami Sivananda, the founder of the Divine Life Society in Rishikesh. Swami Venkatesananda translated the *Yogavāsiṣṭha* while he was teaching in Australia. In late 1981, shortly before his death in 1982, twelve video recordings were made of the Swami's last talks on the text. I am grateful to Swami Ambikananda and Florine Clomegah for this information, and for sending me copies of the videos.

termed the 'Kashmir version' because of its close associations with that geographical area, or the 'Śāradā transmission' on account of the preferred script. This version never once refers to itself by the name *Yogavāsiṣṭha*. According to the Kashmir sources, the self-designated title is either *Mokṣopāya* or *Mokṣopāya-śāstra*. The term *śāstra* denotes what Slaje calls 'a theoretical textbook': this places the work in the general category of philosophical texts on salvation (*mokṣaśāstra*); more precisely, it is a philosophical discussion of the means (*upāya*) of attaining salvation.[66] Slaje dates the anonymous core text to about the tenth century CE. As he puts it, 'the *Mokṣopāya* can hardly have taken shape before 700 [CE] and must have existed as a completed work by 1000 [CE]' (2001a: 6).[67] A version of this lost core text continued to circulate in Kashmir until the eighteenth century (2000a: 171–2).[68] This *Mokṣopāya* text presents itself as the product of human, not divine, authorship. It is based on reasoning (*vicāra*) and rational argument (*yukti*), not divine revelation. In *Mokṣopāya* 2.18.2–3 (Slaje 1993: 138), the lack of any need for divine approval is justified in no uncertain terms:

> The fact that the *śāstra* is of human origin (*pauruṣa*) is no bar to its being accepted, as long as it is based on rational argument. Anything else should be rejected. ... A statement based on rational argument, even if it comes from a child, should be accepted. Anything else should be rejected like straw, even if it comes from Brahmā himself.

The text does not advocate devotionalism in any form, not even Rāma-*bhakti*. It teaches monism (*advaita*), certainly, but not the Advaita Vedānta form associated with Śaṅkara. According to the *Mokṣopāya*, liberation is available to anyone – regardless of sex, caste and education – anyone, that is, who upholds reason and continues to live an active life in the world. The three steps to liberation are: *vicāra* (thinking rationally), *jñāna* (true understanding), and *vairāgya* (detachment, a lasting state of non-involvement). Finally, the format of the discourse is that of an idiosyncratic public lecture and, as such, it is peppered with insulting remarks aimed at an audience too slow to grasp what is being said. To sum up, much of what is associated with the *Yogavāsiṣṭha* today – the brahminical frame stories, the epic setting at Daśaratha's court, Vasiṣṭha teaching Rāma, the underlying *bhakti* context, the overarching frame of the *Rāmāyaṇa* as marked by Vālmīki's presence, even the benevolent tone – is absent. There is no explicit evidence of Vālmīki here.

---

66 Interestingly, even the later *Yogavāsiṣṭha* tends to favour the term *śāstra* when referring to itself. For a list of the self-referential terms used in the *Laghu-Yogavāsiṣṭha* (which was probably earlier than the *Bṛhad-Yogavāsiṣṭha*), see Slaje (1990: 154, Index A1).

67 More recent findings point to the second half of the tenth century (Slaje, personal communication, 9 August 2002).

68 For further information on the Kashmir recension, see Hanneder (2000). For the critical edition of the *Mokṣopāya-Ṭīkā*, the eighteenth-century commentary by Bhāskarakaṇṭha, and thus of the surviving *Mokṣopāya* text embedded within it, see Slaje (1993, 1995, 1996a). For a revised edition of the *Vairāgya-prakaraṇa* (the first chapter on detatchment) in Devanāgarī script, together with an updated introduction, see Hanneder and Slaje (2002).

The second strand of textual transmission is more promising. This version is usually referred to as the 'Vulgate' on account of its popularity, or the 'Nāgarī transmission' on account of its preference for the Devanāgarī script. This is the pan-Indian version that now circulates most often under the title *Yogavāsiṣṭha*. The core text, still discernible in the Kashmir recension, has been altered almost beyond recognition. Reflecting on the changes that have taken place in the transition from *Mokṣopāyaśāstra* to *Yogavāsiṣṭha*, Slaje describes the resulting text as 'a literary forgery of not inconsiderable dimensions' (2001a: 18). Rāma-*bhakti* has been added. Buddhist terms and associations have been erased. Negative statements about scriptures (*śruti*, *veda*) and rituals have been rendered positive. The robust haranguing tone of the public sermon has been polished smooth to be more in keeping with Daśaratha's court, where we now find one earnest but illustrious pupil (Rāma) facing a gracious and kindly teacher (Vasiṣṭha). Unlike in the *Mokṣopāya*, both teacher and pupil are identified in the *Yogavāsiṣṭha*, their identities significant in the larger epic context. The teaching itself has been transformed into a more orthodox Advaita Vedānta. Finally, as the text expanded, a series of enclosing frames was added.

The text as we now have it presents Vālmīki as the narrator of Vasiṣṭha's teachings to Rāma. Precisely how he comes to do this is complicated and involves a series of embedded conversations. In the following summary of *Yogavāsiṣṭha* 1.1–2,[69] I have allocated numbers to the dialogues in order to clarify the levels of embeddedness. The opening question is reminiscent of the *Bhagavadgītā*. At level 1, two *ṛṣi*s converse. Sutīkṣṇa asks Agastya: 'Which is more likely to lead to *mokṣa*: the path of work (*karma*) or the path of knowledge (*jñāna*)?' Agastya responds by telling the story of Kārūṇya (level 2). Having completed his studies, this young man is torn between the two, apparently conflicting, truths he has learned: that one should perform one's duties and that one should abandon all action. He asks his father, Agniveśya, for advice. Agniveśya's response is to tell him the story of the heavenly nymph, Suruci (level 3). When she sees one of Indra's messengers flying over the mountain top where she is sitting, she asks him where he is going. The messenger describes the mission he is unsuccessfully completing (level 4). Indra has spotted a royal sage (*rājarṣi*) by the name of Ariṣṭanemi engaged in extreme ascetic practice, and has sent the messenger to escort him to heaven. However, Ariṣṭanemi is unimpressed by the messenger's description of the rewards awaiting him in Indra's heaven, and has refused to go. Indra's response this time is to suggest that Ariṣṭanemi should seek Vālmīki's advice before making his final decision. Ariṣṭanemi agrees. He then asks Vālmīki (level 5) how best to avoid birth and death. Vālmīki's reply, eventually, is to narrate the dialogue between Rāma and Vasiṣṭha. But first he explains the background story (level 6). His disciple Bharadvāja had related Vālmīki's earlier composition, the *Rāmāyaṇa*, to Brahmā. The god's response was to ask Vālmīki to complete that composition in such a way that it enabled those who heard it to

69 The verses and the divisions of the text vary with each Sanskrit edition and English translation. To simplify matters, therefore, the references used here are taken from the widely available 1993 translation by Swami Venkatesananda, which generally follows the vulgate version.

reach liberation. At Brahmā's command, therefore, Vālmīki had composed this new teaching – the 'secret of the liberation of Rāma' (level 7) – and had revealed it to Bharadvāja. This secret is the teaching contained in the dialogue between Vasiṣṭha and Rāma. In the present constituted by his conversation with Ariṣṭanemi (level 5), Vālmīki proceeds to tell that secret, that story, again (1.3ff.). Within that story, there are many further stories – even stories within stories within stories, just as there are dreams within dreams within dreams – but we need not go into those here.[70]

From the point of view of the structure of the whole, we need only note that levels 1–5 are not mentioned again until the end of the text. By contrast, Vālmīki's composition (that is, his narration to Bharadvāja at level 6) is constantly reaffirmed. He sets the scene in the opening chapter on detachment (*Vairāgya-prakaraṇa*, 1.2–11). He marks the moments when the assembled company takes a break to rest or sleep: when the gathering disperses at the close of the first day (the end of 2.5), for example, and when the sun begins to set on the evening of the second day (3.4).[71] Finally, at appropriate moments, he interjects explanatory or descriptive comments for Bharadvāja's benefit. For example, when Vasiṣṭha does not answer Rāma immediately, Vālmīki explains to Bharadvāja that Rāma's mind is not yet ready for the truth Vasiṣṭha has to offer (4.39). Similarly, Vālmīki records the response of the audience in Daśaratha's court when Vasiṣṭha concludes the main part of his discourse (6.2.200). Sometimes, he does both at once. At the start of the chapter on dissolution (*Upaśānti-prakaraṇa*), for example, Vālmīki both notes the breaks in the teaching (at midday, again in the evening when everyone retires to bed, and the slow start the next morning as preparations are made to hear the next instalment) and explains to Bharadvāja that Rāma is unable to sleep because his mind is grappling with the wisdom that has been imparted to him that day (5.1–3). Similarly, at the start of the chapter on liberation (*Nirvāṇa-prakaraṇa*), Vālmīki describes the moment when the sun sets (a frozen tableau as everyone in the court absorbs Vasiṣṭha's teaching before dispersing for the night), and what Swami Venkatesananda calls the 'pin-drop silence' (1993: 326) of rapt attention when they reassemble the following morning (6.1.1–2).[72] Also in chapter 6, Bharadvāja responds to these personal interjections (6.1.127–8) to create a two-way conversation at level 6. This reinforces the idea that the Vasiṣṭha–Rāma dialogue, composed by Vālmīki, was revealed first to Bharadvāja; only later was it repeated for Ariṣṭanemi's benefit. At the end of 6.2.213, when the Vasiṣṭha-Rāma dialogue is finally

70 For a virtuoso analysis of the role of dreams in Indian thought, including an insightful foray into the complex patterns of dreaming in the *Yogavāsiṣṭha*, see O'Flaherty (1984).

71 See also the end of 6.1.34 and 6.1.60, and the beginning of 6.2.160. Vālmīki is frequently mentioned at the end of the so-called 'days'. These 'days' (18 of them) are clearly part of a late attempt to restructure the work, perhaps along the lines of the *Mahābhārata*.

72 The vulgate version of the *Yogavāsiṣṭha* divides the *Nirvāṇa-prakaraṇa* into two sections (*sarga*), the first half (*pūrvārdha*) and the last (*uttarārdha*), the latter usually being regarded as a later addition and often ignored or omitted on that account. However, the Kashmir recension preserves the full text in an undivided *Nirvāṇa-prakaraṇa*. For further details, see Slaje (1996b).

completed, when Rāma *et al.* have attained liberation, and after Vālmīki has described the week-long festivities held at Daśaratha's court (6.2.214), we are taken back through the levels of story-telling. Vālmīki tells Bharadvāja that, by listening to this text, he is already a *jīvanmukta* (level 6). He then assures Ariṣṭanemi that he will attain the truth through this teaching (level 5). Ariṣṭanemi dismisses Indra's messenger (level 4). At level 3, the messenger is thrilled to have heard the discourse and Suruci feels blessed. At level 2, Kāruṇya informs his father that his delusion has vanished. At level 1, Sutīkṣṇa thanks Agastya for dispelling his ignorance and enabling him to cross the ocean of *saṃsāra* thereby.

The chronological stages of the text's development may be crudely summarized as follows.[73] What Slaje calls 'Stratum A' is the *Mokṣopāya* core, which can only be loosely defined at present. The material probably began as a series of lectures or sermons by one original author to a public audience, thus giving the earliest layer its inherently dialogical structure. As it took shape as a 'text', the work probably came to consist of two parts rather than the eventual six: a *Jāti-* or *Utpatti-prakaraṇa* and a *Nirvāṇa-prakaraṇa*. The original title of this text was the *Mokṣopāyaśāstra*. Not surprisingly, there is considerable interest in the contents of this core text among some of my Valmiki contacts, together with the conviction that the 'original author' was in fact Vālmīki.

Stratum B begins 'somewhere around 1.3.33/2.10.4/2.10.9–43', and ends at 7. 200.[74] Here we see the first steps in the process of reworking the text in the form of a dialogue between Vasiṣṭha as the teacher and Rāma as the pupil. This dialogue is framed by the Brahmā-Vasiṣṭha story.

Stratum C begins with 1.3.18–1.32/2.10 and ends at 7.201–3. This layer inserts parts of the *Bālakāṇḍa* so that the teachings become part of Rāma's training as a *jīvanmukta*, before he accompanies Viśvāmitra to the forest.

Vālmīki does not appear in the text until Stratum D which was probably composed around the eleventh century. This layer is also found in the *Laghu-Yogavāsiṣṭha*, which means that a more precise dating of Stratum D depends on the dating of the *Laghu-Yogavāsiṣṭha*. Stratum D begins with 1.2.3–1.3.17 and ends first at 6.126, and then again at 7.215. At this point, the Vālmīki-Bharadvāja frame is added and the entire composition is ascribed explicitly to Vālmīki. We also find the first mention of a single work called the *Mahā-Rāmāyaṇa* which combines both the *Vālmīki Rāmāyaṇa* and the *Yogavāsiṣṭha*. This frame is clearly a later addition to an already late text, perhaps as late as the fourteenth century when this second strand of textual transmission was almost complete.[75] This suggests that the *mokṣaśāstra* core of what was in origin a philosophical text became increasingly embedded in the devotional context that had

73 I owe the following analysis to Walter Slaje (1994: 99–154, including some helpful explanatory diagrams; 2000a; and further clarifications by email, 11 May and 9 August 2002).

74 The numbering of the two halves of the *Nirvāṇa-prakaraṇa* is a matter of convention: either 6a and 6b (as in Slaje 1994), or 6 and 7 (as in Slaje's later work, and followed here).

75 Chapple (1984: x) summarizes the dates allocated to the *Yogavāsiṣṭha* by scholars writing in the 1920s and 1930s.

overwhelmed the north of India. As a result, the monistic message (reworked according to the more popular Advaita Vedānta) became reframed within the Rāma story. This in turn brought into the text the figure now regarded as the most celebrated narrator of that story: Vālmīki.

There is yet one more layer. Stratum E begins at 1.1 of the *Yogavāsiṣṭha* edition, and ends at 7.216. It represents the latest additions to the text, which can only be found in the vulgate versions. This layer probably took shape as late as the seventeenth or even eighteenth century.

For our purposes, we need to ask only one more question. What does the *Yogavāsiṣṭha* tell us about Vālmīki? First, we are told that he composed the *Yogavāsiṣṭha* as the philosophical sequel to his earlier *Rāmāyaṇa*. In this context, the story of Rāma is perceived primarily as a vehicle for spiritual instruction. The entire text has been inserted into the Rāma story at a particular point: after the prince has returned from his studies and before Viśvāmitra takes him to the forest to destroy the *rākṣasa*s who are impeding the sacrifice; that is, it forms the concluding part of the young man's religious education before he embarks on his worldly duties. Rāma's studies so far have not clarified matters for him. He remains confused about the nature of existence and how one should live in the world (1.12–31). Both at level 7 and at level 6, it is agreed that everyone would benefit from hearing Vasiṣṭha's answer to Rāma's questions. But it is Vālmīki who responds. Second, the primary teaching is that the external world is like a dream, an optical illusion like the blueness of the sky (1.3); one should not therefore allow the mind to be caught up in it. However, as Vālmīki explains to Bharadvāja, those who are unable to attain that state of supreme understanding should 'adopt the adoration of name and form' (6.1.127; Venkatesananda 1993: 482); that is, devotional worship will lead the less spiritually advanced towards liberation. Third, according to the enlightened crow Bhuśuṇḍi in yet another embedded story, time is cyclical without ever repeating itself precisely. Thus Vasiṣṭha has now taken this form for the eighth time. Viṣṇu has incarnated as Rāma for the eleventh time, as Kṛṣṇa for the sixteenth. Similarly, Vālmīki has composed the *Rāmāyaṇa* many times before, and he has now recorded Vasiṣṭha's instructions to Rāma for the twelfth time.[76] Yet all this is illusory, appearing true only to the deluded mind (6.1.22). This suggests that great sages such as Vasiṣṭha and Vālmīki are born in every age in order to reveal the sacred texts and teach the truth. These ideas are significant for several reasons: the implied sanctity of the texts in question, the eternal nature of the truth cyclically conveyed by them (and therefore the irrelevance of linear concepts of time and sequence),[77] and the special role reserved for Vālmīki as the one chosen to compose both the *Rāmāyaṇa* and the *Yogavāsiṣṭha* for each new age.

---

76 According to Bhuśuṇḍi, these spiritual instructions were originally one hundred thousand verses in length. We are also informed that there was once another great religious text known as 'Bharata', which has now been forgotten.

77 Within the tradition, this solves the problem of how Vālmīki can be the original author if he does not appear until Stratum D: he has always known the truth and he keeps coming back to teach it. Linear time is irrelevant.

6. Concluding Remarks

Was Vālmīki a dacoit? The evidence studied in this chapter, drawn from the earliest Sanskrit texts available, says that he was not. There is a hint that he might have belonged to a tribal community, and that some people may have looked down on that community; but there are also hints that a tribal background was not at that time an impediment to either learning or status. Stronger evidence may be found in the three main texts discussed: the two epics and the *Yogavāsiṣṭha*. While there is no external evidence to speak of, all the internal evidence points to a man of ascetic prowess, great learning and high status. There is little here with which to validate the much later dacoit legend discussed in chapter 4.

Before this chapter comes to a close, however, there are three themes that require further comment: the ascetic motif, the question of Vālmīki's lineage, and the notion of blame. I shall return to the first of these at the start of chapter 4. Here, I need only note that ascetic practice (*tapas*) is an important theme common to most, if not all, of the passages discussed in this chapter. The search for the poet Vālmīki has led repeatedly to the discovery of his ascetic prowess. This leads me to wonder whether these two key elements (poet and ascetic) should for the moment be kept apart. None the less, by the time of the seven-*kāṇḍa* version of the *Vālmīki Rāmāyaṇa*, certainly by the time the vulgate text of the *Yogavāsiṣṭha* had taken shape, these two elements are inextricably linked.

The question of Vālmīki's lineage is equally complicated. I have already noted, in relation to the passages discussed above, that two quite different patronymics are applied to Vālmīki: *prācetasa* or 'descendant of Pracetas' and *bhārgava* or 'descendant of Bhṛgu'.[78] Unfortunately, neither academic scholars nor traditional commentators are certain about the identity of Pracetas. According to one school of thought, he is a *muni* or *ṛṣi*, perhaps even one belonging to the Bhārgava line. According to another, the name 'Pracetas' refers to the god Varuṇa. Govindarāja's commentary offers both possibilities (Goldman 1976: 100). Hari Prasad Shastri's translation opts for the second (1976: 611 n. 2). In his widely used Purāṇic encyclopaedia, Vettam Mani declares without further comment that Vālmīki is 'the tenth son of Varuṇa' (1975: 822). The idea that Pracetas is a *muni* or *ṛṣi* is hard to dispute. However, there is little evidence to support the link with Bhṛgu, certainly nothing early enough to be convincing. For example, the *Mahābhārata* lists of Bhārgavas do not include the name 'Pracetas'. Moreover, the epithet 'son of Pracetas' is more frequently applied to Dakṣa and Prajāpati, neither of whom are considered Bhārgavas (Sörensen 1904). As Goldman points out, the inclusion of the name 'Pracetas' in the list of Bhārgavas in various Purāṇas could simply be derived from the *Rāmāyaṇa* references cited above (1976: 100). The idea that the name 'Pracetas' refers to the god Varuṇa is intriguing in another way entirely. The rationale given by Govindarāja and others is that – according to their version of the termite-mound legend – Vālmīki was released from the termite mound by a downpour of rain sent by

78 For further references to both epithets in relation to Vālmīki, see John Brockington (1998: 395 n. 117).

Varuṇa. But, as we have shown, there is no evidence that the termite-mound story was associated with Vālmīki until well after the *Vālmīki Rāmāyaṇa*, a fact which renders this explanation unacceptable. More interesting is Goldman's suggestion that Bhṛgu is sometimes considered to be Varuṇa's son (1976: 100). I shall discuss the Bhārgava question in chapter 4.

Finally, there is the issue of blame. In the above accounts, blame has taken several forms. First, there is the Vālmīki who belongs to the *suparṇa*-folk who are described as killers and therefore classified as unruly *kṣatriya*s. Second, there is the passage where Vālmīki recounts how his fellow ascetics once accused him of being a brahmin-killer. While his companion, Rāma Jāmadagnya, freely admits his own guilt on that score, Vālmīki does not; but he asks Śiva to cleanse him of the sin anyway.[79] A third example is found in the *Vālmīki Rāmāyaṇa* and relates to Sītā, not Vālmīki. In chapter 44, Rāma learns about the rumours circulating in the city, accusations of infidelity against Sītā. Like Vālmīki in the *Mahābhārata* passage, Sītā is innocent. Like him, she must suffer the consequences anyway: she must purge herself publicly of guilt. My final example is the one that caused all the trouble in Birmingham: the legend that Vālmīki was once a murderous robber, a dacoit who killed not only brahmins but anyone who came his way. At this point, I shall note only that there are two closely connected themes here: sin followed by the need for absolution from that sin, and false accusation followed by the need for a public demonstration of innocence. I shall return to this idea too in chapter 4.

Chapter 3 has focused mainly on the two Indian epics. I shall conclude by quoting the exasperated comment of one scholar who has taken this particular academic path before me. As Goldman puts it (1976: 101):

> It appears little short of extraordinary that the Sanskrit epics which revel in the accounts of the deeds, origins and antecedents of even the most trivial characters, should offer such scanty and muddled evidence concerning a figure of the stature of Vālmīki.

The evidence examined above is certainly less informative than might have been hoped or expected. It is none the less my considered view that any account of the life and character of Vālmīki must begin with these early Sanskrit passages. That said, it is not entirely clear what these texts are telling us. Both Indian epics illustrate the growing tension between the social demands of orthodox *dharma*, the individual powers available through ascetic practice (*tapas*), and the universal salvation afforded through devotion to God (*bhakti*). By virtue of his asceticism, the brahmin-born Jāmadagnya takes up the sword and kills all the *kṣatriya*s whose *dharma* it is to protect brahmins (Mbh. 3.117). In defence of *dharma*, Rāma beheads Śambūka, the *śūdra* who has forgotten his ordained status in the search for personal divinity through ascetic practice (Rām. 7.67.3–4). When Yudhiṣṭhira asks about Śiva, some of the *ṛṣi*s speak about the powers they have

79 Bulcke raises the possibility that Vālmīki is insulted by the brahmins because he is an itinerant singer of tales (*kuśīlava*), hence also Vālmīki's insistence on his own purity on the occasion of Rāma's horse sacrifice (1960: 54). Certainly, both scenarios can be taken to imply blame.

attained through asceticism, others of the salvation afforded to them by his divine grace. In both Sanskrit epics, Vālmīki himself remains to a large extent a character from the old ascetic school. He is revered as a learned and holy man, his reputation derived from years of ascetic practice in remote places. But he is also 'one who knows what is right' (*dharmavid*), and so he uses his ascetic powers to convey and maintain *dharma*. Finally, despite his role in the development of the Rāma story, and therefore in the widespread worship of Rāma as God, Vālmīki himself seems as yet unaffected by the call of *bhakti*.

Chapter 4

Tracing Motifs in Sanskrit and Vernacular Texts

1. Orality and Text

After considering the earliest textual evidence for Vālmīki, I now turn to the legend that has grown up around him. Three key motifs become apparent in the Sanskrit material: the ascetic enclosed in a termite mound, the sinner who becomes a saint, and the idea that an evil or ignorant person is not worthy to recite the name of God. A fourth element, hinted at in the Sanskrit material but only made explicit in the vernacular texts, is the redefining of the sinner as an 'untouchable'. This brings our study full circle.

Before getting to grips with the detail, however, there are two important issues to be raised. First, something must be said about the implications of what is usually called 'the oral tradition', in particular about the relationship between orality and textual evidence. Second, with regard to the texts that I shall be discussing below, it is important to appreciate the wealth of material at our disposal, whether in Sanskrit, in the Indian vernaculars, or in non-Indian languages. In relation to both these points, any discussion of text is inevitably selective.

The very notion of an oral tradition is fraught with misunderstanding. At one level, as discussed earlier, both Sanskrit epics found their origin in oral composition. This is emphasized by the format of reciters and audience. If we follow John Brockington's analysis of the development of the *Rāmāyaṇa* outlined on pp. 94–5, it is in the third phase in particular that the definitive framework is provided in the form of episodes involving Vālmīki. The poet's presence serves to emphasize the importance of the format, the reciter/audience relationship, and the underlying theme of orality. As a gifted 'singer of tales', he has transformed popular stories, including contemporary events, into the ongoing oral epic. Able to narrate the full story of Rāma's life even while that story is incomplete, he is the ideal 'participant observer' of the oral tradition. This image of Vālmīki as participant observer is reinforced by Hiltebeitel's suggestion that Sītā is already living in Vālmīki's hermitage when he sees the courting Sarus Cranes. In that case, the description of the grieving female is intended to remind us, as it does Vālmīki, of Sītā's desperate circumstances (2001: 320).[1]

---

1 Both the Amar Chitra Katha comic and the *Vālmīki Rāmāyaṇa* agree that Vālmīki composed the epic story all at once, including both what had already taken place and what was yet to come. Since the comic-book assumes the dacoit and termite-mound stories, it depicts the poet writing the epic first (that is, immediately on emerging from the termite mound) and Sītā coming to his hermitage only 'years later' (Pai 1994: 17–20). By contrast, the *Vālmīki Rāmāyaṇa*

At another level, both Indian epics continue to function as fluid (that is, unfixed) compositions. This need not be a problem, certainly not for the reciters and audiences directly concerned. I shall discuss only one example here, the Śambūka episode mentioned earlier. In a minor incident in the *Vālmīki Rāmāyaṇa*, the *śūdra* Śambūka is believed to be a threat to the *dharma* of the entire kingdom when he practises *tapas*, and he is consequently beheaded by Rāma (7.67.4; see Plate 3.1).[2] In Maharashtra, according to the local folk tradition, this event took place on Rāmṭek Hill (Rāmagiri), north of Nagpur, and the story has a different ending. Before he died, Śambūka received three boons from Rāma: that Rāma should stay at Rāmṭek, that Śambūka's body should be transformed into a *śivaliṅga*, and that pilgrims should worship Śambūka before they worship Rāma (Sontheimer 1991: 119–20). We may assume that the natural sympathy for Śambūka experienced by lower-caste audiences in the locality influenced the reciters to such an extent that, over time, the outcome of the story was adjusted in his and their favour. In the context of this particular regional and religious experience, the shift in meaning seems to be unproblematic. However, changes of this kind can be controversial. Like the legend of Śambūka, the legend of Vālmīki emerged in response to the pressures of religious experience – mainly *bhakti* – through the usual processes of oral composition. While the lower-caste devotees of Rāmṭek Hill seem to endorse the Śambūka story, however, the Valmiki community rejects outright the legend commonly associated with Vālmīki elsewhere. For the devotee, the key issues are self-representation and consensus.

For textual scholars, the oral basis of the epics can itself be a problem. While few would wish to deny the importance of orality in the ongoing composition of the epics – that is, in past, present and future – there is a tendency to give greater weight to the textual lineage. In relation to Peter Brook's celebrated staging of the *Mahābhārata* in 1985, for example, John Brockington comments that the opening image of Vyāsa dictating the text to Gaṇeśa – so effective in performance – 'has in fact no basis whatsoever in the [critical] text, from which indeed Gaṇeśa is absent in any capacity' (1998: 2–3). While there is no explicit disapproval, the textual scholar's expectations and focus are clear.[3] Thus the term 'oral' is often applied, not to the nature of epic composition in general, but to variants for which no prior textual evidence can be found. If a textual antecedent is found, then it is assumed to be the source of later textual versions. Raghavan, for example, justifies his selection of early texts for an anthology of Sanskrit

---

does not mention any part of the dacoit story and it is less clear when exactly in the unfolding Rāma narrative the composition of the epic occurs. Hiltebeitel's suggestion that Vālmīki responds with such emotion at the sight of the mourning crane precisely because the mourning Sītā is already in his hermitage is perceptive. Certainly, this order of events is reflected in *Padma Purāṇa* 5, summarized on p. 124.

2 This story reappears in a range of texts. For the *Padma Purāṇa* account, see Deshpande (1989: part 2, pp. 460–7.) For the *Ānanda Rāmāyaṇa*'s reworking of the story in order to highlight the implications of *bhakti*, see Aklujkar (2000: 94ff.).

3 For an English translation of the (originally French) text of Brook's play, see Carrière (1988).

literature with the assertion that, 'in substance and message, the later phases of this literature are but an extension of the earlier' (1958: xi). The all-encompassing oral backdrop of epic storytelling is too often played down or ignored. It is the textual scholar's concern with provenance and precedence, this search for the 'original' or 'definitive' text, that provides both the best and the worst of the various critical edition projects. At its best, the Baroda critical edition of the *Vālmīki Rāmāyaṇa* (for example) sets out in its critical apparatus and its appendices much of what scholars need to know in order to understand, or at least to debate, the evolution of the text. At its worst, it gives the stamp of approval to text itself: all those manuscripts copied generation after generation by educated (and therefore probably high-caste) scribes for the benefit of the wealthy (and therefore probably high-caste) literati of the time. The same may be said of the Poona critical edition of the *Mahābhārata*. This approach serves to undermine still further the importance of orality, and the significance of the reciter and audience responding to each other *in situ*.[4]

While my concern in this study remains a study of text – specifically, a study of the evolution of the Vālmīki legend in Sanskrit texts – my watchword is 'multiplicity'. I am reminded here of the distinction Paula Richman makes between what she calls the 'Valmiki and Others' model (also termed the 'genealogical' or 'chronological' model) and the 'Many Ramayanas' model first elaborated by A. K. Ramanujan.[5] For Richman, the 'Valmiki and Others' model views all later tellings of the Rāma story as 'deviations' from Vālmīki's text. This, she claims, automatically creates a hierarchy of tellings, the authority of each one being dependent on how closely it resembles its putative source. By contrast, the 'Many Ramayanas' model establishes a non-hierarchical set of relationships, one in which each telling is valid in its own right. For my part, I believe it is possible to combine the best of both models. My pattern of work and the particular issue that I am investigating – the evolution of the Vālmīki legend – require the chronological, text-historical approach, but without the implication that all tellings after the *Vālmīki Rāmāyaṇa* are inferior. The larger question of religious authority and meaning requires a close look at the 'Many Ramayanas' paradigm. My fundamental position as a historian of Indian religions requires an appreciation of multiplicity: oral as well as text-based tellings, within and across religious divides, in relation to a range of regional and caste groups, within India and beyond. What is important is the realization that all these tellings, including the *Vālmīki Rāmāyaṇa*, find their origins in oral composition as a response to the specific social, political and religious frameworks of the time. Our task as scholars is to comprehend these different responses, to explore the reasons for them and the relationships between them, in the hope that the complexities of the

---

4 For a brief discussion of the oral tradition in India, see William Smith (1988: 20–2). For further examples of oral narratives, see Bhattacharya (1980), Kapp (1991), Sontheimer (1991) and Nilsson (2000). For performance traditions, see Awasthi (1980), Sweeney (1980), Anuradha Kapur (1990), Lutgendorf (1991a, 1991b) and Blackburn (1991, 1996). For women's oral traditions, see Flueckiger (1991) and Narayana Rao (1991).

5 Ramanujan's essay may be found in Richman's first edited volume (1991: 22–49), while Richman's discussion of the two models is in her second (2000: 3–5).

whole can be maintained without damage to the constituent parts. One component of that task is to articulate the discomfort experienced by (for example) the Valmiki community when the version of the Rāma story given the greatest prominence and authority in the wider Indian community is one that they believe demeans their own religious tradition. It is at this point, and for this reason, that questions of hierarchy and equal validity need to be taken more seriously.

The second point I wish to raise in this introductory section relates to the extraordinary range of 'texts' at our disposal. In the following discussion, my focus is on the written text. However, I have not forgotten either the lack of a written form for many 'texts', even today, or the oral nature of those 'texts' that have been written down.

Over the centuries, the story of Rāma has spread across the world, the precise format of its message adapting itself to the literary form, the host culture and the religious and political preferences of the place and time.[6] There are numerous versions of the Rāma story,[7] and several accounts of its cross-cultural spread.[8] Sometimes, the celebration of the Rāma story is simultaneously a celebration of Vālmīki as the poet who provided its lyrical form; sometimes Vālmīki is not even mentioned. While it is impossible in a study of this kind to provide details of every version of the story, and every take on the role played by Vālmīki in it, a brief overview of the chronology of related literature is in order.

Unsurprisingly, the earliest versions of the Rāma story (or elements of it) tell us little about Vālmīki, certainly little that is new. For example, like the Sanskrit *Rāmopākhyāna* episode from the *Mahābhārata* discussed in chapter 3, the Pali *Daśaratha Jātaka* of the Buddhist tradition is almost certainly derived from the *Vālmīki Rāmāyaṇa*, but it too does not mention the poet by name.[9] However, the

---

6 For explorations of the religious and political meanings underlying some Rāma narratives, see several of the articles in Richman (1991).

7 For an early overview of the expansion of the story in Sanskrit literature, see Raghavan (1973). For adaptations of the Rāma story into languages other than Sanskrit, see John Brockington (1984: 260–306 and 1998: 499–505). For an index of what Yardi describes as the most important Rāma texts in Sanskrit, Prakrit and other Indian and non-Indian languages, see Yardi (1994: 280–6). For a bibliography of Rāma texts in Assamese, Bengali, Oriya, Sanskrit, Prakrit and Hindi, see William Smith (1988: 195–8).

8 For studies of the Rāma story in South Asia, see Thiel-Horstman (1991) and Richman (1991, 2000); for Asia generally, see Raghavan (1980a), Iyengar (1983) and Vyas (1992); for Assam, Bengal and Orissa, see William Smith (1988); for Assam alone, see Goswami (1994). For the Tamil version by Kampaṉ (also written 'Kamban'), see Aiyar (1987) and Srinivasan (1994); for a comparison between Kampaṉ's Tamil telling and Ranganatha's Telugu one, see Sarma (1994); for a comparison between Kampaṉ's Tamil telling and Eḻuttacchan's Malayalam one, see Thampi (1996). For a recent summary of scholarship in this and related areas, see John Brockington (1998: 486ff.).

9 Despite the assertions of several early scholars, it is now generally agreed that the brief *Daśaratha Jātaka* is a later (not, as previously believed, an earlier) version of the Rāma narrative; judging by the prose, it may be as late as the fifth century CE. According to Richard Gombrich, 'the whole thing was a spoof', a collection of 'absurdities clobbered together by an author intent on treating a revered Hindu

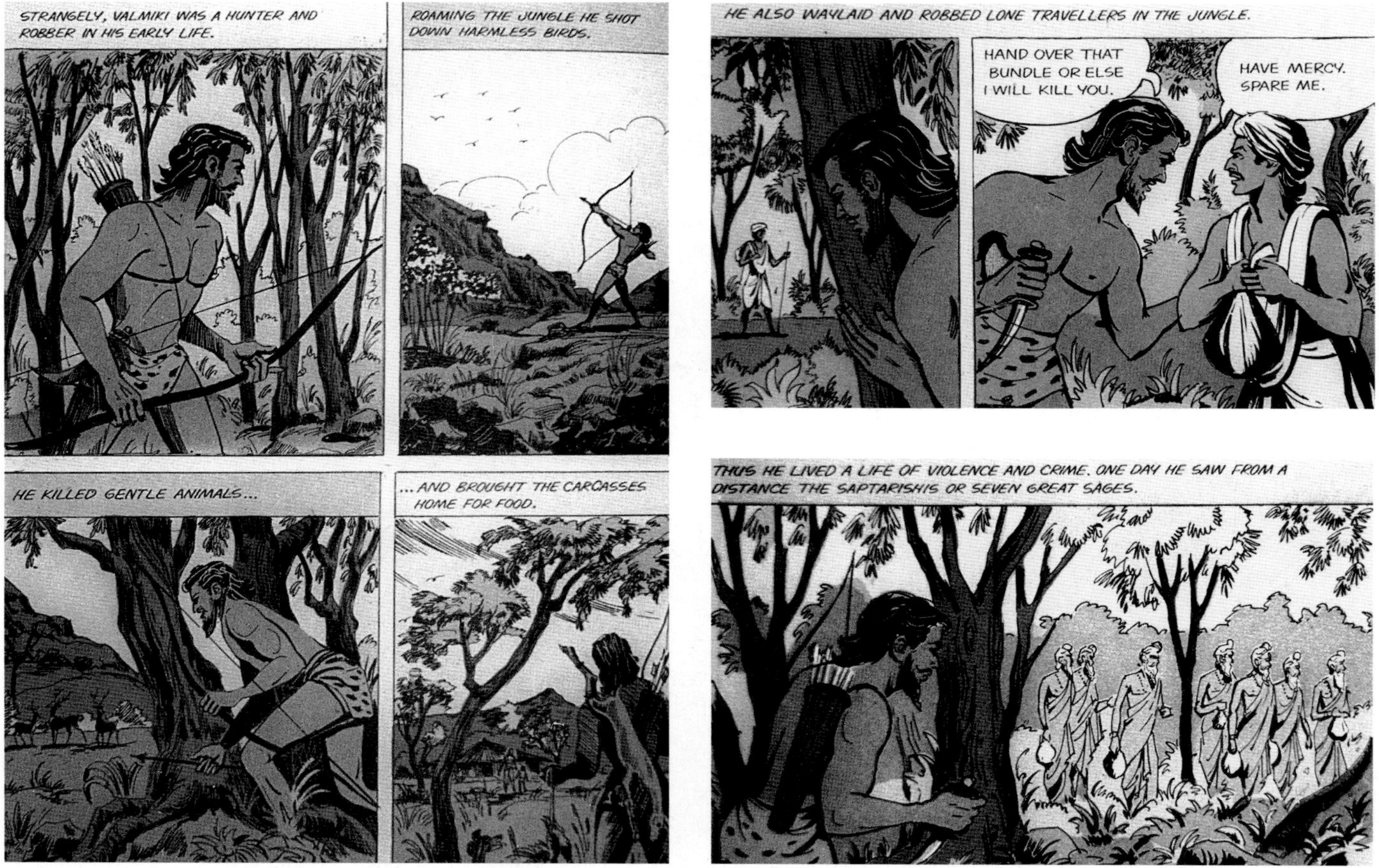

Plate 1.1 The dacoit legend

Plate 1.2 Guru Valmik meditating in the forest

Plate 1.3 Guru Valmik inside the termite mound

Plate 1.4 The killing of the crane

Plate 1.5 The birth of the śloka

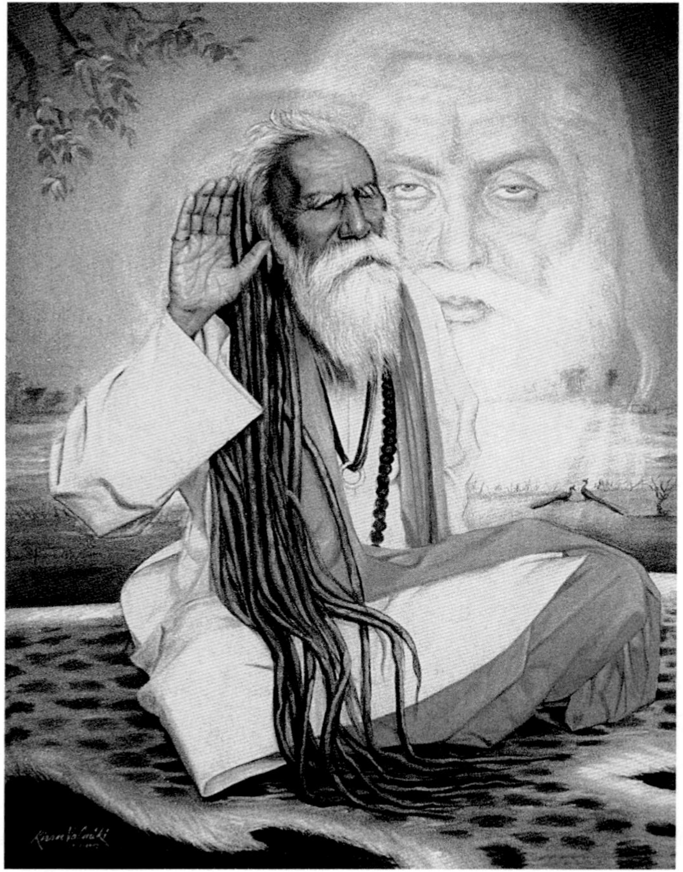

Plate 2.1 Portrait of Sahib Sri Sri 108 Sat Guru Gian Nath Ji Maharaj

Plate 2.2 Guru Valmik, the amrit, and Amritsar

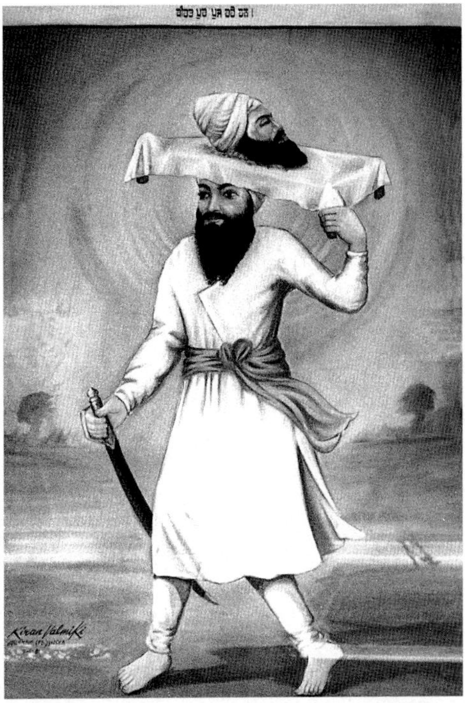

Plate 2.3 Jiwan Singh carrying the head of Guru Tegh Bahadur

Plate 2.4 Image of Bhagwan Valmik in the prayer hall in Southall

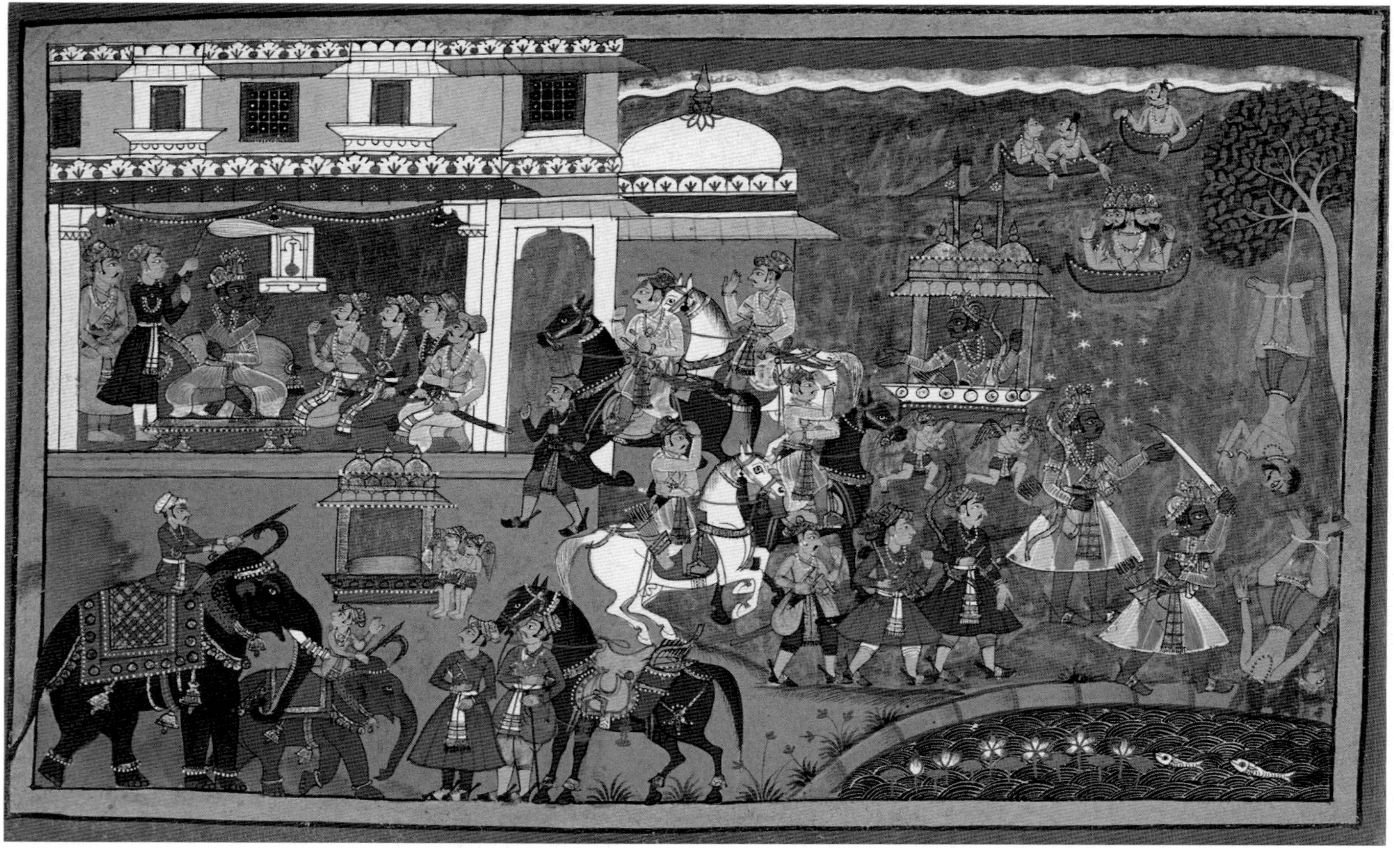

Plate 3.1 Rāma beheads Śambūka

Plate 5.1 Guru Valmik as a baby

Plate 5.2 Full-length portrait of Guru Valmik

Plate 5.3 Guru Valmik watches Vasiṣṭha teaching Rāma

Plate 5.4 Bhagwan Valmik, the power behind the gods

Pali *Buddhacarita* by Aśvaghoṣa, probably composed in the second century CE,[10] does mention the name 'Vālmīki'. This text shows evidence of borrowing from books 2 and 5 of the *Vālmīki Rāmāyaṇa*, and its author – unlike that of the *Rāmopākhyāna* – may well have known books 1 and 7 as well.[11] However, Aśvaghoṣa's only reference to Vālmīki is the statement that the descendants of great men often make more impressive contributions than their ancestors, illustrated by several examples. One of these exemplars is Vālmīki who, according to Aśvaghoṣa, created the *śloka* (*sasarja padyam*, v. 43) which his illustrious ancestor, the *maharṣi* Cyavana, had been unable to create before him (v. 46).[12] In its context, this is a minor detail but it has important ramifications. For the point that Aśvaghoṣa is making depends on the widespread but, as we shall see, mistaken assumption that Vālmīki belonged to the Bhārgava lineage, and was thus a descendant of Cyavana. Johnston, following Leumann, compounds the error. In his footnote to verse 43, he writes that Cyavana, 'on an occasion similar to that which caused Vālmīki to make the first *śloka*, failed to make his outcry in the metre'. But Johnston has elided two quite separate scenarios: the termite-mound motif that over time was applied to both men, and the *krauñca-vadha* ('killing of the crane') episode which is peculiar to Vālmīki. It is therefore incorrect to say, as Johnston does, that on a 'similar' occasion Cyavana failed to produce that *śloka*; there was no similar occasion. I shall return to the issue of the Bhārgava lineage in section 2.

In addition to these early Buddhist tellings of the Rāma story, there are early Jain versions, composed in Sanskrit, Prakrit and Apabhraṃśa. Kulkarni lists fifteen Jain Rāmāyaṇas composed between the third and the seventeenth century, followed by a longer list of later derivative works (1980: 12–14). The first text listed, and the best known, is Vimalasūri's Prakrit *Paümacariya*, dated to the late third century CE. Kulkarni notes that at least eight other texts are derived from it. For example, parts of Vimalasūri's work are incorporated into a number of later Jain texts such as Saṅghadāsa's Prakrit *Vāsudevahiṇḍī* (fifth century), Puṣpadanta's Apabhraṃśa *Mahāpurāṇa* (965 CE) and Bhadreśvara's Prakrit *Kahāvalī* (eleventh century). The rest (such as Guṇabhadra's ninth-

---

story with irreverence'; that is, it was an elaborate joke at the expense of an already existing story (1985: 435–6). For further discussions of this issue, see Goldman (1984: 32–3), John Brockington (1998: 377–8, 499) and Mary Brockington (2002: 139–41). For details of the August 1993 protest by the Vishwa Hindu Parishad against this Buddhist telling of the Rāma story, on the grounds that the text's portrayal of Rāma and Sītā as siblings is 'objectionable', see *SAHMAT* (October 1993, including a report on the incident by Geeta Kapur). See also Reynolds (1991).

10 Aśvaghoṣa is usually located in the first half of the first century (e.g. Johnston 1936: II, xiii–xxiv). However, recent evidence for the associated date of Kanishka (Sims-Williams and Cribb 1996, and Cribb 1999) now places him more persuasively in the first half of the second century.

11 For some early views on the relationship between the *Buddhacarita* and the *Vālmīki Rāmāyaṇa*, and for a detailed account of the borrowings by the former, see Raghavan (1956).

12 For text and translation, see 1.43, 46 in Johnston (1936: I, 4; II, 10) and 1.48, 52 in Cowell (1894: I, 9; II, 6–7).

century *Uttarapurāṇa*) take their lead either from the *Vālmīki Rāmāyaṇa* or from the *Mahābhārata*'s *Rāmopākhyāna*. According to Vimalasūri's account, the Rāma story was originally told by Mahāvīra, not Vālmīki, and was then passed down from disciple to disciple. Indeed, Vimalasūri accuses Vālmīki of deliberate deception: according to the Jain author, Vālmīki has presented a false account of the life of Rāma (called 'Padma' in the Jain text) and it is Vimalasūri's task to put the record straight. None the less, as Kulkarni demonstrates, Vimalasūri's text is deeply indebted to the *Vālmīki Rāmāyaṇa*. The main difference between the two narratives is that Vimalasūri's priority is to expound Jain rather than Hindu teachings. The result is a strikingly different Rāma narrative constructed around Rāvaṇa as the Jain hero.

Turning now to early Sanskrit tellings, I begin with the dramatic or poetic literature – the genre termed *kāvya* – simply because these texts are more easily dated than religious or mythological material. Kālidāsa's contribution to the Vālmīki discussion lies in his lyric narrative, the *Raghuvaṃśa* ('The lineage of Raghu'). Since Kālidāsa is usually associated with the reign of Candra Gupta II (*c*. 375–415), we may allocate this poem to about 400 CE. The Rāma story forms the central theme of this poem in praise of the Ikṣvāku lineage: cantos 1–9 recount events relating to Rāma's four predecessors, cantos 10–15 focus on the life of Rāma, while cantos 16–19 continue the story from Rāma's departure to Agnivarṇa's ignominious death. There are several references to Vālmīki. Although he is not mentioned by name, he is usually assumed to be included in the homage given by Kālidāsa to his learned predecessors. For example, Kālidāsa's phrase 'ancient poets' (*pūrvasūribhiḥ*, 1.4) is glossed by Mallinātha as 'poets such as Vālmīki' (*kavibhir vālmīkādibhiḥ*; see Devadhar and Suru 1934: 4). Later on, there are more specific allusions to the poet whose grief took the form of a *śloka*, who found Sītā by following the sound of her weeping (*ruditānusārī kaviḥ*, 14.70), who blessed her and her unborn children and took them in, the compassionate poet (*kaviḥ kāruṇikaḥ*, 15.71). There is also a description of Vālmīki's hermitage where Sītā raises her sons (canto 14). Finally, Kālidāsa credits Vālmīki with providing the first template for poets (*kaviprathama-paddhati*, 15.32–3): the story may be Rāma's, he says, but the creative work belongs to Vālmīki (15.64).[13]

After Kālidāsa, Rāma is usually presented as an avatar of Viṣṇu, his heroic nature superseded by his divinity, God in his own right. As Matchett has demonstrated (2000), the flexibility of the *avatāra* framework allows for the status of both the supreme deity and the apparently subordinate form of the avatar to be in place simultaneously. Kumāradāsa's *Jānakīharaṇa* ('The abduction of Jānakī'), written in perhaps the sixth century, was probably modelled on the *Raghuvaṃśa* as well as being directly influenced by Vālmīki's text. In the sixth or early seventh century, Bhaṭṭi's *Rāvaṇavadha* ('The killing of Rāvaṇa', also called the *Bhaṭṭikāvya*) retells most of the Rāma story but omits the *Uttarakāṇḍa* and some of the *Bālakāṇḍa* too. In terms of historical development, there is at this point still remarkably little change in the information provided regarding

---

13 For further details of Kālidāsa, his world and his plays, see Stoler Miller (1984). For a brief analysis of the *Raghuvaṃśa*, see Raghavan (1980c: 27–41).

Vālmīki's character and background. Most important of all, there is still no evidence of the Vālmīki of popular legend.

Turning now to plays, the earliest Sanskrit plays based on the Rāma story are probably the two ascribed to the south Indian playwright, Bhāsa: the *Pratimānāṭaka* ('The drama of the ancestral image') and the *Abhiṣekanāṭaka* ('The drama of the coronation').[14] Neither mentions Vālmīki. In the first half of the eighth century, Bhavabhūti probably functioned as a poet at the court of King Yaśovarman. His two plays – the *Mahāvīracarita* ('The story of the great hero') and the better-known *Uttararāmacarita* ('The later story of Rāma') – relate the full Rāma narrative. In the second play, Act 2 is set in the Daṇḍaka forest where a female ascetic (*tāpasī*) tells a forest goddess (*vanadevatā*) what happened on that very spot twelve years earlier. Bhavabhūti thus places in the female ascetic's mouth his version of the events leading up to Vālmīki's composition of the *Rāmāyaṇa* epic, as follows. One day, when the *brahmarṣi* Vālmīki went to the river Tamasā to bathe, he saw a hunter shoot down one of a pair of cranes. When he instinctively cursed the hunter, the words emerged in the divine form of a *śloka*. At once, Brahmā appeared, praised Vālmīki for his enlightened (*prabuddha*) response, and instructed him to compose the story of Rāma in the same poetic form. Bhavabhūti refers to Vālmīki as 'the first poet' (*ādyaḥ kavir asi*) and 'the blessed son of Pracetas' (*bhagavān pracetasaḥ*). This eighth-century retelling is much the same as that found in the *Vālmīki Rāmāyaṇa*: the focus is on the *krauñca-vadha* incident, that is, on the killing of the Sarus Crane, and on the compassion that this incident arouses in Vālmīki.[15] There is still no 'Vālmīki legend': no wicked past, no termite mound, and no appearance of the Seven *Ṛṣis*. Yet, despite the fact that Bhavabhūti's text contains no reference to the termite-mound story, Kale's 1934 edition supplies it. On page 42 of the notes section (each section is numbered separately), Kale glosses *vālmīki* as follows: 'So called from Valmîka or an ant-hill, full of the nests of termites, with which he was covered as he sat down repeating the word Marâ, Marâ'. This twentieth-century gloss on an eighth-century text is both unwarranted and misleading.

The list of Sanskrit poets and playwrights who have drawn on the Rāma story continues. I mention only some of these here and, where appropriate, summarize the information they contain about Vālmīki. According to John Brockington, for example, Anaṅgaharṣa Māyurāja composed the *Udattarāghava* in the eighth century or earlier, while Śaktibhadra wrote the *Āścaryacūḍāmaṇi* in the ninth (1998: 489). According to Karin Steiner, Murāri composed his *Anargharāghava*

14 While the 'real Bhāsa' may be as early as the second century, the so-called 'Trivandrum plays' are usually placed in the seventh century, although they may well be later still (John Brockington, email communication, 17 June 2002). For previous discussions of the date and authorship of the plays ascribed to Bhāsa, see Devadhar (1927). For a text-historical analysis of the relationship between Bhāsa's plays and the *Vālmīki Rāmāyaṇa*, see Słuszkiewicz (1957). For an English translation of the *Pratimānāṭaka*, see Janaki (1978).

15 For a detailed discussion of the relationship between Bhavabhūti's two plays and the *Vālmīki Rāmāyaṇa*, see Raghavan (1968). For an analysis of the multiple tellings of the Rāma story in the *Uttararāmacarita*, see Shulman (2000).

somewhere between the first half of the eighth century and 950 CE, probably in Orissa (1997: 12–15). Although Murāri considers himself to be following in Vālmīki's footsteps, and even refers to himself in the prologue as a 'young Vālmīki' (*bālavālmīki*), Vālmīki himself does not appear in the play. We learn only that he was a *ṛṣi* and, yet again, a descendant of Pracetas (*prācetasa*, 1.9–12).[16] In the tenth century, Rājaśekhara composed what is probably the longest Sanskrit play ever written, a retelling of the complete *Rāmāyaṇa* plot, in his drama entitled *Bālarāmāyaṇa*, 'The Little Rāmāyaṇa'. Legend has it that Rājaśekhara had the honour of reading this play and two others to the great Śaṅkarācārya (Suru 1960: 1–2). He also wrote the first two acts of the *Bālabhārata*, 'The Little Mahābhārata', a drama that promised to be longer still. In the latter play, the prelude to the first act presents an encounter between the authors of the two epics, Vyāsa and Vālmīki, in which the latter admonishes the former for writing at such enormous length (Tubb 1996).[17] But there is no support for the Vālmīki legend in either play. In the eleventh century, we find the works of Bhoja, Kṣemendra and Dhīranāga, in the twelfth century Sandhyākaranandin, and so on. Vālmīki's text even becomes a topic for discussion by the greatly respected literary theorists, Ānandavardhana and Abhinavagupta (tenth–eleventh century). Both dwell on the famous, and in my view pivotal, *krauñca-vadha* episode and on Vālmīki's dramatic invention of the Sanskrit *śloka*.[18] For them, as for most of these early writers, Vālmīki's compassionate response to the killing of the crane remains his defining moment, his signature story as it were, the key motif in his life. This is important.

If we now turn to the Sanskrit Purāṇas, dating becomes more difficult.[19] That said, it is still useful to consider the developing Vālmīki legend in the context of a relative chronology. For example, none of the three oldest Purāṇas – *Mārkaṇḍeya*, *Brahmāṇḍa* and *Matsya* – mentions the Rāma story at all, let alone the Vālmīki legend.

Brief versions of the Rāma story, but not the Vālmīki legend, appear in several Purāṇas. In the *Vāyu Purāṇa*, for example, the chapter on the Ikṣvāku dynasty

---

16 The *Anargharāghava* was first brought to the attention of the West in 1827 by H. H. Wilson who dismissed the work as having 'no dramatic merit, being deficient in character, action, situation, and interest', and described Murāri's language as 'as far from good taste as his ideas' (see Wilson 1955: 136). This immoderate judgement prompted Steiner to take a closer look at the play, and to offer the first complete translation in a European language (1997: 9–11, citing the 1827 edition of Wilson). With regard to the date of the *Anargharāghava*, John Brockington prefers the tenth century CE (1998: 489).

17 For a biographical sketch of Rājaśekhara, see Suru (1960: lvii–cxi); see also Mitra (1983), cited in Tubb (1996: 85).

18 For a brief account of these and other texts, see John Brockington (1998: 489–91). For the influence of the *Vālmīki Rāmāyaṇa* and Kālidāsa's *Raghuvaṃśa* on Bhoja's *Campūrāmāyaṇa*, see Słuszkiewicz (1927). For an analysis of Abhinavagupta's approach to the *krauñca-vadha* incident, see Masson (1969). For a collection of articles on Abhinavagupta's work, see Raghavan (1980d).

19 For a detailed early account of the Rāma story in the Purāṇas, see Raghavan (1973: 33–73). For more recent summaries, see William Smith (1988: 13–14) and John Brockington (1998: 491–2).

includes an account of the Rāma narrative (26.183–96), but it is short. There is no abandonment of Sītā, and no mention of Vālmīki.[20] Briefer still is the account in the *Brahma Purāṇa*. A chapter devoted to sacred sites such as Rāmatīrtha includes the brief story of Daśaratha (53.2ff.). While Rāma's birth and subsequent story is mentioned in passing, the main focus of this account rests on Daśaratha's inadvertent sin of brahmin-murder. There is no mention either of Sītā's abandonment or of Vālmīki.[21] The *Bhāgavata Purāṇa* despatches the Rāma story in three short chapters (9–11). The special feature of this telling is that Sītā does not undergo the fire ordeal after the death of Rāvaṇa; she simply joins Rāma in triumph in Ayodhyā. Later, when she has been abandoned by Rāma, she comes to the hermitage of 'Vālmīki, son of Pracetas', where she gives birth to twin boys (11.9–11). Sītā entrusts the boys to Vālmīki's care and enters the earth (11.15). She does not appear in the story again, and there is no further mention of Vālmīki.[22] The issue of Rāma's divinity is given a Śaiva gloss in the *Śiva Purāṇa* (*Rudrasaṃhitā*, section 2, chapters 24–5). When Śiva sees Rāma lamenting the loss of Sītā, he bows to him, to the great surprise of his consort, Satī (24.27–9). Śiva explains that Rāma and Lakṣmaṇa are the sons of Daśaratha, that the former is a complete incarnation of Viṣṇu, the latter a partial incarnation of Śeṣa (24.38–9). Seeing Satī's disbelief, Śiva suggests that she test Rāma for herself. She assumes the form of Sītā. When Rāma greets her as Satī, she admits his divinity. Chapter 25 contains Rāma's explanation of the honour bestowed on him by Śiva, including a reference to the abduction of Sītā (v. 35).[23] But there is nothing more about Vālmīki.

Longer versions of the Rāma story may be found in the *Kūrma* and *Agni Purāṇas*. In the *Kūrma*, the story is told in chapters 21 of the *Pūrvabhāga* and 34 of the *Uttarabhāga*, with the addition of a magical or illusory Sītā (*māyā-sītā*) created by Agni to take Sītā's place for the abduction.[24] It is the *māyā-sītā* who enters the fire: she is destroyed while the real (unblemished) Sītā is restored by Agni to a delighted Rāma. The *Agni Purāṇa* contains an uneven list of some of the avatars of Viṣṇu, including seven chapters devoted to Rāma. The avatars mentioned are: the fish (*matsya*, ch. 2), the tortoise (*kūrma*, ch. 3), the boar (*varāha*, ch. 4), Rāma (chs 5–11), Kṛṣṇa (ch. 12), and the Buddha and Kalki together (ch. 16); the Rāma incarnation is evidently the important one here. But Vālmīki's role is brief. At the start, we are told only that the Rāma story was told by Nārada to Vālmīki (5.1). At the end, we learn that Rāma's two sons were born in Vālmīki's hermitage to Sītā who had been abandoned there on account of a rumour (11.10). We are then told

---

20 For an English translation of the relevant verses of the *Vāyu Purāṇa*, see Tagare (1988: part 2, pp. 688–9).

21 For an English translation of this chapter, see Bhatt (1986: part 4, pp. 973–91). The editors describe part 4 as an independent text, separate from the rest of this Purāṇa.

22 For an English translation of the relevant chapters, see Tagare (1976: part 3, pp. 1177–90). For other brief accounts of the Rāma story, see *Garuḍa Purāṇa* (*Pūrvakhaṇḍa*, chs 142, 143) and *Viṣṇu Purāṇa* (4.4; cf. Wilson 1961: 307).

23 For an English translation of these two chapters, see Kunst and Shastri (1969: part 1, pp. 384–9).

24 For the 'shadow Sītā' (*chāyā-sītā*) tradition, see *Brahmavaivarta Purāṇa* 6.60.28–35, cited in Raghavan (1973: 45); see also Doniger (1999: 12ff.).

that Vālmīki composed the *Rāmāyaṇa* after hearing the story from Nārada (11. 12). Finally, what William Smith calls 'peripheral' or 'apocryphal' material may be found in a number of Purāṇas, such as the *Vāmana* and *Padma*, while *śākta* and Tantric elements have been added in the *Bṛhaddharma*, *Mahābhāgavata* and *Devībhāgavata Purāṇa*s. I shall consider the *Padma Purāṇa* here.

Book 6 of the *Padma Purāṇa* covers the Rāma narrative in three chapters: the main story (6.242), Rāma's consecration (6.243), and his ascent to heaven (6.244). Vālmīki is mentioned only in the last of these: he takes Sītā in when she is abandoned; then, when Rāma comes that way for the horse sacrifice, Vālmīki asks him to take her back (6.244.1–22).[25] Book 5 gives a longer, if more disjointed account: from Rāma's journey with Sītā in the aerial chariot back to Ayodhyā (5.1) and the release of the sacrificial horse (5.11) to the abandonment of Sītā in the forest (5.58) and the great sacrifice where Kuśa and Lava recite the *Rāmāyaṇa* (5.66–7), interspersed with a wealth of other inserted tales. Vālmīki's role is as expected: he welcomes Sītā to his hermitage, and initiates her boys into Vedic study (5.59.40–86); able to see the future, he composes the *Rāmāyaṇa* and teaches the boys to recite it (5.66.16–20); he asks Rāma to take back wife and sons (5.66.44–51); and the *krauñca-vadha* episode is told (5.66.143–57). This is followed by a summary of the entire *Vālmīki Rāmāyaṇa* (6.66.164–82).[26] Book 4 (the *Pātālakhaṇḍa*) provides the longest version of the Rāma story: from the horse sacrifice (4.1) to Vālmīki's ashram (4.54), with accounts of both the golden image of Sītā (4.67.16) and the *krauñca-vadha* episode (4.86.161–2), and then the narrative starts up all over again (4.100). But there is yet another version of the *Rāmāyaṇa* in the *Padma Purāṇa*. This one, described as *not* the one narrated by Vālmīki, is told to Rāma at another point in book 5. In this telling, there is no *krauñca-vadha* sequence, no abandonment of Sītā and no reference to Vālmīki (5.116).[27] These two themes are evidently associated not with the Rāma narrative *per se* but with Vālmīki's telling of it. In my view, this is significant.

This is not a comprehensive account of the Rāma stories as narrated in the Sanskrit Purāṇas. However, even a summary like this one allows us to draw some preliminary conclusions about this genre of material. First, the Rāma story is so well known that even the briefest reference to it is sufficient to prod the collective memory. Second, it is widely understood that the *Vālmīki Rāmāyaṇa* is one among many versions of the story; even Rāma is treated to another telling. Third, the idea of providing 'flash-back' explanations for events is commonplace. A prime example of this tendency in the Rāma story is the justification given for the washerman's unkind remark about Sītā, the unfortunate comment that gave rise to the rumour that led to Rāma's decision to abandon her in the forest. According to the *Padma Purāṇa* (5.57), for example, that remark is the direct result of Sītā's thoughtless treatment of a pair of parakeets (*śuka*).[28] It seems that

---

25 For an English translation of these chapters, see Deshpande (1991: part 9, pp. 3221–47).

26 See Deshpande (1990b: part 5, pp. 1646ff.).

27 See Deshpande (1990c: part 6, pp. 2267–94).

28 The Sanskrit term *śuka* is almost always translated by the English word 'parrot'. However, there are no parrots in India, only parakeets. The stereotypical 'talking' parakeets are the Roseringed (often kept as a pet) and the larger Alexandrine.

when she was a girl, long before she knew anything about Rāma, she overheard the parakeets talking about him as a great king who would marry a woman named Sītā. Eager to learn more, she has the birds captured. The parakeets explain that Vālmīki has composed a poem about Rāma's future, including his marriage to Sītā, and then they describe at length Rāma's great physical beauty. Sītā's response is to keep the parakeets in captivity, despite their entreaties and distress, despite even the female's pregnancy. Before she dies, the female curses Sītā to be similarly separated from her husband when pregnant. The male swears revenge before he also dies. It is he who is then reborn as the washerman who will cause Sītā such pain.[29] In the context of the Purāṇas, it is understandable if a similar flash-back explanation is provided for Vālmīki in the form of the dacoit legend. What is also clear, however, is that there is no evidence in earlier texts to validate this supposed 'flash-back'.

One further conclusion may be drawn from these accounts. Generally speaking, there are two main aspects to these portrayals of Vālmīki: his composition of an epic narrative of the Rāma story, usually after hearing the story from Nārada; and his compassion for Sītā which leads him to take care of her and her sons. I believe that this constitutes a change of emphasis. Whereas earlier presentations of Vālmīki focus on the *krauñca-vadha* episode – that is, on the ascetic's compassion for the grieving crane, his instinctive creation of the *śloka* form, and the subsequent use of that verse form in the composition of the *Rāmāyaṇa* – the focus in the Purāṇas is placed more emphatically on Vālmīki's response to the abandoned Sītā. In my view, Hiltebeitel's suggestion that Sītā is already in his hermitage when he composes the poem (2001: 320) reflects this Purāṇic emphasis.[30]

The rest of this chapter falls into four sections. Sections 2–4 focus on the key motifs of the Vālmīki legend, each contextualized within the genre of material in which it appears: the ascetic overgrown, the sinner redeemed, and the special mantra for the unworthy. Section 5 explores the role played by some vernacular accounts in making the idea that Vālmīki was an 'untouchable' a fixture in the legend of popular culture. I am reminded here of what Hopkins wrote about both Indian epics over a century ago:

> When we have peeled off the outer layer (and in it are included with one exception, if it be an exception, all the references to Vālmīki in the great epic), we have left two epics, one of which is a complete whole, the other a congeries of incongruous stories grouped around a central tale.[31]

Hopkins's depiction of the *Mahābhārata* as a collection of 'incongruous stories' is useful: these stories are the results of the accumulating, proliferating oral

29 For an English translation of this episode, see Deshpande (1990b: part 5, pp. 1879–83).

30 A further example of the *krauñca-vadha* episode is provided by the later *Bṛhaddharma Purāṇa* (2.25–30).

31 Hopkins (1901: 79). The possible exception is *Mahābhārata* 7.118.48, which in this study is discussed in chapter 3. For the discussion by Hopkins of all the references to Vālmīki, see pp. 58–64.

tradition. Vālmīki too was a 'singer of tales': continuing the tradition, he transformed popular stories current at the time into epic poetry. But this process persisted after Vālmīki as well; indeed, it continues today.[32] My concern in the rest of this chapter is to disentangle some of the 'incongruous stories' that have emerged in relation to Vālmīki – elements of which will form part of the so-called 'popular' legend – to reveal three distinct threads. I begin with the motif of the ascetic enclosed within the termite mound.

2. The Ascetic Overgrown

The name 'Vālmīki' is usually traced back to the Sanskrit term *valmī* ('termite'), hence *valmīka* ('termite mound') and *vālmīki* ('one who is related in some way to a termite mound'). This derivation – widely accepted by Indian tradition, and quite explicit in the Vālmīki legend – is rejected outright by the Valmiki community, and with good reason. Chapter 3 has already established that there is no evidence of a link with termite mounds in the earliest occurrences of the name 'Vālmīki'. This section will demonstrate that, as a result of popular etymology, that link was applied retrospectively. Conversely, the earliest reference to the termite-mound motif has no connection whatever with 'our' Vālmīki. Indeed, this powerful motif has a lively history in its own right.[33] Before embarking on the relevant details of that history, however, I shall consider this striking motif within the wider context of Indian asceticism or *tapas*.

Ascetic practice in the Indian epics involves a bewildering range of techniques. Some ascetics engage in practices involving fire or water, or submit their bodies to extremes of heat, wind and cold. Some regulate their breathing, or refuse to speak. Others reduce their intake of food, or consume only water or air. Some go naked, or wear only rags or garments made of tree bark or animal skins, and let their hair become long and matted (*jaṭā*). Still others sit or stand in an unusual position (on one leg, for example, or with one arm raised above their heads). A particularly challenging practice is to keep the body completely motionless like a log of wood (e.g. *sthāṇu*, *kāṣṭha*).[34] Most of these techniques are still in evidence

32 There is a growing body of work on modern Indian epics. For a comprehensive study of India's oral and classical epics, with particular reference to the cult of Draupadī, see Hiltebeitel (1999b). For the Avadhī and Bhojpurī versions of the ancient Hindi tale of Lorik and Candā, collected from Varanasi, Allahabad and Mirzapur, see Pandey (1979, 1982, 1987). For the Tamil folk epic of the twin 'elder brothers' who, with their marginally younger sister, make a set of triplets, see Beck (1982). For the Rajasthani epic of Pābūjī, still performed in Rajasthan today by singer-priests (*bhopo*) in front of stylized cloth paintings, see John Smith (1990, 1991). For the Siri epic of Tulunāḍu, a lengthy oral narrative concerning three generations of divine or sacred women in Tulu society, and for the creative role of the singer, see Honko (1998) and Honko *et al.* (1998).

33 For a detailed study of this motif, see König (1984; for the etymology and implications of the term *valmīka*, see pp. 19–23).

34 For studies of *tapas* in the *Mahābhārata*, see Hara (1979) and Shee (1986). For a

today, as anyone who attended or watched television reports of the 2001 Kumbh Mela would know.[35] Like so many visitors to South Asia, I have seen ascetics with matted hair, naked or barely clothed, standing on one leg, keeping one arm permanently raised above their heads, refusing ever to sit or lie down, keeping silent, and so on. Perhaps my most striking experience was in the 1980s, when my esteemed teacher, Tarkatīrtha Lakṣmaṇśāstrī Jośī, took me to meet His Holiness Śrī Candraśekharendrasarasvatī of the Kāmakoṭipīṭh when the latter was giving *darśan* in northern Maharashtra. We found His Holiness in a covered cart, unmoving and silent, engaged in a one-week vow (*vrata*) of *kāṣṭhamauna*, that is, keeping still and silent like a log of wood. The termite-mound motif offers an even more powerful image: here the *tapasvin* engages in such an extended period of immobility that his body becomes hidden from view by the termite mound slowly growing up over it. But there are other examples of the practice of immobility too.

An important element of this idea is that the ascetic must not move whatever the provocation. Several stories demonstrate this point. In the *Mahābhārata*, for example, the *Ādiparvan* contains two versions of the story of King Parikṣit's meeting with the ascetic Śamīka (1.36–8 and 1.45–6). While hunting in the forest, the king shoots a deer. He is searching for the wounded animal when he comes across a motionless ascetic. Śamīka has taken a vow of silence (*mauna-vrata*, 36.18, 37.8, 38.23, 45.24, 46.7) but also, it transpires, one of immobility: he keeps so still that he appears to the king to be an inanimate wooden post (*sthāṇubhūta*, 37.7; *sthāṇuvat*, 45.26). The king asks the ascetic for help in his search but, even when a response is angrily demanded of him, Śamīka neither speaks nor moves. Parikṣit becomes so enraged by the lack of attention being paid to him that he deliberately insults the ascetic by draping a dead snake over the man's shoulder. This is a mistake. For Śamīka's son, Śṛṅgin, belongs to the old school of irascible and dangerous ascetics. Śṛṅgin is furious when he hears about the insult to his meek father. He curses the king who in due course dies.[36] As Shee points out, there is a significant point to be made here. In this portrayal of the contrasting asceticisms of father and son, we find a reversal in biological terms of what was in fact a text-historical development. In biological terms, the father precedes the son. In text-historical terms, Śamīka's gentle embodiment of inner spirituality develops later than (that is, becomes textually visible later than) his son's fiery demonstration of ascetic power. This historical progression

---

detailed account of ascetic techniques and a list of relevant citations, see Shee (1986: 243–346 and 347–70).

35 The Kumbh Mela is held every three years, at each of the four sacred spots in rotation: that is, at Haridwar, Nasik, Ujjain and – the most sacred of the four – at Prayag, today known as Allahabad. According to Hindu astrology, the planets come into alignment every 144 years to produce the most auspicious *melā* of all. This last occurred in 2001: an estimated 100 million people came to bathe at Allahabad, along with virtually every ascetic in India. For images of some of the remarkable ascetics who participated, women as well as men, see Dixie (2001).

36 For English translations of the two versions, see van Buitenen (1973: 97–8, 110–11; however, he reads 'Śāmīka' throughout). For studies of the implications of one or both of these stories, see Hacker (1978: 342–5), Wezler (1979) and Shee (1986: 1–30).

reflects the increasing influence of Buddhism and Jainism on Hindu ascetic practice. Thus when Śṛṅgin curses Parikṣit for the insult to his father, Śamīka does not congratulate him. He admonishes his son for his lack of restraint, and sends a messenger to the king in the hope of sidestepping the younger man's unruly curse. The important thing now is self-control and equanimity (*śama*), not irascible cursing, the hot anger of ascetic power that is more often associated with earlier forms of Hindu asceticism.[37] The religious authority now vested in the new ascetic mode is reflected in the narrative by the parental authority of the father.

Returning to the unmoving ascetic being deliberately insulted or tormented by an irreverent onlooker, we should note that this theme is not peculiar to the Parikṣit incident. In one form or another, it is widely known throughout the Indian sub-continent, across the centuries, and in all three of the religious traditions of classical India. To prove the ubiquity of this particular aspect of the immobility theme, I shall refer here to a cluster of stories found in both the Jain and the Buddhist traditions.

There are isolated instances of the motif in the literature and art of each tradition. In Vimalasūri's text, for example, Rāvaṇa engages in severe forms of *tapas*, including long periods of standing calm and motionless in the face of fearful apparitions sent by the *yakṣa*s (Kulkarni 1990: 18 n. 17). More interesting still is the evidence for a shared sub-narrative which relates how both Mahāvīra and Gautama were tormented as they sat unmoving in meditation. According to the eleventh-century *Triṣaṣṭiśalākāpuruṣacaritra* by the Jain monk Hemacandra, for example, we read that Mahāvīra was once standing outside a village, meditating in a fixed upright posture (*kāyotsarga*). A local cowherd comes by, searching for his missing animals, and asks for help. When Mahāvīra fails to respond, the cowherd begins to insult him, suggesting that his ears are useless. When there is still no response, true to type, the cowherd becomes enraged. He shoves the points of the hard stalks of *kāśa* grass deep into the ascetic's ears, so deep that they meet, and then he breaks the ends off so that they cannot be removed. The rest of the narrative explains how these painful foreign objects are eventually removed. But the point of the story is that Mahāvīra neither complains nor moves throughout the ordeal.[38] A similar incident is related in the *Ācārāṅgasūtra.* Again, Mahāvīra is sitting in meditation, without moving. This time, his tormentors need no excuse: they beat him, stab him, tear out his hair, cover him with dust, and generally toss him about. The point of this story is the same: Mahāvīra bears all without comment, without complaint, and still without moving.

In Buddhist literature, similar narratives are applied to the Bodhisattva Gautama. In the Pali *Mahāsīhanādasutta* of the *Majjhimanikāya*, for example, Gautama is engaged in the ascetic practice of sleeping in a cemetery. The same cowherd hooligans, or others just like them, deliberately torment him: they spit at him, urinate on him, cover him with dust, and then stick spikes into his ears.

37 For a discussion of the potential danger inherent in the unthinking anger or deliberate curse of an ascetic, see Shee (1986: 371–87).

38 For a translation of this episode, see Johnson (1962: vol. 6, pp. 120–3).

But Gautama's ascetic vow is as strong as Mahāvīra's: he does not respond in any way. Another version of the story is found in the Sanskrit *Lalitavistara*. This time, the hooligans think (or pretend) that Gautama is a 'dust-goblin' (*pāṃśupiśāca*), and they 'play' with him mercilessly, enveloping him yet further in dust and dirt. The trick with the grass is 'played' to such an extent, the text informs us, that the blade thrust into Gautama's ears or nose or mouth comes out of his nose and ears and mouth in every possible combination. This is all rather distressing unless, of course, the story is another exaggerated spoof aimed at ridiculing Hindu ascetic practice (unlikely, since the protagonist is Gautama). For the purpose of our discussion, however, one point is important. These different accounts, found in both literature and art, suggest a tradition shared across religions, languages, regions and time. The stories are found in Hindu, Jain and Buddhist scriptures, preserved in Sanskrit, Prakrit and Pali. The work of visual artists locates the story in Gujarat, in the Deccan and in Bengal: the cave painting in Ajaṇṭā probably dates to the fifth century CE; manuscript illustrations began in the eleventh century, paper ones in the fourteenth.[39] We may conclude that stories of torments inflicted on immobile ascetics are both ancient and widespread.[40]

More interesting for our purposes is the version of the immobility motif that shows the ascetic staying still long enough for nature to envelop him. A particularly arresting example is provided in the *Śāntiparvan* of the *Mahābhārata* by the story of the ascetic Jājali (Mbh. 12.253). We learn that he habitually practised several ascetic techniques at once. For example, he lives in isolation in the forest (v. 2) but he also engages in the advanced technique of living underwater and then leaving his physical body, to roam the world without it (v. 4). In addition, he restricts his intake of food, his clothing consists of strips of bark and skins, his hair is tangled into matted locks, his body is filthy, and he is silent (*muniḥ*, v. 3). Determined to be the most impressive ascetic of all, Jājali tries everything: he sleeps in the open during the monsoon rains, he immerses himself in water in the cold season and he exposes his body to heat and wind in the hot season (vv. 15–6). At one point, Jājali stops eating altogether and stands motionless in the forest like a wooden post or the trunk of a tree (*kāṣṭhavat*, *sthāṇubhūta*, vv. 19, 20, 22). Again, this particular form of *tapas* is not peculiar to Jājali. Sāvitrī does something similar when she needs to accumulate enough ascetic power to protect her husband from his predicted death. She undertakes the *vrata* of standing motionless, without food or drink, for three days and nights (Mbh. 3.280.3); that is, she stands in a rigid upright posture as if she has turned into a wooden post (*kāṣṭhabhūteva lakṣyate*, v. 8). In Jājali's case, however, he stands so still for so long that drongos[41] bring blades of grass to

39 For an analysis of both the Jain and the Buddhist accounts, together with a discussion of the Ajaṇṭā painting and related manuscript illustrations, see Wujastyk (1984).

40 Of course, the temptation to tease or torment someone who is not supposed to move is not peculiar either to South Asia or to the past. In a secular but significantly ceremonial context, for example, tourists and children regularly seek to disrupt the fixed posture and staring gaze of the guardsmen outside Buckingham Palace.

41 The term *kuliṅga* (vv. 20, 28; literally, 'having bad characteristics') denotes the

add to his matted locks and build a nest on his head (vv. 20–1). When the female lays her eggs in the nest (v. 24), Jājali resolves not to disturb the natural process. He continues to stand there unmoving while the eggs hatch, the fledglings grow up, and the young birds slowly learn to fly and fend for themselves. Only when their exploratory flights extend to an absence of a month, does Jājali move once more (v. 37).[42]

But the best-known practitioner of immobility techniques in the *Mahābhārata* is the famous Bhārgava figure, Cyavana. There are two distinct episodes to consider. The first involves the ascetic practice of living underwater, noted above in relation to Jājali. In the *Anuśāsanaparvan*, we read that Cyavana (described as the 'great Bhārgava *ṛṣi*') engages in the discipline of living with his body submerged in water (Mbh. 13.50.3). He enters the river at its most turbulent point, where the Gaṅgā meets the Yamunā, and he stays there in the midst of that current for twelve years (v. 4) without moving: sometimes he lies down, sometimes he stands up, but otherwise he is as motionless as a log of wood (*sthāṇubhūta*, v. 6; *kāṣṭhabhūta*, v. 9). One day, his body becomes entangled in a fisherman's net and he is dragged up to the surface. To the astonishment of the assembled fishermen, Cyavana emerges from the water completely overgrown by aquatic life: he is plastered in duckweed, his beard and hair have turned a greenish-yellow colour and he is covered in clinging masses of hard-shelled molluscs (Mbh. 13.50.19).[43] In the epic context, the point of the story is the fear experienced by the fishermen and their desire to avoid the ascetic's powerful curse. For our purposes, the story constitutes a remarkable example of the *tapas* of immobility taken to such an extreme that the ascetic in question becomes incorporated by the natural world.

The second episode involving Cyavana constitutes the earliest textual example of the motif of the ascetic in the termite mound. In the *Āraṇyakaparvan*, the incident is narrated as a significant detail in the much longer story of a conflict of

Black Drongo (*Dicrurus adsimilis*, familiarly known as the 'king crow') on account of its pugnacious attitude to other, even larger, birds (Dave 1985: 63; Ali and Ripley 1983: 353ff., #963, Plate 61.5). Dave does not refer to this episode directly. Despite John Brockington's more recent identification of this bird as *Dicrurus paradiseus L.*, the Racket-Tailed Drongo (1998: 196), in the absence of any mention of crests or especially long tails we may reasonably accept that Jājali's birds are Black Drongos. Certainly, the descriptive evidence fits: the preference for an exposed look-out post for hunting, the habit of nesting between 4 and 12 metres from the ground in or on a tree standing by itself in the open, the use of grass and other materials to fix the nest to its 'substrate', and the fact that both sexes take part in nest-building. Later in the episode, the word *caṭaka* is used to denote the same birds (vv. 41, 50). While this term is often taken to mean 'sparrow', it can also (as in this case) denote any smallish noisy bird (Dave 1985: 92–3); this is a further indication that the bird in question is the smaller Black Drongo and not the more impressive long-tailed variety.

42 For an English translation of the full story, see Ganguli (1970: III, Santi Parvan part 2, pp. 230–33; that is, in section 241).

43 The complete episode may be found in chapters 50–1; for an English translation, see Ganguli (1970: IV, Anusasana Parvan part 2, sections 50–1, pp. 38–42). In his analysis of this incident, Goldman implies incorrectly that Cyavana immerses himself in the sea rather than in a river (1977: 50 n. 1).

wills between Indra, king of the gods, and Cyavana, a conflict which resulted in Indra agreeing to allow the Aśvins to drink *soma* (Mbh. 3.121–5).[44] The elderly Bhārgava has been given as his wife the young and beautiful princess, Sukanyā. In the hope of persuading her to choose one of them as her husband instead, the Aśvins use their healing powers to rejuvenate the old man. In a Nala-like episode, Sukanyā has to choose between the three, now identical, young men. She chooses Cyavana who then rewards the Aśvins for his new-found youth and beauty with the promise that he will force Indra to let them share in the *soma* sacrifice.[45] The part of the story that we are interested in comes before all this.

The termite-mound episode explains how the old ascetic came to be given so young and beautiful a wife in the first place. Chapter 122 begins by declaring that Cyavana Bhārgava is the son of the great *ṛṣi*, Bhṛgu (v. 1). One day, he is practising austerities (*tapas*) beside a lake near the river Narmadā. (Another distinction between termite mounds and anthills is that the former are often found near water.) The particular form of Cyavana's practice is precisely described: he stands there without moving in the so-called 'heroic' posture (*vīrasthāna*), as still and rigid as the stump of a tree or a wooden post (*sthāṇubhūta*), and he stays there in that one spot (*eke deśe*) for a long time (v. 2). In fact, he remains in that position for so long that he 'becomes' a termite mound (*sa valmīko 'bhavad*), a mound which itself becomes hidden from view because of the creepers growing up over it, a mound completely covered with termites (v. 3).[46] This is the non-obstruction of nature with a vengeance. By not moving, Cyavana allows his body to be overgrown by a termite mound which in turn becomes overgrown with creepers, until he resembles nothing more than a great lump of earth from all sides (*mṛtpiṇḍa iva sarvaśaḥ*), the whole thing crawling with termites. He continues to stand like this, his body completely enclosed by the termite mound (*valmīkena samāvṛtaḥ*, v. 4), motionless, doing *tapas*.

The next part of the story demonstrates an important point. Immobility on the part of an ascetic like Cyavana does not constitute a lack of awareness of his surroundings. On the contrary, all these 'wooden posts' are fully aware of what is going on around them. I still remember the bright eyes of His Holiness Śrī Candraśekharendrasarasvatī glowing at me in the dark recesses of his cart as I paid him homage twenty years ago. Certainly, Jājali knows exactly when the drongos have no further need of the nest they have constructed on his head (Mbh. 12.253.37). Cyavana too, standing there inside his termite mound with only his eyes showing, knows perfectly well what is going on. He sees the beautiful princess come to the lakeside spot with her friends. When the friends drift

---

44 For English translations of this episode, see van Buitenen (1975: 458–61) and Goldman (1977: 50–9).

45 An early source for the story of the Aśvins can be found in *Ṛgveda* 1.116.10, where they are credited with stripping the skin off Cyavana's body, extending his life span and making him the husband of young girls. For an English translation, see Griffith (1973: 77). For a detailed analysis of the early development of the story of Cyavana and the Aśvins, see Witzel (1987). The story of Cyavana is also a favourite theme in the work of Wendy Doniger [O'Flaherty] (1973, 1985, 1999).

46 The term used here, *pipīlika*, usually means 'ant'. In this context, however, the word must be taken to denote the termites visible on and around the termite mound.

away, he continues to watch her, admiring her beauty, falling in love. He even tries to speak to her but his parched throat means that she cannot hear him.[47] But then she spots his eyes shining in the side of the termite mound. Inquisitively, thinking they are some kind of creature that gives out light (as she explains later, v. 19), she takes a sharp stick or thorn (v. 12) and pokes him in the eye (v. 13).[48] This is strongly reminiscent of the spikes-in-the-ears motif examined earlier in relation to both the Jain Mahāvīra and the Bodhisattva Gautama. Like those protagonists, Cyavana does not move; unlike them, he becomes angry. He is unwilling to harm the beautiful Sukanyā who did not intend to hurt him, so he uses his ascetic powers to alert the king: he prevents the royal troops from relieving themselves, both bladder and bowel (vv. 13–14). Mass constipation among his men soon makes the king realize that someone has upset the irascible (if not yet apparent) Cyavana, and the truth is out. The two kinds of asceticism displayed in the Śamīka and Śṛṅgin narrative, as discussed above, are both present to some extent in this story. Śamīka's refusal to react is reflected in Cyavana's continued immobility. Śṛṅgin's irascible nature is paralleled in Cyavana's, the former's angry curse in the latter's instinctive desire to take revenge on someone. For our purposes, however, the crucial point here is that this is the earliest textual evidence of the motif of the ascetic in the termite mound, and it has nothing whatever to do with Vālmīki.

We may note in parentheses that, without the termite-mound motif, this story is far older than the epic context in which we find it. In the *Śatapatha Brāhmaṇa* (4.1.5.1ff.), for example, the king's sons torment the 'decrepit and ghostlike' ascetic (Cyavana) by throwing clods of earth at him, yet further evidence that tormenting ascetics is an old Indic theme (Eggeling 1885: 1–2; cf. Witzel 1987: 382). Here and in the *Taittirīya Saṃhitā* (6.4.9.1ff.), the issue is whether or not the Aśvins (and, by extension, all human healers and doctors) are fit to participate in the *soma* sacrifice. In the field of *rasāyana* ('rejuvenation', one of the eight traditional branches of *āyurveda*), by contrast, the point of the story is the

47 Simon Brodbeck's response to all this is to wonder whether these descriptions of immobility reflect some kind of 'shamanic, drug-assisted practice'. The fact that the protagonist can see and hear what is going on around him but is unable (rather than unwilling) to move or speak may suggest the use of a substance that disables the motor functions without affecting one's consciousness. As Brodbeck remarks, 'the weirdness of this experience would quickly acquire religious ramifications' and, if one were to die before the drug wore off, one would have 'a first-class ticket ... into the glorious beyond'. There is also the graphic identification of *karman* (usually translated 'action' in the sense of a deliberate undertaking) with bodily movement of any kind. Finally, the frequent tales of ascetics being tortured by cowherds may be linked with the expansion of pastoralists into land already occupied by hunter-gatherer tribes, with the 'ascetic' or shaman symbolizing the tribal communities being displaced. In this context, the constant theme of the ascetic's curse would indicate that the advance of the pastoralists was not unopposed (personal communication, 8 June 2002). This is of particular interest in view of the contemporary portrayal of Vālmīki as belonging to an early tribal (*ādi*) people.

48 According to the account in the *Devībhāgavata Purāṇa* (7.2–7), Sukanyā blinds Cyavana deliberately, that is, despite his verbal warning (cited in Tagare 1976: part 3, p. 1134 n. 1).

rejuvenation of Cyavana by means of a special formula, the *cyavana-prāśa*. According to Mukhopadhyaya, this formula is 'still much used' in India today (1922–29: vol. 2, p. 258). Indeed, Cohen discusses what he calls the 'ubiquitous Chyawanprash' preparation in the treatment for ageing in India (1998: 109–13, 131–3). *Soma* is used in rejuvenation rituals within the context of *āyurveda* too (Wujastyk 2001: 119–21). As we shall see in chapter 5, the idea of a splendid rebirth, of being reborn in a particularly radiant form, applies to all these contexts, including that of the ascetic in the termite mound. The Cyavana story, with and without the termite-mound motif, continues to reappear in the Purāṇas in various forms.[49] For example, book 5 of the *Skanda Purāṇa* contains both a brief allusion to the story and a longer narrative. The former does not refer directly to the termite-mound incident. Instead, there is a description of a sacred place called 'Cyavana's hermitage' (or 'ashram', *cyavanāśrama*) where Śiva may be worshipped in the form of Cyavaneśvara. This *tīrtha* is said to mark the spot where Cyavana attained perfection (*siddhi*), and where he regained his sight thanks to the healing power of the Aśvins. Anyone who bathes at that place will therefore attain divine vision (5.1.56.61–4). The second telling includes the termite-mound incident but, like the epic version, it does not tell us explicitly that Cyavana was blinded by Sukanyā. What it does tell us is that Cyavana worshipped Śiva in order to have the power to make Indra allow the Aśvins to drink the *soma* (5.2.30.1–58). In both cases, an ancient story is retold in a devotional context and with an entirely different emphasis.

It is clear that termite-mound asceticism has long been associated with Cyavana, but it is not peculiar to him. The theme is in fact characteristic of Indian ascetic practice in general, as was well known to early Buddhists. In the second century, for example, in Aśvaghoṣa's *Buddhacarita*, the different kinds of Indian ascetics are described for the benefit of the Bodhisattva (7.14–18). The list includes those who peck from the ground like birds, those who graze on grass like deer, those who live with the fishes underwater, and so on. Among these extreme groups are those who, 'having become termite mounds' (*valmīkabhūtā*), live on air (literally, 'on the forest wind', *vanamārutena*) with the snakes (*bhujaṅgaiḥ saha vartayanti*, v.15). Johnston's critical apparatus offers the reading preferred by Cowell: *valmīkibhūtā iva mārutena* (1936: I, 70; cf. Cowell 1894: II, 56). In the context of termite-mound asceticism, my translation is unproblematic. Johnston, however, is unaware of that context and argues for a different scenario. His translation reads: 'and others pass their time with the snakes, turned into anthills by the forest wind'. His explanation is unnecessarily complex: 'the wind piles up earth round the motionless ascetics lying on the ground, turning them into anthills, and thus giving them an additional resemblance to snakes who are often mentioned as living in anthills' (II, p. 95 n. 15). In fact, what we have here is a straightforward allusion to the ascetic practice of remaining in an upright standing posture, without moving or eating, until the practitioner is enclosed within (or, at least, looks like) a termite mound. At this point he is often actually mistaken for a termite mound, which might explain the

---

49 For a translation of the version found in *Bhāgavata Purāṇa* 9.3, see Tagare (1976: part 3, pp. 1134–8).

allocation of the honorific term (*valmīka* or *vālmīki*) to commemorate what he has done. The mention of snakes is yet another indication that the mounds associated with ascetics are made by termites, not ants. The ventilation shafts which are so ideal for snakes are found in termite mounds but not in anthills which are therefore never occupied by snakes (see König 1984: 210–35).

The Bodhisattva is unimpressed by all this; he is heading for the middle path. By contrast, the Jain tradition provides its own celebrated example: Bāhubali, also known as Gomata or Gomateśvara. Bhārata and Bāhubali were the oldest and the youngest sons respectively of Ṛṣabha, once a king and subsequently the first Jain Tīrthaṅkara of the current era. To cut a long story short, when their father abdicates in order to take up the renunciate's life, the two brothers fight for his throne. Bāhubali wins, and then he too renounces the throne in favour of the ascetic path. He is said to have stood upright in meditation – motionless, naked, silent and without food or drink – for so long that creepers entwined themselves around his legs and arms, birds nested in his beard,[50] wild animals rested amicably together at his feet, and snake-inhabited termite mounds rose up around his legs. The termite mound enclosing but not obscuring Bāhubali's feet and legs is especially clear in the immense tenth-century image at Śravana-belagola in the state of Karnataka.[51]

We find the termite-mound motif associated with other individuals in the Hindu Purāṇas too. According to *Padma Purāṇa* 2.61, for example, a brahmin ascetic named Pippalāda performs *tapas* out in the open, enduring all weather conditions, for three thousand years. His immobility – likened to a stone, to a log of wood, to a mountain, to a post – enables a great termite mound to grow up over him. He remains motionless inside it, despite being repeatedly bitten by the snakes living in there with him.[52] Another example is provided by the *asura* Hiraṇyakaśipu. He chooses this form of *tapas* in order to challenge the power of the gods, and he too finds himself encased in the termite's clay mound, physical proof of his success (*Bhāgavata Purāṇa* 7.3.17–23).

The motif even turns up in Indian Sufism, albeit with a twist that mocks the gullible Hindu. According to a twentieth-century narrative, the famous Sufi saint Shāh Nūr meditated for so long that he became completely covered by a termite mound. The mound was worshipped by local Hindus who believed that it housed

---

50 This detail is provided by Nagar (1999: 427) but I have yet to find a textual reference for it.

51 For a brief account of the tussle for power between the brothers before Bāhubali's renunciation, and for representations of the latter's posture of immobility, see Titze (1998: 7–11 *et passim*) and Nagar (1999: 425–7, black-and-white Plates 116–20; for a similar motif identified as Ṛṣabha, see Plates 25, 29). For a translation of the earliest extant account of the story of Bhārata and Bāhubali taken from the *Ādipurāṇa*, a ninth-century Jain text composed in Sanskrit by Jinasena, see Strohl (1990; for details of Bāhubali's ascetic practice, see pp. 237–43).

52 For a translation of this episode, see Deshpande (1990a: part 3, pp. 1125–9). In this late Purāṇa context, the story is told in order to demonstrate that devotion in the form of caring for one's parents brings greater merit than even extreme forms of ascetic practice like this.

a deity.[53] For a while, the locals quarrelled about the identity of the mound's occupant; when the saint eventually emerged, all the Hindus converted to Islam (Green 2002: 224ff.). This is an intriguing story for at least two reasons: the shared termite-mound motif, and the Sufi saint whose name recalls the Bhagwan Valmik shrines named 'Bāla Shāh'. We may note in particular the Sufi shrine's mixed Hindu–Muslim clientele, and the suggestion that the ignorant 'Hindus' in the story represent 'the topos of the uncultured tribal' (p. 227), one more link in the *ādi* chain of meaning. Finally, Green's comments regarding oral narratives as a rich source of pre-modern discourse ('the memory of the saints, shored-up by shrine, narrative and cult', p. 233) suggest that the Valmiki traditions regarding 'Bāla Shāh' deserve much closer examination.[54] In the context of the termite-mound motif, however, my point is that the idea of someone remaining motionless for so long that a termite mound grows up around him is widespread, whether that someone is a Hindu ascetic doing *tapas*, a Jain monk meditating, or a Sufi saint thinking of God. The story may well have begun with Cyavana, but it soon became a pan-Indian motif. This means that it was never restricted to, or even primarily evocative of, the *Rāmāyaṇa* poet Vālmīki.

We may now return to the Bhārgava question alluded to earlier. Why is Vālmīki so often referred to as a 'Bhārgava', a 'descendant of Bhṛgu'? The answer almost certainly lies in the workings of popular etymology, that is, by the gradual association of Cyavana's termite-mound story with the poet Vālmīki's name. According to Goldman (1977: 79–80), the 'oldest attested Bhārgava myth' is the conflict between Indra and Cyavana, described above. At the time of the reshaping of the epic at the hands of the Bhārgavas, due to the increased interest in *tapas* generally, the termite-mound motif (which was probably older still) became associated with one of the greatest Bhārgavas, Cyavana. Its purpose in this context was no doubt to increase yet further the fame of a man already renowned for his ascetic practices. As we have seen, the termite-mound story represents the epitome of the *tapasvin*. Such an ascetic lives for years beyond human habitation, neither eating nor drinking, remaining constantly aware yet motionless. The heat (*tapas*) of renunciation, of voluntary suffering, gives rise to a purifying inner power that burns away the impurities of human existence. When the ascetic emerges from the termite mound, the fragile clay outer 'body' disintegrates, and he is reborn as a purified higher being. So important is this story as the marker of supreme asceticism that it becomes associated with Bhṛgu himself.[55] At some point, as will become explicit in section 3, this powerful motif also became associated with the *Rāmāyaṇa* poet, Vālmīki.

53 For other tales of deities residing in termite mounds, see König (1984: 272–6).

53 For oral traditions relating to Shāh Nūr, whose devotees are said to have included Awrangzeb himself, see Green (2002: chapter 5). The historical Shāh Nūr Hammāmī (literally, 'he of the bath-house') died in 1692; a more modern version of his name is 'Hamāwī'. He was probably from north-east India (Pūrāb), and came to Awrangabad around the time of its re-foundation by Awrangzeb in 1681 (Nile Green, personal communication, 16 May 2002). For termite-mound imagery in Sufi tales from the Tamil south, see Bayly (1989: 122–3; cited in Green 2002: 208 n. 19).

55 For details of the Bhṛgu family according to the various Purāṇas, including this particular story taken from *Padma Purāṇa* 20, see Mani (1975: 139–41).

The process of conflation is clear. According to the evidence gathered in chapter 3, the name 'Vālmīki' existed first, independent of the later legend. What I have called 'termite-mound asceticism' came next, associated in the earliest recorded instance with Cyavana. But while Cyavana evidently 'became a termite mound' (*sa valmīko 'bhavad*), he was never called 'Vālmīki'. This suggests that the process of popular etymology came third: the term *vālmīki* ('derived from' or, better still, 'born of the termite mound') became an honorary epithet, a mark of respect to the greatest ascetics. Termite-mound asceticism emerged as the marker *par excellence* of extreme *tapas*, hence its appearance in relation to saints and ascetics in a range of religious traditions. The fact that both Cyavana and Vālmīki were renowned ascetic *ṛṣi*s facilitated the building of further connections between the two men. The parallels already noted are striking, even in the detail. Yet another parallel is that both men are celebrated for performing a 'truth act',[56] that is, for making a formulaic declaration that they have never told a lie. In each case, the great man swears a public oath on his truthfulness before saying something that he wants his audience to believe. Cyavana's oath reads: 'Just as [it is true that] I have never spoken falsely [or in vain], so … '.[57] While truth acts are archetypical in epic and Purāṇic narratives, the parallels between Cyavana and Vālmīki are particularly telling. At some point, the similarities between the two men must have been so persuasive that the combination of Cyavana's termite-mound story and the popular etymology for Vālmīki's name eventually led to the assumption that the ascetic Cyavana and the poet-ascetic Vālmīki were related. Hence we find Aśvaghoṣa's remark, noted earlier, that Vālmīki had made an even greater contribution than his renowned ancestor, Cyavana. It was no doubt in honour of that perceived relationship that Vālmīki was given the name 'Bhārgava', which properly belongs to Cyavana. In the fourth phase, the termite-mound incident was probably borrowed from Cyavana, Vālmīki's supposed relative, and used for the construction of the Vālmīki legend in such a way that the name became the resulting title. In the fifth and final phase, the termite-mound story was attributed directly to 'our' Vālmīki, but with a somewhat different purpose. In view of the next development in the legend, this change of focus is important.

3. The Sinner Redeemed

The point of the Vālmīki legend is that the protagonist was once a wicked person who had a transformative experience, after which he was supremely good. As a general theme, this one is common to most religious traditions. The best-known Christian example is that of Saul of Tarsus. Others include Saint Augustine and Luther, each of whom presented himself as a great sinner until he 'saw the light',

---

56 The Sanskrit term for 'truth act' (*satyakriyā*) may be traced back to the *Ṛgveda* where its role is essentially magical (Thompson 1998).

57 *na vṛthā vyāhṛtaṃ pūrvaṃ yan mayā* ... (Mbh. 13.53.54). For Vālmīki's declaration, see Rām. 7.87.17 and variant readings in the critical apparatus of the Baroda edition, as discussed briefly in chapter 3.

hence the former's 'confessions'. Luther's transformation was said to have taken place when he 'met' Jesus in a vision. For the early Christians, Saul was the epitome of evil, for he went out of his way to persecute believers until, in one transformative moment, he was blinded by the truth on the road to Damascus. The fullest account occurs in Acts 9 of the New Testament (see also 22.1–16 and 16.4–18). Before his conversion, Saul repeatedly threatens the disciples of Jesus with death (v. 1); even after his conversion, he continues to be known as the man who arrests believers and has them killed (v. 21).[58] This is the villain who becomes Saint Paul, the paradigm of instantaneous conversion in the Christian tradition. For the psychologist William James, Saint Paul is a pivotal figure. For example, James understands the classic Christian distinction between the 'once-born' and the 'twice-born' in terms of 'healthy-mindedness' (epitomized by Walt Whitman, for whom life is and always was wonderful) and the 'sick soul'. The latter, epitomized by Saul of Tarsus, must repent and be born again (1982: 80–7 *et passim*).[59] While the interpretation given to the second birth varies with the religious tradition, the parallels remain.

A Buddhist example may be found in the *Avadānaśataka*. According to this compendium of legends and oral traditions, Aśoka too was a murdering brute before he became the ideal Buddhist ruler.[60] But the best-known Buddhist parallel is provided by the story of Aṅgulimāla (literally, 'Finger-Necklace'). Like some versions of the Vālmīki legend, Aṅgulimāla was born into a brahmin family, the son of the royal priest. As a result of the jealousy of his fellow students, he left his teacher and became a dacoit. He earned his name from his notorious habit of severing his murdered victims' fingers and wearing them on a thread around his neck. But one day the Buddha came his way. That was the transformative moment for Aṅgulimāla: he realized the error of his ways, took his vows, and in time came to be revered as the perfect Buddhist monk. Gombrich presents an imaginative analysis of this episode as evidence of Tantric practice in the early Buddhist period (1996). His discussion is based on two accounts in the Pali Canon (*Theragāthā* 866–91 and the *Aṅgulimāla Sutta*, see *Majjima Nikāya* II, 97–105) and two commentaries (the *Papañcasūdanī* ascribed to Buddhaghoṣa, and the *Paramatthadīpanī* ascribed to Dhammapāla). The Amar Chitra Katha version of the story, which offers remarkable echoes of the Vālmīki legend, is described as an 'adaptation' from the *Paramatthadīpanī* (Pai 2000). For Gombrich, Aṅgulimāla's violence serves to fulfil a Tantric *vrata*; for Pai, and for the popular Buddhist tradition, it has the robber's more prosaic goal of material gain. Finally, in a further parallel with both Vālmīki and Cyavana, Aṅgulimāla too performs a truth act (Gombrich 1996: 136).

In all three traditions, a callous villain – either himself a murderer or responsible through others for the deaths of his victims – undergoes a transformative

58 For further discussion and illustrations, see Karen Armstrong (1983: 40–66) and Porter (1995: 226–7).

59 I am grateful to Paul Gifford for reminding me of William James's work.

60 This popular view is supported by the recent Bollywood film, *Ashoka*. The film focuses on Aśoka's early, pre-Buddhist life and culminates in the bloody battle against the Kaliṅgans.

experience. The sinner is redeemed. In time he becomes not merely good but a saint. Clearly, this motif is not peculiar to the Indian traditions. Within India, it is not even specific to Vālmīki. For example, it is said that the Maharashtrian *bhakti* poet, Nāmdev, was once a dacoit too. On one occasion, we are told, he slaughtered eighty-four horsemen. His transformative moment came when, on visiting a temple, he overheard a woman rebuking her hungry child for crying. On enquiring further, Nāmdev learned that, because he had murdered the woman's husband, she was now a widow, the child was an orphan, and they were both starving. Nāmdev instantly abandoned his wicked ways: he went to Pandharpur to take up the life of a saint for which he has been revered ever since.[61] My concern in this section is to examine – as far as is possible with largely undateable texts – the gradual accumulation of the elements of this motif around the figure of the author of the *Vālmīki Rāmāyaṇa*. In order to do this, we need to pick up the thread from section 2.

Perhaps the earliest reference to the termite-mound story in relation to the name 'Vālmīki' occurs in the *Skanda Purāṇa*.[62] As one might expect of the Purāṇas generally, however, the context and thrust of the story have changed. In the epic versions of the Cyavana story, the stress is placed squarely on the ascetic context. The practitioner is already an ascetic; he embarks on the *tapas* of immobility in order to attain power; he achieves this goal by means of renunciation, physical suffering and the consequent burning away of impurities. As a result, the ascetic is reborn as a purified and more powerful being. The Purāṇic versions tend to be strikingly different: both context and emphasis have shifted towards devotionalism. The protagonist is no longer an ascetic but a sinner of one form or another: a hunter, a robber, a dacoit. In the course of the story, he attains not the perfection of the autonomous ascetic but the redemption from sin that is acquired by the grace of God in response to an act of devotion. The key elements here are: *bhakti*, divine grace, and redemption.

As indicated earlier, there are references to Vālmīki, even to the Vālmīki legend, in several Purāṇas. Here, however, my primary focus will be on the *Skanda Purāṇa* because it contains four separate tellings of the story, which may be deemed to reflect some of the steps in the construction of the Vālmīki legend. But first we need to understand something of the complexity of the text in question.

The *Skanda Purāṇa* was once widely known in north India where, until about the thirteenth century CE, it was regarded as authoritative. However, a distinction must be made at the outset between this title and the text it supposedly denotes. Hazra, writing in 1940, bases his overview of the text on the two printed editions then available: the 1910 Bombay edition (Veṅkateśvara Press) and the 1911 Calcutta edition (Vaṅgavāsī Press), the latter being a deliberate enlargement of the former. But these editions prove to be little more than 'collections of *khaṇḍa*s'; there are no extant manuscripts to match either printed text (Adriaensen, Bakker and Isaacson 1994: 325). Dating these collections is

61 For further details of this story, see Ranade (1983: 186). I am grateful to Susan Prill for bringing this story to my attention.

62 For references in the *Skanda Purāṇa* to the Rāma story, see Raghavan (1973: 40–3).

haphazard. For example, after a brief discussion of passages which he considers to be earlier than 1300 (or 1200 or 1050), Hazra declares that there is little in the printed vulgate which can be dated before 700 CE (1975: 157–66). Later scholars such as Bulcke place most of the text in the ninth century CE at the earliest, while admitting that 'much of its material belongs to a later date' (1958: 126). Over thirty years later, Tagare revisits the issue at the start of his projected nineteen-volume English translation based on both printed texts and manuscripts. He locates 'the last redaction' of the *Skanda Purāṇa* somewhere between the seventh and the ninth century CE, with numerous later interpolations (1992: lx–lxi).

The discovery of an incomplete Nepalese palm-leaf manuscript dated 810 CE has brought greater clarity. It is described by Adriaensen *et al.* as 'the oldest dated Nepalese manuscript known to us, and probably the oldest surviving manuscript of a Purāṇic text' (1994: 326). Based largely on this manuscript, Kṛṣṇa Prasāda Bhaṭṭarāī's edition was published in 1988, entitled *Skanda-purāṇasya Ambikākhaṇḍaḥ*.[63] A team of scholars at the University of Groningen is currently engaged on the critical edition of the 'oldest extant text that calls itself Skandapurāṇa' (Bakker 1996: 5).[64] The Groningen project reflects several recensions. All three of the manuscripts belonging to the oldest recension (including the Nepalese one mentioned above) bear the colophon title *Skanda Purāṇa*, and not one of them is divided into *khaṇḍa*s. The single manuscript of the second (later) recension bears the colophon title *Revākhaṇḍa* of the *Skanda Purāṇa*. Finally, four manuscripts of the third (latest) recension bear the colophon title *Ambikākhaṇḍa* of the *Skanda Purāṇa*. The title of Bhaṭṭarāī's edition thus indicates the use of a manuscript from this third recension. All these manuscripts contain a text considerably shorter than that of the printed vulgate. As a result of their work so far, Adriaensen *et al.* suggest a tentative date for the 'core text' of between the sixth and eighth centuries CE. In their view, it is 'very improbable that the text could have arisen earlier than ca. AD 500'. They therefore situate it 'tentatively' in the seventh or eighth centuries (1994: 328), later adjusting that estimate to 'between the sixth and eighth' centuries (1998: 5). Evidence for a possible sixth-century origin is provided by Yokochi (1999). All these early recensions are associated with the north-east: with Nepal in the case of the palm-leaf manuscript, with Bengal in the case of the *Revākhaṇḍa* and the *Ambikākhaṇḍa* (Adriaensen *et al.* 1998: 18). It was in the twelfth century, according to the editors of the Groningen project, that 'the practice of calling newly composed texts *khaṇḍas* of the *Skandapurāṇa* might have started' (1994: 326). Until the end of the twelfth century, the *Skanda Purāṇa* was probably known in northern India in forms relating to these three recensions. Subsequently, more and more texts appeared in the guise of *khaṇḍa*s of the *Skanda Purāṇa*. As these became more widespread and prominent, the 'original' (that is, the earliest attested) recension appears to have dropped out of sight, even in the north-east of India (1998: 18). By perhaps the thirteenth century, certainly by the

63 I am indebted to Albrecht Wezler for kindly sending me a copy of this text.

64 For further information on the Groningen project and on the first completed volume, see Adriaensen *et al.* (1994, 1998), Bakker (1996, 2000) and Yokochi (1999, 2000).

fourteenth, few people would have known for certain what material belonged in the text called the 'Skanda Purāṇa' (1998: 6).

If these preliminary investigations prove to be correct, then the early accounts of the Vālmīki legend discussed in this section are all late developments. Unfortunately, until we have critical editions of the mass of *dharma* texts that cite the relevant passages from the *Skanda Purāṇa*, it is impossible to be more precise. These early versions of the legend belong to the 'collections of *khaṇḍa*s' compiled well after the ninth century, probably after the twelfth, possibly later still.[65] The important point for our purposes, however, is that the printed vulgate text of the *Skanda Purāṇa* provides four different accounts of the story. Each of these makes a direct, but not especially persuasive, link to the author of the *Vālmīki Rāmāyaṇa*. Basing my comments on the Veṅkateśvara Press edition, I shall consider each account in turn, in narrative order, in the hope of teasing out some of the mechanics in the evolution of the Vālmīki legend.

The ostensible aim of the *Skanda Purāṇa* is to recount the life of Skanda. The result is a collection of stories that glorify both Skanda and his parents, Śiva and Devī. As the editors of the Groningen project put it, the text is 'entirely permeated by ascetic and yogic values' (Adriaensen *et al.* 1994: 327). As is typical of a Purāṇa, however, portions of the text are devoted to Viṣṇu too. The first version of the Vālmīki story occurs in one such portion: in book 2 (the *Vaiṣṇavakhaṇḍa*), section 7 (the *Vaiśākhamāsa-māhātmya*), chapters 17–21.[66] According to the Groningen team, the *Vaiṣṇavakhaṇḍa* of the printed *Skanda Purāṇa* was probably composed at the end of the thirteenth or the beginning of the fourteenth century, and may have been the work of one editor.[67] Section 7 functions as an independent work in praise of the month of Vaiśākha so beloved of Viṣṇu. Several stories are told to illustrate the general point that merit obtained during this period is deemed of special significance. For our purposes, we should note at the outset the highly devotional context. The story we are interested in begins in chapter 17. When a pious brahmin named Śaṅkha enters the forest, an unnamed hunter (*vyādha*) robs him of everything he owns, including his sandals. Here, we should note the appearance of the paradigmatic sinner: hunting in the forest marks him as a tribesman, as a dacoit he is evil, and the text tells us he looks like the god of death. Watching Śaṅkha's progress after the robbery, however, this hunter is moved by the brahmin's physical distress and subsequently returns his sandals to him. Śaṅkha blesses him for this, referring to the special merit his action has acquired because it was performed in the month of Vaiśākha. Startled by this response, the hunter asks for religious instruction. Eventually, he lays down his weapons and asks Śaṅkha to explain both his current birth as a low-caste hunter and his therefore supposedly inappropriate interest in *dharma* (2.7.18.35–6). Śaṅkha's answer is long and complicated. In brief, the hunter's previous life (as a brahmin named Stambha) was selfish and empty of religion: despite the attentions

65 A search of the Bhaṭṭarāī edition yields no evidence of the Vālmīki legend (Hans Bakker, personal communication, 19 January 2002).

66 For an English translation of this first account, see Tagare (1995: part 7, pp. 106–11).

67 See Bakker (1986: part 1, pp. 129, 130 n. 1) and Adriaensen *et al.* (1998: 14–15).

of his devoted wife, he died thinking of a prostitute on whom he had wasted his attentions. Since he had a natural inclination for violence and was always causing trouble, he was reborn as a terrifying (*ghorarūpa*, v. 76) hunter. Thanks to his wife's devotions on his behalf, however, he retained a small interest in religious matters. After further instruction and additional storytelling, we come to the crux of the story. When it is time for Śaṅkha to leave, the brahmin gives the hunter a mantra to recite: the two-syllable name of God, *rā-ma* (2.7.21.53). The brahmin explains that reciting the name of Rāma brings the same benefits as reciting all the thousand names of Viṣṇu. If the hunter recites this one mantra for the rest of that lifetime, he will be reborn in the family of a *ṛṣi* called 'Termite Mound' (*valmīka*), and he himself will attain great fame under the name 'Son-of-Termite-Mound' (*vālmīki*, v. 56). Interestingly, the wicked person in this version of the story is not the individual who is later named 'Vālmīki' but one of his forebears.

Here, we should note the devotional motif of reciting the name of God. Regardless of the other details provided in different versions of the story, the key theme is always the extraordinary power unleashed by reciting Rāma's name. We should not be surprised, therefore, to discover that an incomplete manuscript of the Vālmīki legend, listed as part of the *Jaiminīya Rāmāyaṇa*, offers an alternative name in the colophon: the *Rāma-nāma-māhātmya*, or 'In praise of the name of Rāma'.[68] This is the point of the story. According to the *Padma Purāṇa*, if one is unable to recite the thousand names of Viṣṇu, then it is enough to recite the single name of Rāma. The verse in question (*Uttarakhaṇḍa* 72.135) literally resonates with his holy name:

> *rāma rāmeti rāmeti rāma rāma manorāma /*
> *sahasranāma tat tulyaṃ rāma nāma varānane //*

This verse is still recited at the end of the *Viṣṇusahasranāmastotra* today. In the various versions of the Vālmīki legend, then, the power of Rāma's name is responsible for the salvation of the sinner.[69]

In this first account, the story reaches its conclusion by jumping forward in time to tell us about the hunter's father in his next life, a *ṛṣi* called Kṛṇu. This takes us straight back to the epic context of ascetic practice, discussed in section 2. As we might expect, the practice in question is the immobility technique. Kṛṇu performs this extreme act of *tapas* for so long that a termite mound grows up over his body. In fact, it appears as if he has turned into a termite mound, so much so that when he finally emerges from within it, people begin to call him 'Termite Mound' (*valmīka*).[70] In terms of the five phases in the development of the Vālmīki legend, outlined at the end of section 2, this story represents the fourth phase. But the story goes on. Once more in the world and now thinking about women, Kṛṇu ejaculates. An actress (or dancer, *śailuṣī*) seizes his seed and,

68 The manuscript is in the Madras Government Oriental Manuscripts Library (Raghavan 1973: 68 n. 1).

69 This constitutes another powerful reason for the Valmikis' dislike of the legend: it places Rāma, a mere human being, above Bhagwan Valmik.

70 *vālmīkam abhavad dehe tasya kālena bhūyasā / valmīka iti taṃ prāhur ato vai munipuṃgavam // Skanda Purāṇa* 2.7.21.65.

as foretold, the hunter is reborn as Kṛṇu-the-Termite-Mound's son. He is therefore called 'Son-of-Termite-Mound', that is, 'Vālmīki' (v. 67). Here, the father's honorific title becomes a patronymic, apparently taken by his son as a personal name. We are then told that 'Son-of-Termite-Mound' goes on to compose the 'divine Rāma story' (*rāmakathāṃ divyām*, v. 68). Here we have a compromise of sorts between phase four (in which 'Vālmīka' is an honorific) and phase five (in which a direct link is made with the author of the *Vālmīki Rāmāyaṇa*). In the *Skanda Purāṇa*, the point of the story is that extraordinary benefits may be obtained in the month of Vaiśākha through devotion to Viṣṇu. Because of his devotion at that particular time, the hunter is reborn as the son of an ascetic brahmin *ṛṣi*. Here, rebirth is seen as an effective way of linking the epic theme of the protagonist-as-ascetic to the *bhakti* theme of the protagonist-as-sinner, except that the hunter is reborn not as the ascetic himself but as the ascetic's son. According to this account, it is the son who eventually writes the *Rāmāyaṇa*, on the strength of his devotion in his previous life; that is, his poetic achievement has nothing to do with his own ascetic practice. The last link in the chain is awkward: the ascetic who is honoured with the name 'Termite Mound' ('Valmīka') is the father of the ex-sinner who writes the *Rāmāyaṇa*. In fact, the entire chain of events seems awkward. Perhaps what we have here is really rather simple: the ancient stereotype of the ascetic doing *tapas* within a termite mound, combined with the increasing likelihood that people referred to such ascetics by the honorific 'Termite Mound' ('Valmīka'), leading to the simple association of 'Valmīka' with 'Vālmīki', the similarly named poet of the *Rāmāyaṇa*. The train of thought seems transparent in the retelling.

The second account occurs in book 5 (the *Āvantyakhaṇḍa*), section 1 (the *Avantīkṣetra-māhātmya*), chapter 24.[71] The devotional context here relates to Śiva not Viṣṇu: the story is told as one of many explanations for the construction of a *śivaliṅga* in a sacred place of pilgrimage (*tīrtha*). In this particular case, both *liṅga* and *tīrtha* are named 'Vālmīkeśvara' ('Lord of the one who was born from the termite mound'), hence the need to explain why Śiva should be worshipped here in this form. The story begins with a good brahmin couple, Sumati and his wife Kauśikī, and their son Agniśarmā. Despite the encouragement of his parents, Agniśarmā is not interested in studying the Vedas (vv. 3–4). When drought and famine strike, Sumati moves his family into the forest (v. 6).[72] There Agniśarmā takes up with local robbers (*ābhīrair dasyubhiḥ sārdhaṃ*, v. 7); the Sanskrit terms

71 For an English translation of this second account, see Tagare (1997: part 12, pp. 77–80).

72 Brodbeck notes (personal communication, 8 June 2002) that this relocation to the forest, combined with the allocation of evil to the people who live there, constitutes a stereotypical demonization of the tribal as 'other'. As we saw in chapter 2, and in the story of the Sufi saint in this chapter, this is a constant theme in Indian religions. Indeed, the subjugation of tribal peoples by the spread of 'civilization' seems to be a widespread phenomenon. A Western example is provided by the English word 'brigand', derived from 'Brigantes', the name of a powerful tribe in ancient Ireland and northern Britain (Partridge 1966: 59). In this context, both the disparaging remarks about tribals that are so often made in early Indian texts, and the dacoit motif in general, make perfect sense.

suggest both local tribesmen (*ābhīra*) and low-caste or 'untouchable' robbers (*dasyu*). They kill passing travellers for material gain. Agniśarmā forgets about the sacred texts and his superior origins (*gotra*), forgets that he is a brahmin,[73] until one day he comes across the celebrated 'Seven *Ṛṣi*s'.

We may note in passing that the tradition of the Seven *Ṛṣi*s provides two main lists. In Vedic sources, the list is based on *gotra*: Viśvāmitra, Jamadagni, Bharadvāja, Gotama, Atri, Vasiṣṭha and Kaśyapa, with Agastya as an occasional eighth. In the *Mahābhārata*, the list reads: Mārici, Atri, Aṅgiras, Pulastya, Pulaha, Kratu and Vasiṣṭha. This second list, based on regions, is developed further in the Purāṇas, sometimes with the addition of other names (such as Bhṛgu and Dakṣa); the number can be increased to eight, nine, ten or, occasionally, more. In symbolic terms, the Seven *Ṛṣi*s represent transformation through ascetic practice: the pursuit of *tapas* in order to build up inner heat, to 'see', to become divine, and to effect similar changes in those around them (Mitchiner 1982). In the Vālmīki legend, the seven are not usually named, but their transformative powers are clear.

Agniśarmā is on the point of killing the *ṛṣi*s when the leader of the group, Atri, asks him why he wants to attack ascetics who are engaged in a pilgrimage (v. 11). Agniśarmā replies that he has a family to support. Atri's response intrigues him. The *ṛṣi* suggests that Agniśarmā should ask the members of his family what they really think about his profession. Who incurs the sin that is involved in dacoity? Perhaps his family does not believe in killing living beings for this reason? (vv. 13–14). Agniśarmā complies. One by one, each member of his family – father, mother, wife and son – informs him that the sin of killing is his alone (vv. 17–20). In shock, Agniśarmā throws down his cudgel (*laguḍa*) and rushes back to the Seven *Ṛṣi*s (v. 22). Prostrating himself in front of them 'like a dropped stick',[74] he asks for their help. Atri instructs Agniśarmā to sit at the base of a nearby tree and to meditate 'while reciting the great mantra' (v. 27), that is, the name of Rāma.[75]

---

73 I shall return to the implications of this 'forgetting' in chapter 5.

74 The Sankrit phrase used (*praṇamya daṇḍapātena*, v. 23) suggests that he prostrates himself suddenly and totally. Tagare translates *daṇḍapātena* as 'like a log of wood' (1997: 79). This seems to be a deliberate evocation of the immobility technique associated with ascetics like Cyavana in the epic and, of course, with the legend later associated with Vālmīki. My translation is an equally deliberate ploy to differentiate between these similar, but in my view not yet conflated, scenarios. A more idiomatic English expression might be 'like a felled tree'. In Daṇḍin's *Daśakumāracarita* (Kale 1966: I, 25), the term *daṇḍapraṇāmam (akaravam)* is translated by Kale as 'fell prostrate' (II, 16), by Böhtlingk and Roth as 'eine steife Verneigung, bei der man wie ein Stock niederfällt' (1990: III, 498), and by Monier-Williams as 'prostration of the body at full length (like a stick)' (1899: 467).

75 Identifying which 'great mantra' is intended depends on the context, of course. In the fifteenth-century Jain text, the *Kumārapālacaritramahākāvya* of Cāritrasundaragaṇi, for example, the term *mahāmantra* relates to the worship of the Jinas (Granoff 1998: 232). In the context of the *Skanda Purāṇa*, the editor of the Veṅkateśvara edition quite rightly understands the term *mahāmantrajapena* (v. 27) as *rāmamahāmantrajapena*. However, Tagare goes two steps too far. In a footnote to this verse, he first informs us incorrectly that the mantra concerned is *ma-rā* 'as per traditional story', and then conflates the termite-mound motif with the poet

The Seven *Ṛṣi*s leave. Agniśarmā remains seated in meditation for thirteen years. He keeps so still that a termite mound grows up over him (v. 29). When the *ṛṣi*s return that way, they are amazed to hear a voice from within the mound and they dig him out (vv. 29–31). Despite the long years of severe *tapas*, Agniśarmā emerges radiant (*dīptatejasaḥ*, v. 32), visibly purified of his sins. In effect, he is 'reborn' from the termite mound. As the *ṛṣi*s explain, since he has remained focused and motionless within the termite mound for so long, he will become known by the name 'Vālmīki' (that is, 'Son-of-the-termite-mound' or 'Born-from-the-termite-mound', v. 34). Once the *ṛṣi*s have left, Vālmīki worships Śiva and then goes on to compose the *Rāmāyaṇa*. Ever since then, the chapter concludes, Śiva in the form of Vālmīkeśvara has been known to bestow poetic ability on those who worship him: whoever visits the *śivaliṅga* in that place will be able to compose poetry.

This version of the Vālmīki legend recalls several elements of the ascetic motif associated with epic narrative and, in particular, with Cyavana. The technique of immobility is captured here as so often elsewhere in the vivid image of the motionless ascetic completely enclosed by a termite mound, that marker of supreme *tapas*. The continued self-awareness of the ascetic within that mound is demonstrated here by the sound of *japa* recitation rather than (as in Cyavana's case) by glowing eyes. Only the familiar epic metaphor provided by Tagare's 'like a log of wood' jars: the image is produced at the wrong moment in the narrative, both psychologically and technically speaking. This awkwardness suggests that the ascetic milieu is no longer of primary significance, hence my preference for the simile 'like a dropped stick'. There are several elements in this telling that fit better in the Purāṇic context of devotionalism, not all of them appropriate to the Vālmīki legend: the sinner redeemed; the recitation of Rāma's name as a means to redemption; the propitiation of Śiva which enables Vālmīki to compose the *Rāmāyaṇa*; and the subsequent construction of a *śivaliṅga* to mark the sacred spot. Finally, the sinner in this case is not a hunter by birth but a brahmin who, forgetting his origins, has descended to dacoity. In the context of the *Skanda Purāṇa*, we may conclude that this account is narrated as a simple *sthalapurāṇa*, a story to explain a sacred place. Its connection with the Rāma narrative is minimal, while the attempt to link the incident with the poet's name seems forced. The *sthalapurāṇa* idea finds further support in Hans Bakker's work on Ayodhyā (1986). He describes a sacred bathing place on the bank of the Sarayū river nearby where a variant of the legend is still recounted. According to the relevant Sanskrit *māhātmya*, a hunter named Ḍiṇḍira, belonging to the Kirāta tribe, once came to this spot. Inspired by the sight of ascetics engaged in *tapas*, he joined them until, in time, he 'became' a termite mound (*valmīkam abhavat tadā*, OA/B, 23). Rāma, then a boy, was playing in the area. Touched by him, Ḍiṇḍira at once gained a divine form and went to heaven. According to Bakker, the Valmīkatīrtha site is still sacred today: there is an ashram with practising ascetics or hermits and a Hanumān temple containing images of Hanumān, Rāma, Sītā, Lakṣmaṇa, and the figure of an ascetic, presumably Ḍiṇḍira-the-Termite-

Vālmīki without textual support (1997: 79 n. 1). This is a typical example of the kind of problem we are dealing with.

Mound. Unlike the two *Skanda Purāṇa* examples, however, this version of the story appears to make no explicit mention of the composition of the *Vālmīki Rāmāyaṇa* (1986: 353–62).

The third account in the *Skanda Purāṇa* occurs in book 6 (the *Nāgarakhaṇḍa*), chapter 124,[76] in relation to a brahmin named Lohajaṅgha. When famine strikes the region, Lohajaṅgha becomes a dacoit or thief (*caurya*) in order to feed his ageing parents to whom he is devoted. The Seven *Ṛṣi*s appear as before, this time led by Marīci. Seeing Lohajaṅgha looking like a messenger of death yet wearing the sacred thread of a brahmin, the *ṛṣi*s castigate him for behaving like a barbarian (*mleccha*). Then they ask their all-important question. Shocked by his family's response and now fearful on his own behalf, Lohajaṅgha asks the sages for advice. This time, the mantra they give him to chant is nonsensical (*jāṭaghoṭa*, v. 64). Years later, the *ṛṣi*s return to find him still chanting, but now enclosed within a great termite mound (*mahatā valmīkena samāvṛtaḥ*, v. 69). They declare that, since Lohajaṅgha attained his supreme religious goal within the termite mound, he will henceforth be celebrated thoughout the world by the name 'Vālmīki'.[77] As verse 89 explicitly states, the name is an honorific title intended to commemorate this particular form of extreme ascetic practice. A literal translation reads: He who performs *tapas* in such a place (that is, in a termite mound) becomes known as 'Son (descendant) of (Born from) the termite mound' (*vālmīki*).[78] This evidently belongs to what I have called phase four in the development of the Vālmīki legend. The account adds a new element to the story: the sages give Lohajaṅgha (as both fallen brahmin and penitent dacoit) a mantra to recite, but one without any obvious meaning. This detail, which is elaborated further in yet later versions of the story, is discussed in section 4 of this chapter.

The fourth account occurs in *Skanda Purāṇa* book 7 (the *Prabhāsakhaṇḍa*), chapter 278. This time the protagonist is named Vaiśākha. The name may be an allusion to the first account, that is, to the title of the chapter (*Vaiśākhamāsamāhātmya*) and thus to the devotional context in general. Born a brahmin, Vaiśākha supports his family by dacoity. The Seven *Ṛṣi*s appear as before, again led by Marīci, but this time Aṅgiras is their spokesman. They ask their question. Shocked by his family's response, Vaiśākha renounces the world (vv. 26–8). The *ṛṣi*s instruct him to recite a slightly different (but equally cryptic) four-syllable mantra: *jñāṭaghoṭa* (v. 35).[79] Vaiśākha practises *tapas* for thousands of years until he becomes enclosed by a termite mound (*valmīkena sa veṣṭitaḥ*, v. 45). Eventually, the Seven *Ṛṣi*s return. Surprised to hear the sound of recitation (*śabdam uttamam*) emanating from a termite mound, they dig Vaiśākha out. When he emerges still reciting his mantra, the *ṛṣi*s realize that he has attained

---

76 I am unaware of any English translation of either the third or the fourth account.

77 *vālmīkāntaḥ sthito yasmāt saṃsiddhāṃ paramāṃ gataḥ / vālmīkir nāma vikhyātas tasmāl loke bhaviṣyasi // Skanda Purāṇa* 6.124.85.

78 *tapaḥsthaḥ so 'pi tatraiva vālmīkir iti yaḥ smṛtaḥ / Skanda Purāṇa* 6.124.89.

79 I am following the text of the Veṅkateśvara Press edition here. The two mantras cited – *jāṭaghoṭa* (6.124.64) and *jñāṭaghoṭa* (7.278.35) – are almost certainly variant readings of the same phrase.

samādhi. Since he achieved this level of concentration within a termite mound, they proclaim that Vaiśākha will become known throughout the world as 'Born-from-the-termite-mound' (v. 57).[80] Finally, they prophesy that he will now compose the *Rāmāyaṇa* and then attain final liberation.[81] We may note that, after this speech by the *ṛṣi*s, our protagonist is still referred to as 'Vaiśākha' (that is, before verse 59); but it is not long before he is referred to directly as 'Vālmīki' (for example, before verse 62). In effect, the redeemed sinner has become the composer of the *Vālmīki Rāmāyaṇa*. We have shifted into phase five.

Several conclusions may be drawn from these accounts in the *Skanda Purāṇa*. First, they support the point made earlier that the ascetic-in-the-termite-mound motif is not peculiar to Cyavana; here it is described in relation to a variety of differently named individuals. Second, according to these accounts, the practitioner of this particular form of *tapas* is always a brahmin. Third, it is not always the practitioner of termite-mound asceticism who earns the honorific title 'Vālmīki'. Fourth, the sinner (whether hunter or dacoit) invariably abandons his wicked ways. Fifth, the name 'Vālmīki' ('Son-of-Termite-Mound' or, better still, 'Reborn-from-the-termite-mound') becomes the postscript to each version of the story. Sixth and last, on the strength of that name and through the workings of popular etymology, all the elements of the story become associated with the author of the *Vālmīki Rāmāyaṇa*.

There is one final point to consider in this section: the possibility that 'our' Vālmīki might have been seen as in some sense a sinner prior to these Purāṇic reconstructions. As indicated in my concluding remarks to chapter 3, there are some hints to this effect. To summarize the main incident here, Bhīṣma is lying on his bed of arrows being questioned by Yudhiṣṭhira, while Kṛṣṇa speaks about Śiva; afterwards, the assembled *ṛṣi*s relate their own experiences of Śiva's grace (Mbh. 13.18.1ff.). Vālmīki's contribution is to say that he was once called a killer of brahmins (v. 7).[82] Although the epic narrative suggests that he was accused falsely, it is quite possible that the idea remained within the tradition in some way. Certainly, the theme of apparent sin and false accusation is a powerful one. The most celebrated example, of course, is Sītā herself: she is abandoned by her husband because of an apparent sin, falsely accused by rumours in the town. This is perhaps the most heartrending element in the Rāma story. It seems to me quite possible that a theme of such power in the main narrative might have been reinforced by replication – at least within the oral tradition – in relation to another key character, particularly when there is already in existence an apparently authoritative suggestion to that effect. Whether it begins with a hint or a rumour, this is the stuff of which false accusations are made. Either way, the motif of the sinner redeemed did in fact become an established part of the Vālmīki legend. For the implications of the special mantra given to that sinner, the next stage in the textual evolution of that legend needs to be examined.

---

81 *yasmāt tva mantram ekāgro dhyāyan valmīkam āśritaḥ / tasmād vālmīkinamā tvaṃ bhaviṣyasi mahītale // Skanda Purāṇa* 7.278.57.

81 *kṛtvā rāmāyaṇaṃ kāvyaṃ tato mokṣaṃ gamiṣyasi // Skanda Purāṇa* 7.278.58.

82 In this context, we may recall Daśaratha's inadvertent sin of brahmin-murder referred to earlier (p. 123).

4. A Special Mantra for the Unworthy

The third element of the Vālmīki legend is the idea that the sinner in question needs to be given a personalized mantra, one that is appropriate either to the evil actions of the dacoit or to the tribal (and therefore supposedly 'low-caste') birth of the hunter, or both. There are two parts to this motif: the 'low' status of the sinner and the consequently unusual form of the mantra. Judging by the four early accounts of the story found in the *Skanda Purāṇa*, this motif is the last of the three to fall into place. With regard to the caste status of the protagonist, he is a brahmin in all four accounts, albeit a fallen brahmin; only in the first account are we told that the brahmin was a hunter in his previous life. With regard to the mantra, in the first two accounts the dacoit is required to recite the name of Rāma. In the context of *bhakti* religion, even in a text devoted to Śiva, this makes sense. In each of the last two accounts, he is given a deliberately cryptic mantra; perhaps surprisingly, in neither of these accounts is the protagonist a hunter in his previous life. My concern in this section is to examine the earliest extant Sanskrit text in which all three of the motifs that make up the Vālmīki legend (including the *marā-marā* mantra) are in place, and to look more closely at the implications of the special mantra.

The earliest text containing all three motifs is the *Adhyātma Rāmāyaṇa*. This is, without doubt, the most influential version of the Vālmīki legend. Manuscripts of the complete text have been found all over India, especially among Rāma devotees in the north of India, and at least thirteen commentaries have been written on it (Raghavan 1998: 23). Usually dated to the fourteenth or fifteenth century CE, this text is technically part of the *Brahmāṇḍa Purāṇa*. However, it has traditionally been transmitted separately, and is therefore generally viewed as an independent text.[83] According to tradition, it was composed by the fourteenth-century saint Rāmānanda. Certainly, the work is the primary text of the Rāmānandin sect retrospectively attributed to him. Whoever the author was, however, the *Adhyātma Rāmāyaṇa* was obviously composed after the spread of Rāma-*bhakti* in the north of India. Rāma's divinity is explicit: all the characters in the story are aware that he is God (that is, both hero and avatar), and the *bhakti* context is repeatedly stressed. Within the framework of an abbreviated Rāma story, however, the author introduces long philosophical digressions according to which Rāma is the Supreme Being (*paramātman*) and Sītā the creative power of illusion (*māyāśakti*). Chief among these digressions is the *Rāmagītā* (7.5), almost certainly an earlier text but traditionally viewed as the heart of the *Adhyātma Rāmāyaṇa* and consequently often transmitted separately too. Generally speaking, the *Adhyātma Rāmāyaṇa*'s philosophical retelling of the Rāma story is today the best known of the Sanskrit versions, second only to that of the *Vālmīki Rāmāyaṇa*. The main storyline is much the same, but the 24,000 *śloka*s of the *Vālmīki Rāmāyaṇa* have been reduced to 4,000. Furthermore, Vālmīki's role in the two texts is in some ways similar. For example, he takes Sītā in when she is abandoned near his hermitage (7.4.53–6); he teaches his epic poem to her sons, Kuśa and Lava (7.6.24–6); and he makes his famous declaration at

83 For independent English translations, see Baij Nath (1913) and Dhody (1995).

the assembly when Rāma invites Sītā to swear that she is pure (7.7.21–7).[84] These are important similarities.

In several crucial ways, however, the *Adhyātma Rāmāyaṇa* is strikingly different. First, there is no *krauñca-vadha* scene in which the mourning of the female Sarus Crane at the death of her mate serves to inspire Vālmīki to compose the first Sanskrit *śloka*. To put it another way, the epic signifier of Vālmīki as compassionate poet has now been replaced by the late Purāṇic signifier of the Vālmīki legend. Second, Vālmīki is not the author of the poem. The narrator here is the archetypal bard (*sūta*) who repeats a conversation between Śiva and Pārvatī, which has been passed on by Brahmā to Nārada, and by Nārada to him. This new setting marks the parameters of this retelling: the bard signals the generally Purāṇic format, while the Śaiva dialogue places a Tantric emphasis on the earlier narrative.[85] Third, a major component of this mystical overlay is the emphasis on the magical effects of mantra recitation (*japa*) and, in particular, of the recitation of the Name. The restriction of the use of Vedic mantras to twice-born males had led to an increase in popular mantras (that is, mantras available to *śūdra*s and women) in the post-Vedic *bhakti* period. In the context of *bhakti*, the name of the deity is central; for many devotees, the Name is God. In fact, the religious life of north India from the thirteenth to the sixteenth century was marked by the cult of the Name; furthermore, by the fifteenth and sixteenth centuries, 'Rāma' was the most common word for 'God' (Bakker 1986: 119, 124).[86] Fourth, when Rāma visits Vālmīki's ashram together with Sītā and Lakṣmaṇa, looking for a suitable place to live during their forest exile,[87] the poet himself relates what I have termed the 'Vālmīki legend' as his own life-story (2.6. 61–80).[88] According to the *Adhyātma Rāmāyaṇa* account, Vālmīki regards that first meeting with Rāma as the ultimate goal of his years of ascetic practice (2.6. 34), a clear demonstration that the epic context of *tapas* has been superseded by the Purāṇic context of *bhakti*. The following day, Vālmīki explains to Rāma the power of the latter's name: 'Whoever recites your mantra takes refuge in you alone, … [and] his [or her] heart becomes a beautiful temple to you' (v. 53). Reciting Rāma's name has the power to destroy all impurities (v. 59). 'Who can describe the greatness of your name, and how?' asks Vālmīki. '[For] it was by the

84 In Baij Nath's differently numbered translation (1913), these passages may be located at 7.4.58–61 (p. 202), 7.6.26–8 (p. 214) and 7.7.25–34 (pp. 216–17) respectively. See also Dhody (1995: 229, 236, 240).

85 Of course, one may argue, as Alper does, that 'for at least the past millenium, all of Hinduism has been Tantricized' (1989: 358).

86 For a brief overview of studies on mantra recitation in the context of 'Hinduism', and on the significance of the names of gods, see Alper (1989: 358–63). For a brief summary of the rise of devotion to Rāma in north India, with special reference to the cult of the Name (both in its *saguṇa* aspect and in the *nirguṇa* form of the *sant*s), see Bakker (1986: 119–24).

87 In the *Vālmīki Rāmāyaṇa*, the ashram they visit belongs to Bharadvāja.

88 In Baij Nath's translation (1913), this story may be located at 2.6.65–86 (pp. 46–7), and the verses in the following paragraph are numbered 36, 56, 63 and 65 respectively; see also Dhody (1995: 56). For further discussion of the *Adhyātma Rāmāyaṇa*, see Siddhantaratna (1935) and Raghavan (1998: 23ff.).

power of that name that I became a *brahmarṣi*' (v. 60).[89] In order to exemplify that magical power, Vālmīki proceeds to tell his own story, as follows.

He was raised among low-caste Kirāta tribals, a twice-born (brahmin) by birth (but by birth only, *janmamātradvijatvaṃ me*), always delighting in the *śūdra* life-style (*śūdrācāraratah sadā*, v. 61). Described as being by nature undisciplined (*'jitātmanaḥ*), he had many children with a *śūdra* woman. By associating with thieves (*corais ca saṃgamya*), he became a thief himself (v. 62). He preyed on passing travellers, armed with a bow and arrow. One day, he sees the Seven *Ṛṣi*s (here called *muni*s) and tries to rob them; but they are unafraid. They address him as 'vilest of twice-born' (*dvijādhama*, v. 65), and ask their pivotal question. As in the versions of the story discussed earlier, this robber too is stunned by his family's response: he throws away his weapons and begs the *ṛṣi*s to help him. At this point, significantly, the *ṛṣi*s look at each other (*parasparaṃ samālocya*), saying, 'This vile brahmin is a very wicked person' (*durvṛtto 'yaṃ dvijādhamaḥ*). They realize that he should be shunned by good people; and yet he has asked for help and therefore deserves to be given religious instruction (v. 73). Wanting both to keep their distance and to help him, the *ṛṣi*s find a compromise. They reverse the syllables of Rāma's name and tell the dacoit to recite that mantra (that is, *ma-rā*) with a concentrated mind until they return. While the text gives no reason for this choice of mantra, the tradition assumes that low-caste habits and a career as a dacoit have rendered him unworthy to pronounce the name of God, despite his brahmin birth. As before, the dacoit does as he is told. He sits motionless (*niścalarūpiṇaḥ*) in one place until a termite mound rises up over him (*valmīko 'bhūn māmopari*, v. 77). A thousand years later, the *ṛṣi*s return and summon him from the mound. The former dacoit comes out of the mound transformed, like the sun emerging from the mist (*nīhārād iva bhāskaraḥ*, v. 78). The *ṛṣi*s greet him according to his new status – 'O lord of *muni*s' – and bestow on him the title he has now earned: 'Born-from-the-termite-mound' (*vālmīkis tvaṃ*). 'For when you came out of that termite mound,' they explain, 'you were born for the second time'.[90] At the end of his story, Vālmīki returns to the main point of his narrative: he has earned his title, and thus become who he is, by the power of Rāma's name.[91] My point is a related one. According to this story, the most effective means to salvation is the recitation of Rāma's name.[92] Even the worst sinner – including the brahmin who behaves like a *śūdra* and a dacoit – can be saved.[93] According to the Vālmīki legend, however, to be effective the Name must be tailored to the sinner's low status.

It seems that the evolving legend has added two further elements to the story, placing both in the mouth of Vālmīki for maximum effect. First, the apparent contradiction – between the brahmin who takes up ascetic practice and the low-

89 We must note once again that this portrayal of Vālmīki as subordinate to Rāma is rejected by the Valmiki community today.

90 *valmīkāt sambhavo yasmāt dvitīyaṃ janma te 'bhavat* (v. 79).

91 *ahaṃ te rāma nāmnaś ca prabhāvād īdṛśo 'bhavam* (v. 80).

92 *rāmanāmnaiva muktiḥ syāt kalau nānyena kenacit* // *Adhyātma Rāmāyaṇa* 2.5.27.

93 *rāma rameti yadvāṇī madhuraṃ gāyati kṣaṇam* / *sa brahmahā surāpo vā mucyate sarvapātakaiḥ* // *Bhāgavata Purāṇa* 4.1.84.

caste hunter or dacoit who repents of his wicked ways – is resolved by having a brahmin boy raised by tribals. The high-caste child raised by low-caste parents is another ancient motif, exemplified in the *Mahābhārata* by the figure of Karṇa (Karve 1974). Second, the nonsensical mantra is now explained within an explicitly devotional context by the assumed unworthiness of the recipient to pronounce the name of God. Interestingly, different explanations are offered for the word *marā* in different parts of India: in Tamilnadu, the hunter is insensitive to the divine and so prefers to repeat the word for 'tree'; in Maharashtra, the word is taken to mean 'to die' (Raghavan 1998: 65 n. 12). The point of the story is clear: even when the syllables are reversed and are then recited by a man ignorant of their potential meaning, God's name has the power to bring salvation. We may assume that, by the time the (now purified, now reborn) ex-dacoit emerges from his termite mound, he is knowingly reciting the name of God. This is obviously a story about *bhakti*.

Moreover, the fact that there is no mention of the composition of the *Rāmāyaṇa* in relation to the redeemed sinner supports the argument that this was not originally intended as a story about the poet. In fact, much the same story is told about a pupil of Rāmānanda who is credited with the conversion of Muslims in Ayodhyā. According to the tradition, Rāmānanda reversed his own mantra (that is, he changed 'Rāma' to *marā*) for their use, and at once (the story goes) the Vaiṣṇava mark appeared on their foreheads, *tulasī* beads circled their necks, and their tongues unwittingly recited the name of God (Bakker 1986: 120 n. 5). Vālmīki is not even mentioned here. The story merely demonstrates an easy way for barbarians (*mleccha*) or ignorant sinners to pronounce the name of God. Another celebrated story makes the same point, but without mentioning either Vālmīki or Rāma. Here the protagonist is the brahmin Ajāmila who falls in love with a *śūdra* woman, marries her and takes up the supposed 'vices' of the *śūdra* way of life. When it is time for him to die, the messengers of death (*yamadūta*) come for him. Terrified out of his wits, Ajāmila repeatedly calls out to his eldest son – 'Nārāyaṇa!' – thus unwittingly calling out one of the names of Viṣṇu. Despite the lack of devotional intent on Ajāmila's part, Viṣṇu appears and saves him.[94] The moral of this story is the same: the recitation of God's name, even by a wicked and ignorant person (here again a fallen brahmin unaware of what he is saying), brings salvation. The application of the story to Vālmīki is unnecessary.

The problem of the brahmin who behaves likes a *śūdra* is also tackled in the *Ānanda Rāmāyaṇa*. This later and much longer text was composed somewhere between the fifteenth and seventeenth centuries, probably in Maharashtra.[95] The

94 See *Bhāgavata Purāṇa* 6.2.14.

95 This is John Brockington's estimate (1998: 495). Vidyut Aklujkar explains her preference for the fifteenth century in relative terms: the text must have been composed after the *Adhyātma Rāmāyaṇa* which it mentions, but before both Narahari's Kannada *Torave Rāmāyaṇa* (*c.* 1500–90) and Eknāth's Marathi *Bhāvārtha Rāmāyaṇa* (1533–99) for which it serves as a source (1995: 107 n. 2). Raghavan suggests a later date and a south Indian origin: perhaps during Maratha rule in the south, possibly Thanjavur, at the end of the seventeenth or the beginning of the eighteenth century (1998: 121). For further discussion of the *Ānanda Rāmāyaṇa*, see Bulcke (1958: 129–30), Aklujkar (1995) and Raghavan (1998: 72ff.).

first chapter is devoted to retelling the whole story of the *Vālmīki Rāmāyaṇa*. The remaining eight chapters provide a string of new episodes that have since become popular: we learn about Rāma's sacrifices, donations and pilgrimages, about his other marriages, his children and grandchildren, and so on. A particularly interesting episode concerns Sītā's abandonment in the forest. Rāma instructs Lakṣmaṇa to kill Sītā and, to prove that he has done so, to bring him her severed arm (2.3). When Lakṣmaṇa is unable to do this, Viśvakarman creates an exact replica of Sītā's arm for him to take back to Rāma (2.4). But the most remarkable addition is the extended recasting of characters and incidents from the Rāma narrative to explain characters and incidents in the Kṛṣṇa story. We may also note that Vālmīki's role as the holy author of the *Vālmīki Rāmāyaṇa* is extended to include his authorship of the *Ānanda Rāmāyaṇa* too (Aklujkar 1995). Indeed the text both demonstrates an awareness of multiple, often divergent, post-Vālmīki tellings of the Rāma story and claims to be itself the best example of Vālmīki's creative work (Aklujkar 2000). The past history of Vālmīki narrated in this text (2.14) follows the first account of the *Skanda Purāṇa* extremely closely in places, sometimes verbatim. As before, the problem of the poet's earlier caste-status is solved by means of three consecutive life-stories. Many of the elements are discussed above. First, he is a brahmin named Stambha who falls in love with a prostitute and adopts the life of a *śūdra*. In his next life, Stambha is reborn as a hunter who lives the life of a dacoit; one day, he robs a brahmin named Śaṅkha, then feels pity for him and returns his sandals. In his third life, the former dacoit is reborn from a snake that has swallowed the semen of the ascetic Kṛṇu; the child is raised by the Kirātas as a *śūdra*, and eventually meets the Seven *Ṛṣi*s. The rest of the tale is predictable, including the *Adhyātma Rāmāyaṇa* mantra, *ma-rā*, the name of God with its syllables reversed.

The next step in the development of the Vālmīki legend is to make the sinner not simply a low-level brahmin who has fallen among dacoits but a supposedly 'untouchable' hunter. This step had evidently been taken by the time of the *Tattvasaṃgraha Rāmāyaṇa*, which was probably composed in the seventeenth century, possibly in the eighteenth.[96] Rāmabrahmānanda Sarasvatī compiled this immensely ambitious compendium (*saṃgraha*) with two primary aims. First, he would summarize all the versions of the Rāma narrative available to him at the time; second, he would provide the esoteric meaning (*tattva*) of the incidents recounted. This seems to be the last great devotional retelling of the Rāma story in Sanskrit. The narrative opens with a gathering of sages on the banks of the river Gomatī. Vālmīki's arrival puts them in mind of Rāma and they ask the bard (*sūta*) to speak about him. The bard's response takes the typically Purāṇic form of reporting a conversation between Śiva and Pārvatī (1.1). In book 2, when Rāma pays a visit to Vālmīki, the latter refers to his own story (2.22). Prompted by Pārvatī, Śiva then relates in full the story of the hunter who became Vālmīki.

96 For discussions of the *Tattvasaṃgraha Rāmāyaṇa*, including a summary of its contents, see Raghavan (1952–3); see also Bulcke (1958: 128–9), and John Brockington (1998: 495). With regard to dates, the seventeenth century is preferred by Bulcke and Brockington, the eighteenth by Raghavan (1980b: 19; see also 1952–3: 4–6).

The hunter makes his living as a dacoit, preying on travellers in the forest. The Seven *Ṛṣi*s appear; he attacks them too, whereupon they ask their crucial question. Shocked by his family's refusal to share the sin of dacoity, the hunter repents of his wickedness and asks for spiritual instruction. While the *ṛṣi*s are wondering what kind of instruction they can possibly give to a hunter, a celestial voice announces that they should teach him a special mantra: *ma-rā*. They do so. The hunter embarks on his ascetic practice and, in time, becomes completely enclosed within a termite mound. Indra begins to worry about the possible consequences of such extreme *tapas*. Bṛhaspati reassures him: it will result in the creation of a great *ṛṣi* (*brahmarṣi*) who will compose the epic *Rāmāyaṇa*. Much later, the Seven *Ṛṣi*s return. They break open the termite mound to find their pupil reciting Rāma's name. The gods rejoice. Greeting him as 'Vālmīki', Viṣṇu pronounces him the future author of the *Rāmāyaṇa*. At this point, legend and epic meet. Vālmīki makes his home on the banks of the Tamasā river, meets Nārada who tells him the Rāma story and, finally, composes the *Rāmāyaṇa* (2.22–30). Raghavan's summary does not mention the *krauñca-vadha* incident, the signifying motif of the epic; that said, Vālmīki's famous *śloka*-curse (*mā niṣāda* … ; see above, p. 97) is later specified as one of the *Rāmāyaṇa* verses worth reciting (7.21). Either way, the devotional context is uppermost in this retelling. Moreover, there is no doubt about the low status of the sinner in question: he is born a tribal hunter and consequently accorded 'untouchable' status.[97]

As one would expect, Vālmīki makes another appearance in the *Tattvasaṃgraha Rāmāyaṇa*, this time in the *Uttarakāṇḍa*. Śiva explains to Pārvatī that, when rumours began to circulate about Sītā, Rāma decided to have her taken to Vālmīki's hermitage. Pārvatī asks why that hermitage in particular. Śiva replies that Vālmīki once performed *tapas* for the honour of having the goddess Lakṣmī born as his own daughter. But Lakṣmī refused to be born from a human female; instead, she agreed to emerge from the furrows of the earth as Sītā (meaning 'furrow') and be adopted by Janaka. In order to enable Vālmīki to have the experience of treating her like his own daughter, Lakṣmī created the gossip about Sītā that would cause her to be taken to his hermitage. Vālmīki would then have the honour of caring for both Sītā and her two sons. Śiva continues the narrative: the boys are born in the hermitage, Rāma performs the horse-sacrifice, Vālmīki's

97 For a study of the ambivalent attitudes towards hunting expressed in Sanskrit texts – including the glorification of the 'righteous' royal huntsman and his consumption of meat, the ascetic doctrine of *ahiṃsā* with its ban on taking life and the resulting trend towards vegetarianism, and the widespread contempt for the tribal hunter as 'degraded' – see Wilhelm (1991). For an exploration of folk traditions about hunting in relation to the cult of Khaṇḍobā in Maharashtra, see Sontheimer (1997). The main centre of Khaṇḍobā worship is the temple of Jejurī, where the local version of the legend of Vālmīki as a dacoit is located. Sontheimer suggests that the 'environmental and historical core' of the story is that robbers would raid merchant caravans passing through the crossroads at Jejurī (1997: 287); another example perhaps of the conflict between tribespeople and the more 'civilized' settlers encroaching on their land, noted earlier. For the Marathi version of the story which depicts Vālmīki as a member of the Koḷī tribe, one of several variants to be found in the Deccan, see Sontheimer (1989: 174–6).

young pupils sing his epic poem, Vālmīki asks Rāma to take Sītā back, and Sītā returns to the earth (7.5–9).

There are several other late Sanskrit adaptations of the story, all termed 'Rāmāyaṇas'. I shall mention only two more here. First, the voluminous fourteenth-century *Bhuśuṇḍi Rāmāyaṇa* takes the form of a conversation between Brahmā and a violence-prone crow (hence the name 'Bhuśuṇḍi', denoting a type of weapon).[98] Once a 'traditional secret' circulated only in 'the limited circle of the Rāma Bhaktas of the *Rasika* cult' (B. P. Singh 1980: 476), this remarkable text relates the early life of Rāma along the lines of the juvenile and erotic stories of Kṛṣṇa. The credit for the first narration of the Rāma story is given here to Rāma himself: he told Sītā, who told Lakṣmaṇa, who told Bhārata, and so on. The main sources of inspiration for this work seem to be the *Vālmīki Rāmāyaṇa* and the *Bhāgavata Purāṇa*, together with clear evidence of Tantric influence. In its turn, the *Bhuśuṇḍi Rāmāyaṇa* seems to have influenced at least two major Rāma narratives: the Sanskrit *Adhyātma Rāmāyaṇa* (discussed on pp. 147–50) and the Hindi *Rāmcaritmānas* by Tulsīdās (discussed briefly in chapter 5). In the *Bhuśuṇḍi Rāmāyaṇa*, however, Vālmīki's dramatic role is minimal: even his final declaration of Sītā's innocence is dropped.[99]

Another interesting Sanskrit version of the Rāma narrative is provided by the brief, and decidedly *śākta* or Goddess-oriented, *Adbhuta Rāmāyaṇa*, sometimes called *Adbhutottara Rāmāyaṇa* or *Adbhutottara-kāṇḍa*. This work presents itself as dictated by Vālmīki to his pupil Bharadvāja in the form of an appendix to the *Vālmīki Rāmāyaṇa*. Also a popular work, as is demonstrated by the manuscripts found all over India, it was probably composed in the north in the fourteenth or fifteenth century (Raghavan 1998: 4). This text relates the origin and primordial (*mūlaprakṛti*) greatness of Sītā within the context of music as yoga (*gānayoga*).[100] Sītā is portrayed here as a multi-armed Devī who has to enter the fray in order to protect her husband from Rāvaṇa's even more terrifying brother. John Brockington is not mistaken when he comments that Sītā enters the battlefield 'in a manner which would delight modern militant feminists' (1998: 495). Sītā assumes a terrible form, kills the second Rāvaṇa, then dances on the battlefield, shrieking with laughter until Śiva places himself beneath her feet in order to protect the universe. Called 'Kālī', Sītā carries the marks of Śiva (third eye, crescent moon, trident) and is identified explicitly with Maheśvarī Śakti, ultimate reality. In a conscious parallel with the *Bhagavadgītā*, she gives Rāma divine vision so that he can see her true form and he praises her as both Supreme Goddess and Supreme Brahman. Finally, she grants him a wish: she will retain

98 For a summary of the main events in the *Bhuśuṇḍi Rāmāyaṇa*, see Raghavan (1975). For further information regarding the ideology and significance of the text, see B. P. Singh (1980) and John Brockington (1998: 494–5). For the date of this text, I have followed Raghavan (p. 21) and John Brockington (p. 494), rather than B. P. Singh's preference for the twelfth century (p. 487).

99 B. P. Singh (1980: 490). With access to only one of the four *khaṇḍa*s of the Sanskrit text, I have been unable to rule out the possibility that one of the others contains a version of the Vālmīki legend; judging by the summaries available, however, this appears not to be the case.

100 For further discussion of this musical context, see Raghavan (1991).

her supreme form in his heart but return to Ayodhyā with him in human guise (Raghavan 1998: 13–19). Another non-Vālmīki element is the idea that Sītā was Rāvaṇa's daughter. More precisely, Sītā is born to Maṇḍodarī, Rāvaṇa's wife: Maṇḍodarī secretly removes the foetus and buries it; later, while ploughing the earth, Janaka finds the baby girl (hence the child's name). The all-important *bhakti* context is provided by the stress on music as a devotional aid, especially in relation to singing the praises of God, and the statement that Rāma's kingdom resounds with the mantra of his Name (*nāmaghoṣa*, 2.47).

I shall not attempt to consider all the potential sources for, and variations of, the Vālmīki legend. The Sanskrit materials considered above are certainly of interest. However, they tell us considerably more about the development of the *bhakti* tradition than they do about Vālmīki. In the final section of this chapter, I shall summarize the effects of the rise of *bhakti* on the portrayal of Vālmīki in Sanskrit texts with some particular questions in mind. How do we explain the text-historical shift from Vālmīki as a learned brahmin to Vālmīki as an ignorant *śūdra* or tribal, to an 'untouchable'? And how might this relate to the discomfort currently being felt by members of the Valmiki community in Britain? How might it relate to the *dalit* discourse? Is it possible simultaneously to elevate Vālmīki as Bhagwan and to defend his *ādi* status, that is, to allow that he might have been a tribal without going so far as to say that he was a 'dacoit'?

5. The 'Untouchable' as Exemplar

I shall begin by summarizing what the early Sanskrit texts tell us about Vālmīki. Although it is hard to prove the point, 'Vālmīki' may have lived in north India around the turn of the fourth century BCE. According to the *Taittirīya Prātiśākhya*, he was an expert in Sanskrit pronunciation; but there is a hint that his mother-tongue was not Sanskrit. The focus of the *Mahābhārata* is on his ascetic prowess; but the *suparṇa* story carries suggestions of tribal origins and non-brahminical behaviour; and there is the dispute about a *sāma* ritual that made the other ritualists call him a 'brahmin-killer'. The later books of the *Vālmīki Rāmāyaṇa* bring him centre stage. By the first century BCE, he is described as a great ascetic (*muni*), a contemporary of Rāma, who lived in a hermitage near the Tamasā and Gaṅgā (Ganges) rivers. By the time of the *Uttarakāṇḍa*, he is described as a famous brahmin who has close links with the royal house of Ayodhyā and belongs to the Bhṛgu clan.[101] In the context of the *Rāmāyaṇa*, Vālmīki is an inspired and gifted poet, a man of high principles and firm morals, a spiritual leader reverenced even by kings, and a gentle saint who feels compassion for all beings. The definitive epic motif for this greatly respected figure is the *krauñca-vadha* episode: the compassion that Vālmīki shows for the cruelly slaughtered crane reflects his caring response to the abandoned Sītā; and that moment of empathy, of shared pain, is the source of his poetry. In the

101 Perhaps, as discussed, the term 'Bhārgava' here provides a hint of the future conflation: the early termite-mound motif connected with Cyavana, the honorific title 'Reborn-from-the-termite-mound', and the etymology of Vālmīki's name.

Yogavāsiṣṭha, Vālmīki is the repository of the highest spiritual truth. So where does the dacoit idea come from? The only source in these texts is the collection of hints regarding his possibly tribal origins.

The legend took shape slowly. In its earliest forms, it contained no reference to the Rāma narrative, let alone to Vālmīki. Somewhere between the twelfth and the fifteenth centuries CE, however, within the context of devotional worship in north India, the Vālmīki legend became so firmly entrenched that few people are surprised to find it in popular children's comic-books today.

The first element is the motif of termite-mound asceticism. But this is no longer the epic symbol of severe *tapas* according to which the immobility technique, usually in a rigid standing position, is practised in pursuit of ascetic power. Nor does it symbolize the advanced meditative states and *kāyotsarga* stance of mendicant Jains. Instead, the termite mound now represents the supreme achievement of *bhakti*: complete and long-term absorption in the *japa*-recitation of the name of God, with the practitioner in the traditional seated posture.

The second element is the motif of the sinner redeemed. With the emergence of Rāma-*bhakti*, the dacoit-turned-devotee becomes the perfect illustration both of the grace of God and of the power of the name of Rāma to save sinners, even when the syllables of that mantra are reversed. Found in one form or another in most religious traditions, this theme assumes a typically Indian form in the dacoit story.

The third element is the personalized mantra. This reinforces the idea that the protagonist is a sinner in urgent need of redemption. From the vague early hints that Vālmīki might once have been in some sense an outsider (non-Sanskrit, a non-brahmin *suparṇa*, or accused by brahmins of ritual error), we have reached a point where he is described as a 'fallen brahmin', one who behaves like a *śūdra* and a dacoit. By the seventeenth century, the final touch is added: the sinner, once a brahmin, is redefined as a hunter in the forest, in effect a tribal, and by implication an 'untouchable'.

Why? Why do *bhakti* stories so often have an 'untouchable' protagonist? From the brahminical point of view, the answer is clear: the ritual path is barred to the 'lower' castes; by contrast, the path of *bhakti* is in many ways tailored to them. Thus the 'untouchable' protagonist may simply be a mechanism for emphasizing the extraordinary power of *bhakti*, with or without the recitation of the Name. The following two examples demonstrate that this scenario need have nothing to do with Vālmīki *per se*.

The first episode, taken from the *Śiva Purāṇa*, relates to the worship of Śiva rather than Viṣṇu or Rāma. Chapter 9 of the *Koṭirudrasaṃhitā* section tells the story of a particularly dramatic brahmin-to-'untouchable' transformation. After the death of her husband, a brahmin girl proves incapable of controlling her sexual desires and is banished by her husband's family. Following her natural inclinations, she marries a *śūdra* (v. 10). In time, she becomes obsessed with sex, eating meat and drinking alcohol. One day, she is so drunk and so desperate for meat that she unwittingly kills a calf in the darkness of the night. On realizing what she has done, she blurts out 'Śiva! Śiva!' (v. 15). But then her desire for meat overcomes her, and she cooks and eats the meat anyway. As a result, when she later dies, Yama decrees an appropriate rebirth: she is born blind and with a dark complexion to an 'untouchable' woman (*caṇḍālā*). Her life is one of unmitigated suffering: her parents die when she is still a baby, she fails to find a husband, she develops leprosy, and she becomes a beggar, learning to survive by eating the leftovers of other 'untouchables' (v. 21). One day, however, someone tosses her a bunch of inedible leaves which she casts aside without thinking. By chance, the leaves land on a nearby *śivaliṅga* (v. 28). When she dies this time, she goes straight to heaven in an aerial chariot (v. 33). The story ends with the anticipated devotional explanation: she had instinctively called out Śiva's name when, as a brahmin, she killed the calf; as an 'untouchable', she had unwittingly worshipped the *śivaliṅga* with leaves; and, by begging all night, she had managed to stay awake during the auspicious all-night vigil of Śiva Caturdaśī.[102] The brahmin perspective is glaringly obvious: impure behaviour (epitomized here by uncontrolled sexuality, especially that between a brahmin girl and low-caste men) and the consumption of meat and alcohol lead to birth as an 'untouchable'. But even the worst behaviour (exemplified here by the killing, cooking and eating of a sacred calf), even the lowest of 'untouchables' (exemplified here by the dark-skinned, blind female 'untouchable' who eats the leftovers of other 'untouchables'), can be redeemed by the power of the Name, by a simple offering to God, by a vigil on his special day. The brahminical moral of the story, then, is that no action is too despicable, no person too low, for the grace of God to work its miracles.[103]

The second story, taken from the *Nārada Purāṇa*, brings us closer to the Vālmīki legend. In fact, without mentioning Vālmīki at all, it serves as a model for the dacoit part of the legend. First, the story concerns a hunter, in this case named 'Gulika'. Second, an explicit link is made between caste status and the worship of Viṣṇu: whoever refuses to bow to Viṣṇu is in effect a *caṇḍāla*, a *śvapaka* (1.3); putting it another way, the *caṇḍāla* who worships Viṣṇu is in reality an excellent person (v. 12). The strikingly familiar story runs as follows. A hunter preys on other people as a dacoit. He robs them, abducts women, and kills both people (including brahmins) and animals (including cows, v. 20). One day, he is on the point of killing the brahmin Uttaṅka, when the latter points out to him his precarious position in words that could have come straight from the Vālmīki legend. 'You kill and steal in order to support your family,' he says. 'But they only support you because you bring in money' (vv. 40–2). Uttaṅka continues: 'They enjoy the wealth you give them, but you alone are the doer, you alone will suffer the effects of your sins' (v. 51). Gulika becomes afraid when he hears this, and begs Uttaṅka's forgiveness (v. 52). He blames his birth as a hunter and his life as a dacoit on sins in a previous life (v. 56); then, in an agony of remorse, he dies (v. 59). Uttaṅka sprinkles his body with water that has washed the feet of Viṣṇu. Instantly freed of his sins, Gulika speeds to heaven on an aerial chariot (v. 60ff.).

102 For an English translation of this episode, see Shastri (1970: part 3, pp. 1287–90).
103 As Apratim Barua rightly points out, it is possible to read this and similar stories from the *dalit* point of view: unlike brahmins, *dalit*s are so close to God that even the smallest and unintended gesture takes them to heaven (personal communication, 27 May 2002). For a further discussion of the theme of undeserved grace, see Doniger (1993).

Again, the brahminical moral of the story is obvious. Even the worst behaviour (epitomized here by the killing of brahmins and cows), even the lowest of 'untouchables' (defined here as *caṇḍāla*, *śvapaka*), can be redeemed by the grace of God.

The figure of Vālmīki evidently became entangled in similar threads of *bhakti* storytelling. During that period in north India when Rāma-*bhakti* and the cult of the Name was on the rise, the story of the composition of the *Rāmāyaṇa* was gradually reworked along the lines of these other tales. But we may still ask why Vālmīki in particular became reclassified as an 'untouchable'. Might it have had something to do with his possibly tribal origins? The contempt for tribal as opposed to royal hunters in late Sanskrit literature is well known. The Sanskrit terms (such as *kirāta*, *niṣāda*) are regularly glossed as 'degraded', 'savage', 'outcast' (Wilhelm 1991: 7–8). Were these aspects of the tribal 'other' perhaps thrust upon Vālmīki in order to make a dharmic rather than a devotional (let alone an epic) point? Within the context of brahminical discourse, the label 'untouchable' is certainly a mighty stick with which to beat those considered to be out of place. On occasion, even Śiva, the archetypal out-of-place 'other' in the Vedic ritual arena, is classed by indignant brahmin ritualists as an 'untouchable' (O'Flaherty 1976: 277ff.).[104] As we shall see in chapter 5, the untouchability of Vālmīki becomes even more explicit in the vernacular tellings of the legend. I shall pick up the thread of his tribal or *ādi* identity there.

104 For the related Bhairava myths, see White (1991).

Chapter 5

Drawing Conclusions for Today

1. Introduction

Chapter 1 of this study laid out the problem under discussion: the dispute in Birmingham in February 2000, the legend at issue, the principles at stake. Chapter 2 contextualized the people involved: the origins of 'untouchability' in early India, the myths and politics of *dalit* self-representation, the implications for the Valmiki community in Britain. The next two chapters focused on texts. Chapter 3 located the implications of the name 'Vālmīki' in early Sanskrit texts: a Sanskrit expert in the *Taittirīya Prātiśākhya*, an ascetic *ṛṣi* in the *Mahābhārata*, the compassionate poet of the *Vālmīki Rāmāyaṇa* and the enlightened saint of the *Yogavāsiṣṭha*. Chapter 4 traced each of the elements of what I have called 'the Vālmīki legend', also in Sanskrit texts: the ascetic technique of immobility celebrated in the 'termite-mound motif'; the *bhakti* theme of sinner-to-saint transformation through the power of God's name; and the *marā-marā* mantra, with its implications of low status and ignorance on the one hand and the irrelevance of intellectual understanding on the other. It also raised the possibility of Vālmīki's *ādi* status.

Chapter 5 is intended to pull all these disparate threads together. The resulting 'conclusion' is the end point of several quite different approaches, based on radically different kinds of evidence. Section 2 focuses on the continuing development of the *bhakti* tradition as it is demonstrated in the vernacular languages of India. References to Vālmīki and to the Vālmīki legend are traced beyond the Sanskrit sources considered above to some of the vernacular tellings of the Rāma story. In particular, the dacoit motif is explored further by a brief consideration of some of the hagiographical materials of northern India. This section is intended to illustrate the implications of the some of the ideas discussed above in the context of Sanskrit texts (some of which seem to be the result of vernacular discourse) as they are expressed in vernacular forms.

Section 3 focuses both on Vālmīki as a deity in general and on the 'Bhagwan Valmik' of the Valmiki community. Evidence for the past worship of Vālmīki is sought in epigraphical records and in the earliest available text on Hindu iconography. Evidence for the God of British Valmikis today is drawn from contemporary materials. This section is intended to facilitate comparisons between the earliest portrayals of Vālmīki as a deity and contemporary forms of worship in their current socio-political context.

Section 4 revisits the complex relationship between caste and salvation: the *dalit* agenda, the stories of 'fallen brahmins' and 'untouchable saints', and the potentially liberating notion of the 'true brahmin'. This section is intended to explore some of the possible responses of the devotee to the apparent disjunction between the textual evidence about Vālmīki and contemporary felt reality.

Section 5, the final section of this book, turns to the broader implications of the title: the relationship between textual authority and religious meaning.

2. The Role of Vernacular Tellings

The first point to stress is the crucial role played by vernacular languages in the spread of devotional religion. The use of the languages of the common people for religious composition instead of Sanskrit was tantamount to a rejection of brahminical control: now the truths hidden in the scriptures could be revealed in forms that anyone could hear and understand. As a result, vernacular versions of the Rāma story, both in India and beyond, are even more numerous than those in Sanskrit. Since my primary concern in this study is the Sankritic tradition, I shall discuss only a few of the oldest extant versions in selected Indian languages. Tamil and Malayalam will serve to represent southern India, Bengali and Hindi the north.[1] Finally, I shall return to the context of the recent incident in Birmingham by exploring the possible references to Vālmīki in the Sikh holy book, the *Ādi Granth*.

Tamil provides the earliest extant retelling of the Rāma story in any Indian vernacular. The *Irāmāvatāram* or 'Descent of Rāma' – composed by Kampaṉ, a poet at the Cōḻa court of Kulottuṅga II – was deliberately modelled on the Sanskrit *Vālmīki Rāmāyaṇa* (but without the *Uttarakāṇḍa* which, according to Tamil tradition, was composed by someone else). The result is a poetic re-imagining rather than a translation. The dates suggested for this text range from the eighth to the thirteenth century CE, with the most likely answer lying somewhere in the twelfth. Maharajan opts for the ninth century (1972: 7), and this is the date printed on the Kamban postage stamp issued by the Government of India in 1964 (Sarma 1994: 26 n. 56). I prefer to follow Zvelebil who argues for the twelfth century (1975: 181–4; cf. Thampi 1996: 9–10). Steeped in the devotional mood of its Āḻvār predecessors, the *Irāmāvatāram* portrays Rāma as God in human form, whose name alone brings salvation.[2] Rāma's divinity is assumed, while Rāvaṇa takes on the aura of a tragic hero. In more recent times, as a result of the anti-brahmin, anti-Sanskrit movement of south India, the values of the Rāma story as told by both Vālmīki and Kampaṉ have been reversed: Rāvaṇa has become a Dravidian hero, pitted unfairly against the invading 'Aryan' villain, Rāma.[3] Like

1 For the Rāmāyaṇa tradition in other parts of India and Asia, see William Smith (1988) and the essays in Raghavan (1980a), Thiel-Horstmann (1991) and Richman (1991, 2001).

2 For a summary of the contents of the *Irāmāvatāram*, see Maharajan (1972) and Aiyar (1987: 6–26). For further information on Kampaṉ and his work, see Hart and Heifetz (1988: 1–33). For evidence that the Rāma story, including the *Vālmīki Rāmāyaṇa*, was well known in the Tamil-speaking south well before Kampaṉ, see Thampi (1996: 3–4). For a comparative study of the Rāmāyaṇa tellings in Tamil and Telugu, see Sarma (1994).

3 See Zvelebil (1988). For the Tamil folktale about the great battle between Hanumān and Rāvaṇa's younger brother, the terrifying sorceror-warrior called Mayilirāvaṇaṉ

Vālmīki's text in the north, Kampaṉ's Tamil telling is still revered and expounded throughout the south of India.[4] However, Kampaṉ dispenses altogether with the frame-story constituted by the role of Vālmīki, and tells us nothing whatever about the poet's past history. It seems that Kampaṉ is not one of the links in this particular chain of meaning.

In Malayalam, the earliest extant Rāma narrative is Eḻuttacchan's *Adhyātma-rāmāyaṇam Kiḷippāṭṭu*. Composed in the form of a conversation between Śiva and Pārvatī, this work is heavily dependent on the Sanskrit *Adhyātma Rāmāyaṇa* discussed earlier. The term *kiḷippāṭṭu* describes the indigenous metrical form in which it is written. Nair translates *kiḷippāṭṭu* as 'birdsong'; that is, the work was composed as if it were issuing from the throat of a parakeet. The author offers the bird milk and honey, coaxing it to sing the story of Rāma (1978: 95).[5] The author – Tuñcattu Ramanujan Eḻuttacchan, commonly called 'Tuñcan' – is widely praised as the greatest writer in the history of Malayalam language and literature (p. 89). The date assigned to Eḻuttacchan's work varies from the fifteenth to the seventeenth century, with the most likely date being the sixteenth century (Thampi 1996: 23). The text became enormously popular, was deemed sacred even in its author's lifetime, and is still revered today (Nair 1978: 92–3). Like Kampaṉ, Eḻuttacchan dispenses with the frame-story constituted by Vālmīki's role in the *Vālmīki Rāmāyaṇa*.[6] Unlike Kampaṉ, Eḻuttacchan follows the *Adhyātma Rāmāyaṇa* to make Vālmīki (not Bharadvāja) advise the exiles on where to live. Before doing so, Vālmīki tells Rāma about his past: a brahmin by birth, he had lived as a *śūdra*, supporting his family by hunting and dacoity; after meeting the Seven *Ṛṣi*s, he had recited the syllables *ma-rā*, and become enclosed within a termite mound; on emerging, he was transformed into Vālmīki, poet and sage.[7]

If we now turn to north India, the earliest extant Rāma narrative seems to be the Bengali *Rāmāyaṇa* attributed to Kṛttibās Ojhā. Generally agreed to be 'the most popular single book in all of premodern Bengal', the *Kṛttibāsī Rāmāyaṇa* is even more widely read today: 'a popular story for popular consumption', available 'at any given moment' in half a dozen cheap editions (Stewart and Dimock 2000: 243).[8] This influential telling was composed initially in the fifteenth or

---

or 'Peacock Rāvaṇa', conducted prior to Rāma's defeat of Rāvaṇa, see Zvelebil (1987: xxxv–xlvi, 173–222). For another Tamil folktale, in which Sītā becomes the aggressor, see Shulman (1979).

4 According to Srinivasan, Kampaṉ's text may well have influenced Tulsīdās: the Tamil text was taken to Varanasi, while Tulsī himself is known to have visited the south (1978: 12).

5 For *kiḷippāṭṭu*, Eḻuttacchan and the history of Malayalam literature in general, see also George (1968) and Chaitanya (1971).

6 For a comprehensive comparison between Kampaṉ's Tamil and Eḻuttacchan's Malayalam versions of the Rāma story, see Thampi (1996).

7 Eḻuttacchan's version of this story (vv. 1995–2108), taken directly from the *Adhyātma Rāmāyaṇa*, is summarized in Thampi (1996: 222).

8 There is still no faithful English translation of this text. For a free English rendering of a popular edition, see Mazumdar (1958). A more accurate sense of Kṛttibās' text may be gained from reading the extracts translated in Stewart and Dimock (2000).

sixteenth century, probably in the last half of the fifteenth (William Smith 1981: 229, 239 n. 1). The text as we now find it reflects 'the living *Rāmāyaṇa* tradition' rather than being a 'frozen' reconstruction of the classical text (p. 236). Smith's article explores the emendations made to the text – even to the author's name (from 'Kīrttibās' to 'Kṛttibās', p. 231) – by early nineteenth-century Bengali *paṇḍits* in search of the 'correct' original, and by later editors inserting new material. He notes that the latter process continues today (p. 238; see also Datta 1980). Smith concludes that this 'mass of *Rāmāyaṇa* material stamped with the name of Kṛttibās' is a 'summation of the *Rāmāyaṇa* tradition in Bengal, ... the result of five hundred years of growth and an unknown number of contributors, and in both form and authorship, the collective product of an entire culture' (p. 238). Since Kṛttibās wrote in the late fifteenth century (that is, before Caitanya introduced popular Vaiṣṇava *bhakti* to Bengal), Smith argues that the pronounced emphasis on *bhakti* must belong to the later revisions to his text. Furthermore, because of the closeness in the dates between the two texts, he does not consider it likely that Kṛttibās himself borrowed from the Sanskrit *Adhyātma Rāmāyaṇa* (p. 232). Be that as it may, the text as we have it today follows the Sanskrit *Adhyātma Rāmāyaṇa* rather than the *Vālmīki Rāmāyaṇa* in two important ways: in the devotional emphasis in general, and in the pre-history of Vālmīki in particular. With regard to the first aspect, Rāma is God incarnate, Sītā is Lakṣmī, the villains long to be killed (and therefore saved) by Rāma, and the entire story is divine play (*līlā*). With regard to the second aspect, Vālmīki was once Ratnākara, a cruel and uneducated robber who, at the prompting of Brahmā and Nārada, repents of his ways. According to this version, Brahmā asks Ratnākara to say the name of Rāma but the dacoit cannot. The Bengali text explains what happened next:

> But his tongue was stiff with sin, so he could not say 'Rāma'.
> He replied, 'My mouth will not form that word.'
> When he heard this, Brahmā, very concerned,
> wondered how he could get that mouth to utter the *rāma nāma*.
> 'If he says the syllable *ma* first and then *rā*,
> the *rāma nāma* will come from this sinner's mouth.'
> Finding a solution, Brahmā said,
> 'Son, when someone dies, what do you shout?'
> Hearing Brahmā, Ratnākara said,
> 'Dead men are called *maṛā* (corpse).'
> 'Don't say *maṛā*, say *marā* unceasingly,' said Brahmā,
> 'then the name of Rāma will come from your mouth'.[9]

So Ratnākara learned to pronounce the name of God and became purified thereby. After some time, on account of the termite mound that had grown up around him, he became known as 'Vālmīki' ('Born-of-the-termite-mound'). Finally, he composed the *Rāmāyaṇa*. It can be no surprise if this is the Vālmīki familiar to Bengali-speakers today.

---

9 For this translation, and for Kṛttibās' Bengali original, see William Smith (2000: 250).

But Hindi provides what is probably the best-known vernacular version of all. Throughout the Hindi-speaking north of India, any reference to the Rāma story is taken to be a reference to the immensely popular *Rāmcaritmānas*, 'The holy lake of the deeds of Rāma', composed in the sixteenth century by Tulsīdās (*c.* 1532–*c.* 1623) in the Avadhi dialect of Hindi. As William Smith's survey of hagiographical literature in north India demonstrates, Tulsī is widely regarded as an incarnation of Vālmīki himself (2000: 20, 22, 124). Tulsī's text, however, is modelled on both the *Vālmīki Rāmāyaṇa* and the later *Adhyātma Rāmāyaṇa*; that is, Rāma is portrayed as both perfect man and God incarnate. While these two texts constitute Tulsī's primary influences, he borrowed from other tellings as well. Examples of borrowing from the *Adhyātma Rāmāyaṇa* include Tulsī's use of a conversation between Śiva and Pārvatī as the overarching framework, and his portrayal of Vālmīki's meeting with Rāma in the forest. The latter element includes the idea that Vālmīki accepts all three exiles as divine, but offers particular adoration to Rāma. Borrowing from that forest episode means, of course, that Tulsī would have been familiar with the *Adhyātma Rāmāyaṇa* account of the Vālmīki legend. Tulsī's other Sanskrit sources include the *Yogavāsiṣṭha*, the *Adbhuta Rāmāyaṇa* and the *Bhāgavata Purāṇa* (Vaudeville 1955: 144–5).

It is important not to underestimate the significance of the *Rāmcaritmānas*, even in recent decades. Writing in 1978, for example, Madan Gopal declares that 'there is no village in northern India where the story is not recited or staged every year at the time of Dussehra' (p. 110). In 1984, the 'hottest-selling' cassette recording in the north was an abridged version of the *Rāmcaritmānas*.[10] In 1987–88, Ramanand Sagar's hugely successful television serial, *Rāmāyaṇa*, was based on Tulsī's text.[11] The audience figures for the serial shown on India's national television network are said to have exceeded 'the estimated 50 million aggregate circulation of all the journals in India'; and, as Dalmia-Lüderitz put it, '12,000 cinema halls cannot compete with the half million video sets' (1991: 207 n. 1). The commercial implications are astounding: video-cassettes, books for adults, comic-books for children, prayer-books, calendars, posters, dolls, toys, and so on (see Tripathi *et al.* 1988). Thanks to Florine Clomegah, I own a splendid example of this burgeoning commercialism: a board game entitled *India's epic Ramayana game*, with the invitation, 'Experience an ancient epic adventure'. Two large illustrations adorn the cover: an earnest Vālmīki with his twin disciples to the left; Rāma, Sītā and Lakṣmaṇa to the right. There are also four smaller pictures: Śiva with his wife, their sons, his bull and her lion; Viṣṇu enthroned on Śeṣa floating on the cosmic ocean, with Lakṣmī at his feet, and Brahmā on his airborne lotus in the air above; Durgā seated on her tiger; and Vālmīki talking to Nārada, while Brahmā hovers above. Finally, there is a map of India showing Rāma's route. The only character shown twice is Vālmīki. Even

10 Scott Marcus, personal communication, cited in Lutgendorf (1991a: 410).

11 For an analysis of the 'feast of *darśan*' offered by Sagar's television serial, including his effective mix of tradition and innovation and with particular reference to the character of Kaikeyī, see Lutgendorf (1995a). For Lutgendorf, the Sagar serial is 'an independent *Rāmāyaṇa*: an original retelling in a new medium' (p. 237).

in this children's game, it seems that Vālmīki is far more than a poet: he is the stereotypical traditional sage, the sublime spiritual teacher, a divine personage venerated at the level of gods. More important, the popularity of the television serial has reinforced still further the centrality of Tulsī's particular telling. However, the *Rāmcaritmānas* version of the story is not accepted by everyone. For example, it omits the story of Sītā's banishment by Rāma; when it looked as if the television *Rāmāyaṇa* might follow suit and leave out Vālmīki's significant role in the resolution of the story, the *dalit* communities in several major cities in the north went on strike, refusing to collect refuse until the episode was reinstated (Richman 1991: 3). Despite this significant omission, by 1991 the recitation of the *Rāmcaritmānas* had become 'one of the most visible (and audible) forms of popular religious activity in Northern India' (Lutgendorf 1991c: 185).[12] For all these reasons, it is worth looking more closely at the references to Vālmīki to be found in the *Rāmcaritmānas*.

Book 1 (*Bālakāṇḍa*) opens with Sanskrit *śloka*s. *Śloka* 4 pays homage to the 'lord of poets' (*kavīśvara*), an epithet for Vālmīki as author of the first Sanskrit *Rāmāyaṇa* (Prasad 1990: 1). The next reference to Vālmīki is more ambiguous. Devotion to Rāma is likened to bathing in the Gaṅgā: after such a bath, crows (*kāka*) become koels (*pika*) and herons (*baka*) become 'swans' (*marāla*). Prasad's Hindi translation replaces *pika* with *koyal*, *baka* with *bagulā*, and *marāla* with *haṃsa*. Both *pika* and *koyal* denote the 'koel' or 'Indian cuckoo'. Both *baka* and *bagulā* can mean either 'heron' or 'egret' but not 'crane', the more usual translation. It is the hunched posture of the first two, the neck drawn back between the shoulders, that reminds the poet of the hypocritical brahmin (Leslie 1998b: 464–5). Both *marāla* and *haṃsa* can denote a range of large aquatic birds from 'duck' to 'flamingo'. For largely poetic reasons, the term *haṃsa* is usually translated as 'swan', despite Vogel's insistence on 'goose' (1962); in my view, the implications of the term require still further investigation. In Tulsī's verse, the poet imagines the crow's harsh cawing being transformed into the melodious notes of the koel, while the religious hypocrisy popularly attributed to herons skulking at the water's edge is replaced by the noble piety associated with the *haṃsa*, symbol of the soul.

We are then informed that a similar miraculous transformation was experienced by Vālmīki, Nārada and Agastya (Prasad 1990: 3–4). We may note that disrespect need not be intended here. In *Kavitāvalī* 7.58, for example, Tulsī uses this image of heron-to-'swan' transformation with regard to himself. Similar images may be found in the verses of the *Ādi Granth* (e.g. Dass 2000: 238). However, translators and commentators on the passage invariably explain this reference to Vālmīki in terms of his early life as 'a hunter and highway robber' (Prasad 1990: 4 n. 1; Growse 1987: 6 n. 1), often recounting in full the *Adhyātma Rāmāyaṇa* episode (Dhody 1987: 4–5, 560). Tulsī makes a direct reference to the *Adhyātma* account in his own text a little later on. In the midst

12 For further discussion of Tulsī's life and works, and the impact of the *Rāmcaritmānas* from the sixteenth century to the present day, see Lutgendorf (1991a: 1–52); see also the critical essays by Indian and Western scholars in Prasad (1990: 721–42). For the *Rāmcaritmānas* in the UK, see Nesbitt (1999).

of praising the power of Rāma's two-syllable name, Tulsī tells us that the first great poet (*ādikavi*, that is, Vālmīki) was purified by these two syllables even though he recited them in the wrong order (Dhody 1987: 17; Growse 1987: 20; Prasad 1990: 15). But at the point where we would expect Vālmīki's past history to be recounted – that is, at the point in the *Adhyātma Rāmāyaṇa* when Rāma, Lakṣmaṇa and Sītā arrive at Vālmīki's ashram in the forest – Tulsī tells us only that Vālmīki is a great ascetic and a brahmin, nothing more (Dhody 1987: 232ff.; Growse 1987: 297ff.; Prasad 1990: 273ff.). At the end of the *Rāmcaritmānas*, Tulsī returns to the theme of the purification of the wicked and, in this context, mentions Vālmīki's supposedly sinful past once again. In Prasad's translation (1990: 663), the passage (including Prasad's glosses) reads as follows:

> Listen, O stupid soul! Who has not found salvation by worshipping Rama, the purifier of the fallen? The harlot (Pingala), Ajamila, the huntsman (Valmiki), the vulture (Jatayu), the elephant and many other wretches have been delivered by him. An Abhir, a Yavana, a Kirata, a Khasha, a Chandal, and all who are the very embodiments of sin are purified if they but once repeat the name of Rama whom I adore.

The point is simple and familiar: even the worst sinner can find salvation by reciting Rāma's name. All the traditional examples are here. The 'harlot' or courtesan is Piṅgalā, whose pet parakeet has learned from its previous owner how to repeat the name of God ('Rāma'); merely by hearing this constant repetition, Piṅgalā attains salvation. Ajāmila is the brahmin mentioned in chapter 4, the one who abandoned his brahmin duties and took up with a *śūdra* woman, a prostitute according to some. On his deathbed, he calls out in fear to his son ('Nārāyaṇa') and, even though it is unintentional, the mere sound of God's name ensures his salvation. The hunter (*vyādha*) is identified by both Prasad and Growse (1987: 718) as Vālmīki, according to the tradition recorded in the *Adhyātma Rāmāyaṇa*.[13] The vulture is a flesh-eater and thus the lowest of birds; and yet Jaṭāyu finds salvation because he too repeats Rāma's name. Finally, the elephant is the famous Gajendra: due to sins in his previous life, he becomes trapped in the jaws of a mighty crocodile; but he recites a hymn to Viṣṇu (traditionally entitled the *Gajendramokṣastotra*) and is saved. After this list of individual sinners saved by reciting God's name, Tulsī provides a list of the categories of sinful people who can be saved in a similar way. These include: tribals such as Ahīrs (*ābhīra*), Kirātas and Khaśas (*khasa*); foreigners, including Muslims;[14] and

13 Dhody is less certain, vaguely describing an unnamed hunter who took to singing God's name and earned thereby the title of 'Righteous Hunter' (1987: 521 n. 5).

14 The Hindi term for 'foreigner' (*jamana*) is derived from the Sanskrit *yavana*, which has changed its denotation over time. In its earliest use, as the Sanskrit equivalent of 'Ionian', the word denoted the Greeks, that is, the participants in and successors to Alexander's campaign in the fourth century BCE (Karttunen 1997: 268; see also v, 13 n. 54, 14). The term was subsequently applied to any foreigner, especially one who came to India to rule. In this respect, the term has been applied at different times to both the Muslims and the British.

'untouchables'.[15] Interestingly, Prasad's Hindi translation refers in parentheses to a man saying '*Harām*' (1990: 663). The reference is to a popular story of the time. When an old Muslim man is knocked down by a pig, he cries out, '*Harām! Harām!*' ('Unclean! Unclean!'). Since he has unwittingly called out the name of God (*Ha Rām! Ha Rām!*), even this foreigner, this unbeliever, is saved (cf. *Kavitāvalī* 7.76; Allchin 1964: 160 and 1966: 27). The implication of both this story and Tulsī's list is that everyone can be saved by reciting Rāma's name, even if they do so unintentionally, even those deemed to be the very embodiment of sin. The common denominator of all these examples, including both the named individuals and the general categories, is an embodied form that demonstrates, and thus represents, great sin.[16]

It is no surprise to find these links and implications in Tulsī's other works too. For example, similar sentiments can be found in two of his best-known texts, the *Kavitāvalī* and the *Vinayapatrikā* (Allchin 1964, 1966), independent collections of verses, both composed in the contemporary language of Vraj (Brajbhāṣā). According to *Kavitāvalī* 7.138, after hearing the teaching of the Seven *Ṛṣi*s, Vālmīki is transformed from a hunter (*vyādha*) into the 'moon of sages' (*munīndu*) merely by saying, '*Marā, marā*'. According to *Kavitāvalī* 7.89, all the faults of the 'cuckoo of poets' (*kavikokila*, Vālmīki) are removed when he says, 'Kill! Kill!' (*marā, marā*); that is, Vālmīki does not even have to say Rāma's name properly to be saved. These verses are to be found alongside the same exemplars and categories of sinners that we found before: the prostitute, the elephant, the vulture, and Ajāmil (7.7); Prahlād and the crocodile (7.8); the tribal woman Śabarī, and the vulture (7.10); the vulture, Śabarī, and the 'aboriginal Kol' (7. 15); Ajāmil, the elephant, and the Bhīl woman (7.18); a Kirāt, the Kol woman (7. 19); and so on. Śabarī, also called the 'Bhīl woman', is the tribal who offers Rāma roots and fruit when he comes to Mataṅga's hermitage. In later tellings, she tastes each item to ensure its goodness before offering it to Rāma; in orthodox terms, these offerings are defiled (both by her touch and by her saliva) but Rāma, unconcerned, accepts.[17] The 'cuckoo of poets' reference is followed immediately by a line about the elephant, Ajāmil and the harlot. In this way, Tulsī identifies Vālmīki repeatedly as a tribal hunter and places him in the same sinful category as the lowest of the low: the hunter and Ajāmil (7.92); the hunter, Ajāmil and the harlot (7.93); and so on. The *Vinayapatrikā* does much the same thing. Vālmīki is identified as the hunter who became a sage by reciting the syllables of Rāma's name in the wrong order (151.7), and he is listed alongside 'untouchables' (*śvapaca*), tribals (*niṣāda*, Khal, Bhīl) and foreigners (Yavana), alongside the vulture, the prostitute and the crocodile (46.9, 57.3, 144.4, 236.3, etc.). As Allchin concludes, it was 'a favourite ploy of Tulsī' that Vālmīki was once a hunter who

---

15 The Hindi term here is *svapac*, glossed by McGregor as 'dog-cooker, or dog-feeder: an outcaste' (1993). The word is derived from the Sanskrit *śvapaca*, noted earlier.

16 For a discussion of the implications of the physical body, see Leslie (1999).

17 See William Smith (2000: 207–8). Śabarī is a devotee of the revered low-caste teacher and ascetic, Mataṅga. As her name implies, she belongs to the Śabara tribe, a designation that (like Bhīl and Kirāta) is on a par with 'untouchable'. For a discussion of the Śabarī story in a range of tellings, see Lutgendorf (2000).

'gained enlightenment' by reciting 'Kill! Kill!', even though he failed to recognize the saving syllables of Rāma's name and recited them in the wrong order (1966: 187). This recurring idea that Vālmīki is an ignorant tribal, 'untouchable' both by birth and by behaviour, may be contrasted with the complete absence of such an identification in the earliest Sanskrit texts. I shall return to the issue of Vālmīki's implied tribal origins in section 4.

Even this brief overview of vernacular retellings is instructive. The texts discussed have all proved influential in the dispersal of the Rāma story, in terms of both region and language.[18] Before moving on, however, it is necessary to demonstrate beyond any further doubt that the elements of the Vālmīki legend are not peculiar to Vālmīki. On the contrary, they belong to the rich patchwork of themes common to the hagiographical tradition of north India, what William Smith prefers to call its 'sacred biography'.[19] As Smith points out, the dacoit motif is applied to a range of individuals apart from Aṅgulimāla and Vālmīki. Thus Guru Nānak is waylaid by a robber named Bholā: Nānak sends him to ask his family if they will share his sin; when Bholā hears their answer, he abandons the dacoit path and follows Nānak. Similar stories are told of Caitanya too.[20] The pattern is the same in that the sinners are redeemed; it is different in that the saint is the perpetrator in the Aṅgulimāla-Vālmīki model but the victim in the Nānak-Caitanya model. The brahmin-turned-brigand is another recurring theme, as is the association of the 'renegade brahmin' with Kirāta tribals (William Smith 2000: 242).

The notion of 'the accidental devotee' (p. 245) gathers under one heading many of the motifs and individuals already discussed. The message is the same, always presented from the brahmin point of view. Even the lowest of the low can be saved by the grace of God: animals like the elephant, disgusting creatures like the vulture, practitioners of the most impure professions such as the prostitute and the hunter, and members of the lowest castes such as the so-called 'dog-eating untouchable'. Each in turn is saved, not because of his or her own worth, but by some felicitous accident or by unwittingly pronouncing the name of God. Thus the vulture whose flesh is carried clockwise round a Viṣṇu temple by a scavenging dog is deemed to have performed a *pradakṣiṇā*. Similarly, two aimlessly drunken sinners are deemed to have danced a *pradakṣiṇā* around a ruined temple and placed a 'banner' upon it. The unintentional recitation of the name of God is an equally frequent motif. Here we find, yet again, the stories of Ajāmila calling out the name of his son Nārāyaṇa and being rewarded for calling out to God, of Piṅgalā and her pet parakeet, of the Muslim calling out 'Unclean' (*harām*), and so on. According to Caitanya, Muslims are particularly lucky in this regard: since all Muslims say '*Harām, Harām*', they will all be saved (William Smith 2000: 253). Thus every element of the Vālmīki legend is part of the north Indian (in some respects, pan-Indian) hagiographical tradition.

---

18 For the particular contribution of the Panjab to the Rāma story, see Sahdev (1983).

19 William Smith (2000: 11; for a thoughtful and comprehensive discussion of the nature of hagiography, see pp. 1–18).

20 For these and other examples of the dacoit motif, see William Smith (2000: 239–45). For a further Sanskrit example, see the first ten chapters of the *Gaṇeśa Purāṇa*.

In the context of the Birmingham dispute, one further source is important: the *Ādi Granth*, also known as the *Gurū Granth Sāhib*, the sacred text of the Sikhs. As Mandair suggests in his report for the Radio Authority, it seems likely that the broadcaster at the centre of the dispute based his remarks on the *Ādi Granth*, or perhaps on a Panjabi text that was itself based on the *Ādi Granth* such as Sodhi Teja Singh's *Bhakt Māl* (2000: 2). It is therefore necessary to consider the relevant passages in the *Ādi Granth* in some detail.

The *Ādi Granth* or 'First Book' of the Sikh tradition is a compilation of verses composed largely in the 'language of holy men' (*santbhāṣā*, *sādhukkaṛī*, *santbolī*).[21] This language was the preferred means of communication between religious mendicants in medieval north India, and was based partly on the Hindi dialect spoken near Delhi.[22] The *Granth* is written in the Gurmukhi script (*gurumukhī*, 'from the mouth of the Guru'), the script used by most Sikhs today when they write in Panjabi. According to the Sikh tradition, the first compilation of the *Ādi Granth* was dictated by the fifth Guru Arjan to his disciple (who was also his uncle) in 1603–4. This 'first compilation' is known as the Kartārpur manuscript (or the Gurdās recension, after Arjan's uncle) and believed to have been based on a number of volumes of verses composed by the first four Gurus. It is said that a copy was made, with additional materials and some difference in organization, by a Sikh named Banno; this text is referred to as the 'Banno' or 'Khārā recension'. The modern printed text is said to be based on a third recension (the Damdaṃ or Damdamī), dictated from memory by Guru Gobind Singh in 1706. Modern scholars of Sikhism are more likely to speak of the gradual compilation of verses over time. This process began with Nānak in the sixteenth century, reached some kind of closure in 1708 (when the granting of Guru-ship to the *Granth* created a greater investment in textual accuracy), and it continues to evolve today.[23] Callewaert notes that one third of the text consists of compositions by Guru Arjan (1996: vol. 2, p. 13). The *Granth* is now regarded as the physical embodiment of the ten Gurus, the 'Eternal' or 'Living' Guru, and is paid homage accordingly. Most of the resulting text takes the form of a collection of hymns (*pad*) and verses (*salok*) classified according to the melody (*rāga*) to which they were sung, a clear indication of their oral origins. In each case, the hymns and verses are sandwiched between a liturgical prologue and a devotional composition serving as an epilogue.

In its current form, then, this material is later than most of the other sources considered in this study. We may further assume that any references to Vālmīki in

---

21 My primary source for the *Ādi Granth* is Winand Callewaert's rendering of the Gurmukhi text into the Devanāgarī script (1996). For the text in Gurmukhi script, with different transliteration and an English translation, see Chahil (1998). For the compositions by Ravidās, I have also consulted the Hindi critical edition by Callewaert and Friedlander (1992). The last of these is based on a number of manuscripts from other traditions as well as on the Panjabi tradition of the *Ādi Granth*; we may also note that the earliest manuscript consulted for this collection is from Fatehpur and dated 1582.

22 For further information regarding the linguistic variety of the *Ādi Granth*, see Shackle (1983) and Pashaura Singh (2000: 167ff.).

23 For recent studies on the formation of the *Ādi Granth*, see Pashaura Singh (2000), Deol (2001a) and Mann (2001a, 2001b).

the *Ādi Granth* reflect the ideas and stories in circulation at the time of compilation. I am aware, of course, of the potential problems surrounding even this cautious statement. To put it simply, in the current climate of politicized religion, it is provocative to speak of the historical evolution of any sacred text. The Sikh scriptures are no exception, particularly in the discourses conducted in the diaspora. The recent work of Piar Singh (1996), Pashaura Singh (1998), McLeod (1999) and Oberoi (2001) illustrates all too clearly some of the problems inherent in the textual study of Sikh scriptures, including the not infrequent charge of blasphemy.

Before moving on to consider the references at issue, it is worth pausing to note a particular feature of this text, a feature that is especially relevant in the context of the Valmiki community. The *Ādi Granth*, this sacred body of writings elevated to the level of 'Living Guru', contains repeated denunciations of caste prejudice. According to a composition by Ravidās (*Ādi Granth* 858, *Rāga bilāvalu* 2), for example, it is irrelevant whether one is a brahmin, a *kṣatriya*, a *vaiśya* or a *śūdra*, even a cremation-ground attendant (*ḍom*), an 'untouchable' (*caṇḍār*) or a foreign barbarian (*malech*); one can be purified simply by praising God (Callewaert 1996: 858). This verse can also be found in the edition by Callewaert and Friedlander of Ravidās' work in Hindi; another version replaces 'cremation ground attendant' (*ḍom*) with 'woman' (*nārī*), making gender discrimination equally irrelevant to the world of *bhakti* (Callewaert and Friedlander 1992: *pad* 106, pp. 164–5). The *Ādi Granth* verse demonstrates another significant feature of the Sikh text: the inclusion of material composed by low-caste saints or *bhagat*s. These include members of *śūdra* castes (such as the weaver Kabīr, the calico-printer Nāmdev and the barber Sain) and even so-called 'untouchables' (such as the cobbler Ravidās and the butcher Sadhna).[24] Ravidās is especially famous in this regard. He is known as the 'poor Chamār' (Hindi, *camār*; Sanskrit, *carmakāra*; 'leather-worker') who 'regularly carried cattle carcasses' and 'mended shoes in the middle of the road' (Callewaert and Friedlander 1992: 12); and yet he became a *sant*. There can thus be no question of prejudice against 'untouchables' in the philosophy of the *Ādi Granth*. The separate issue of conflicting truth claims in relation to the pre-history of Vālmīki is more complicated. I shall return to this point after a brief consideration of some of the key passages.

None of the allusions to Vālmīki that I have located in the *Ādi Granth* mentions the composition of the *Rāmāyaṇa* epic. *Pace* Dass (2000: 266, 298), this does not mean that the name 'Bālmīk' denotes someone else. It means that the primary concern of these devotional compilers is the familiar legend of Vālmīki's redemption from sin and not the epic poem. While the composition of the *Vālmīki Rāmāyaṇa* is not specified, it is assumed: in fact, it demonstrates his sanctity. Interestingly, there is one verse attributed to Ravidās which does link the Vālmīki of devotional tradition with the *ṛṣi* of the ancient past. In the critical

24 For free translations of some of the best-known songs attributed to these saints, see Dass (2000). For a scholarly analysis of the life and works of Ravidās, see Callewaert and Friedlander (1992); despite the arguments put forward here in favour of the form of the *sant*'s name used by most Hindi speakers ('Raidās', p. 22), I have followed the Panjabi-speakers' preference for 'Ravidās'.

edition of Ravidās' work, verse 1 of *pad* 84 lists some of the 'countless' significant individuals whose lives were spent absorbed in devotion to God (Callewaert and Friedlander 1992: 153). Vālmīki is listed alongside some of the most illustrious figures of the epic or generally pre-*bhakti* past. These include celebrated *ṛṣi*s such as Viśvāmitra, Vyāsa, Mārkaṇḍeya, Kapila, Atri, and Agastya, the great ascetic Cyavana, and even gods such as Gaṇeśa and Śiva. In my view, this demonstrates at least a general awareness of the epic associations circulating in relation to Vālmīki. But this hymn is not included in the *Ādi Granth*. All the references to Vālmīki in the *Granth* relate not to the epic context but to the efficacy of the Divine Name to redeem even the worst of sinners, including those regarded by 'higher' castes as the lowest of the low-born. There is no interest in, or concern for, Vālmīki in his own right.

The first passage occurs within a composition attributed to the fourth Guru Rāmdās (*Ādi Granth* 995, *Rāga mārū*). The relevant parts of Chahil's translation (1998: vol. 3) read as follows:

> By contemplating the Name, one is emancipated. Dhru, Prahlad and Bidar ... [are saved.] ... All the blemishes of Nam Dev, Jaidev, Kabir, Trilochan and Ravi Dass, the cobbler, were cast off. ... and Ajamal who mated with whores ... [and] Ugar Sain ... [and] Nanak. ... by contemplating the Name, one is saved. Dhanna, the farmer, and Balmik, the highway robber, ... [were saved].

The list begins with well-known saintly or heroic figures from classical Hindu mythology, individuals who were saved by calling on God's name: Sukdev and Janak (cited in the preceding passage), Dhrū, Prahlād and Bidar. The next category of people saved by the Name consists of eminent saints and devotees within the *sant* tradition: Nāmdev, Jaidev, Kabīr, Trilocan, Ravidās, Nānak, and 'Dhannā the *jaṭ*'. Tradition has it that the 'Jaidev' mentioned here is Jayadeva, the brahmin author of the celebrated twelfth-century Sanskrit work, the *Gītagovinda* or 'Song of the Lord' (Callewaert 1996: vol. 2, p. 9 n. 2). The third category comprises a number of well-known redeemed sinners, individuals who were once notorious for their wickedness and are now celebrated for having been saved by the all-powerful name of God: Ajāmal who is said to have consorted with prostitutes, Ugar Sain (Ugrasena) the father of wicked King Kaṃsa, and Vālmīki 'the highway robber' (*bālmīku baṭvārā*). The last of these three is an explicit allusion to the Vālmīki legend.

The second reference occurs a few pages later, this time in a composition attributed to the fifth Guru Arjan (*Ādi Granth* 999, *Rāga mārū*). To provide the context, I again quote selectively from Chahil's translation:

> Dhru became immortal [by meditating on God]. Ajamal, for the love of his son, uttered Naryan, the Lord, who ... drove away [the messengers of death]. ... Balmik of low caste was saved and also was saved the poor huntsman. ... [and] the great elephant ... [and] Prahlad ... and Bidar ...

We find Vālmīki in the same sort of company as before, joined this time by the elephant (Gajendra) associated with both the Purāṇas and Tulsī's poems. In this passage, the reference to 'Balmik' (*bālmīku*) occurs alongside the word *supcār*, meaning 'untouchable'.[25] The reference to a poor hunter (*badhik tare bicāre*) suggests, in this passage at least, yet another individual, despite the fact that the two aspects (hunter and low caste) are repeatedly conflated in the familiar Vālmīki legend. There is in fact other evidence for a hunter who may not be Vālmīki. In the *Rāga Gaūṛī* section of the *Ādi Granth*, in a list of similarly redeemed sinners (including the prostitute, Ajāmal and Ugar Sain), we find 'that hunter who shot the fatal arrow'. This is understood by Dass to refer to the hunter who accidentally killed Kṛṣṇa by shooting a poisoned arrow into his heel (2000: 28, 243–4). However, an allusion to Kṛṣṇa's hunter in one verse does not necessarily conflict with an allusion to the hunter of Vālmīki legend in another. Either way, we find in these two *Ādi Granth* passages an explicit portrayal of Vālmīki as a dacoit and as an 'untouchable'. That said, we must also stress that the whole point of these passages is to demonstrate the efficacy of the Name, and not primarily to make any pronouncements regarding the character or background of Vālmīki.

A third passage makes this clear. In *Ādi Granth* 1124, *Rāga kedārā*, Ravidās speaks of the baseness of the high-born who do not love God. He reminds his listeners that Vālmīki was an 'untouchable' too, and he was saved:[26]

1. You may perform the six sacred duties,
   be endowed with a noble birth,
   if you have no devotion for Hari in your heart,
   not pleased by tales of His lotus feet,
   you are considered the equal of an outcaste (*supaca*).
   [*Refrain*:] Mind, awake! Aware or unaware
   why do you not look at Vālmīki?
   He reached such a high state from such a low caste,
   through his special devotion to Rām.

2. The enemy of dogs (*suāna satru*), an outcaste (*ajātu*) from all other men,
   he fixed his love on Krishna.
   How can wretched men praise him,
   whose praise enters into all three worlds?

3. Ajāmil, Piṅgalā, the hunter and the elephant
   have gone to be with Hari.
   When such evil-minded ones were liberated,
   why should you not be saved, Ravidās?

Vālmīki ('Bālmīk' in the *Ādi Granth*) is explicitly named in the refrain that links the verses together. He is described as an 'untouchable' (*supaca*) and as a man without caste (*ajātu*). The epithet, 'enemy of dogs', may be interpreted in at least two different ways: it may be a consequence of the supposedly low-caste or

25 This seems to be the only use of the term in the *Ādi Granth*. It is glossed by commentators as 'dog-eater' (Christopher Shackle, personal communication, 25 April 2002).

26 In the following, the translation is by Callewaert and Friedlander (1992: *pad* 53, p. 136) while the vernacular terms are taken from Callewaert (1996).

tribal habit of eating dog-meat, or it may be a reference to the fact that dogs habitually bark at 'untouchables' who live beyond the boundaries of caste settlements.[27] Finally, verse 3 identifies this 'untouchable' as the legendary hunter in his usual company of redeemed sinners: Ajāmala, Piṅgalā and Gajendra. Yet Dass insists that this 'untouchable' hunter is the one associated with Kṛṣṇa. According to Dass, this is the hunter who is turned away from Kṛṣṇa's celebratory feast because of his untouchability; when Kṛṣṇa learns of this, he orders Draupadī to feed the hunter herself while he washes the man's feet. Dass concludes: 'The *chandal* Valmiki should not be confused with Valmiki the Brahmin, the author of *The Ramayana*' (pp. 265–6). This statement may be politically wise in the current climate, but in my view it is wrong. As a result of the shared hagiographical traditions of north India in general, and the emergence of the 'Vālmīki legend' in particular, Vālmīki the brahmin author of the epic and Bālmīk the 'untouchable' hunter and dacoit have at this point become conflated. Along with so much else in north India, the *Ādi Granth* simply reflects this fact.

What conclusions may be drawn from this discussion? Broadly speaking, only two aspects of the story are crucial to the Sikh religious context: the importance of *bhakti* in general and the efficacy of the divine Name. The historicity of Vālmīki is unimportant. The references to him merely reflect the stories in circulation in north India at the time when the *Ādi Granth* was being compiled, stories that are to a large extent still in circulation today. Is it necessary to assume that, because they are found in a sacred text, these references to Vālmīki constitute a truth claim? A fundamentalist Sikh would think so. Conversely, if one wishes to reject the legend about Vālmīki, is it necessary to reject the text in which it is found? Some Valmikis might think so. This is the problem.

The scholar's solution is much simpler. As this study has clearly demonstrated, the Vālmīki legend is found in many *bhakti* compositions, both in Sanskrit and in vernacular languages. Its function is always the same: it serves to encourage devotional practice, in particular the recitation of the name of God, even in the case of sinners, even when the protagonist does not know what he (for example, Ajāmila) or she (for example, Piṅgalā) is doing. For this purpose, the Vālmīki legend is strengthened by the *marā marā* mantra. The hunter/dacoit's failure to recognize the significance of the sounds he is making mirrors both the dying Ajāmila's uncomprehending shout to his son and the prostitute Piṅgalā's idle registering of the squawking of her pet bird. That is all. In the context of devotional religion, questions of historicity, coherence, even verifiability, are irrelevant when set beside the spiritual message being taught.

---

27 The first meaning is assumed by Dass's translation, 'dog-eater' (2000: 121), the second by Callewaert and Friedlander (1992: 136 n. 70). My preference is for the first meaning, as a reflection of the erroneous popular etymology of the term. The second meaning does not fit with the probably prior sense of 'dog-keeper'; see my earlier discussion of the Sanskrit terms, *śvapaca* and *śvapāka* on p. 28.

3. Worshipping Vālmīki

The first part of this section examines the earliest archaeological evidence for the worship of Vālmīki as a deity, with particular reference to a seventh-century inscription found in what is now central Vietnam. The second part analyses the earliest textual evidence for the worship of Vālmīki, with particular reference to the earliest extant Sanskrit text on the creation of religious images. The third part focuses briefly on contemporary practice by considering some of the materials disseminated to devotees by Valmiki communities in Britain. The combination of these three rather different approaches to the worship of Vālmīki throws further light on the evolution of ideas relating to this important cultural figure.

To begin with the archaeological evidence, the tradition of Vālmīki worship dates back at least fourteen centuries to the reign of King Prakāśadharma (*c*. 653–679 CE) of Campā.[28] The term 'Campā' denotes a series of kingdoms and cultures that existed on the coast of what is now central Vietnam over a period of approximately a thousand years (Southworth 2001: 21). The Campā culture is usually associated with the Caṃ-speaking peoples of southern Vietnam, known as 'Cham' (p. 22 n. 2). Indigenous materials on the history and culture of Campā are sparse (Sarkar 1985: 9–11). However, its inscriptions, written in both Sanskrit and Caṃ, are some of the earliest epigraphic records so far discovered anywhere in Southeast Asia. With regard to scholarly research, the first comprehensive study of the culture was R. C. Majumdar's classic work (1927). According to the more recent work of Sarkar, Campā entered the pages of history as a political force in the second century CE.[29] The ongoing relationship between Campā and India is evident in the social and cultural institutions of the culture, and especially in the religious lives of the people. While there is more evidence for the worship of deities belonging to the Śaiva pantheon, Vaiṣṇava worship was also popular, as was Buddhism. Some Campā rulers even considered themselves incarnations of Viṣṇu. As the figures at the end of Southworth's dissertation (2001) demonstrate, there is evidence of a range of Indian religious icons and allegiances at the time. Further evidence of Indian influence is provided by the hundreds of Sanskrit inscriptions (over a hundred in Campā alone), and by the key role played by the *Manusmṛti* in the indigenous legal system. In Southeast Asia generally, both Indian epics were popular. Moreover, there is evidence of familiarity with all seven *kāṇḍa*s of the *Vālmīki Rāmāyaṇa*. In Campā in particular, there are rock inscriptions that indicate knowledge of both the *Bāla*- and the *Uttarakāṇḍa*s.

Before commenting on the remains of the Vālmīki temple discovered in Campā, however, something needs to be said about King Prakāśadharma. He belonged to the dynasty of Gaṅgarāja, the king who was said to have abdicated

---

28 According to recent research, archaeological evidence for the worship of Viṣṇu and Śiva is found in India as early as *c*. 600 BCE, while the first Viṣṇu temples probably date from the third century BCE (Chakrabarti 2001: 48–51).

29 The following summary is based on Sarkar (1985: 156–8, 180–2, 285–6, 312). For further information, see Majumdar (1927) and Southworth (2001).

in order to live out his life on the banks of the Gaṅgā.[30] Before 1927, scholars knew of several Sanskrit rock inscriptions bearing Prakāśadharma's name.[31] These inscriptions tell us that the king promoted the worship of a range of Hindu deities: Amareśa (that is, Śiva; perhaps with a *śivaliṅga*), Viṣṇu the 'Supreme Person' (*puruṣottama*; with a temple), Īśāneśvara and Prabhāseśvara (donations), Śambhubhadreśvara (an image and a donation) and 'Maheśvara's friend', Kuvera (a temple). The epigraphical reference to Kuvera as 'the yellow one with one eye' (*ekākṣapiṅgala*; no. 14, v. 2), together with the allusion to his friendship with Śiva, suggests an awareness of the story found in the *Uttarakāṇḍa* of the *Vālmīki Rāmāyaṇa* (7.13.24, 30–1; Shastri 1976: 410–12). There is also a reference to Lakṣmī, goddess of wealth, who is said to follow the king everywhere because he reminds her of Rāma, son of Daśaratha (no. 12, v. 25). We may conclude that, although Prakāśadharma's religious allegiance embraced both Śaiva and Vaiṣṇava deities, the evidence suggests that he showed a particular interest in the Rāma story.

In 1927, however, a new Prakāśadharma inscription (C. 173) was found near the south-west corner of the citadel of what was probably the first capital of Campā: Trá-Kiêu.[32] As Claeys describes, a stone plinth functioning as a paving slab on the outer threshold of a contemporary Vietnamese dwelling proved to belong to the seventh-century citadel. The plinth bears an inscription consisting of four lines of Sanskrit in what Claeys describes as a seventh-century script (1927: 477–9). The inscription is carved onto two of the lateral faces of the stone, at right angles to each other: four lines, each line forming a *śloka*, two lines on each face. The stone plinth is now in the History Museum in Hanoi, numbered B2/38, but its current condition is unknown. For those who wish to take a closer look at the evidence, a rubbing is kept in the library of the École Française d'Extrême Orient in Paris (no. 508).[33] The inscription commemorates the construction of a temple to Vālmīki on the orders of King Prakāśadharma. More precisely, as Mus explains, it commemorates the consecration of an image and the reconstruction of a temple, both in honour of Vālmīki. The following translation is based on Mus's decipherment of the damaged Sanskrit text, with numerals added by me for clarity:

> Now that the enemy of autumn[34] has disappeared, King Prakāśadharma – he who is beloved by all the world, who is endowed with the good qualities of sacred knowledge, creative power, serenity, good fortune (*lakṣmī*), fame and fortitude, the destroyer of all the enemy hosts – … who

30 Majumdar (1927: 35). For a revised lineage of Prakāśadharma, see Southworth (2001: 331).

31 The following information is taken from Majumdar (1927: Book 3, pp. 13–28, inscriptions nos 9–15). See also Finot (1904) and Huber (1911).

32 Southworth indicates the precise location on maps 9–10 of his dissertation (2001: 247–9), with the excavation sites on plans 117–19.

33 William Southworth (email communication, 27 November 2001).

34 The Sanskrit term translated here is *sārada*, one of the classical six seasons of South and Southeast Asia. The idea that the year has only two parts, 'wet' and 'dry', is also very old; it goes back to the opposition between Agni and Soma (Wujastyk 2001: chapter 6).

[1] performed the pious act (*kṛtyaṃ*) of consecrating (*abhiṣecanam*) in this place [a statue of] Vālmīki – the great *ṛṣi*, the first poet (*kaver ādyasya*), the man whose *śloka*, so greatly honoured (*abhipūj[itam?]*) by Brahmā, arose out of grief (*śokāt*), the one who is himself an incarnation in human form (*mānuṣasyātmarūpiṇaḥ*) of Viṣṇu, the Primeval Male (*pumsaḥ purāṇasya*) – [and] …

[2] reconstructed (*punas … kṛta[ṃ]*) his [Vālmīki's] temple (*pūjāsthānam*) … [35]

The inscription is incomplete. However, there is no doubt that what remains is a partial record of King Prakāśadharma's celebration of Vālmīki as a great sage (*ṛṣi*), as the first poet (*kavi*), and as the creator of the verse-form (*śloka*) that arose out of the famous *krauñca-vadha* episode described in the *Vālmīki Rāmāyaṇa*. The description of Vālmīki as an incarnation of Viṣṇu, as God in human form, is equally indisputable. The insertion of the word 'statue' in the translation is justified by Mus on the grounds that the epigraphy of Campā never separates the image (or, rather, the deity) from the temple. Thus the 'consecration of Vālmīki' means the consecration of the deity Vālmīki in both his statue and his temple, one within the other. The allusion to building that temple 'again' (*punas*) also requires explanation. Mus convincingly argues that Prakāśadharma had already constructed this temple to Vālmīki once; it was then destroyed by his enemies (now annihilated in their turn, according to the inscription), and finally rebuilt on the same site. Following Finot, Mus takes the allusion to the 'enemy of autumn' to suggest that the frequent battle campaigns of the period were likely to have been conducted in the autumn, against either invaders or rebels. The appropriate time for endowing religious institutions damaged in the process would therefore be at the end of that season (1928: 148).

What may we conclude from all this? First, the Rāma story (and, in particular, the Sanskrit text of the *Vālmīki Rāmāyaṇa*) seems to have played a significant role in the classical culture of Campā. As a result, it was appropriate for the king to celebrate Vālmīki both as a great *ṛṣi* and as the first poet. Second, from at least the seventh century, Vālmīki was worshipped as a deity, as a manifestation of Viṣṇu in human form. He received official recognition as such in the form of a temple and an image, both consecrated twice by the king himself. Southworth argues convincingly that the My Son inscription comparing Prakāśadharma to Rāma, the Duong Mong inscription to Viṣṇu Puruṣottama, and the Trá-Kiêu inscription about the Vālmīki temple are related. The two temples (at Duong Mong and Trá-Kiêu respectively) are the only ones formally dedicated to Viṣṇu in the epigraphy of Campā. Prakāśadharma's personal interest in Viṣṇu was no doubt due to the perceived religious link between Viṣṇu and kingship, hence perhaps the carefully chosen epithets for Viṣṇu ('Supreme Person' and 'Primeval Man'). The popularity of the *Vālmīki Rāmāyaṇa* would have reinforced the explicit parallel drawn between Prakāśadharma and Rāma, and thus the king's

35 The Sanskrit text as reconstructed by Mus (1928: 149) reads as follows: *yasya śokāt samutpannaṃ ślokam brahmābhipūj[ati] | viṣṇoḥ pumsaḥ purāṇasya mānuṣasyātma-rūpiṇaḥ || … ritam kṛtyaṃ kṛtaṃ yenābhiṣecanaṃ | kaver ādyasya maharṣṣer v-vālmikeś śru… …r iha || pūjāsthānam punas tasya kṛta … y … | prakāśa- dharmmanṛpatis sarvārigaṇasūdanaḥ || vidyāśaktikṣamālakṣmīkīrttidhairyya [guṇān- vitaḥ] | … ty eṣa jagatkāntaś śārade 'ntarite [r]i[pau] ||*

links with both Viṣṇu and Vālmīki. Together, all these elements would have established Prakāśadharma as the ideal king and Vālmīki as a divinized poet (2001: 234–5). Third, it must not be forgotten that Prakāśadharma's support for the worship of Viṣṇu – and, within that context, of Vālmīki – exists in the margins of a greater preponderance of inscriptions in favour of Śaiva deities. Finally, as Mus suggests, the king's devotion to Viṣṇu seems somewhat abstract rather than heartfelt, literary rather than deeply religious (1928: 158). The deification of Vālmīki, and the official cult inaugurated by it, suggests something similarly cerebral. Perhaps it is primarily a political gesture: Vālmīki's divinity is no doubt being used here to justify and support the current ruler. There is certainly no evidence either of the *bhakti* passion of medieval India or of the notion of the Supreme God conveyed by the Valmiki community today. I conclude that, in seventh-century Campā, Vālmīki was little more than the divinized poet of the Sanskrit *Rāmāyaṇa*, a minor deity among many.

For an idea of what an image of this deity might have looked like, we must turn to the *Viṣṇudharmottara*. This Sanskrit work is usually treated as an independent Purāṇa whose primary aim is the glorification of Viṣṇu. Certainly, the first printed text was published under the title *Viṣṇudharmottara-Mahāpurāṇa*, by the Veṅkateśvara Press in Bombay (1912).[36] Of the three *khaṇḍa*s, the first two are predictably Purāṇic in content. We may also note that the first *khaṇḍa* contains descriptions of Ayodhyā and a version of the Rāma story. But it is the third *khaṇḍa* that concerns us here. In 1924, Stella Kramrisch translated two of its best-known sections into English: the *Citrasūtra* on the art of religious painting (chapters 35–43), and the *Pratimālakṣaṇa* on the art of making religious images (chapters 44–85). Since then, these sections have been celebrated as the earliest detailed accounts of painting and image-making respectively. Other sections in the third *khaṇḍa* are devoted to music, dancing, acting and the building of temples, among other topics.[37] The dating of the text has been much discussed. After assessing the evidence, Priyabala Shah tentatively places the *Viṣṇudharmottara* as a whole somewhere between the second half of the fifth century and the first half of the seventh, that is, in the Gupta age between *c.* 450 and *c.* 650 CE. Focusing solely on the *Pratimālakṣaṇa*, Bhattacharyya suggests 650 CE.[38] According to Rocher, the text was probably composed in north India, perhaps in southern Kashmir or northern Panjab (1986: 252). It is not unreasonable, then, to postulate a link between this seventh-century north Indian manual on iconography (or one like it) and the missing image of Vālmīki in seventh-century Campā.

36 For a summary of the contents of the *Viṣṇudharmottara*, and for related scholarly literature, see Rocher (1986: 250–2). For the possible relationship between this text and the *Viṣṇu Purāṇa*, see Priyabala Shah (1958: xix–xxii) and Bhattacharyya (1991: xxi–xxii).

37 For a critical edition of the third *khaṇḍa*, see Priyabala Shah (1958). For an English translation and a preliminary bibliography, see Bhattacharyya (1991; for a summary of previous scholarship, see pp. xxiii–xxvii).

38 For the conclusions of other scholars – before 1000 CE (Rocher), between 600 and 1000 CE (Kane), between 500 and 600 CE (Hazra), the seventh century (Kramrisch), the first half of the fifth century (Pingree), and so on – see Rocher (1986: 252). For some of the evidence discussed, see Priyabala Shah (1958: xxii–xxviii) and Bhattacharyya (1991: lxvii–lxxiii).

Be that as it may, the *Pratimālakṣaṇa* tells us what an image of Vālmīki ought to look like. The outer frame of the text is a learned conversation between King Vajra and the great *ṛṣi* Mārkaṇḍeya. According to the colophons, the topic they are discussing is *rūpanirmāṇa*, that is, the creation of the physical forms of particular deities. But the first step is to establish the supremacy of Viṣṇu over both Śiva and Brahmā, in accordance with Vaiṣṇava theology. This is achieved by declaring that all three forms (that is, including the *saguṇa* forms, those 'with qualities') are but manifestations of the Supreme Lord (that is, the *nirguṇa*, 'quality-less', or unmanifest form of Viṣṇu), here named 'Janārdana' (44.2–4). The text then proceeds to describe in detail the many iconographic forms of Viṣṇu. The result, to borrow Bhattacharyya's phrase, is 'an iconographical and iconological eulogy (*māhātmya*) of the lord Viṣṇu' (1991: xxxii). Almost every divinity, Śaiva as well as Vaiṣṇava, is presented here as a manifestation, emanation or incarnation of Viṣṇu. One might reasonably ask where, in this plethora of divinities, Vālmīki is placed. The answer takes a somewhat literary form, one reminiscent perhaps of the Campā inscription. In the final chapter of the *Pratimālakṣaṇa*, within the wider context of the avatars of Viṣṇu, Vālmīki appears alongside the characters of the Rāma story and not far away from the characters of the *Mahābhārata*.

While the *Pratimālakṣaṇa* refers to several avatars, only some of them are described in iconographic detail: Varāha, in animal and man-boar forms (85.52b); Narasiṃha, the man-lion (85.54–55a); the Vāmana incarnation, described both as the dwarf and as Trivikrama, the divinity who takes three strides (85.55a–57b); Matsya and Kūrma in their non-human forms (85.59a); Paraśurāma, the son of Bhṛgu (*bhārgavo rāmo*), with his matted hair, axe and deer-skin (85.61b–62a); and Rāma, the son of Daśaratha (v. 62b), together with his three brothers, Bharata, Lakṣmaṇa and Śatrughna (v. 63). The next verse reads as follows:

> Vālmīki should be made with a fair complexion. He should be awe-inspiring on account of the matted hair twisted into a knot. He should look like someone who engages in ascetic practices, serene, but neither emaciated nor plump.[39]

We are then told that the same characteristics should be given to Dattātreya (v. 65a), another celebrated ascetic who is widely believed to be an incarnation of Viṣṇu. By contrast, Vyāsa, the author of the *Mahābhārata*, should have a dark complexion, an emaciated body, and piled up, red-brown matted locks (v. 65b). In addition, Vyāsa should be shown in the company of his four disciples (*śiṣya*): Sumantra, Jaimini,[40] Paila and Vaiśampāyana (v. 66). The *Pratimālakṣaṇa* then describes the way some of the characters in the *Mahābhārata* should look: Yudhiṣṭhira (v. 67a), Vṛkodara (Bhīma, v. 67b), Arjuna (vv. 68b–69a), the twins Nakula and Sahadeva (vv. 69b–70a), and Kṛṣṇā (Draupadī, v. 70b),

39 *gauras tu kāryo vālmīkir jaṭāmaṇḍaladurdṛśaḥ / tapasy abhirataḥ śānto na kṛśo na ca pīvaraḥ* // 85.64.

40 In this context and with regard to Southeast Asia, it is an intriguing coincidence that, in addition to the Trá-kiêu inscription describing an image of Vālmīki, an inscribed pedestal has been found in Sambor Prei Kuk indicating a lost statue of Jaimini (Mus 1928: 149).

followed by several characters from the Kṛṣṇa story. There is no disputing the fact that Vālmīki is classed here, along with all the others, as a manifestation of Viṣṇu. However, he is also viewed as a divinized author[41] and as a revered ascetic. There is nothing here to suggest subsequent developments in his orientation. In particular, the 'fair complexion' stipulated for the iconographic representation of Vālmīki effectively excludes the dark-skinned tribal or 'untouchable' of later legend. However, there is also no indication of the monotheistic supreme being of contemporary worship. For that we need to return to the twentieth century.

Before doing so, however, I wish to consider briefly a statue currently housed in the Nagpur Central Museum. For Hans Bakker, in his book on the 'iconology' of the Vākāṭaka dynasty, the statue represents an as yet unidentified *kavi* or poet (1997: 124–7, Plate XXVI).[42] The image was found in 1987 in the village of Nagardhan (believed to be the site of Nandivardhana, the ancient Vākāṭaka capital), some six kilometres south of Rāmṭek Hill (Rāmagiri) in what is now Maharashtra. This dates the image to somewhere between the mid-fourth and the early sixth centuries CE, most probably to the fifth. It also places it in the same vicinity as the contemporary version of the story of Śambūka discussed in chapter 4 (see Sontheimer 1991: 119–20). The question I wish to raise here is whether this image might represent Vālmīki. This is one of the two possible identifications discussed by Bakker, the other being Kālidāsa. The figure is that of a male seated on the ground in the *paryaṅka* position, the legs not fully crossed but with one foot placed on the opposite thigh and the other against the ground. As stipulated in the *Viṣṇudharmottara*, he is neither emaciated nor plump. The lack of a beard suggests that he is young. He wears a simple necklace and earrings, and his upper garment is draped loosely across his body from the left shoulder. According to Bakker, the hair is curly in a style peculiar to certain archaeological sites near the village of Mandhal; however, the other images to which Bakker directs the reader for comparison seem to have more formal hair-styles. Might the style of the *kavi* image be a local version of matted hair twisted untidily into a knot, as stipulated for Vālmīki? But the most intriguing aspect of this image is the book (*pothī*) that the figure is holding in his left hand. The right arm is broken off above the elbow but it is conceivable that its hand was gesturing in some way towards the book held conspicuously open in the other hand, or towards a listener. This possibility is reinforced by the fact that the figure's eyes are looking sideways as if focused on the book or on a pupil to one side. As Bakker points out, the representation of the *pothī* is extremely unusual. Books and manuscripts held by deities such as Brahmā and Sarasvatī are usually shown closed and in a vertical position, symbolizing a religious tradition open only to the élite. This book is not only held open, it is firmly angled towards the viewer; if the letters

41 I deduce this from Vālmīki's placing between Rāma and his brothers on the one hand and Vyāsa, the other great epic author, on the other. Dattātreya's intervention between Vālmīki and Vyāsa might suggest that the last two are included here as epic characters rather than as epic authors (Simon Brodbeck, personal communication, 8 June 2002).

42 I am grateful to Phyllis Granoff for drawing my attention to this image.

marked on the open pages were decipherable, they would be clearly legible to all who glanced in that direction (see photograph, Bakker p. 125). The symbolism is clear. Moreover, anyone familiar with contemporary portraits of Bhagwan Valmik will be struck by the similarities between them and this Vākāṭaka image. In devotional prints and paintings, Valmik is often shown sitting in a similar position on the ground with a book or manuscript open in one hand while he uses the other for teaching purposes. Often the eyes of the portrait are directed towards his audience: sometimes, he appears to be offering the book; sometimes he is teaching from it, or writing in it. But the symbol of the open book is constant: the wisdom contained within it is accessible to all. The same message is displayed on the walls of Valmiki temples in Britain today.

I conclude this section by presenting briefly the main attributes of Bhagwan Valmik as they may be understood from some of the other temple paintings on display, and from some of the literature circulating within the Valmiki community.[43] This account is not intended to be exhaustive; nor indeed could it be in a study of this scope. An in-depth study would require a close examination of the Panjabi-language materials available; indeed, this would constitute a significant research project for a scholar with the requisite language skills. None the less, I believe that it is useful to present here, even in this restricted form, the qualities attributed to Bhagwan Valmik by some of his British devotees. Judging by the material at my disposal, then, I suggest that Bhagwan Valmik is primarily worshipped in two aspects: in his embodied, manifest or *saguṇa* form, and as the unmanifest or *nirguṇa* Ultimate Reality. For the sake of clarity, I shall refer to the first as 'Guru Valmik', and to the second as 'Bhagwan Valmik'. The embodied human form is especially striking in two temple paintings that show Guru Valmik as a baby (see Plate 5.1).[44] In general terms, however, the *saguṇa* aspect (Guru Valmik) may be divided into four, often overlapping, manifestations: as an ancient *ṛṣi*; as a poet, the celebrated author of the first Sanskrit *Rāmāyaṇa*; as the spiritual preceptor of the *Yogavāsiṣṭha*; and as an inspiring figurehead for *dalit*s everywhere. I shall begin by considering in turn each of the manifestations of his *saguṇa* form.

The identification of Guru Valmik as an ancient *ṛṣi*, a wise and disciplined ascetic, is evident in almost every illustration. The line drawing on the front cover of the first issue of the Southall-based journal *Valmik Jagriti* offers a perfect example. Guru Valmik sits on the ground in the open with his right hand raised in blessing. He is wearing a robe draped across his left shoulder. His white beard is long and bushy, his white moustache luxuriant. His hair is also white, long at the back, the rest coiled up on the top of his head. While Guru Valmik lacks here the matted locks of the Indian ascetic tradition, the effect conveyed is one of calm authority and ancient wisdom. His head is enclosed in a red-tinted halo and his expression is serene. Another example is provided by the cover picture for all but

43 I am indebted to Lekh Raj Manjdadria for making this material available to me.

44 The painting in the Bhagwan Valmik Ashram in Birmingham uses the baby's jewellery and the fine clothes of the mother to suggest a high-status family. A second mother-and-baby painting, in a different style, may be found in the Bhagwan Valmik Mandir in Southall.

two of the issues in my possession of the journal *The Service*. All carry the same head-and-shoulders portrait of 'Jagat Guru Valmiki Ji' by the popular local artist, Kiran Valmiki.[45] The marks of the ascetic (matted locks, topknot, *rudrākṣa* beads) are absent, but the marks of wisdom and serenity remain: halo, long white hair, bushy white beard and the half-lidded contemplative gaze. The most dramatic example of this manifestation is found in the full-length portraits painted by Kiran Valmiki.[46] In this first category, I also place the frequent attribution to Guru Valmiki of an ancient lineage and great antiquity.[47]

The second category, Guru Valmik as the author of the *Rāmāyaṇa*, is also exemplified in much of the illustrative material. For example, later issues of *Valmik Jagriti* have preferred a cover depicting the same ascetic figure, but this time he is engaged in writing out a text with the aid of a feather quill. In the background, a simple hut stands by the bank of a river; in the foreground Rāma and Sītā, enclosed in their own shared halo of sanctity, offer obeisance. The same picture may be found in *Valmikism* (opposite p. 4). It is significant that Rāma and Sītā are shown bowing to Guru Valmik, and not vice versa. For, in contrast with most Hindus today (but in accord with text-historical criticism of the early development of the Rāmāyaṇa story), Valmikis regard Rāma and Sītā as human beings, not gods. Rāma is the ideal king, Sītā the ideal wife, Lakṣmaṇa the ideal brother and Hanumān 'the most loyal of followers'.[48] In addition to the illustrative and written material in Valmiki publications, Guru Valmik's authorship of the *Rāmāyaṇa* is frequently celebrated in temple paintings: the *krauñca-vadha* incident or 'birth of the *śloka*', Guru Valmik writing the text in the shade of his hermitage, Guru Valmik handing over the finished manuscript to the two boys. Other paintings stress Valmik's compassionate nature: he rescues Sītā, raises and educates her sons, teaches them archery and spiritual knowledge as they grow up, uses his pot of amrit to bring everyone back to life after the final battle, and helps to reconcile them all with Rāma. The gentle and generous personality of Guru Valmik is a favourite topic, one that extends to the community's understanding of his teachings. According to *Valmik Jagriti*, 2, p. 4, Guru Valmik teaches ethical values, how to live within the family and within the wider society. Some of these values are listed among the seven 'Principles of Living': not gambling, not stealing and not exploiting the poor; not 'clouding the mind'; respecting the

45 Kiran Valmiki was born in Jalandhar in the Panjab on 2 January 1957. Although his family name is Gill, his school teacher in India insisted on calling him by the (for the teacher, caste-related and therefore derogatory) name 'Valmiki'. Later, when Kiran decided to become a religious artist, he deliberately chose this name as a mark of pride. He studied Indian painting for many years, living and working with his guru, before coming to Britain. Judging by the large number of paintings bearing his signature that now hang in the various temples in Britain, Kiran Valmiki is without doubt the most popular religious artist for the British Valmiki community today.

46 For the one at the Bhagwan Valmik Mandir in Bedford, see Plate 5.2. Similar paintings by the same artist may be found in the Bhagwan Valmik Ashram in Birmingham, and in the Jagat Guru Valmik Ji Maharaj Temple in Coventry.

47 See, for example, *Valmik Jagriti* (2, pp. 19–20 and p. 26; 3, pp. 23–5) and *The Service* (1.1, p. 10).

48 See *Valmikism* (pp. 4, 9) and *The Service* (1.1, p. 11).

individuality of others and their beliefs; and meditation as the path towards understanding oneself.[49] A later provisional list of 'Principles of Valmiki Dharma' suggests four fundamental elements: self-control, a spirit of enquiry, contentment, and keeping good company (*Valmik Jagriti*, 3, p. 44).

The third category presents Guru Valmik as the community's spiritual preceptor, particularly in relation to the *Yogavāsiṣṭha*. I have already described the cover picture used for the later issues of *Valmik Jagriti*: an ascetic figure engaged in writing a Sanskrit text. The caption beneath that picture reads: 'Bhagwan Valmik Ji composing the Maha Ramayana'. The implication here, stated explicitly elsewhere,[50] is that Guru Valmik is the author of a single text entitled the *Mahā-Rāmāyaṇa*, of which the *Rāmāyaṇa* forms the first half and the *Yogavāsiṣṭha* the second. Since these texts are believed to be two halves of the same work by one author, devotees naturally perceive a considerable overlap between what I have separated as the second and third 'categories'. For the textual scholar, however, the two texts are quite distinct, of different periods, by different 'authors', and with different evolutionary histories (see chapter 3). The shared context preferred by the Valmiki community is illustrated on the front cover of the first issue of the monthly newsletter *The Service* (1982). Guru Valmik is shown seated cross-legged on the top of a flattened mound of earth, beside him a water-pot, in front of him a text open on a low stool or dais. His right hand is raised in blessing, his left in the gesture of teaching, as he preaches to the assembled multitude sketched into the foreground. The stress on teaching is made abundantly clear in two temple paintings relating to the *Yogavāsiṣṭha*: Guru Valmik giving his blessing to Vasiṣṭha before handing over the text of the *Yogavāsiṣṭha* in front of a waiting crowd of devotees (in the Bhagwan Valmik Ashram in Birmingham); and Guru Valmik gazing down benevolently as Vasiṣṭha conveys the teachings he has received to Prince Rāma (in the Bhagwan Valmik Mandir in Bedford; see Plate 5.3). The emphasis is no longer on the writing but on the teaching.[51]

---

49 The full text of the 'Principles of living: VALMIKI DHARAM' reads as follows: '1. We believe in One Absolute God. "WOHI EK BRAHM", Bhagwan Valmik Ji. 2. We meditate via reciting Bhajans. 3. We discard gambling, stealing and exploitation of poors. 4. We abstain from clouding the mind. 5. We respect the individuality of others and their beliefs. 6. We stand for truth and our right to defend us. 7. Meditation has crucial importance. It is a means to know oneself and learning how to change to enlightened state of mind.' (*Valmik Jagriti*, 2, p. 26).

50 See, for example, *Valmik Jagriti*, 2, pp. 4, 20; *Valmikism*, p. 1.

51 According to *Valmik Jagriti*, 1, p. 3, the importance of the *Yogavāsiṣṭha* is directly connected to the community's need to understand and then put into practice 'the principles of living within Valmiki Dharam'. The text has also become part of a political process of unification. Thus an article entitled 'An Important Message to All Valmikis' exhorts its readers to 'unite to create a Yoga Vasistha in simple Punjabi', adding that, 'until we all read from one holy book, we cannot unite' (*Valmik Jagriti*, 2, p. 27). In 2001, the Valmik Sabhas of Southall and Jalandhar re-released the Panjabi edition of the *Yogavāsiṣṭha* in order to 'bring back the teachings of our past in a modern context' (*Valmik Yog Vasistha*, front cover). Reprints of B. L. Atreya's 1930s lectures on the text (2000a and 2000b) are enthusiastically recommended in order to 'build a Common World Culture' (p. 9), within which everyone can know 'how he can become God' (p. 11).

One of the key points of Guru Valmik's teaching relates to *karma* and caste. We are repeatedly informed that he did not believe in the caste system and held that all human beings were 'equal in the sight of God' (*Valmikism*, p. 9). This is why, today, devotees congregate in the 'Langer hall' after worship in order to share food. The custom is designed 'to unite people from all sections of the society and to promote social equality between all human beings'. For the same reason 'Karah Parshad' is distributed from a common bowl (*Valmikism*, p. 13). In the distant past, *The Service* explains, 'the caste system was thrust upon us as divinely originated' (1.1, p. 12). An explicit link is drawn between 'Hinduism', caste, and the persistent fiction of 'untouchability' even after its formal abolition. Since caste is integral to 'Hinduism', and 'untouchability' to caste, only the destruction of 'Hinduism' will achieve the abolition of 'untouchability' (*The Service*, 1.6, pp. 15–18). Therefore anything in either of Guru Valmik's texts that contradicts this basic anti-caste principle must have been added by another hand. Thus Baaghaa warns his readers to be alert to the 'wily interpolations craftily interwoven by pillars of Brahmanical Imperialism in the original text of Valmik's Ramayan with the purpose of diluting the bright image of the grand divine who conceived and produced this marvellous work' (*Valmik Jagriti*, 1, p. 7). This idea is widespread. For example, an article in *The Service* declares that 'we know for a fact that parts of Ramayana were later deleted, distorted and added to by the crafty Brahmin priests and writers' (1.1, p. 9). Baaghaa cites one of the examples that many people, including non-Valmikis, have found most disturbing: the story of the *śūdra* Shambuk or Śambūka. In most versions of the *Rāmāyaṇa*, Śambūka performs *tapas* to become divine, thereby contravening the socio-religious laws of class (*varṇadharma*) with disturbing consequence for the kingdom as a whole. As soon as the connection is made clear to him, Rāma decapitates Śambūka (see Plate 3.1). Baaghaa concludes that stories like this could never have been formulated by Guru Valmik; they should therefore be expunged from his text.[52] Moreover, Valmikis are expected to defend this judgement. In fact, according to Baaghaa, 'the credit for purifying Valmik's Ramayan by deleting anti-Shudar blight from it should go to Valmiki Brotherhood' (*Valmik Jagriti*, 1, p. 7). The call to action is clear. It is the concern of the Valmiki community both in and beyond India to preserve the image of their Guru from what are deemed to be malicious slurs on his character. In this context, their heated response to the casual airing of the dacoit legend in Birmingham is hardly surprising.

This brings us to the fourth way in which Guru Valmik is revered: as a unifying figurehead for all *dalit*s. This idea is derived from the belief that, in this manifest form, Guru Valmik himself was of tribal origin, that he was a *dalit* (*Valmikism*, p. 1). For example, the first issue of *The Service* claims that Valmik was born 'in the Naga nation', and explicitly identifies 'Nagas' with 'non-Aryans' and 'Dravidians'.[53]

---

52 In the context of the Valmiki community's need for the unspoilt, 'original' text of the *Vālmīki Rāmāyaṇa*, we can look forward with some interest to the forthcoming English translation by John and Mary Brockington of what they term the 'core' text.

53 For a comprehensive, if now somewhat dated, study of the *nāga*s in Indian literature and art, see Vogel (1926), including the suggestion that Vālmīki's name may be derived from the 'sanctity attached to the abode of the cobra' (p. 30).

According to this argument, Valmik is the 'ancestor' of the 'original' (*ādi*) inhabitants of India, prior to the so-called 'Aryan invasion', the 'first recorded dalit hero' (1.1, p. 9). Several temple paintings reinforce the *dalit* angle. A prime example is the painting by Kiran Valmiki of Ek Lava (Ekalavya), found in the Bhagwan Valmik Mandir in Southall. Ekalavya was a prince of the Niṣāda tribe; from the brahminical point of view, this made him an 'untouchable'. When he proved to be a brilliant archer likely to outshine even Arjuna, the Pāṇḍavas' teacher Droṇa demanded as his fee Ekalavya's thumb, thus destroying for ever the prince's ability to compete against the 'higher' castes. Valmikis are encouraged to learn about such early *dalit* role models, and about Guru Valmik himself, so that they can discover their own cultural past and in the process develop some control over their future. Thus the editorial of the first issue of *Valmik Jagriti* declares that its aim is to 'trace our rich cultural roots', to 'preserve our heritage', and to 'stand for truth and our right to defend [ourselves]'. The second issue contains a detailed article on the Sanskrit term *anārya* ('non-Aryan'), as a means of debunking the widespread idea that 'Hinduism' is essentially 'Aryan' when in reality 'the best part of what is called Hinduism is not Aryan but indigenous' (*Valmik Jagriti*, 2, p. 17).[54] As discussed in chapter 2,[55] current scholarship no longer promotes the idea of a 'original' clash between 'Aryan' and 'indigenous' (read 'Dravidian') people. The more complex notions relating to the spread of languages does, however, still allow for the fundamental *dalit* claim that their tribal forebears were at some point and in some way subjugated by encroaching pastoral settlers. Hence the power of the story of Ekalavya, prince of the Niṣādas, reclassified by brahminical discourse as 'untouchables'. Acceptance of these ideas has led to a new era of hope and aspiration.[56] The emphasis is now on knowledge, for education has been denied to *dalit*s for too long (*Valmik Jagriti*, 3, p. 3).[57]

---

54 The article refers to the indigenous worship of snakes, monkeys, bulls, trees and stones; to the Dravidian origins of Gaṇeśa, Garuḍa, Hanumān, Nandi, the Nāgas, Kumāra, Śiva, Viṣṇu; and so on. While there is certainly historical evidence to support many of these assertions, it is beyond the scope of this study to enter into this discussion here.

55 For the problems inherent in the 'Aryan invasion theory', see chapter 2, section 3.

56 This is clear in the rousing address by Gurpal Gill, President of the Southall Sabha, to 'all members of Valmiki Brotherhood at home and abroad'. 'After centuries of oppression and deprivation,' he declares, 'Valmikis are joyfully astir with hopes and aspirations sky-high'. Their aim must be for 'total unity among Valmiki ranks' and, for this purpose, 'Bhagwan Valmik Ji remains the pivot and matrix of our cultural expanse' (*Valmik Jagriti*, 2, p. 3). It should be no surprise that oppression, both past and present, is a recurring topic in Valmiki publications. For the 'bloody catalogue of Hindu crimes' against 'untouchables', see *The Service*, 1.3, pp. 16–18, and Amarjit Singh's series of articles on the caste system (1982–83). Subsequent issues of *The Service* contain similar articles on the origins of *dalit*s, on their present-day sufferings, and on the achievements of key individuals such as Ambedkar and Ravidās.

57 Education is the primary motive behind the publication of *Valmikism*, a booklet produced by WAVE (the Wolverhampton Association for Valmiki Education) in collaboration with the Wolverhampton Valmik Sabha. This booklet, printed 'in response to the increasing number of young Valmikis being brought up in Britain', aims to teach these young people about 'the culture and traditions of Valmikis' in order to encourage greater awareness of Valmiki 'identity' within the community as a

But education is only the first step. The impulse behind this education, and therefore unification, programme is not simply to promote the cultural unity of those now calling themselves 'Valmikis'. The intention is rather to create from that cultural unity a global religion. As *Valmik Jagriti*, 3, p. 23 declares:

> Shri Valmik Ji is Bhagwan and Guru.
> We believe in the philosophy of Guru Valmik Ji
> as given in Ramayana and the Yoga-Vasistha.
> That is why we are called Valmikis.
> As believers of Christ are called Christians.

The long-standing bond between Valmikis and Indian Christians, a bond born of shared *dalit* ancestry, is reinforced by the cover picture of *The Service* (1.3): a portrait of 'Jesus Christ', both hands raised to demonstrate the crucifixion wounds, to welcome and to bless (see also pp. 14–15). The publication of this third issue was timed to coincide with the conference on 'Valmiki-Unity', held in the Panjab on 5 April 1998. Special emphasis is placed on maintaining and building on the links between non-resident Indian (NRI) Valmikis in the UK and their counterparts in the Panjab. There is even a separate section devoted to 'NRI information for Valmik Sabhas in the UK'. The aims of the 'NRI Sabha' include such things as helping Valmiki NRIs to protect their rights in the Panjab, providing facilities for them when they visit, maintaining 'cultural and ethnic bonds' between the Panjab and NRIs, 'especially the new generation', promoting 'social welfare' in the Panjab, and so on (*Valmik Jagriti*, 3, p. 51).

More important, the journal urges the global community to embrace fourteen proposals under the heading 'VALMIKI UNITY'. The first proposal urges both delegates to the conference and readers of the journal:

> To stop wandering into different religions. Adopting
> another religion will destroy our Valmiki roots.
> Be a Valmiki and be proud of it.

Further proposals include the following: to have complete faith in the teachings given in the *Rāmāyaṇa* and the *Yogavāsiṣṭha*; to create common rituals, notably but not exclusively Valmiki marriage ceremonies and Valmiki death rituals; to ensure that all Valmiki communities across the world use the same 'approved' texts for worship in temples and homes; to have rituals performed by 'Valmiki pujaris'; to have their own researchers; to establish a Valmiki Press to publish 'Valmikian research' for 'promotion in all languages'; to educate all Valmiki children; to build Valmiki temples 'in every town and village'; and, reflecting the UK environment,

---

whole (p. 1). An earlier initiative is represented by the publications of the Valmiki Research Unit (VRU). The VRU is the creation of an independent group of British Valmikis intent on producing and promoting 'qualitative and academic research' on issues important to their community and to their religious tradition. Six issues were produced between October 1995 and August 1997. These were made available free of cost to all who showed interest, either in printed form or via the VRU website. I am grateful to Lekh Raj Manjdadria for sending me printed copies of all six issues.

to attend one's local temple every Sunday. This idea that Valmikis should differentiate themselves from – to some extent, distance themselves from – both Hindus and Sikhs is significant, especially in the context of Eleanor Nesbitt's research in Coventry where no such distinction is made (see chapter 2). This suggests that not all the Valmiki Sabhas in the UK are in agreement on this matter.[58]

The fifth category of contemporary Valmik worship embraces and overshadows the other four: Bhagwan Valmik in his *nirguṇa* aspect, unmanifest Ultimate Reality. For example, the first issue of the *Valmik Jagriti* declares: 'We believe in One Absolute God' (1, p. 3). The first of the seven 'Principles of Living' ('Valmiki Dharam') reads: 'We believe in One Absolute God. "WOHI EK BRAHM", Bhagwan Valmik Ji' (2, p. 26). This statement is explained at length in the third issue (3, pp. 10–21). For example, the word 'Brahm' is glossed as 'the formless God' and the central affirmation, 'WOHI EK BRAHM' ('The formless God is One'), is described as 'the Mahavakya for us Valmikis' (p. 10). This is a deliberate link with the 'great assertions' (*mahāvākya*) of monistic philosophy in the Upaniṣads. The specific *mahāvākya*s cited are the four best-known and best-loved pronouncements of the Upaniṣads. 'I am Brahman' (*ahaṃ brahmāsmi*) is from the *Bṛhadāraṇyaka Upaniṣad* (1.4.10, 2.5.19). 'That you are' (*tat tvam asi*)[59] is from the *Chāndogya Upaniṣad* (6.8.7, 6.9.4, etc.). 'This self is Brahman' (*ayam ātmā brahma*) is found in both the *Bṛhadāraṇyaka Upaniṣad* (4.4.5) and in the *Māṇḍūkya Upaniṣad* (2). Finally, 'Consciousness is Brahman' (*prajñāṇaṃ brahma*) is from the *Aitareya Upaniṣad* (3.3). From these and other passages, it is clear that Valmik is celebrated in his *nirguṇa* aspect of the Absolute, as Bhagwan, as well as in his *saguṇa* manifestation as an incarnation of God in human form. The *nirguṇa* aspect is reinforced by several temple paintings that are both dramatic and informative: Bhagwan Valmik holding the universe in one hand (see frontispiece); and Bhagwan Valmik as the power behind all the gods (see Plate 5.4). The latter painting shows light emanating from Bhagwan Valmik, passing to Devī, and then from her to the three main male deities of the Hindu pantheon.[60] This notion of the unmanifest as light is reminiscent of the early teachings of Sri Sat Guru Gian Nath Ji Maharaj, the charismatic saint who first came to England in 1972 (see Plate 2.1), and it underlies much of the Valmiki teachings today.

---

58 For those which are, the implications of 'Valmikism' are pursued in proposal 13: 'Valmiki Mandirs [are] to preach Valmikism only. A Valmiki Mandir must not have any other form of worship except Puja and readings from the Ramayana and Yoga-Vasistha. We give you an example. "Non[e] else to be praised except Allaha." This is written outside Mosques. And thus theirs is the largest religion in the world' (*Valmik Jagriti*, 3, p. 6ff.). While this journal may represent the more radical wing of the 'global' Valmiki community, it demonstrates the direction that at least some in Britain would like the community to take.

59 Despite Joel Brereton's 1986 article demonstrating that this interpretation of *tat tvam asi* is grammatically impossible, it is still the one generally accepted outside academic circles. See also Olivelle (1996: 349).

60 Another version of this scene is to be found in the Lord Valmik Ji Nirankar Holy Temple Gian Ashram Bhavnashan in Ampthill Road, Bedford. I have no information on the painter of either work.

The problem of the dacoit story should now become clear. For a community of people who believe that Prince Rāma is as human as Prince Ekalavya and that Bhagwan Valmik is divine, the idea that God was once a 'petty bandit who achieved salvation by inadvertently reciting the name of Rama' is totally unacceptable. As *The Service* exclaims, 'What cheek!' (1.1, p. 12).

To summarize this section, there seems to have been a remarkable progression in the evolution of thought about Vālmīki as a deity. The epigraphical evidence of the seventh-century Campā culture shows him as Viṣṇu in human form, worthy of independent worship in a temple of his own, a temple in honour of Vālmīki's poetic gifts and his compassion, one that was constructed personally (twice) by King Prakāśadharma. The textual evidence of the *Pratimālakṣaṇa* reinforces the idea of Vālmīki as an incarnation of Viṣṇu and describes how he should look in iconographical form: fair-skinned, ascetic but not emaciated, and serene. Together, epigraphy and text present explicit external evidence to support the assertion that Vālmīki was worshipped as a deity, certainly by the seventh century CE, probably by the fifth.[61] His main characteristics at that point were: authority and god-like power, by virtue of his ascetic practices; poetic prowess, exemplified by his authorship of the *Vālmīki Rāmāyaṇa*; a serene and compassionate nature, demonstrated by his iconographical image, by the definitive *krauñca-vadha* episode and by his behaviour towards Sītā and the twins; and an identification with Viṣṇu by association with the Rāma story. There is no mention of the *Yogavāsiṣṭha* in either source. Equally, there is no reference to the dacoit legend. But Vālmīki's status as a deity is clear. His popularity in the seventh century is illustrated by the fact that, even in what is now Vietnam, a temple to him and an image of him were created by an influential king of the time. Coincidentally, as I have also discussed in this section, the so-far-unidentified Vākāṭaka statue dated to around the fifth century may also be of Vālmīki. Be that as it may, it was not until the early twentieth century that Bhagwan Valmik became the centre of a monotheistic religious movement of his own, first in northern India, and subsequently in Britain.

4. Caste and Salvation

There are many reasons for the striking change in the traditional portrayal and popular understanding of Vālmīki. In this study, I have focused on the legend that Vālmīki was once a dacoit. Once the fully developed legend emerges from the cultural mix, two important elements come into focus: Vālmīki as the archetypical redeemed sinner of the *bhakti* tradition and Vālmīki as the vaguely 'ancestral' figure of the *dalit* movement in much of north India. To take the second element first, the part of the legend that is still valued by Valmikis today is the idea of a shared ancestral link: that Vālmīki, like them, was an 'aboriginal' (*ādi*) inhabitant of India, a 'tribal', a *dalit*. Without the legend, this link might never

---

61 As Greg Bailey points out, however, we cannot make a judgement about the extent of his worship; the *Pratimālakṣaṇa* may have included Vālmīki purely for the sake of completeness (personal communication, 15 July 2002).

have been made. But this supremely uplifting and now unifying element appears to bring with it the part of the legend that Valmikis hate: the idea that their ancestor/saint/God was once a sinner; that he was impure and ignorant; that he was a thieving, murdering dacoit. At first sight, it seems difficult to defend the *dalit* identity while demolishing the dacoit. Text-historically speaking, they appear to stand or fall together.

If we read between the lines, however, this is not the case. What I hope this study of authority and meaning has demonstrated is that, for centuries, the text-producers of high-caste Sanskrit culture (in particular the 'Bhārgava' brahmins) denigrated and stigmatized what I have called the 'tribals'. Even high-status tribal princes like Ekalavya were dismissed as without caste (*avarṇa*) and re-classified as 'untouchable', let alone the ordinary people hunting in the forests and fishing in the rivers as they went about their lives. The violence anticipated by these brahmins at the hands of the forest people was probably the result of their own temerity in invading the latter's space: the tribal response would surely have been to defend that space, the brahmin counter-response to vilify their assailants as 'dacoits'. But the only extant version of these events is the one-sided account of those astonishingly self-assured brahmin redactors. Quite simply, they twisted the evidence. They used their so-called 'sacred' texts effectively as 'tools in an extended campaign of ethnic subjugation'.[62] But where does that leave the Valmiki devotees? Can they in fact defend the tribal and reject the dacoit?

While there is evidently a conundrum here, I believe that they can. Purushottam Lal Bhargava disagrees: regardless of the political aspirations of certain castes, he declares, Vālmīki could not possibly have been a tribal; as the composer of the first Sanskrit poem, he must have belonged to the Sanskrit-speaking élite.[63] Judging by the evidence discussed in chapter 3, I would respond that he has focused too closely on the 'poetic' aspects relating to Vālmīki at the expense of the alternative evidence of a 'non-Sanskritic other'. Sahdev reaches similar conclusions to those of P. L. Bhargava, but expresses them more gently. She maintains that there is no early evidence to support the idea that the poet Vālmīki might have belonged to a group classified as 'low-caste', and suggests that the dacoit story was the result of a confusion between several individuals sharing the same name: the poet, a well-known dacoit, and a 'Svapaca'.[64] Judging by the evidence discussed in chapters 3 and 4, I would respond that the acceptance of tribal origins (the high-status 'other' whose mother-tongue is not Sanskrit) is not necessarily an acceptance of the 'low-caste'

62 Simon Brodbeck, personal communication, 8 June 2002.

63 P. L. Bhargava (1984: 79 n. 2). In my presentation of Bhargava's views here, I have omitted his outdated references to 'non-Aryan' tribesmen and an 'Aryan' élite; the principle by which one group subjugates another does not require these distinctions.

64 Sahdev makes a firm distinction between the epic poet and one or more low-caste figures of the same name, including one who is said to have died at Thaneshwar near Karnal. She points out that this Vālmīki is described by Ravidās as *śvapac*, and concludes that he was an 'untouchable'. This is the Vālmīki revered by the 'Chuhras', she suggests, not the epic poet. Over time, she maintains, due to pressures from outside (on the part of either colonial officials or orthodox Hindus, or both), the *dalit* figure and the epic poet became conflated (1986: 14–16). Prashad's discussion of this point (2000: 73) cites Sahdev's Panjabi-language study (1980: 100, 112, 120–2).

status so often conferred on the 'other' by brahmins. If Ekalavya was a prince of the Niṣādas, could Vālmīki not have been a prince of the Suparṇas? Is this more unreasonable than re-classifying one tribal group as 'untouchable' and the other as winged monsters that eat snakes? Surely not. More important, if we reject the tribal hints (the non-Sanskrit-mother-tongue strands) in the pre-history of Vālmīki, then we must reject *dalit* ancestry as well as dacoit behaviour. Few will mourn the loss of the dacoit in relation to Vālmīki. As Benjamin Khan puts it, 'the theory that Vālmīki began his career as a highway robber is a legend ill-conceived and unfounded' (1983: 12).[65] But what of the millions of devotees who venerate Bhagwan Valmik as a *dalit* forebear?

I suggest two quite different ways forward. The first relates to the workings of caste and is already outlined above: meticulous text-historical study to reveal as plainly as possible the reconstruction of the 'other' (including, but not exclusively, the tribal populations) within the caste-driven, brahminical universe. This is the work of scholars. There is plenty to do but it will bring the necessary clarity of vision. The alternative is to grasp the nettle of caste and salvation in another way entirely, that of the *jīvanmukta* as described in the *Yogavāsiṣṭha*. Let me put the two together.

In early Vedic contexts, the term *ārya* ('noble') distinguished the Sanskrit-speaking élite from the rest of the population (termed *dāsa* or *dasyu*), largely for ritual purposes. Over time, the *ārya/dāsa* distinction became the *varṇa*-related distinction between *dvija* ('twice-born') and *śūdra* (glossed as *ekajāti*, 'having one birth').[66] The boundary between the so-called 'élite' and the rest of the population was not as clear-cut as later texts and commentators, both Indian and 'Orientalist', suggest: some tribal princes and ritual specialists would almost certainly have been incorporated into the *kṣatriya* and brahmin classes. In time, however, the *varṇa* system became crystallized, in principle (if not in fact) fixed.[67] By the time of the Buddha, the assumption of superiority on the part of the orthodox brahmin was widespread. In the *Dīgha Nikāya*, for example, two Buddhist monks complain to the Buddha of the arrogance of brahmins. The brahmin boast (27.3) is translated by William Smith (2000: 209) as follows:

> Brahmans are the best caste (*seṭṭho vaṇṇo*), the other castes are inferior (*hīno*); Brahmans are of a fair color (*sukko vaṇṇo*), others are black (*kaṇho*); Brahmans are pure, not non-Brahmans; Brahmans are the sons of the god Brahmā, born from his mouth, born of Brahmā, created by Brahmā, heirs to Brahmā.

65 See also van Nooten (1976: xiii).

66 The gradual enslavement of members of the second group gave Sanskrit its word for 'slave' (*dāsa*), just as the enslavement of the Slavonic population in Europe led in time to the English word 'slave'. Interestingly, the word for 'slave' in the Finnish language is *orja*, which appears to go back to a protoform **orya*, derived from *ārya*, the ethnic name of Aryan-speakers who lived in the regions south of the ancient Finnic-speakers (Carpelan and Parpola 2001: 112ff.).

67 For a comprehensive account of *varṇa* (first tripartite, later quadripartite) as the fundamental principle of classification in early Indian society, see Brian Smith (1994). For the racial essentialism inherent in the 'Aryan idea' from the late nineteenth century onwards, 'the racial theory of Indian civilization', see Trautmann (1997).

But there is also an ancient tradition in India of resistance to brahminical *varṇa-dharma*. The Buddhist *Dhammapada*, for example, devotes the whole of chapter 26 to the 'brahmin path' (*brāhmaṇa-vaggo*) and concludes that a 'true brahmin' is one who acts 'nobly', that is, as a brahmin should (Carter and Palihawadana 1987: 391–416). In this context, the 'noble' person (*ariya*) is one whose actions are noble, not one born into a noble family. According to this view, physical birth is irrelevant. A verse in the *Mahābhārata* goes further still:

> Not the act of physical birth, nor the performance of the sacraments, not Vedic learning, nor respectful bowing: none of these lead to the twice-born state; conduct alone [does that].[68]

Here, the concept *ārya*, the very foundation of brahminhood, is radically undermined. High status is derived from behaviour, not birth.

But what does this mean for the normative religious hierarchies of *varṇa* and *jāti*? It is generally assumed – certainly by the voluminous *dharma* literature – that only males of the higher *varṇa*s are capable of the spiritual heights implied. Even in the epic literature there is a marked tendency for the stories of spiritual and physical renewal to be told only in relation to high-caste, usually brahmin, males. This is essentially what the concept *dvija* ('twice-born') simultaneously reveals and conceals. At one level, the term is the mark of spiritual rebirth and is thus, theoretically, applicable to anyone who undergoes such a transformation. At another level, as the Vedic ritual of initiation (*upanayana*) has long demonstrated, it is restricted to those whose physical birth places them in the appropriate sex and *varṇa*. The same basic *dvija* idea is found in the termite-mound motif: in the epic, the ascetic (in the *bhakti* context, the sinner) is 'born again' from the termite mound, transformed and purified, in what seems to be a deliberate mirroring of the *upanayana*. The rebirth theme may be found in a number of other rituals and stories too. For example, the *Aitareya Brāhmaṇa* describes a symbolic rebirth enacted during the *soma* ritual, while the *Suśruta Saṃhitā* describes a physical rejuvenation ritual, also by means of *soma*, by which a man may obtain a new body. In both cases, the protagonist enters a special hut and emerges 'reborn' (Wujastyk 2001: 119–21, 174–9). The story of Cyavana was discussed earlier: by bathing at a sacred spot, an elderly ascetic gains a god-like physical form to reflect his inner transformation; he too is 'reborn'. But all these rebirth scenarios are applied to high-caste males. Clearly, beneath the theory lies the fairly constant assumption that the candidate for spiritual rebirth (*dvija* in one sense) will first be born into a higher *varṇa* (*dvija* in the other sense).[69] It is similarly assumed that the person most likely to understand *brahman* ('the Absolute'), and therefore be termed a *brāhmaṇa* (that is, a brahmin), will first be born

68 *na yonir nāpi saṃskāro na śrutaṃ na ca saṃnatiḥ / kāraṇāni dvijatvasya vṛttam eva tu kāraṇam // Mahābhārata* 13.131.49.

69 In this context, we may note Caraka's insistence that a doctor does not enjoy the title *vaidya* by virtue of his first, physical birth. At the end of his study (*vidyā*), he is deemed to have experienced a second birth (*dvitīyā jātir ucyate*): the *vaidya* is known as 'twice-born' (*dvija*) because of the knowledge he has attained (*Caraka Saṃhitā, cikitsāsthāna* 1(4).52–3).

into the brahmin *varṇa*. At some point, this assumption became explicit. According to Bhattacharji, it was the Bhārgavas who introduced the concept of *jāti-brāhmaṇa*, that is, the idea that one might be a brahmin by birth alone (1991: 477). The classic statement reads:

> A man who is devoid of asceticism and Vedic knowledge is a brahmin by birth alone.[70]

Not only is such a man still classed as a brahmin, he is on those grounds alone deemed worthy of reverence.[71] It is this idea that gives rise to the extravagant praise of brahmins that one finds in epic and *dharma* literature, including the notion that they are gods in human form.

The tension between this brahminical utopia and the real world is apparent in many ways. At one end of the spectrum lies the unsettling notion of the 'fallen brahmin'; at the other, lurks the (from the brahmin's point of view) even more disturbing idea of the *śūdra* with religious aspirations. The 'fallen brahmin' is a stock figure in early Indian literature: the brahmin by birth who – whether out of ignorance, forgetfulness or wilfulness – adopts the morals and lifestyle of the *śūdra* or tribal. In the *Yogavāsiṣṭha*, in the context of illusionist philosophy, the high-caste protagonist (sometimes a brahmin, sometimes a king) dreams that he is an 'untouchable'.[72] In the *Skanda Purāṇa*, in the context of *bhakti*, the brahmin 'forgets' that he is a brahmin and becomes 'like' an 'untouchable'. In both cases, the status quo is preserved: in the *Yogavāsiṣṭha*, the dreamer awakens to the 'reality' of high-caste existence; in the *Skanda Purāṇa*, by means of the termite-mound experience, the forgetful brahmin is returned to his proper state. As Doniger points out, the social facts of 'untouchability' are not challenged in any way: 'the gruesome description of the life lived by the Untouchables shows not how unhappy they are but how horrid they are' (O'Flaherty 1984: 159). The suffering at issue is that of the temporarily transplanted king or brahmin not the miseries of permanent 'untouchability'. For the brahminical conception of the universe, the 'untouchable' world represents not real suffering but everything that is dark, disgusting and wrong. We may also add that the much-lamented miseries of the so-called 'untouchables' constitute yet more evidence of the brahminical projection of the 'other'.

Since the literature reflects only the concerns of its supposedly high-caste authors, there are no stories of 'untouchables' who 'forget' their social origins and become 'like' brahmins, not even stories of 'untouchables' who dream that they are brahmins. Perhaps the closest is the story of Mataṅga who thinks he is a brahmin until a female donkey informs him that he is in fact the offspring of a brahmin father and a *śūdra* mother, which makes him a *caṇḍāla*. Once Mataṅga realizes this, he spends the rest of his life doing *tapas* in order to attain the brahmin status

70 *tapaḥśrutābhyāṃ vihīno jātibrāhmaṇa eva saḥ* (Patañjali's *Mahābhāṣya* commentary on *Aṣṭādhyāyī* 2.2.6; see Kielhorn 1962: 410). I am grateful to Ashok Aklujkar for locating this reference for me.

71 *brāhmaṇo nāma bhagavāñ janmaprabhṛti pūjyate* (*Mahābhārata* 12.261.11).

72 For some of the variants of this idea, all taken from the *Yogavāsiṣṭha*, see O'Flaherty (1984: chapter 4).

he had believed was already his. But his efforts are in vain. As Indra explains to him repeatedly, it is impossible for a *caṇḍāla* to become a brahmin (Mbh. 13.28–30).[73] We find here, still well within the brahminical universe, the equally stereotypical figure of the 'religious *śūdra*'. A contradiction in terms, this figure stands in direct opposition to the 'fallen brahmin'. The best-known example of this paradox is provided by the *Vālmīki Rāmāyaṇa* account of the death of the over-ambitious *śūdra* Śambūka. I have already alluded to this episode more than once, but it is worth examining it more closely here. First, a crisis is signalled by the premature death of a thirteen-year-old brahmin boy. This tragedy is formulated by the child's father as proof that Rāma is an unrighteous or adharmic king (7.64). Rāma summons an emergency council to explain and redress the catastrophe. Nārada informs the king that only brahmins perform *tapas* in the *kṛta-yuga*, brahmins and *kṣatriyas* in the *treta*, while *vaiśyas* join them in the *dvāpara*; but only in the degenerate *kali-yuga* is *tapas* permitted to *śūdras*. The death of the brahmin boy in the current *dvāpara* age is due to the fact that a *śūdra* is performing *tapas* (7.65). Rāma tracks down the illegitimate ascetic at once. He finds Śambūka engaged in a particularly rigorous form of long-term *tapas*, hanging upside down (7.66.12–13). First, Rāma greets Śambūka with the respect due to a great ascetic, then he demands to know both Śambūka's *varṇa* and the reason for his ascetic practice. His head still hanging downwards, Śambūka replies without evasion (7.67.1):

> 'O Rāma, I was born in a *śūdra* womb, and I am performing this fierce *tapas* in order to become divine in this body. I am not telling a lie, O king. I do this out of a great desire to attain heaven. Know that I am a *śūdra*, Rāma, and my name is Śambūka.'[74]

Even before Śambūka has finished speaking, Rāma has drawn his sword and cut off the still hanging head (see Plate 3.1). In that instant, the brahmin boy revives. As the gods rain down flowers from the heavens above, the divine order represented by *varṇadharma* is restored. This story is evidently yet another brahmin (possibly Bhārgava) insertion intended to reinforce *varṇadharma*, in this case to resist the caste mobility implied, and thus to block even the remote possibility of marriage across the *varṇas*. Whatever the original intentions of those distant redactors, however, the story is certainly intended to bar the supposedly inappropriate redemption of the *śūdra*.[75]

---

73 Depending on the context, stories about Mataṅga describe him either as an acolyte hankering after knowledge or as an ascetic teacher, or again as a major contributor to ancient Indian musical traditions. In every story, however, there lurks the notion of a once marginal (that is, 'untouchable' or tribal) status (R. N. Mishra 1995). I am grateful to Richard Widdess for bringing this paper to my attention, along with other material from the Conference on Mataṅga's *Bṛhaddeśī* held at the Department of Tribal Studies, Kannada University, Hampi, in July 1995. The proceedings of this conference remain unpublished.

74 *śūdrayonyāṃ prasūto 'smi tapa ugraṃ samāsthitaḥ / devatvaṃ prārthaye rāma saśarīro mahāyaśaḥ // na mithyāhaṃ vade rājan devalokajigīṣayā / śūdraṃ māṃ viddhi kākutstha śambūkaṃ nāma nāmataḥ //* Vālmīki Rāmāyaṇa 7.67.2–3.

75 For a comparison of versions of the Śambūka story found in the *Vālmīki Rāmāyaṇa* and the *Ānanda Rāmāyaṇa*, see Vidyut Aklujkar (2000: 94–7).

Patterns like these are revealed by text-historical study. In my view, this makes it easier to draw conclusions more appropriate for today. In the mainstream *bhakti* context of contemporary India, let alone in contemporary Britain, the liberation of *dalits* does not depend on caste-related status. Far more important are the qualities deemed necessary for liberation, and who may therefore attain it. In terms of *bhakti*, for example, the 'true brahmin' is one who has devotion. As Ravidās himself put it, 'without devotion, the whole world is *śūdra*'.[76] According to the teaching of the *Mokṣopāyaśāstra* as it is embedded within the current form of the *Yogavāsiṣṭha*, liberation is open to everyone: men, women, children, even animals. It is what Slaje calls 'an attitude of mind', not a quality attached to the physical body (2000a: 183). Contrary to the stories told of Mataṅga and Śambūka, caste status is immaterial. Anyone can be a *jīvanmukta* in this life, internally detached, externally carrying out his or her normal worldly duties. The key issue here is the individual's spiritual state, not his or her status, nor the physical characteristics carried in the body. Despite the terrible punishment meted out to Śambūka in the *Vālmīki Rāmāyaṇa*, *dalits* today can be 'true brahmins', devotional or gnostic *āryas*. We can only hope that the widespread belief in the inherent superiority of the 'born brahmin', by both brahmins and others, will soon become a thing of the past.

5. Sacred Text and Religious Meaning

Much has been written about 'scripture'.[77] As a result, it is no longer possible to approach a sacred text as mere text. While a 'text' may be studied objectively, a 'sacred text' must be explored in relation to the community or communities that hold it sacred. For the individuals involved, the sacred text forms a bridge of meaning between the transcendent and the mundane world in which they live. In order to grasp the complexity of that meaning, we have to examine the text, the community, and what Wilfred Cantwell Smith calls the 'engagement' of the community with that text (1993: 239). By means of this 'engagement', a symbol or a figure becomes laden with meaning beyond itself. The multiple meanings invested in the figure of Vālmīki by South Asian communities lie not so much in their sacred texts as in the minds of those who read or hear them. These meanings are immensely powerful and, as we saw in Birmingham in February 2000, potentially explosive. It is precisely because of this potential that we need to formulate ways out of the conflicts that arise.

As I noted in chapter 1, this book began as an academic response to a question put to me by one of my students: Was Vālmīki a dacoit? It soon became apparent that this deceptively simple question concealed two more, entirely separate, questions: How is Vālmīki portrayed in the earliest Sanskrit texts? Where does the dacoit legend come from? The first question is addressed in chapter 3, the second

76 *bhakti vināṃ sabahi jaga sūdā*, cited in William Smith (2000: 209 n. 30). For the popular calendar picture of Ravidās cutting open his own chest to reveal the sacred thread beneath his skin, see Nesbitt (1991: 29).

77 For an excellent overview of this topic, see Wilfred Cantwell Smith (1993).

in chapter 4. As these chapters began to take shape, however, it became clear that my study of texts lacked the all-important element of 'engagement'. The dispute in Birmingham that had provoked the question in the first place only made sense in the context of diaspora communities from the Panjab; they in turn required some understanding of *dalit* religion and politics in north India; and that led me back to an enquiry into the far-reaching concept of untouchability. Chapter 2, 'Contextualizing the person', was intended to provide the missing elements of community and 'engagement'.

The resulting study is an exploration of text and meaning in relation to the figure of Vālmīki and the community of individuals who worship him as Guru and Bhagwan Valmik. The question now is how to make sense of the overlapping clusters of ideas that have been revealed in the process. I conclude by bringing together what I see as two separate strands in the formation of meaning surrounding Vālmīki. One strand presents the dominant voice of the 'Hindu' tradition as it has been preserved in both Sanskrit and vernacular texts. The other reveals the more muted *dalit* voice as expressed in early ethnographic accounts of the so-called 'Chuhras' and in more recent studies of the Valmikis in India. As I see it, these two strands are now being pulled together by the demands of the British Valmiki community to find (or make) one meaning, a meaning by which they all can live.

The earliest evidence belongs to the brahminical voice of the Hindu textual tradition. This strand delineates the complexes of meaning preserved in sacred texts (see chapters 3 and 4). At some point between 350 and 150 BCE, and in some region in central India, the *Taittirīya Prātiśākhya* gives us an expert in Sanskrit pronunciation who may have had a non-Sanskrit mother-tongue. At various points prior to 400 CE, the *Mahābhārata* gives us a superlative ascetic (*tapasvin*, *muni*), a semi-divine ancestral figure with visionary powers (*ṛṣi*), and an exemplary brahmin (*dvija*, *brāhmaṇa*). As discussed, it seems likely that the *Mahābhārata* references that stress Vālmīki's ascetic prowess belong to an earlier period than those emphasizing his gifts as a poet. But the *Mahābhārata* also gives us some hints of a counter-rhetoric: the tribal origins and anti-brahmin behaviour implied by the *suparṇa* story, and the currents of 'otherness' suggested by the dispute at the *sāma* ritual.

The references to Vālmīki in the *Vālmīki Rāmāyaṇa* belong to the third stage of development outlined by John Brockington, usually dated between the first and third centuries CE. The undercurrents relating to Vālmīki's origins and status have been erased: he is a brahmin ascetic, a respected member of the community, the protector of the vulnerable, and his Sanskrit is perfect. The only evidence that he might have a different background from the other Sanskrit-speakers is the fact that he is credited with inventing a new kind of Sanskrit verse-form.

Judging by the *Skanda Purāṇa*, however, all this changed at some point after the ninth century, probably after the twelfth, possibly later still. By this time, the central feature of the Vālmīki story is the dacoit legend: termite-mound asceticism, the sinner redeemed and the special mantra. In order to fit the needs of north Indian *bhakti* and the ensuing cult of the divine Name, Vālmīki has been transformed into a sinner, a dacoit, a fallen brahmin. As the story is elaborated still further in vernacular tellings, the fallen brahmin becomes an 'untouchable', a tribal. The downward spiral culminates in the cruel and ignorant dacoit of the twentieth-century comic strip with which this book began.

For the *dalit* strand of interconnected meanings, however, we need to adopt the Valmiki perspective. I begin with what Pauline Moller Mahar describes as 'the shamanistic and polytheistic' religious practices of early 'Chuhras': a focus on spirit possession, the worship of 'caste godlings', and the propitiation of disease goddesses (1960: 280–2).[78] Unfortunately, we can no longer reconstruct an 'original Chuhra religion'. The earliest records of 'Chuhra' beliefs and practices are those compiled by Temple (1884), Greeven (1894) and Youngson (1906, 1907). By that time, as we have seen, the so-called 'Chuhras' already venerated a number of saints with Muslim-sounding names such as Lāl Beg and Bāla Shāh, the latter in particular being worshipped as both ancestral hero figure and semi-divine intermediary, at least according to the records of ethnographers. This evidence of Muslim terminology and forms of worship can be explained either by the general pattern of conversion of 'untouchables' to Islam or as proof of the need to camouflage traditional beliefs. The latter interpretation is reinforced by the fact that the songs of Bāla Shāh prophesy that Muslims as well as Hindus will perish at the end of time: only Bāla's followers will be saved. So harsh a prophecy suggests that there was already a marked note of separatism in place with regard to both religions. The link between the Muslim name 'Bāla Shāh' and the Hindu name 'Bālmīk' remains unclear, despite the connections made between them by colonial officials, later generations of scholars and Valmikis themselves. Prashad blames the initial elision of Bāla Shāh and Vālmīki on colonial officers intent on seeing everything in brahminical terms (2000: 67–74). But the almost complete suppression of Bāla Shāh in favour of the epic poet seems to be the work of the Arya Samaj from the 1930s onwards. Their militant programme of 'purification' was aimed precisely at the so-called 'untouchables', especially those who had converted to Islam or Christianity. Prashad also holds the Arya Samaj responsible for circulating stories about Vālmīki being kidnapped and brought up by tribals, in this case Bhīls (pp. 91–9).

Whatever the truth of all this, we should note that, already in 1881, the *Report on the Census of the Panjab* informs us that Bāla Shāh is another name for the hunter 'Bāl Mīk' (Ibbetson 1916: 294). Almost eight decades later, the 1961 Census report explains that 'Valmiki was a Bhil, a race of mountaineers, who used to rob and kill travellers passing through the forest'.[79] The idea is still intact in 1993: according to K. S. Singh, 'the Balmiki living in Delhi … trace their descent from Saint Balmiki whom they describe as a Bhil' (1993: 109). Even the

78 Mahar describes 'the three dominant modes of religious worship represented in Chuhra life': the 'original' practices, the 'Valmiki cult' as influenced by the Arya Samaj, and the ideas of the 'new Nationalism'. In this particular village in Uttar Pradesh at that time, it was the young men who were the ardent Valmiki devotees; women tended to 'cling to their polytheism, their vows and sacrifices' (1960: 287). It would be interesting to explore gender differences in Valmiki beliefs and practices today, both in India and in Britain.

79 The report continues with the rest of the well-known dacoit legend (vol. 13, part A: 88–9).

oldest record of 'Chuhra' beliefs, that compiled by Youngson in Sialkot in 1891, contains a version of the dacoit legend (1906: 349–50). Thus the ideas that I have been trying to separate are presented by the earliest reconstituted 'text' of 'Chuhra' oral tradition as already overlapping. This is the nature of the phenomenon under investigation. While it is impossible to prove this point, there is almost certainly a tribal core to this complex of beliefs: a belief in a priestly ancestor, both member and champion of the 'dark race' (Youngson 1906: 353), a powerful figure with a special relationship to God. The oral traditions of the 'Chuhras' as recorded by Youngson (1906–7) explain how this once noble people became separate, one of many myths of origin to explain away untouchability. While the link between the 'Chuhras' and Bālmīk was already in place before the Hinduization programme of the Arya Samaj, that programme undoubtedly reinforced it. This brought two major changes, the first resisted by the Arya Samaj, the second encouraged by them. According to the first, Vālmīki was perceived not only as a combination of heroic *dalit* ancestor, enlightened saint and teacher, but as God. According to the second, the group as a whole changed its name from 'Chuhra' to 'Balmik' or 'Valmiki', while many individuals changed their own Muslim names to Hindu ones. The new nomenclature constituted a formal rejection of both Islam and the general practice of 'untouchable' conversions, while simultaneously celebrating the reinclusion of 'purified ex-untouchables' within the Hindu fold. Most significant of all, certainly from the point of view of the Valmikis themselves, this new name became a proud marker of self-respect.

So what happens when these two strands are brought together? Which elements of the textual tradition survive when required to blend with, and yet support, the *dalit* perspective? The dacoit legend is the first element to go, but it need not take with it the celebration of extreme termite-mound asceticism embedded in the famous honorific and bestowed retrospectively on Vālmīki by way of popular etymology. The motif of the slaughtered crane remains intact, as does Vālmīki's rescue of Sītā in the forest. These two episodes combine to present Vālmīki as the ever-present protector of the vulnerable. The image of the inspirational teacher, educator of the younger generation, is derived both from Vālmīki's relationship with Sītā's sons, Kuśa and Lava, and from his authorial function in the *Yogavāsiṣṭha*. Finally, the notion that Vālmīki was the original *dalit* hero bringing both social advancement and religious salvation to a beleagured community has several compelling sources: the lingering evidence in early texts that he had a tribal past; the increasingly vigorous pan-Indian *dalit* movement; and the inspiring principle of the 'true brahmin' found in the *Yogavāsiṣṭha*. The result is a complex mix of multiple meanings still in the process of being made.

Glossary

Abhir, Ahīr (*ābhīra*): member of a particular tribal caste, traditionally herders.

Ācamana (*ācamana*): purifying ceremony of sipping water from the palm of the hand.

Achut (*achūt*): 'untouchable'.

Ad Dharm (*ādi dharm*, *ād dharm*): first or original religion.

Adharma (*adharma*): incorrect behaviour.

Adi (*ādi*): first, original; aboriginal.

Adi Dravida (*ādi drāviḍa*): 'original Dravidian'; self-appellation of several groups traditionally classified by others as 'untouchable'.

Adi Karnataka (*ādi karṇāṭaka*): 'original inhabitant of Karnataka'; self-appellation of several groups traditionally classified by others as 'untouchable'.

Adibasi: *see* Adivasi.

Ādikavi (*ādikavi*): 'first poet'; epithet of Vālmīki.

Adivasi, Adibasi (*ādivāsī*): original inhabitant; indigene.

Advaita Vedānta (*advaita vedānta*): monistic philosophical school epitomized by Śaṅkara (eighth–ninth centuries CE).

Ahiṃsā (*ahiṃsā*): 'absence of the desire to harm'; non-violence.

Ahīr: *see* Abhir.

Āḻvār (*āḻvār*): one of a group of twelve devotional south Indian Vaiṣṇava poets (seventh–ninth centuries CE).

Amrit (*amṛta*): 'deathless'; a mythical drink bestowing extraordinary health and longevity.

Añjali (*añjali*): reverential cupping of hands.

Anta (*anta*): end.

Antya (*antya*): last, lowest.

Antyaja (*antyaja*): 'born in the lowest'; traditional group of seven low castes.

Antyāvasāyin (*antyāvasāyin*): traditional group of seven castes even lower than the *antyaja* group.

Āratī (*āratī*): hymn of praise.

Ārya, Ariya (*ārya*): noble; of refined and respectable conduct.

Arya Samaj (*ārya samāj*): 'society of the noble'; Hindu reform movement of the late nineteenth and early twentieth centuries.

Aryan: pertaining to speakers of so-called 'Aryan' (that is, Indo-European) languages.

Ashram (*āśrama*): refuge or retreat, usually associated with a sage or a religious community.

Aspṛśya (*aspṛśya*): 'not to be touched'.

Asura (*asura*): often translated 'demon'; one of a group of supernatural beings antagonistic to the gods.

Aśvamedha (*aśvamedha*): Vedic ritual culminating in the sacrifice of a horse, undertaken by a king to establish his empire.

Ātman (*ātman*): transmigrating entity (roughly 'soul' or 'self'); reflexive pronoun 'oneself'.

Avarṇa (*avarṇa*): falling outside the four social classes (*varṇa*s).

Avatāra, Avatar (*avatāra*): 'descent'; the incarnation of God in human or animal form.

Āyurveda (*āyurveda*): the science of health and longevity.

Baba (*bābā*): father; grandfather; respectful term of address.

Bal Mik, Bāl Mīk: *see* Valmiki, Vālmīki.

Bāla Shāh: Valmiki shrine; figure revered by many Valmiki communities in India, usually now identified with Valmiki himself.

Balmik, Bālmīk: *see* Valmiki, Vālmīki.

Balmiki: *see* Valmiki.

Bālmīku: *see* Vālmīki.

Bhagwan, Bhagavan, Bhagavat (*bhagavat*): Lord; blessed or holy one.

Bhairava (*bhairava*): 'terrible', 'horrific'; a form or group of forms of Śiva as ritually impure.

Bhajan (*bhajan*): devotional song.

Bhakta (*bhakta*): devotee.

Bhakti (*bhakti*): devotion.

Bhangi (*bhaṅgī*): member of a particular caste, traditionally 'sweepers', and traditionally classified by others as 'untouchable'.

Bharatiya Janata Party, BJP (*bhāratīya janatā*): 'People of India' political party.

Bhārgava (*bhārgava*): descendant of Bhṛgu.

Bhīl, Bhil (*bhīl*): member of a particular tribal caste, traditionally classified by others as 'untouchable'.

Bodhisattva (*bodhisattva*): Buddha-to-be; Buddhist saint; person who is enlightened but sustains embodiment due to compassion for all sentient beings.

Brahman (*brahman*): the Absolute, the Godhead; see also Brahmin.

Brāhmaṇa (*brāhmaṇa*): a genre of Vedic texts; a brahmin.

Brahmarṣi (*brahmarṣi*): brahmin sage.

Brahmin, Brahman (*brāhmaṇa*): member of the first *varṇa.*

Bṛhad (*bṛhad*): great, large.

Chamar, Chamār, Camār (*camār*): member of a particular caste, traditionally leather-workers, and traditionally classified by others as 'untouchable'.

Caṇḍāla, Chandal, Cāṇḍāla, Caṇḍār (*caṇḍāla, cāṇḍāla*): low-caste person, traditionally classified by others as 'untouchable'.

Chuhra, Chohra, Cuhḍā (*cuhḍā*): member of a particular caste, traditionally 'sweepers', and traditionally classified by others as 'untouchable'.

Dacoit, Daku, Ḍākū (*ḍākū*): robber; bandit.

Daitya (*daitya*): descendant of the *asura* Diti; one of a group of supernatural beings antagonistic to the gods.

Daku, Ḍākū: *see* Dacoit.

Dalit (*dalit*): non-derogatory self-appellation of persons or groups traditionally classified by others as 'untouchable'.

Dānava (*dānava*): descendant of Danu; one of a group of supernatural beings antagonistic to the gods.

Darbha (*darbha*): grass used as a ritual seat for meditation.

Darśan (*darśan*): 'view'; spiritually beneficial viewing of a holy person or god.

Dāsa (*dāsa*): member of a group pilloried by the Vedic poets; often translated 'savage' or 'barbarian'.

Dasyu (*dasyu*): member of a group pilloried by the Vedic poets; often translated 'savage' or 'barbarian'.

Devanāgarī (*devanāgarī*): 'of the divine city'; Indian script used for Sanskrit and Hindi, for example.

Devarṣi (*devarṣi*): divine sage.

Dharma, Dharm, Dharam (*dharma, dharm*): correct behaviour; religion; merit.

Dharmaśāstra (*dharmaśāstra*): genre of texts giving details of *dharma*.

Dharmasūtra (*dharmasūtra*): genre of texts giving details of *dharma* (older than the Dharmaśāstras and more closely tied to the Vedic ritual schools).

Doab (*doābā, duābā*): an area of land between two rivers.

Dom, Ḍom (*ḍom*): member of a particular caste, traditionally cremation-ground attendants, basket-weavers and performers, and traditionally classified by others as 'untouchable'.

Dussehra (*daśahrā*): ten-day festival in September/October, celebrating Durgā's victory over the buffalo demon and/or Rāma's over Rāvaṇa.

Dvāpara (*dvāpara*): name of the third of the four *yuga*s or world-ages.

Dvija (*dvija*): 'twice-born'; initiated into the Vedic community; member of one of the first three *varṇa*s; brahmin.

Fatwa (*fatwā*): a legal judgement issued by an Islamic authority.

Gajendramokṣastotra (*Gajendramokṣastotra*): hymn resulting in the release of Gajendra.

Gian (*giānī*): a scripturally learned person.

Gotra (*gotra*): lineage, family.

Gurdwara, Gurdwārā, Gurudwara (*gurudvārā*): 'threshold of the *guru*'; temple, usually Sikh.

Gurmukhi (*gurumukhī*): 'from the mouth of the *guru*'; script in which the Sikh scriptures were written.

Guru (*guru*): spiritual teacher.

Gurudwara: *see* Gurdwara.

Harijan (*harijan*): 'born of God'; term coined by Gandhi to denote persons or groups traditionally classified by others as 'untouchable'.

Hindutva (*hindutva*): 'Hindu-ness'; modern Hindu reform movement.

Jagat (*jagat*): 'that which moves'; the world.

Japa (*japa*): repeated muttering of a mantra.

Jatav (*jātav*): member of a particular caste traditionally classified by others as 'untouchable'.

Jat (*jaṭ*): member of a particular caste, many of whom converted to Sikhism in the late Moghul period.

Jātaka (*jātaka*): genre of texts telling stories about the Buddha's previous lives.

Jāti (*jāti*): 'birth'; caste.

Jīvanmukta (*jīvanmukta*): an enlightened but still embodied being.

Jīvanmukti (*jīvanmukti*): enlightenment while still embodied.

Ji (*jī*): respectful or affectionate name suffix.

Kali-yuga, Kal yug (*kaliyuga*): the last and most degenerate of the four world-ages.

Kāṇḍa (*kāṇḍa*): section, book; subdivision of the *Rāmāyaṇa*.

Karah Parshad (*kaṛāh praśād*): sacramental food distributed to Gurdwara congregation.

Karma (*karma*): action and/or its power to influence the future in unpredictable ways.

Kāśa (*kāśa*): a type of stiff grass.

Kavi (*kavi*): poet.

Kāvya (*kāvya*): poetry, including drama.

Kāyotsarga (*kāyotsarga*): meditative ascetic posture of standing with arms hanging slightly away from the body.

Khalsa (*khālsā*): initiated subsection of the Sikh community, established in 1699 by Guru Gobind Singh.

Khaṇḍa (*khaṇḍa*): section; subdivision of a Purāṇa.

Kirāta, Kirata, Kirāt (*kirāta*): member of a particular tribal caste, traditionally hunters, and traditionally classified by others as 'untouchable'.

Kol, Koli (*kol*): member of a particular tribal caste, traditionally classified by others as 'untouchable'.

Krauñca (*krauñca*): Sarus Crane.

Krauñca-vadha (*krauñcavadha*): 'killing of the Sarus Crane', an episode in the *Vālmīki Rāmāyaṇa*.

Kṛta-yuga (*kṛtayuga*): the first and purest of the four world-ages (see also Sat yug).

Kṣatriya (*kṣatriya*): warrior; member of the second *varṇa*.

Kūrma (*kūrma*): tortoise; Viṣṇu's tortoise avatar.

Kuśīlava (*kuśīlava*): a bard or rhapsodist, usually itinerant.

Laghu (*laghu*): light; little.

Lāl Beg: figure revered by many Valmiki communities in India, usually now identified with Valmiki himself.

Langer (*laṅgar*): community kitchen, usually attached to a place of worship.

Līlā (*līlā*): divine play.

Liṅga (*liṅga*): *see* Śivaliṅga.

Lok Sabha (*lok sabhā*): lower house of the Indian parliament.

Mahā- (*mahā-*): great.

Mahāmantra (*mahāmantra*): great mantra.

Mahar (*mahār*): member of a particular caste, traditionally classified by others as 'untouchable'.

Maharaj (*mahārāja*): great chief or king.

Maharshi, Maharishi (*maharṣi*): great sage.

Mahatma (*mahātmā*): 'great-souled', 'high-minded'; M. K. Gandhi.

Māhātmya (*māhātmya*): eulogy, often of a deity or holy place, typically found in Purāṇic texts.

Maheśvara (*maheśvara*): 'great Lord'; Śiva.

Mahiṣāsuramardinī (*mahiṣāsuramardinī*): the female destroyer of the buffalo demon; the Goddess.

Manas (*manas*): mind.

Mandal (*maṇḍal*): 'circle'; organization.

Mandir (*mandir*): temple, usually Hindu.

Mantra (*mantra*): sequence of syllables, the repetition of which has salvific value.

Marā-Marā, Mara Mara (*marā marā*): mantra consisting of the syllables of Rāma's name in reverse order; sometimes translated 'kill, kill'.

Matsya (*matsya*): fish; Viṣṇu's fish avatar.

Mazhabi (*mazhabī*): 'religious'; subsection of the Sikh community consisting of converted 'Chuhras'.

Mehtar (*mehtar*): member of a particular caste, traditionally refuse collectors, and traditionally classified by others as 'untouchable'.

Melā (*melā*): large gathering or festival.

Mokṣa (*mokṣa*): release from the cycle of repeated birth and death.

Muni (*muni*): ascetic or sage, especially one under a vow of silence.

Nag, Naga (*nāga*): snake; member of an ancient tribal group; sometimes used as a synonym of Adivasi.

Nāgarī (*nāgarī*): *see* Devanāgarī.

Nambudiri (*nambudiri*): member of a particular brahmin caste.

Nath (*nāth*): Lord; master.

Nirankar (*niraṅkār*): formless; epithet of God.

Nirguṇa, Nirguṇ (*nirguṇa, nirguṇ*): without qualities; impersonal.

Niṣāda (*niṣāda*): low-caste tribal person, traditionally a hunter or fisher, and traditionally classified by others as 'untouchable'.

Pad (*pad*): hymn.

Pada (*pada, pāda*): 'foot'; a quarter-verse.

Panchama (*pañcama*): 'fifth'; a person not categorised under any of the four *varṇas*.

Paṇḍit (*paṇḍit*): learned expert.

Panth (*panth*): spiritual path based on a specific *guru* or lineage of *gurus*.

Paṟaiyar (*paṟaiyar*): member of a particular caste, traditionally classified by others as 'untouchable'.

Parvan (*parvan*): section, book; subdivision of the *Mahābhārata*.

Pīr (*pīr*): religious leader(s); elder(s).

Pīyārai (*pīyārai*): the five founder members of the Sikh Khalsa.

Pothī (*pothī*): book.

Pradakṣiṇā (*pradakṣiṇa*): reverential clockwise circumambulation.

Prakaraṇa (*prakaraṇa*): a text section dealing with a distinct topic.

Prātiśākhya (*prātiśākhya*): a manual of Vedic pronunciation.

Prāśa (*prāśa*): food.

Puja (*pūjā*): reverential worship, usually involving an offering of flowers, incense and/or vegetarian food.

Pujari (*pujārī*): *pūjā* specialist; priest.

Purāṇa, Purana (*purāṇa*): genre of Indian texts.

Puruṣottama (*puruṣottama*): 'supreme person'; theological honorific.

Qaum (*qaum*): sizeable community united by faith.

Rāga (*rāga*): 'melody'; subdivision of the *Ādi Granth*.

Rājarṣi (*rājarṣi*): royal sage.

Rāma nāma (*rāma nāma*): the name 'Rāma'.

Rākṣasa (*rākṣasa*): a malignant being; sometimes translated 'ogre'.

Rāmacarita (*rāmacarita*): 'the story of Rāma'.

Ravidasi (*ravidāsī*): member of a certain religious community focused on the fifteenth or sixteenth century 'Chamar' *sant* Ravidās.

Rishi (*ṛṣi*): poet, sage; self-appellation of a particular caste, traditionally classified by others as 'untouchable'.

Rudrākṣa (*rudrākṣa*): 'Rudra-eyed'; item of Indian ascetic paraphernalia, a rosary of beads made from the berries of a particular plant.

Sabha, Sabhā (*sabhā*): assembly hall; religious community.

Saguṇa (*saguṇa*): with qualities; personal.

Sahib (*sāhab*): honorary term of address.

Śaiva (*śaiva*): pertaining to Śiva or his worship.

Sakhā (*sakhā*): friend.

Śākta (*śākta*): pertaining to the worship of the Goddess or feminine principle.

Sāma (*sāma*): litany in the form of song.

Samādhi (*samādhi*): the highest state of yogic attainment, in which the mind is completely stilled.

Saṃsāra (*saṃsāra*): repeated embodiment.

Sant (*sant*): 'true one'; one of a series of north Indian poet-saints emphasizing internal rather than external religion.

Śāradā (*śāradā*): old Indian script, used particularly in Kashmir.

Sat (*sat*): true; pure; real.

Sat yug (*sat yug*): the first and purest of the four world-ages (see also Kṛta-yuga).

Shastar (*śāstra*): treatise.

Shri, Shree: *see* Sri.

Shudar: *see* Śūdra.

Śivaliṅga (*śivaliṅga*): phallic Śaiva icon.

Śloka (*śloka*): Sanskrit verse with four sections of eight syllables each.

Smṛti (*smṛti*): 'that which is remembered'; Hindu sacred texts not part of the Veda.

Soma (*soma*): ancient Indo-Iranian psychoactive drink, especially beloved of Indra.

Sri, Shri, Shree (*śrī*): glorious, splendid, radiant; honorific.

Śūdra, Shudar (*śūdra*): the fourth *varṇa*; the serving class.

Sūkaramaddava (*sūkaramaddava*): pork dish that featured in the Buddha's last meal.

Suparṇa (*suparṇa*): 'fine-winged'; snake-eating bird.

Sūta (*sūta*): a courtly bard.

Śvapaca, Śvapaka, Śvapāka, Svapaca (*śvapaca, śvapaka, śvapāka*): low-caste person, traditionally classified by others as 'untouchable'.

Tantric: pertaining to the genre of texts known as Tantras or to their esoteric ritual and cosmological ideas.

Tapas (*tapas*): ascetic practice.

Tapasvin (*tapasvin*): ascetic practitioner.

Tejas (*tejas*): fiery ascetic energy.

Thamam (*tamām*): 'complete'; term used to denote mainstream religions.

Tīrtha (*tīrtha*): 'ford'; pilgrimage site.

Tīrthaṅkara (*tīrthaṅkara*): 'ford-maker'; perfected Jain saint.

Treta (*treta*): name of the second of the four *yuga*s or world-ages.

Tulasī (*tulasī*): sacred basil plant.

Upanayana (*upanayana*): Vedic initiation ritual at which an adolescent male receives the sacred thread and becomes 'twice-born' (*see* Dvija).

Uttara (*uttara*): later, subsequent; name of the last section of the *Rāmāyaṇa*.

Vaidya (*vaidya*): a learned person, especially in medicine.

Vaiṣṇava (*vaiṣṇava*): pertaining to Viṣṇu or his worship.

Vaiśya (*vaiśya*): member of the third *varṇa*, comprising the class of agriculturists, artisans and merchants.

Valamiki: *see* Valmiki.

Valmīka (*valmīka*): termite mound.

Valmiki, Valmik, Valamiki, Balmiki, Balmik, Bālmīk, Bal Mik: member of a certain religious community; object of this community's worship.

Vālmīki, Valmiki, Balmik, Bālmīku, Bālmīk, Bāl Mīk (*vālmīki*): ancient Indian poet and/or saint; one who is related in some way to the term '*valmīka*'.

Vāmana (*vāmana*): dwarf; Viṣṇu's dwarf avatar.

Varāha (*varāha*): boar; Viṣṇu's boar avatar.

Varṇa (*varṇa*): any one of four distinct types or classes of person.

Varṇa-dharma (*varṇadharma*): behaviour appropriate to social class.

Vishwa Hindu Parishad, VHP (*viśva hindu pariṣad*): 'council of all Hindus'; organization associated with Hindutva agenda.

Viṣṇusahasranāmastotra (*viṣṇusahasranāmastotra*): hymn in praise of Viṣṇu's one thousand names.

Vrata (*vrata*): religious or ascetic vow.

Vrātya (*vrātya*): someone who has – or whose family has – supposedly fallen from higher caste through negligence of Vedic rites of passage.

Yakṣa (*yakṣa*): semi-divine being, usually associated with non-Vedic tradition and with water or vegetation.

Yavana (*yavana*): foreigner.

Zamindar (*zamindār*): landowner or officer of land revenue.

Bibliography

Aadi Kavi Valmiki Foundation. Charity registration no. 293313. Membership form and publicity leaflet. Southall, no date.

Adhyātma Rāmāyaṇa. Adhyātmarāmāyaṇam with the commentaries of Narottama, Ramavarman and Gopala Chakravarti, 2 vols, ed. Nagendranath Siddhantaratna. Calcutta Sanskrit Series, 11. Calcutta: Metropolitan Printing and Publishing House, 1935.

Ādi Granth. Śrī Gurū Granth Sāhib, with complete index, 2 vols, ed. Winand M. Callewaert. Delhi: Motilal Banarsidass, 1996.

Adriaensen, R., H. T. Bakker and H. Isaacson (1994). 'Towards a critical edition of the *Skandapurāṇa*.' *Indo-Iranian Journal*, 37, 325–31.

Adriaensen, R., H. T. Bakker and H. Isaacson, eds (1998). *The Skandapurāṇa, volume 1, adhyāyas 1–25, critically edited with prolegomena and English synopsis*. Groningen: Egbert Forsten.

Agrawala, V. S. (1956). 'The Mahābhārata: a cultural commentary.' *Annals of the Bhandarkar Oriental Research Institute*, 37, 1–26.

Aiyar, V. V. Subramanya (1987). *Kamba Ramayana: a study*, third edition. Bombay: Bharatiya Vidya Bhavan.

Aiyer, K. Narayanaswami, tr. (1975). *Laghu-Yoga-Vāsiṣṭha*, translated into English, third edition. Adyar Library general series, 3. Madras: Adyar Library and Research Centre.

Aklujkar, Vidyut (1995). 'Rāmāvatāra recycled.' *Annals of the Bhandarkar Oriental Research Institute*, 76, 107–18.

Aklujkar, Vidyut (2000). 'Crying dogs and laughing trees in Rāma's kingdom: self-reflexivity in *Ānanda Rāmāyaṇa*.' In Richman, ed., *Questioning Rāmāyaṇas*, pp. 83–103.

Aktor, Mikael (1997). 'Ritualisation and segregation: the untouchability complex in the scholarly Indian literature on *dharma* with special reference to *Parāśarasmṛti* and *Parāśaramādhavīya*.' Dissertation submitted to the University of Copenhagen for the PhD degree.

Aktor, Mikael (2000). 'Untouchables, women and territories: rituals of lordship in the Parāśara Smṛti.' In Julia Leslie and Mary Mcgee, eds, *Invented identities: the interplay of gender, religion and politics in India*, pp. 133–56. Delhi: Oxford University Press.

Ali, Salim, and S. Dillon Ripley (1983). *Handbook of the birds of India and Pakistan, together with those of Bangladesh, Nepal, Bhutan and Sri Lanka*. Compact edition: second edition of vols 1–3, first edition of vols 4–10, and 113 colour plates. Delhi: Oxford University Press.

Allchin, F. R., tr. (1964). *Tulsī Dās: Kavitāvalī*. London: George Allen and Unwin Ltd.

Allchin, F. R., tr. (1966). *Tulsī Dās: the petition to Rām. Hindi devotional hymns of the seventeenth century: a translation of the Vinaya-Patrikā*. London: George Allen and Unwin Ltd.

Alper, Harvey P. (1989). 'A working bibliography for the study of mantras.' In Alper, ed., *Understanding mantras*, pp. 327–443. SUNY Series in Religious Studies. Albany: State University of New York Press.

Alter, Robert (1981). *The art of Biblical narrative.* New York: Basic Books.

Ambedkar, B. R. (1948). *The untouchables. Who were they? And why they became untouchables?* Delhi: Amrit Book Co.

Anand, Mulk Raj (1935). *Untouchable.* With a preface by E. M. Forster. Reprint, London: Penguin, 1986.

Ānanda Rāmāyaṇa. Ananda-Rāmāyaṇam, ed. Pandit Yugal Kishor Dvivedi with commentary, *Jyotsnā*, by Pandey Ramtej Shastri. Varanasi: Pandita Pustakālaya, 1977.

Anargharāghava of Murari. See Steiner (1997).

Anwar, Muhammad (1985). *Pakistanis in Britain: a sociological study*. Incorporating the author's earlier book, *The myth of return: Pakistanis in Britain* (1979). London: New Century Publishers.

Āpastamba Dharmasūtra. Sanskrit text with Haradattamiśra's commentary, the *Ujjvalā*, ed. A. Chinnasvami Sastri and A. Ramanatha Sastri. Kashi Sanskrit Series, 93. Benares, 1932.

Appignanesi, Lisa, and Sara Maitland, eds (1989). *The Rushdie file*. London: Fourth Estate.

Armstrong, Karen (1983). *The first Christian: St. Paul's impact on Christianity*. London and Sydney: Pan Books.

Armstrong, Neil (1998). 'Checks to integration: AKs of Mahepura.' In Charsley and Karanth, eds, *Challenging untouchability*, pp. 154–86.

Atreya, B. L. (1936). *The Vāsiṣṭha-Darśanaṃ, compiled from the Yogavāsiṣṭha Rāmāyaṇa*. The Princess of Wales Saraswati Bhavana Texts, 64. Benares.

Atreya, B. L. (2000a). *From the Yogavāsiṣṭha of Vālmīki: Yogavāsiṣṭha and modern thought, or Agreement of the East and the West on fundamental problems*. Lecture delivered in Benares, first published in *Benares Hindu University Magazine*, reprinted as a book in 1934. Southall, Shri Guru Valmik Sabha.

Atreya, B. L. (2000b). *From the Yogavāsiṣṭha of Vālmīki: Deification of man, its methods and stages according to Yogavāsiṣṭha*. Lecture delivered in Benares in 1935, first published in *Theosophy of India*, reprinted as a book in 1963. Southall, Shri Guru Valmik Sabha, 2000.

Awasthi, Induja (1980). 'Rāmcharitamānas and the performing tradition of Rāmāyaṇa.' In Raghavan, ed., *The Ramayana tradition in Asia*, pp. 504–16.

Ayyangar, Sreenivasa (1991). *The Ramayana of Valmiki*, part 1. Madras: The Little Flower Co.

Baaghaa, Ajeet Singh (undated). 'Bhagwan Valmik.' *Valmik Jagriti*, 1, 6–7. Shri Guru Valmik Sabha, Southall.

Babb, Lawrence A., and Susan S. Wadley, eds (1995). *Media and the transformation of religion in South Asia.* Philadelphia: University of Pennsylvania Press.

Baij Nath, Rai Bahadur Lala, tr. (1913). *The Adhyatma Ramayana*. Sacred Books of the Hindus, extra vol. 1. Reprint, New York: AMS Press.

Bailey, Greg (2002). 'The work of the Indo-American historians and the rewriting of Indian history.' *South Asia: Journal of South Asian Studies* (Australia), 25 (3), December, 165–86.

Bakker, Hans (1986). *Ayodhyā: the history of Ayodhyā from the 7th century BC to the middle of the 18th century, its development into a sacred centre with reference to the Ayodhyāmāhātmya and to the worship of Rāma according to the Agastya Saṃhitā*. Groningen: Egbert Forsten.

Bakker, Hans (1996). 'Pārvatī's svayaṃvara: studies in the *SkandaPurāṇa*, I.' *Wiener Zeitschrift für die Kunde Südasiens*, 40, 5–43.

Bakker, Hans T. (1997). *The Vākāṭakas: an essay in Hindu iconology*. Groningen: Egbert Forsten.

Bakker, Hans (2000). 'Somaśarman, Somavaṃśa and Somasiddhānta: Pāśupata tradition in seventh-century Dakṣiṇa Kosala. Studies in the *Skandapurāṇa* III.' In Tsuchida and Wezler, eds, *Harānandalaharī*, pp. 1–19.

Bālarāmāyaṇa by Rājaśekhara. *The Bālarāmāyaṇa: a drama by Rājaśekhara*, Sanskrit text ed. Pandit Govinda Deva Śāstri. Benares: Medical Hall Press, 1869.

Ballard, Roger, ed. (1994a). *Desh pardesh: the South Asian presence in Britain*. London: Christopher Hurst.

Ballard, Roger (1994b). 'Introduction.' In Ballard, ed., *Desh pardesh*, pp. 1–34.

Ballard, Roger (1994c). 'Differentiation and disjunction among the Sikhs.' In Ballard, ed., *Desh pardesh*, pp. 88–116.

Ballard, Roger, and Catherine Ballard (1977). 'The Sikhs: the development of South Asian settlements in Britain.' In Watson, ed., *Between two cultures*, pp. 21–56.

Banks, Marcus (1994). 'Jain ways of being.' In Ballard, ed., *Desh pardesh*, pp. 231–50.

Baudhāyana Dharmasūtra. Sanskrit text ed. E. Hultsch. *Zeitschrift der deutschen morgenländischen Gesellschaft*, 8 (4). Leipzig, 1884.

Bayly, Susan (1989). *Saints, goddesses and kings: Muslims and Christians in South Indian society, 1700–1900*. Cambridge: Cambridge University Press.

Beck, Brenda E. F. (1982). *The three twins: the telling of a south Indian folk-epic*. Bloomington: Indiana University Press.

Bell, Michael Mayerfeld (1998). 'Culture as dialogue.' In Bell and Gardiner, eds, *Bakhtin and the human sciences*, pp. 49–62.

Bell, Michael Mayerfeld, and Michael Gardiner, eds (1998). *Bakhtin and the human sciences: no last words*. London: Sage.

Béteille, André (1992). *Society and politics in India: essays in a comparative perspective*. Delhi: Oxford University Press.

Bhachu, Parminder (1985). *Twice migrants: East African Sikh settlers in Britain*. London: Tavistock.

Bhachu, Parminder (1991). 'The East African Sikh diaspora: the British case.' In Vertovec, ed., *Aspects of the South Asian diaspora*, pp. 57–85.

Bhargava, Purushottam Lal (1984). 'Was Vālmīki a robber in his youth?' In *Retrieval of history from Purāṇic myths: exposure of late Purāṇic myths about some great characters of the earliest Indian history*, pp. 76–84. Lucknow: The Upper India Publishing House Pvt. Ltd.

Bhatt, G. H., and U. P. Shah, general eds (1958–75). *The Vālmīki-Rāmāyaṇa: critical edition*, 7 vols. Baroda: Oriental Institute.

Bhatt, G. P., general ed. (1986). *Brahma Purāṇa*, part 4, translated by a board of scholars. Ancient Indian Tradition and Mythology, 36. Delhi: Motilal Banarsidass.

Bhattacharji, S. (1991). 'Social pressures behind the Bhārgava interpolation of the *Mahābhārata*.' *Annals of the Bhandarkar Oriental Research Institute*, 72, 469–82.

Bhattacharya, Asutosh (1980). 'Oral tradition of the Rāmāyaṇa in Bengal.' In V. Raghavan, ed., *The Ramayana tradition in Asia*, pp. 593–616.

Bhattacharyya, D. C., tr. (1991). *Pratimālakṣaṇa of the Viṣṇudharmottara*. New Delhi: Harman Publishing House.

Bhikkhu, Mettanando, and Oskar von Hinüber (2000). 'The cause of the Buddha's death.' *Journal of the Pali Text Society*, 26, 105–17.

Bhuśuṇḍi Rāmāyaṇa. Bhuśuṇḍi Rāmāyaṇa: Pūrva Khaṇḍa, ed. B. P. Singh with assistance from Janardana Śāstrī Pāṇḍeya. English introduction by V. Raghavan, Hindi introduction by B. P. Singh. Varanasi: Vishwavidyalaya Prakashan, 1975.

Blackburn, Stuart H. (1991). 'Descent into performance: Rāma *avatār* in a folk tradition of Kerala.' In Thiel-Horstmann, ed., *Rāmāyaṇa and Rāmāyaṇas*, pp. 69–84.

Blackburn, Stuart H. (1996). *Inside the drama-house: Rāma stories and shadow puppets in south India*. Berkeley: University of California Press.

Böhtlingk, Otto, and Rudolph Roth, eds (1990). *Sanskrit-Wörterbuch*, 7 vols. First edition, 1852–1875; second edition, 1855–1875. Reprint: Delhi, Motilal Banarsidass.

Bowen, David (1987). 'The evolution of Gujarati Hindu organizations in Bradford.' In Burghart, ed., *Hinduism in Great Britain*, pp. 15–31.

Brereton, Joel P. (1986). '"*Tat tvam asi*" in context.' *Zeitschrift der deutschen morgenländischen Gesellschaft*, 136, 98–109.

Briggs, George W. (1920). *The Chamars*. The Religious Life of India series, ed. J. N. Farquhar and N. Macnicol. Calcutta and London: Delhi.

Brockington, J. L. (1978). 'Sanskrit epic tradition I: epic and epitome (*Rāmāyaṇa* and *Rāmopākhyāna*).' *Indologica Taurinensia*, 6, 79–111. Reprinted in Greg Bailey and Mary Brockington, eds, *Epic threads: John Brockington on the Sanskrit epics*, pp. 288–325. Delhi: Oxford University Press.

Brockington, J. L. (1984). *Righteous Rāma: the evolution of an epic*. Delhi: Oxford University Press.

Brockington, J. L. (1995). 'Concepts of the self in the Rāmāyaṇa tradition.' Edinburgh Papers in South Asian Studies, 1. Edinburgh: Centre for South Asian Studies, University of Edinburgh.

Brockington, J. L. (1998). *The Sanskrit epics*. Handbuch der Orientalistik, II. XII. Leiden: Brill.

Brockington, J. L. (2000). '*Tapas* in the *Rāmāyaṇa*.' In Tsuchida and Wezler, eds, *Harānandalaharī*, pp. 39–52.

Brockington, Mary (2002). '"Once upon a time ...": the *Rāmāyaṇa* in traditional tales.' In Danuta Stasik and John Brockington, eds, *Indian epic traditions: past and present*, pp. 133–58. Papers presented at the 16th European Conference on Modern South Asian Studies, Edinburgh, 5–9 September 2000. *Rocznik Orientalistyczny*, 54 (1).

Brockington, Mary, and Peter Schreiner, eds (1999). *Composing a tradition: concepts, techniques and relationships*. Proceedings of the first Dubrovnik International Conference on the Sanskrit Epics and Purāṇas, August 1997. Zagreb: Croatian Academy of Sciences and Arts.

Bryant, Edwin (2001). *The quest for the origins of Vedic culture: the Indo-Aryan migration debate*. New York: Oxford University Press.

Buddhacarita of Aśvaghoṣa. See Johnston (1936) and Cowell (1894).

Bulcke, Camille (1950). *Rāmkathā (utpatti aur vikāś)*. Second edition, 1962. Third revised edition, 1971. Prayāg: Hindī Pariṣad Prakāśan.

Bulcke, Camille (1958). 'About Vālmīki (Materials for the biography of Vālmīki, author of the first *Rāmāyaṇa*).' *Journal of the Oriental Institute, Baroda*, 8 (2), December, 121–31.

Bulcke, Camille (1959). 'More about Vālmīki.' *Journal of the Oriental Institute, Baroda*, 8 (4), June, 346–8.

Bulcke, Camille (1960). 'The Rāmāyaṇa: its history and character.' *Poona Orientalist*, 25, 36–60.

Burghart, Richard, ed. (1987a). *Hinduism in Great Britain: the perpetuation of religion in an alien culture.* London: Tavistock.

Burghart, Richard (1987b). 'Introduction: the diffusion of Hinduism to Great Britain.' In Burghart, ed., *Hinduism in Great Britain*, pp. 1–14.

Burghart, Richard (1987c). 'Conclusion: the perpetuation of Hinduism in an alien cultural milieu.' In Burghart, ed., *Hinduism in Great Britain*, pp. 224–51.

Callewaert, Winand M. (1988). *The Hindī biography of Dādū Dayāl*. Delhi: Motilal Banarsidass.

Callewaert, Winand M., ed. (1996). *Śrī Gurū Granth Sāhib, with complete index*, 2 vols. Delhi: Motilal Banarsidass.

Callewaert, Winand M., and Peter G. Friedlander (1992). *The life and works of Raidās.* New Delhi: Manohar.

Caplan, A. Patricia (1972). *Priests and cobblers: a study of social change in a Hindu village in western Nepal*. Studies in Social and Economic Change series. Aylesbury: International Textbook Company Limited.

Caraka Saṃhitā. *Caraka-saṃhitā: Agniveśa's treatise refined and annotated by Caraka and redacted by Dṛḍhabala (text with English translation)*, 4 vols, by Priya Vrat Sharma. Varanasi and Delhi: Chaukhambha Orientalia, 1981–94.

Cardona, George (1976). *Pāṇini: a survey of research*. Reprint, Delhi: Motilal Banarsidass, 1980.

Carpelan, Christian, and Asko Parpola (2001). 'Emergence, contacts and dispersal of Proto-Indo-European, Proto-Uralic and Proto-Aryan in archaeological perspective.' In Christian Carpelan, Asko Parpola and Petteri Koskikallio, eds, *Early contacts between Uralic and Indo-European: linguistics and archaeological* considerations, pp. 55–150. Mémoires de la Société Finno-Ougrienne, 242. Helsinki: Suomalais-Ugrilainen Seura.

Carrette, Jeremy, and Mary Keller (1999). 'Religions, orientation and critical theory: race, gender and sexuality at the 1998 Lambeth Conference.' *Theology and Sexuality*, 11, 21–43.

Carrière, Jean-Claude (1988). *The Mahabharata: a play based upon the Indian classical epic*. Translated from the French (1985) by Peter Brook. London: Methuen.

Carter, John Ross, and Mahina Palihawadana, tr. (1987). *Buddhism: the Dhammapada*. Special edition: Sacred Writings, 6. New York: Book-of-the-Month Club, 1992.

Census of India (1881). Vol. 1: *Punjab*. See Ibbetson, *Report on the Census of the Panjáb*.

Census of India (1931). Vol. 17: *Punjab*. See Khan Ahmad Hasan Khan, *Report [on the] Census of India*.

Census of India (1961). Vol. 13: *Punjab*.

Chahil, Pritam Singh, tr. (1998). *Sri Guru Granth Sahib*, 4 vols. Text, transliteration and English translation, second edition. Amritsar: B. Chattar Singh Jiwan Singh.

Chaitanya, Krishna (1971). *A history of Malayalam literature*. New Delhi: Orient Longman.

Chakrabarti, Dilip (2001). 'The archaeology of Hinduism.' In T. Insoll, ed., *Archaeology and world religion*, pp. 33–60. London: Routledge.

Chapple, Christopher (1984). 'Introduction.' In Swami Venkatesananda, *The concise Yoga Vāsiṣṭha*, pp. ix–xv. Albany: State University of New York Press.

Charsley, Simon R. (1998a). 'Caste, cultural resources and social mobility.' In Charsley and Karanth, eds, *Challenging untouchability*, pp. 44–71.

Charsley, Simon R. (1998b). 'Increasing autonomy: the Harijans of Rateyur.' In Charsley and Karanth, eds. *Challenging untouchability*, pp. 212–39.

Charsley, Simon R., and G. K. Karanth, eds (1998a). *Challenging untouchability: dalit initiative and experience from Karnataka*. Cultural Subordination and the Dalit Challenge series, 1. Delhi: Sage Publications.

Charsley, Simon R., and G. K. Karanth (1998b). 'Beyond untouchability? Local experience and society-wide implications.' In Charsley and Karanth, eds, *Challenging untouchability*, pp. 265–97.

Claeys, Jean-Yves (1927). 'Chronique.' *Bulletin de l'École Française d'Extrême Orient*, 27, 477–8.

Cohen, Lawrence (1998). *No aging in India: Alzheimer's, the bad family, and other modern things*. Berkeley: University of California Press.

Contursi, J. A. (1993). 'Political theology: text and practice in a Dalit Panther community.' *The Journal of Asian Studies*, 52, 320–39.

Conze, Edward, tr. (1973). *Perfect wisdom: the short Prajnaparamita texts*. Reprint, Totnes: Buddhist Publishing Group, 1993.

Cowell, Edward B. (1894). *The Buddha-karita or life of Buddha by Asvaghosha: Indian poet of the early second century after Christ. Sanskrit text, edited from a Devanagari and two Nepalese manuscripts, with variant readings, and English translation*. Reprint, New Delhi: Cosmo Publications, 1977.

Cribb, Joe (1999). 'The early Kushan kings: new evidence for chronology. Evidence from the Rabatak inscription of Kanishka I.' In M. Alram and D. E.

Klimberg-Salter, eds, *Coins, art, and chronology: essays on the pre-Islamic history of the Indo-Iranian borderlands*, pp. 177–205. Vienna: Verlag der Österreichische Akademie.

Dalmia-Lüderitz, Vasudha (1991). 'Television and tradition: some observations on the serialization of the Rāmāyaṇa.' In Thiel-Horstmann, ed., *Rāmāyaṇa and Rāmāyaṇas*, pp. 207–28. Vienna: Verlag der Österreichische Akademie.

Daśakumāracarita of Daṇḍin. See Kale (1966).

Dass, Nirmal, tr. (2000). *Songs of the saints from the Adi Granth*. Albany: State University of New York.

Datta, Bhabatosh (1980). 'The Rāmāyaṇa in Bengal.' In Raghavan, ed., *The Rāmāyaṇa tradition in Asia*, pp. 546–60.

Dave, K. N. (1985). *Birds in Sanskrit literature, with 105 bird illustrations*. Delhi: Motilal Banarsidass.

De, Sushil Kumar (1940). 'Introduction.' In S. K. De, ed., *The Udyogaparvan, being the fifth book of the Mahābhārata, the great epic of India*, pp. i–xlix. Poona: Bhandarkar Oriental Research Institute.

Deliège, Robert (1985). *The Bhils of western India: some empirical and theoretical issues in anthropology in India.* New Delhi: National Publishing House.

Deliège, Robert (1992). 'Replication and consensus: untouchability, caste and ideology in India.' *Man: The Journal of the Royal Anthropological Institute (n. s.)*, 27, 155–73.

Deliège, Robert (1993). 'The myths of origin of the Indian Untouchables.' *Man: The Journal of the Royal Anthropological Institute (n. s.)*, 28, 533–49.

Deliège, Robert (1997). *The world of the 'untouchables': Paraiyars of Tamil Nadu*. Translated from the French by David Phillips. Delhi: Oxford University Press.

Deliège, Robert (1999). *The untouchables of India*. Originally *Les untouchables en Inde: des castes d'exclus* (1995). Translated from the French by Nora Scott. Oxford: Berg Press.

Deol, Jeevan Singh (2001a). 'Text and lineage in early Sikh history: issues in the study of the Adi Granth.' *Bulletin of the School of Oriental and African Studies*, 64 (1), 34–58.

Deol, Jeevan Singh (2001b). 'Eighteenth century Khalsa identity: discourse, praxis and narrative.' In Christopher Shackle, Gurharpal Singh and Arvindpal Mandair, eds, *Sikh religion, culture and ethnicity*, pp. 25–46. London: Curzon Press.

Deshpande, N. A., tr. (1989, 1990a, 1990b, 1990c, 1991). *The Padma-Purāṇa*, parts 2, 3, 5, 6, 9. Ancient Indian Tradition and Mythology, 40, 41, 43, 44, 47. Delhi: Motilal Banarsidass.

Devadhar, C. R. (1927). *Plays ascribed to Bhasa: their authenticity and merits.* Poona: The Oriental Book Agency.

Devadhar, C. R., and N. G. Suru, eds (1934). *Raghuvaṃśa of Kālidāsa, Cantos I–IV: Mallināthaʼs commentary, introduction, translation and critical and exhaustive notes*. Reprint: 1953. Poona: Aryabhushan Press.

Dhody, Chandan Lal, tr. (1987). *The gospel of love: an English rendering of Tulasī's Shri Rāma Charita Mānasa (The spiritual lake of Rāma's pastimes)*. Delhi: Siddharth Publications.

Dhody, Chandan Lal, tr. (1995). *The Adhyātma Rāmāyaṇa: concise English* version. Delhi: M. D. Publications Pvt. Ltd.

Dirks, Nicholas B. (2001). *Castes of mind: colonialism and the making of modern India*. Princeton and Oxford: Princeton University Press.

Dixie (2001). *Kumbha Mela: a study of India's largest pilgrimage*. A photographic exhibition sponsored by the Bagri Foundation (8 January–21 June), Brunei Gallery, School of Oriental and African Studies, University of London. See *www.positivenegatives.co.uk*.

Doniger, Wendy (1991). 'Fluid and fixed texts in India.' In Flueckiger and Sears, eds, *Boundaries of the text*, pp. 31–40.

Doniger, Wendy (1993). 'The scrapbook of undeserved salvation: the Kedara Khaṇḍa of the Skanda Purāṇa.' In W. Doniger, ed., *Purāṇa perennis: reciprocity and transformation in Hindu and Jaina texts*, pp. 59–83, 262–5. Albany: State University of New York Press.

Doniger, Wendy (1999). *Splitting the difference: gender and myth in ancient Greece and India*. Chicago and London: University of Chicago Press.

Doniger, Wendy, with Brian K. Smith, trs (1991). *The laws of Manu*. London: Penguin Books.

Doniger, Wendy: see also O'Flaherty, Wendy Doniger.

Dumont, Louis (1970). *Homo hierarchicus: the caste system and its implications*. Translated from the French by Mark Sainsbury. London: Weidenfeld & Nicolson.

Dwyer, Rachel (1994). 'Caste, religion and sect in Gujarat: followers of Vallabhacharya and Swaminarayan.' In Ballard, ed., *Desh pardesh*, pp. 165–90.

Eaton, Richard M. (2000). '(Re)imag(in)ing Other^{2}ness: a postmortem for the postmodern in India.' In *Essays on Islam and Indian history*, pp. 133–55. New Delhi: Oxford University Press.

Eggeling, Julius, tr. (1885). *The Śatapatha-Brāhmaṇa according to the text of the Mādhyandina School*, part 2. Sacred Books of the East, 26. Reprint, Delhi: Motilal Banarsidass, 1978.

Falk, Harry (1993). *Schrift im alten Indien: ein Forschungsbericht mit Anmerkungen*. Tübingen: Gunter Narr.

Finot, Louis (1904). 'Notes d'épigraphie'. *Bulletin de l'École Française d'Extrême Orient*, 4, 918–26.

Fitzgerald, James L. (2002) 'The Rāma Jāmadagnya "thread" of the *Mahābhārata*: a new survey of Rāma Jāmadagnya in the Pune text.' In Mary Brockington, ed., *Stages and transitions: temporal and historical frameworks in epic and purāṇic literature*, pp. 89–132. Proceedings of the second Dubrovnik International Conference on the Sanskrit Epics and Purāṇas, August 1999. Zagreb: Croatian Academy of Sciences and Arts.

Flueckiger, Joyce Burkhalter (1991). 'Literacy and the changing concept of text: women's Ramayana *maṇḍalī* in central India.' In Flueckiger and Sears, eds, *Boundaries of the text*, pp. 43–60.

Flueckiger, Joyce Burkhalter, and Laurie J. Sears, eds (1991). *Boundaries of the text: epic performances in South and Southeast Asia*. Michigan Papers on South and Southeast Asia, 35. Ann Arbor, Michigan: The University of Michigan.

Frankl, Viktor E. (1984). *Man's search for meaning*. First published in Austria under the title *Ein Psycholog erlebt das Konzentrationslager* (1946). Translated into English (1959), revised and updated (1984). Reprint, New York etc.: Washington Square Press, 1985.

Freeman, James M. (1979). *Untouchable: an Indian life history*. Stanford: Stanford University Press.

Ganguli, Kisari Mohan, tr. (1970). *The Mahabharata of Krishna-Dwaipayana Vyasa, translated into English prose from the original Sanskrit text*, 4 vols. Originally published anonymously in 100 fascicules between 1883 and 1896, under the editorship of Pratap Chandra Roy. Delhi: Munshiram Manoharlal.

Gardiner, Michael, and Michael Mayerfeld Bell (1998). 'Bakhtin and the human sciences: a brief introduction.' In Bell and Gardiner, eds, *Bakhtin and the human sciences*, pp. 1–12.

Gardner, Katy, and Abdus Shukur (1994). '"I'm Bengali, I'm Asian, and I'm living here": the changing identity of British Bengalis.' In Ballard, ed., *Desh pardesh*, pp. 142–64.

Gautama Dharmasūtra. Gautamapraṇītadharmasutrāṇi, with the commentary of Haradatta, ed. Naraharaśāstrī Talekar and Gaṅgādhara Bāpūrāva Kāle. Ānandāśrama Sanskrit Series, 61. Fourth printing, Pune: Ānandāśrama, 1966.

George, K. M. (1968). *A survey of Malayalam literature*. London: Asia Publishing House.

Ghuman, P. A. S. (1980). 'Bhattra Sikhs in Cardiff: family and kinship organisation.' *New Community: a journal of research and policy on ethnic relations*, 8 (3), 308–16.

Gill, Gurpal (undated). 'Editorial.' *Valmik Jagriti*, 1 (3). Southall: Shri Guru Valmik Sabha.

Gill, Gurpal (undated). 'Vistas new and venues fresh.' *Valmik Jagriti*, 2 (3). Southall: Shri Guru Valmik Sabha.

Gill, Gurpal (1998). [Untitled editorial.] *Valmik Jagriti*, 3 (3). Southall: Shri Guru Valmik Sabha.

Gokhale, Jayashree (1993). *From concessions to confrontation: the politics of an Indian untouchable community*. Bombay: Popular Prakashan.

Gold, Daniel (1987). *The Lord as guru: Hindi sants in the north Indian tradition*. New York: Oxford University Press.

Goldman, Robert P. (1976). 'Vālmīki and the Bhṛgu connection.' *Journal of the American Oriental Society*, 96 (1), 97–101.

Goldman, Robert P. (1977). *Gods, priests, and warriors: the Bhṛgus of the Mahābhārata*. Studies in Oriental Culture, 12, Columbia University. New York: Columbia University Press.

Goldman, Robert P., ed., tr. (1984–). *The Rāmāyaṇa of Vālmīki: an epic of ancient India*. Vol. 1, *Bālakāṇḍa*, tr. R. P. Goldman, annotation by R. P. Goldman and Sally J. Sutherland (1984). Vol. 2, *Ayodhyākāṇḍa*, tr. Sheldon I. Pollock (1986). Vol. 3, *Araṇyakāṇḍa*, tr. S. I. Pollock (1991). Vol. 4, *Kiṣkindhākāṇḍa*, tr. Rosalind Lefeber (1994). Vol. 5, *Sundarakāṇḍa*, tr. R. P. Goldman and Sally J. Sutherland Goldman (1996). Princeton Library of Asian translations. New Jersey: Princeton University Press.

Gombrich, Richard F. (1985). 'The Vessantara Jātaka, the Rāmāyaṇa and the Daśaratha Jātaka.' *Journal of the American Oriental Society*, 105, 427–37.

Gombrich, Richard F. (1996). 'Who was Aṅgulimāla?' In *How Buddhism began: the conditioned genesis of the early teachings*, pp. 135–64. The Jordan Lectures in Comparative Religion, 17 (School of Oriental and African Studies, University of London, 1994). London and Atlantic Highlands, New Jersey: Athlone.

Gopal, Madan (1978). 'Tulasi Das.' In Raghavan, ed., *Rāmāyaṇa, Mahābhārata and Bhāgavata writers*, pp. 96–114.

Goswami, Basanta Kumar Deva (1994). *A critical study of the Rāmāyaṇa tradition of Assam (up to 1826 A.D.)*. Calcutta: Punthi Pustak.

Gough, Kathleen (1973). 'Harijans in Thanjavur.' In K. Gough and Hari P. Sharma, eds, *Imperialism and revolution in South Asia*, pp. 222–45. New York: Monthly Review Press.

Gould, Stephen Jay (1999). *Rocks of ages: science and religion in the fullness of life*. London: Jonathan Cape.

Granoff, Phyllis (1998). 'Cures and karma: healing and being healed in Jain religious literature.' In Albert I. Baumgarten, Jan Assmann, and Gedaliahu G. Stroumsa, eds, *Self, soul, and body in religious experience*, pp. 218–55. Studies in the History of Religions (*Numen* Books series), 78. Leiden and Boston: E. J. Brill.

Gray, Chris (2001). 'Census office feels the Force of followers of the "Jedi faith".' *The Independent*, Thursday 11 October, p. 11.

Green, Nile (2002). 'The Sufi saints of Awrangabad: narratives, contexts, identities.' Unpublished PhD thesis, School of Oriental and African Studies, University of London.

Greeven, R. (1894). *Knights of the broom*. Benares: Medical Hall Press.

Griffith, Ralph T. H. (1973). *The hymns of the Ṛgveda, translated with a popular commentary*, revised edition. Reprint, Delhi: Motilal Banarsidass, 1976.

Griswold, Hervey de Witt (1934). *Insights into modern Hinduism*. Reprint, Delhi: Aryan Books International, 1996.

Growse, F. S., tr. (1987). *The Rāmāyaṇa of Tulasīdāsa*, ed. and revised by R. C. Prasad. Reprint, Delhi: Motilal Banarsidass, 1989.

Gurū Granth Sāhib. See *Ādi Granth*.

Hacker, Paul (1978). *Kleine Schriften*, ed. Lambert Schmithausen. Wiesbaden: Steiner Verlag.

Haley, A. J., and Brian S. Johnston. 'Menaces to management: a developmental view of British soccer hooligans, 1961–1986.' *www.thesportjournal.org/vol1no1/menaces.htm* (16 July 2002).

Hanneder, Jürgen (1998). 'Śaiva Tantric material in the *Yogavāsiṣṭha*.' *Wiener Zeitschrift für die Kunde Südasiens*, 42, 67–76.

Hanneder, Jürgen (2000). 'The Yogavāsiṣṭha and its Kashmirian recension, the Mokṣopāya: notes on their textual quality.' *Wiener Zeitschrift für die Kunde Südasiens*, 44, 183–210.

Hanneder, Jürgen, and Walter Slaje (2002). *Bhāskarakaṇṭha's Mokṣopāya-ṭīkā*, vol. 1: *Vairāgyaprakaraṇam*. Revised edition in Devanāgarī script. Indologica Halensis. Geisteskultur Indiens: Texte und Studien, 1. Aachen: Shaker Verlag.

Hansen, Thomas Blom (1999). *The saffron wave: democracy and Hindu nationalism in modern India*. Princeton: Princeton University Press.

Hara, Minoru (1972). 'Valmiki, the singer of tales.' In R. C. Hazra and S. C. Banerji, eds, *S. K. De memorial volume*, pp. 117–28. Calcutta: Firma K. L. Mukhopadhy.

Hara, Minoru (1979). '*Tapas* in the *Mahābhārata*.' English summary of Japanese book entitled *Koten Indo no kugyō*, pp. 504–18. Tokyo: Shunjūsha.

Hardgrave, Robert L., Jr (1969). *The Nadars of Tamilnad: the political culture of a community in change*. Berkeley: University of California Press.

Harivaṃśa. The Harivaṃśa: the khila or supplement to the Mahābhārata, text as constituted in its critical edition. Vol. 5 of *The Mahābhārata: text as constituted in its critical edition*, ed. V. S. Sukthankar *et al.* Poona: Bhandarkar Oriental Research Institute, 1976.

Harrison, Frances (2001). 'Hindus convert to escape caste.' BBC News, Sunday 4 November 2001 (*http://news.bbc.co.uk/hi/english/world/south_asia*).

Hart, George L. (2001). 'Early evidence for caste in south India.' Email attachment, 16 September 2001. See also online discussion group: *www.indology.org.uk*.

Hart, George L., and Hank Heifetz, trs (1988). *The forest book of the Rāmāyaṇa of Kampaṉ*. Berkeley: University of California Press.

Hawley, John Stratton (1995). 'The saints subdued: domestic virtue and national integration in *Amar Chitra Katha*.' In Babb and Wadley, eds, *Media and the transformation of religion in South Asia*, pp. 107–34.

Hazari (1969). *Untouchable: the autobiography of an Indian outcaste*. London: Pall Mall Press.

Hazra, R. C. (1975). *Studies in the Purāṇic records on Hindu rites and customs*. Delhi, Motilal Banarsidass.

Hess, Linda (1983). *The Bījak of Kabir*, translated with Shukdev Singh. San Francisco: North Point Press.

Hiltebeitel, Alf (1999a). 'Reconsidering Bhṛguization.' In Brockington and Schreiner, eds, *Composing a tradition*, pp. 155–68.

Hiltebeitel, Alf (1999b). *Rethinking India's oral and classical epics: Draupadī among Rajputs, Muslims and Dalits*. Chicago and London: University of Chicago Press.

Hiltebeitel, Alf (2001). *Rethinking the Mahābhārata: a reader's guide to the education of the dharma king*. Chicago and London: University of Chicago Press.

Hinnells, John (1994). 'Parsi Zoroastrians in London.' In Ballard, ed., *Desh pardesh*, pp. 251–71.

Honko, Lauri (1998). *Textualising the Siri epic*. Folklore Fellows' Communications, 118 (264). Helsinki: Suomalainen Tiedeakatemia, Academia Scientiarum Fennica.

Honko, Lauri, in collaboration with Chinnappa Gowda, Anneli Honko and Viveka Rai (1998). *The Siri epic as performed by Gopala Naika*, 2 parts. Folklore Fellows' Communications, 119–20 (265–6). Helsinki: Suomalainen Tiedeakatemia, Academia Scientiarum Fennica.

Hopkins, E. Washburn (1901). *The great epic of India: character and origin of the Mahabharata*. Reprint, Delhi: Motilal Banarsidass, 1993.

http://news.bbc.co.uk/hi/english/world/south_asia. See Harrison (2001).

Huber, Édouard (1911). 'Études indochinoises IX: trois nouvelles inscriptions du roi Prakāçadharma du Campa.' *Bulletin de l'École Française d'Extrême Orient*, 11, 260–4.

Ibbetson, Denzil Charles Jelf (1883). *Report on the Census of the Panjáb taken on the 17th of February 1881*. Lahore: Government of India.

Ibbetson, Denzil Charles Jelf (1916). *Panjab castes*. Reprint of the chapters on the races, castes and tribes of the Panjab in Ibbetson (1883). Reprint, Delhi: B. R. Publishing Corporation, 1974.

Ibbetson, Denzil Charles Jelf (1919). *A glossary of the tribes and castes of the Punjab and North-West-Frontier Province, based on the census report of the Punjab, 1883, by the late Sir Denzil Ibbetson, and the census report for the Punjab, 1892, by Sri Edward Maclagen, and compiled by H. A. Rose*. Vol. 1, Lahore: Government of India. Vol. 2, reprint, Delhi: Amar Prakashan, 1980.

Ilaiah, Kancha (1996). *Why I am not a Hindu: a sudra critique of Hindutva philosophy, culture and political economy*. Calcutta: Samya.

India's epic Ramayana game, English version. New Delhi: Samira Products, 21 February 1998.

Iyengar, K. R. Srinivasa, ed. (1983). *Asian variations in Ramayana*. Delhi: Sahitya Akademi.

Jadhav, Sushrut (1994). 'The myths of origin of the Indian untouchables.' *Man: The Journal of the Royal Anthropological Institute (n. s.)*, 29, 712.

Jain, Madhu (1988). 'Ramayan: the second coming.' *India Today*, 13 (16), 31 August, 16.

James, William (1982). *The varieties of religious experience: a study in human nature* (1902), edited with an introduction by Martin E. Marty. The Penguin American Library. Harmondsworth: Penguin.

Janaki, S. S., tr. (1978). *The statue: Bhāsa's Pratimā in English translation*. Madras: Kuppuswami Sastri Research Institute.

Jogdand, Prahlad Gangaram (1991). *Dalit movement in Maharashtra*. Delhi: Kanak Publications.

Johnson, Helen M., tr. (1962). *Triṣaṣṭiśalākāpuruṣacaritra, or The lives of sixty-three illustrious persons, by Ācārya Śrī Hemacandra*, 6. Baroda: Oriental Institute.

Johnston, E. H., tr. (1936). *Aśvaghoṣa's Buddhacarita or Acts of the Buddha in three parts: Sanskrit text of cantos I–XIV with English translation of cantos I–XXVIII, cantos I to XIV translated from the original Sanskrit supplemented by the Tibetan version and cantos XV to XXVIII from the Tibetan and Chinese versions*. Reprint, Delhi: Motilal Banarsidass, 1984.

Jones, Kenneth W. (1976). *Arya Dharm: Hindu consciousness in 19th-century Punjab*. Berkeley: Berkeley University Press.

Jordens, J. T. F. (1978). *Dayānanda Sarasvatī: his life and ideas*. Delhi: Oxford University Press.

Joshi, Barbara R. (1982). *Democracy in search of equality: untouchable politics and Indian social change*. With a foreword by Owen M. Lynch. Delhi: Hindustan Publishing Corporation (India).

Joshi, Barbara R., ed. (1986). *Untouchables: voices of the Dalit liberation movement*. London: Zed Books Ltd.

Journal of the American Academy of Religion, 68 (4), December 2000. Special issue entitled 'Articles and responses on "Who speaks for Hinduism?"'

Juergensmeyer, Mark (1982). *Religion as social vision: the movement against untouchability in 20th-century Punjab*. Berkeley: University of California Press.

Juergensmeyer, Mark (1988). *Religious rebels in the Punjab: the social vision of the untouchables*. Revised edition of 1982 publication. Delhi: Ajanta Publications.

Kale, M. R., tr. (1925). *The Daśakumāracarita of Daṇḍin with a commentary: with various readings, a literal translation, explanatory and critical notes, and an exhaustive introduction*, second edition. Reprint, Delhi: Motilal Banarsidass, 1966.

Kale, M. R., tr. (1934). *The Uttararāmacharita of Bhavabhūti, with the commentary of Vīrarāghava, various readings, introduction, a literal English translation, exhaustive notes and appendices*, fourth edition. Reprint, Delhi: Motilal Banarsidass, 1993.

Kalsi, Sewa Singh (1992). *The evolution of a Sikh community in Britain: religious and social change among the Sikhs of Leeds and Bradford*. Community Religions Project monograph series. Leeds: Department of Theology and Religious Studies, University of Leeds.

Kalsi, Sewa Singh (1999). 'The Sikhs and caste: the development of Ramgarhia identity in Britain.' In Pashaura Singh and N. Gerald Barrier, eds, *Sikh identity: continuity and change*, pp. 255–73. Delhi: Manohar.

Kane, Pandurang Vaman (1968–77). *History of Dharmaśāstra: ancient and mediaeval religious and civil law*, second edition. Poona: Bhandarkar Oriental Research Institute.

Kapadia, Karin (1995). *Siva and her sisters: gender, caste, and class in rural south India*. Boulder, Colorado: Westview Press.

Kapp, Dieter B. (1991). 'The episode of Ayi- and Mayi-Rāvaṇa in the oral *Rāmāyaṇa* version of the Ālu Kurumbas.' In Thiel-Horstmann, ed., *Rāmāyaṇa and Rāmāyaṇas*, pp. 103–14.

Kapur, Anuradha (1990). *Actors, pilgrims, kings and gods: the Ramlila at Ramnagar*. Calcutta: Seagull.

Kapur, Geeta (1993). 'On the *Hum sab Ayodhya* exhibit.' Included with other extracts from SAHMAT (October 1993) in *Bulletin of Concerned Asian Scholars*, 25 (4), October–December 1993, 70–1.

Karmakar, R. D., tr. (1954). *Raghuvaṃśa of Kālidāsa, Cantos XI–XIV*. Poona: Aryabhushan Mudranalaya.

Karnad, Girish (1993). *Talé-Daṇḍa: A Play*. Originally published in Kannada in 1990. Delhi: Ravi Dayal.

Karttunen, Klaus (1997). *India and the Hellenistic world*. Studia Orientalia, vol. 83. Helsinki: The Finnish Oriental Society.

Karve, Irawati (1974). *Yuganta: the end of an epoch*, revised second edition. Originally published in Marathi in 1967. Reprint, Bombay: Orient Longman.

Kavitāvalī of Tulsīdās. See Allchin (1964).

Khan, Benjamin (1983). *The concept of dharma in Valmiki Ramayana*, second edition. Delhi: Munshiram Manoharlal.

Khan, Khan Ahmad Hasan (1933). *Report [on the] Census of India, 1931*. Vol. 17, *Punjab, part 1*. Lahore: Civil and Military Gazette Press.

Khare, R. S. (1984). *The Untouchable as himself: ideology, identity, and pragmatism among the Lucknow Chamars*. Cambridge: Cambridge University Press.

Khare, R. S. (2000). 'Elusive social justice, distant human rights: untouchable women's struggles and dilemmas in changing India.' In Michael R. Anderson and Sujit Guha, eds, *Changing concepts of rights and justice in South Asia*, pp. 198–219.

Kielhorn, F., ed. (1962). *The Vyākaraṇa-Mahābhāṣya of Patañjali*, vol. 1, third edition, revised by K. V. Abhyankar. Poona: Bhandarkar Oriental Research Institute.

Knott, Kim (1986). *Hinduism in Leeds: a study of religious practice in the Indian Hindu community and in Hindu-related groups.* Community Religions Project Monograph. Leeds: University of Leeds.

Knott, Kim (1991). 'Bound to change? The religions of South Asians in Britain.' In Steven Vertovec, ed., *Aspects of the South Asian diaspora*, pp. 86–111.

Knott, Kim (1994). 'The Gujarati Mochis in Leeds: from leather stockings to surgical boots and beyond.' In Ballard, ed., *Desh pardesh*, pp. 213–30.

König, Ditte (1984). *Das Tor zur Unterwelt: Mythologie und Kult des Termitenhügels in der schriftlichen und mündlichen Tradition Indiens*. Beiträge zur Südasienforschung Südasien-Institut Universität Heidelberg, 97. Wiesbaden: Franz Steiner Verlag.

Kramrisch, Stella (1924). *The Viṣṇudharmottara: a treatise on Indian painting.* Calcutta: Calcutta University.

Kripal, Jeffrey J. (1995). *Kālī's child: the mystical and the erotic in the life and teachings of Ramakrishna*. Chicago and London: University of Chicago Press.

Kripal, Jeffrey J. (1998). *Kālī's child: the mystical and the erotic in the life and teachings of Ramakrishna*, second edition, with a foreword by Wendy Doniger. Chicago and London: University of Chicago Press.

Kripal, Jeffrey J. (2000–1). 'Secret talk: sexual identity and the politics of scholarship in the study of Hindu tantrism.' *Harvard Divinity Bulletin*, 29 (4), winter issue, 14–17.

Kulkarni, V. M. (1980). 'Jain Rāmāyaṇas and their source.' In V. R. Raghavan, ed., *The Rāmāyaṇa tradition in Asia*, pp. 226–41.

Kulkarni, V. M. (1990). *The story of Rāma in Jain literature (as presented by the Śvetāmbara and Digambara poets in the Prakrit, Sanskrit and Apabhraṃśa languages)*. Saraswati Oriental Studies, 3. Ahmedabad: Saraswati Pustak Bhandar.

Kunjukuttan, Matampu (1996). *Outcaste (Bhrushtu)*. Translated from the Malayalam by Vasanthi Shankaranarayanan. Modern Indian Novels in Translation series. Madras: Macmillan India Ltd.

Kunst, Arnold, and J. L. Shastri, eds (1969). *The Śiva-Purāṇa*, translated by a board of scholars, part 1. Ancient Indian Tradition and Mythology, vol. 1. Delhi: Motilal Banarsidass.

Lal, Sheo Kumar, and Umed Raj Nahar (1990). *Extent of untouchability and pattern of discrimination*. Delhi: Mittal Publications.

Leslie, Julia (1994). 'Some traditional Indian views on menstruation and female sexuality.' In Roy Porter and Mikulas Teich, eds, *Sexual knowledge, sexual science: the history of attitudes to sexuality*, pp. 63–81. Cambridge: Cambridge University Press. Reprinted as 'Menstruation myths' in Leslie, ed., *Myth and mythmaking*, pp. 87–105.

Leslie, Julia, ed. (1996). *Myth and mythmaking: continuous evolution in Indian tradition*. Collected Papers on South Asia series, 12. Richmond: Curzon Press.

Leslie, Julia (1998a). 'Understanding Basava: history, hagiography and a modern Kannada drama.' *Bulletin of the School of Oriental and African Studies*, 61 (2), 228–61.

Leslie, Julia (1998b). 'A bird bereaved: the identity and significance of Vālmīki's *krauñca*.' *Journal of Indian Philosophy*, 26, 455–87.

Leslie, Julia (1999). 'The implications of the physical body: health, suffering and *karma* in Hindu thought.' In J. R. Hinnells and R. Porter, eds, *Religion, health and suffering*, pp. 23–45. London: Kegan Paul.

Leslie, Julia (2000). Report for the Bhagavan Valmiki Action Committee (26 June). Unpublished.

Leslie, Julia (in press). 'The implications of *bhakti* for the story of Vālmīki.' In Anna King and J. L. Brockington, eds, *The intimate other: divine love in Indian religions*. Hyderabad: Orient Longman.

Lewis, Philip (1994). 'Being Muslim and being British: the dynamics of Islamic reconstruction in Bradford.' In Ballard, ed., *Desh pardesh*, pp. 58–87.

Lord, A. B. (1960). *The singer of tales*. Harvard Studies in Comparative Literature, 24. Second edition, ed. Stephen Mitchell and Gregory Nagy (2000). Cambridge, Mass.: Harvard University Press.

Lutgendorf, Philip (1991a). *The life of a text: performing the Rāmcaritmānas of Tulsidas*. Berkeley: University of California Press.

Lutgendorf, Philip (1991b). 'Words made flesh: the Banaras *Rāmlīlā* as epic commentary.' In Flueckiger and Sears, eds, *Boundaries of the text*, pp. 83–104.

Lutgendorf, Philip (1991c). 'The "great sacrifice" of Rāmāyaṇa recitation: ritual performance of the *Rāmcaritmānas*.' In Thiel-Horstmann, ed., *Rāmāyaṇa and Rāmāyaṇas*, pp. 185–205.

Lutgendorf, Philip (1995a). 'All in the (Raghu) family: a video epic in cultural context.' In Babb and Wadley, eds, *Media and the transformation of religions in South Asia*, pp. 217–53.

Lutgendorf, Philip (1995b). 'Interpreting Ramraj: reflections on the Ramayan, bhakti, and Hindu nationalism.' In David Lorenzen, ed., *Bhakti religion in north India: community identity and political action*, pp. 253–87. Albany: State University of New York Press.

Lutgendorf, Philip (1997). 'Imagining Ayodhya: utopia and its shadows in a Hindu landscape.' *International Journal of Hindu Studies*, 1 (1), 19–54.

Lutgendorf, Philip (2000). 'Dining out at lake Pampa: the Shabari episode in multiple Ramayanas.' In Richman, ed., *Questioning Rāmāyaṇas*, pp. 119–36.

Lynch, Owen M. (1969). *The politics of untouchability: social mobility and social change in a city of India*. New York: Columbia University Press.

Mahābhārata. Critical edition, 19 vols, 1933–66; 6 vols of *Pratīka*-index, 1967–72. Ed. V. S. Sukthankar *et al.* Poona: Bhandarkar Oriental Research Institute.

Mahābhārata. The Mahābhārata: text as constituted in its critical edition, 4 vols, ed. V. S. Sukthankar *et al.* Poona: Bhandarkar Oriental Research Institute, 1971–5.

Mahar, Michael J., ed. (1972). *The untouchables of contemporary India.* Tucson, Arizona: University of Arizona Press.

Mahar, Pauline Moller (1960). 'Changing religious practices of an untouchable caste.' *Economic Development and Cultural Change*, 8 (3), April, 279–87.

Maharajan, S. (1972). *Kamban*. Makers of Indian Literature series. New Delhi: Sahitya Akademi.

Majumdar, R. C. (1927). *Ancient Indian colonies in the Far East*, vol. 1: *Champa*. Greater India Society, 1. Punjab Oriental (Sanskrit) Series, 16. Lahore: Punjab Sanskrit Book Depot.

Mallory, James P. (1989). *In search of the Indo-Europeans: language, archeology and myth*. London: Thames and Hudson.

Mandair, Arvind-pal (2000). A report for the Radio Authority based on the case of Valmiki Action Committee versus Radio XL (May). Unpublished.

Mandair, Arvind-pal (2001). 'Thinking differently about religion and history: issues for Sikh studies.' In Christopher Shackle, Gurharpal Singh and Arvind-pal Singh Mandair, eds, *Sikh religion, culture and ethnicity*, pp. 47–71. London: Curzon Press.

Mani, Vettam (1975). *Purāṇic encyclopaedia: a comprehensive work with special reference to the epic and Purāṇic literature*. Originally published in Malayalam (Kottayam, Kerala 1964). Delhi: Motilal Banarsidass.

Mann, Gurinder Singh (2001a). 'Canon formation in the Sikh tradition.' In Christopher Shackle, Gurharpal Singh and Arvind-pal Singh Mandair, eds, *Sikh religion, culture and ethnicity*, pp. 1–24.

Mann, Gurinder Singh (2001b). *The making of Sikh scripture.* New Delhi: Oxford University Press.

Manusmṛti. Sanskrit text with the commentaries of Medhātithi, Sarvajña-nārāyaṇa, Kullūka, Rāghavānanda, Nandana, Rāmacandra, Maṇirāma, Govindarāja and Bhāruci, ed. Jayantakrishna Harikrishna Dave. 5 vols. Bombay: Bharatiya Vidya Bhavan, 1972–.

Manusmṛti. Mānava-Dharma-Śāstra. Sanskrit text with the commentaries of Medhātithi, Sarvajña-nārāyaṇa, Kullūka, Rāghavānanda, Nandana, Rāma-candra and Govindarāja, 3 vols, ed. Vishvanath Narayan Mandlik; vol. 3 contains Govindarāja's commentary, ed. Rao Saheb. Bombay: Ganpat Krishnaraji's Press, 1886.

Masson, Jeffrey (1969). '"Who killed cock krauñca?" Abhinavagupta's reflections on the origin of aesthetic experience.' *Journal of the Oriental Institute, Baroda*, 18 (3), 207–24.

Matchett, Freda (2000). *Kṛṣṇa: Lord or avatāra? The relationship between Kṛṣṇa and Viṣṇu in the context of the avatāra myth as presented by the Harivaṃśa, the Viṣṇupurāṇa and the Bhāgavatapurāṇa*. London: Curzon Press.

Mayrhofer, Manfred (1988, 1994). *Etymologisches Wörterbuch des Altindo-arischen*, 1 (4) and 2 (15). Indogermanische Bibliothek, 2: Wörterbücher. Heidelberg: Carl Winter Universitätsverlag.

Mazumdar, Shudha (1958). *Ramayana*. Bombay: Orient Longman.

McGregor, R. Stuart (1993). *The Oxford Hindi–English dictionary*. Oxford and Delhi: Oxford University Press.

McLeod, W. Hew (1999). 'Discord in the Sikh panth.' *Journal of the American Oriental Society*, 119 (3), July–September, 381–9.

Mendelsohn, Oliver, and Marika Vicziany (1998). *The untouchables*: subordination, poverty and the state in modern India. Contemporary South Asia series, 4. Cambridge: Cambridge University Press.

Michael, S. M., ed. (1999a). *Dalits in modern India: vision and values*. Delhi: Vistaar Publications.

Michael, S. M. (1999b). 'Dalit vision of a just society in India.' In Michael, ed., *Dalits in modern India*, pp. 99–117.

Miller, Robert J., and Pramodh Kale (1972). 'The burden on the head is always there.' In Mahar, ed., *The untouchables of contemporary India*, pp. 317–59.

Minkowski, Christopher (1989). 'Janamejaya's *sattra* and ritual structure.' *Journal of the American Oriental Society*, 109 (3), 401–21.

Minkowski, Christopher (1991). 'Snakes, *sattra*s and the *Mahābhārata*.' In Arvind Sharma, ed., *Essays on the Mahābhārata*, pp. 384–400. Brill's Indological Library, ed. Johannes Bronkhorst, 1. Leiden: E. J. Brill.

Mishra, K. C. (1987). *Tribes in the Mahābhārata: a socio-cultural study*. Delhi: National Publishing House.

Mishra, R. N. (1995). 'Matanga as a mythical figure and other historical references.' Unpublished paper delivered at the Conference on Mataṅga's *Bṛhaddeśī*, Department of Tribal Studies, Kannada University, Hampi, 11–17 July.

Mitchiner, John E. (1982). *Traditions of the Seven Ṛṣis*. Delhi: Motilal Banarsidass.

Mitra, Vihari-Lala, tr. (1976–78). *The Yoga-Vásishtha-Mahárámáyana of Válmiki translated from the original Sanskrit*. 4 vols. Delhi: Bharatiya Publishing House.

Moffatt, M. (1979). *An Untouchable community in south India: structure and consensus*. Princeton, New Jersey: Princeton University Press.

Mohan, P. Sanal (1999). 'Dalit discourse and the evolving new self: contest and strategies.' *Review of Development and Change*, 4 (1), January–June, 1–24. Chennai: Madras Institute of Development Studies.

Mohan, P. Sanal (2002). 'Narrativising oppression and sufferings: theorising slavery.' Unpublished paper presented in the Centre of South Asia Studies, School of Oriental and African Studies, University of London, 27 February.

Mohan, P. Sanal (forthcoming). 'Religion, social space and identity: construction of boundary in colonial Kerala.' In M. S. S. Pandian and Shail Mayaram, eds, *Subaltern studies*, 12. New Delhi: Permanent Black.

Mokṣopāya(śāstra). For the reconstituted text, see Slaje (1993, 1995, 1996a).

Mokṣopāya Project. Projektleiter: Prof. Dr Walter Slaje. Projektarbeiter: Dr Jürgen Hanneder. Department of Indology, Martin-Luther Universität, Halle-Wittenberg. See *www.indologie.uni-halle.de/forschung/Moksopaya*.

Molesworth, J. T. (1857). *A dictionary, Marāṭhī and English*, compiled with the assistance of George and Thomas Candy (first edition, 1831). Second edition, revised and enlarged, by J. T. Molesworth. Bombay: Bombay Education Society's Press.

Monier-Williams, Monier (1899). *A Sanskrit–English dictionary, etymologically and philologically arranged with special reference to cognate Indo-European languages*, revised edition. Oxford: Clarendon Press.

Moon, Vasant, *et al.* (2001). *Growing up Untouchable in India: a Dalit autobiography*. Originally published in Marathi as *Vasti*. Translated by Gail Omvedt, with an introduction by Eleanor Zelliot. Lanham, Maryland: Rowman & Littlefield Publishers.

Mosse, C. David F. (1986). 'Caste, Christianity and Hinduism: a study of social organisation and religion in rural Ramnad.' Unpublished DPhil thesis, University of Oxford.

Mosse, C. David F. (1994a). 'Idioms of subordination and styles of protest among Christian and Hindu harijan castes in Tamil Nadu.' *Contributions to Indian Sociology (n. s.)*, 28, 67–106.

Mosse, C. David F. (1994b). 'Catholic saints and the Hindu village pantheon in rural Tamil Nadu, India.' *Man: The Journal of the Royal Anthropological Institute (n. s.)*, 29 (2), 301–32.

Mosse, C. David F. (1994c). 'Comment: replication and consensus among Indian Untouchable (Harijan) castes.' *Man: The Journal of the Royal Anthropological Institute (n. s.)*, 29 (2), 457–60.

Mukherjee, Prabhati (1988). *Beyond the four varṇas: the untouchables in India*. Shimla: Indian Institute of Advanced Study.

Mukhopadhyaya, Girindrinath (1922–29). *History of Indian medicine, containing* notices, biographical and bibliographical, of the ayurvedic physicians and their works on medicine from the earliest ages to the present time, 3 vols. Reprint, Delhi: Munshiram Manoharlal, 1994.

Murugkar, Lata (1991). *Dalit Panther movement in Maharashtra: a sociological appraisal*. Bombay: Popular Prakashan.

Mus, Paul (1928). 'Études indiennes et indochinoises I: l'inscription à Valmiki de Prakaçadharma (Tra-Kieu).' *Bulletin de l'École Française d'Extrême-Orient*, 28, 147–52.

Nagar, Shantilal (1999). *Iconography of Jaina deities*, 2 vols. Delhi: B. R. Publishing Corporation.

Nagaraj, D. R. (1992). *The flaming feet: a study of the dalit movement in India*. Bangalore: South Forum and ICRA.

Nair, K. Bhaskaran (1978). 'Tunchattu Eluttacchan.' In Raghavan, ed., *Rāmāyaṇa, Mahābhārata and Bhāgavata writers*, pp. 89–95.

Narayana Rao, Velcheru (1991). 'A *Rāmāyaṇa* of their own: women's oral tradition in Telugu.' In Paula Richman, ed., *Many Rāmāyaṇas*, pp. 114–36.

Nesbitt, Eleanor (1980). 'Aspects of Sikh tradition in Nottingham.' Unpublished MPhil thesis, University of Nottingham.

Nesbitt, Eleanor (1990a). 'Religion and identity: the Valmiki community in Coventry.' *New Community*, 16 (2), January, 261–74.

Nesbitt, Eleanor (1990b). 'Pitfalls in religious taxonomy: Hindus and Sikhs, Valmikis and Ravidasis.' *Religion Today*, 6 (1), 9–12.

Nesbitt, Eleanor (1991). *'My Dad's Hindu, my Mum's side are Sikh': issues in religious identity*. Arts Culture and Education Research and Curriculum Papers.

Charlbury: The National Foundation for Arts Education in collaboration with the University of Warwick.

Nesbitt, Eleanor (1993). 'The transmission of Christian tradition in an ethnically diverse society.' In Rohit Barot, ed., *Religion and ethnicity: minorities and social change in the metropolis*, pp. 156–69. Kampen: Kok Pharos.

Nesbitt, Eleanor (1994). 'Valmikis in Coventry: the revival and reconstruction of a community.' In Ballard, ed., *Desh pardesh*, pp. 117–41.

Nesbitt, Eleanor (1995). 'Panjabis in Britain: cultural history and cultural choices.' *South Asia Research*, 15 (2), 221–40.

Nesbitt, Eleanor (1997). '"We are all equal": young British Punjabis' and Gujaratis' perceptions of caste.' *International Journal of Punjab Studies*, 4 (2), 201–18.

Nesbitt, Eleanor (1999). 'The impact of Morari Bapu's kathas on young British Hindus.' *Scottish Journal of Religious Studies*, 20 (2), autumn, 177–92.

Nesbitt, Eleanor (in press). 'Young British Sikhs and religious devotion: issues arising from ethnographic research.' In Anna King and J. L. Brockington, eds, *The intimate other: divine love in Indian religions*. Hyderabad: Orient Longman.

Nilsson, Usha (2000). '"Grinding millet but singing of Sita": power and domination in Awadhi and Bhojpuri women's songs.' In Richman, ed., *Questioning Rāmāyaṇas*, pp. 137–58.

Nowell-Smith, Geoffrey, ed. (1996). *The Oxford history of world cinema*. Oxford: Oxford University Press.

Oberlies, Thomas (1995). 'Arjunas Himmelreise und die Tīrthayātrā der Pāṇḍavas: zur Struktur des Tīrthayātrāparvan des Mahābhārata.' *Acta Orientalia*, 56, 106–24.

Oberoi, Harjot (2001). 'What has a whale got to do with it? A tale of pogroms and biblical narratives.' In Christopher Shackle, Gurharpal Singh and Arvind-pal Singh Mandair, eds, *Sikh religion, culture and ethnicity*, pp. 186–206.

O'Flaherty, Wendy Doniger (1973). *Śiva: the erotic ascetic*. London: Oxford University Press.

O'Flaherty, Wendy Doniger (1976). *The origins of evil in Hindu mythology*. Berkeley: University of California Press.

O'Flaherty, Wendy Doniger (1984). *Dreams, illusion and other realities*. Chicago and London: University of Chicago Press.

O'Flaherty, Wendy Doniger (1985). *Tales of sex and violence: folklore, sacrifice, and danger in the Jaiminīya Brāhmaṇa*. Reprint, Delhi: Motilal Banarsidass, 1987.

O'Flaherty, Wendy Doniger (1988). *Other people's myths: the cave of echoes*. New York: Macmillan. Reissued with a new preface, Chicago: University of Chicago Press, 1995.

O'Flaherty, Wendy Doniger: see also Doniger, Wendy.

O'Hanlon, Rosalind (1985). *Caste, conflict and ideology: Mahatma Jotirao Phule and low caste protest in nineteenth-century western India*. Cambridge: Cambridge University Press.

Olivelle, Patrick, tr. (1996). *Upaniṣads*. The World's Classics series. Oxford: Oxford University Press.

Olivelle, Patrick, tr. (1999). *Dharmasūtras: the law codes of Āpastamba, Gautama, Baudhāyana, and Vasiṣṭha, translated from the original Sanskrit*. Oxford World's Classics series. Oxford: Oxford University Press.

Omvedt, Gail (1990). *Violence against women: new movements and new theories in India*. New Delhi: Kali for Women.

Omvedt, Gail (1994). *Dalits and the democratic revolution: Dr Ambedkar and the dalit movement in colonial India*. New Delhi: Sage Publications.

Omvedt, Gail (1995). *Dalit visions: the anti-caste movement and the construction of an Indian identity*. Tracts for the Times, 8. London: Sangam Books.

Padma Purāṇa. 4 vols, Sanskrit text ed. Vishvanath Narayan Mandlik. Pune: Ānandāśrama, 1893–4.

Pai, Anant, ed. (1994). *Valmiki: the story of the author of the epic, 'Ramayana'*. Amar Chitra Katha series, vol. 579. Delhi: India Book House.

Pai, Anant, ed. (2000). *Aṅgulimāla: the robber who became a saint*. Amar Chitra Katha series, vol. 521. Delhi: India Book House.

Pandey, Shyam Manohar (1979, 1982, 1987). *The Hindi oral epic tradition*. Vol. 1: *Loriki, the tale of Lorik and Candā*. Vol. 2: *Canainī, the tale of Lorik and Candā*. Vol. 3: *Lorikāyan, the tale of Lorik and Candā*. Allahabad: Sahitya Bhawan Pvt. Ltd.

Pandurange Rao, Ilapavuluri (1994). *Valmiki*. Makers of Indian Literature series. Delhi: Sahitya Akademi.

Pantawane, Gangadhar (1986). 'Evolving a new identity: the development of a Dalit culture.' In Joshi, ed., *Untouchables*, pp. 79–87.

Parry, Jonathan P. (1979). *Caste and kinship in Kangra*. London: Routledge & Kegan Paul.

Partridge, Eric (1966). *Origins: a short etymological dictionary of modern English*, fourth edition. Reprint, London: Book Club Associates, 1978.

Piar Singh (1996). *Gatha Sri Adi Granth and the controversy*. Michigan: Anant Education and Rural Development Foundation, Inc.

Pillai, Sivashankar (1947). *Scavenger's son (Tottiyute makan)*. Originally published in Malayalam. Translated by R. E. Asher for the Asian Writer's series. Oxford: Heinemann Educational, 1993.

Pillai-Vetschera, Traude (1999). 'Ambedkar's daughters: a study of Mahar women in Ahmednagar district of Maharashtra.' In Michael, ed., *Dalits in modern India*, pp. 229–51.

Pollock, Sheldon (1984a). '*Ātmānaṃ mānuṣaṃ manye: Dharmākūtam* on the divinity of Rāma.' *Journal of the Oriental Institute, Baroda*, 33 (3–4), March–June, 231–43.

Pollock, Sheldon (1984b). 'The divine king in the Indian epic.' *Journal of the American Oriental Society*, 104, 505–28.

Pollock, Sheldon (1998). 'India in the vernacular millenium: literary culture and polity, 1000–1500 CES*.' *Daedalus*, 127 (3), 41–74.

Porter, J. R. (1995). *The illustrated guide to the Bible*. Oxford: Oxford University Press.

Prasad, R. C., ed., tr. (1990). *Tulasidasa's Shriramacharitamanasa: the holy lake of the acts of Rāma*, edited and translated into Hindi and English, compact edition. Delhi: Motilal Banarsidass.

Prashad, Vijay (2000). *Untouchable freedom: a social history of a dalit community*. New Delhi: Oxford University Press.

Pratimālakṣana. See *Viṣṇudharmottara*.

Pratimānāṭaka. *Pratimā Nāṭaka of Makāvi Bhāsa*, ed. V. Raghavan. Madras: Kuppuswami Sastri Research Institute, 1977.

Premchand, Dhanpat Rai Srivastav (1988). *Deliverance and other stories*. Translated from the Hindi by David Rubin. New Delhi: Penguin.

Pritchett, Frances W. (1995) 'The world of *Amar Chitra Katha*.' In Babb and Wadley, eds, *Media and the transformation of religion in South Asia*, pp. 76–106.

Purewal, Anjali (1976). 'Home–school relationships of Punjabis in Bedford.' Unpublished MSc thesis, Cranfield Institute of Technology.

Quigley, Declan (1991). *The interpretation of caste*. Oxford: Oxford University Press.

Radio Authority (2000). 'Radio XL 1296 AM (Birmingham), Thursday 24 February 2000', P022/38, *Radio Authority Quarterly Programming Bulletin: All Complaints, Quarter*, 38, April–June, 17. See *www.radioauthority.co.uk*.

Radio Authority (2001a). First revised adjudication, communicated to Lekh Raj Manjdadria with a letter dated 11 May 2001, but not published.

Radio Authority (2001b). 'Adjudication revision: programming', P022/38, *Radio Authority Quarterly Programming Bulletin: All Complaints, Quarter*, 43, July–September, 52–3. See *www.radioauthority.co.uk*.

Raghavan, V. (1952–3). 'The Tattvasaṃgraharāmāyaṇa of Rāmabrahmānanda.' *Annals of Oriental Research, University of Madras*, 10 (1), 1–55.

Raghavan, V. (1956). 'Buddhological texts and the epics.' *Adyar Library Bulletin*, 20, May, 349–59.

Raghavan, V. (1958). *The Indian heritage: an anthology of Sanskrit literature*, second edition. Reprint, Bangalore: Indian Institute of World Culture, 1980.

Raghavan, V. (1968). 'Rāmāyaṇa: quotations and textual criticism.' In *Mélanges d'Indianisme a la mémoire de Louis Renou*, pp. 595–604. Paris: Institut de Civilisation Indienne. Reprinted in Raghavan, *The greater Rāmāyaṇa*, pp. 277–87.

Raghavan, V. (1973) *The greater Rāmāyaṇa*. The Professor K. Venkataraman Lectures for 1971 in the University of Madras. Varanasi: All India Kashiraj Trust.

Raghavan, V. (1975). 'English Introduction.' In *Bhuśuṇḍi Rāmāyaṇa*, vol. 1, ed. B. P. Singh with assistance from Janardana Śāstrī Pāṇḍeya. Varanasi: Vishwavidyalaya Prakashan.

Raghavan, V., ed. (1978). *Rāmāyaṇa, Mahābhārata and Bhāgavata writers*. New Delhi: Publication Division, Ministry of Information and Broadcasting, Government of India.

Raghavan, V., ed. (1980a). *The Ramayana tradition in Asia.* New Delhi: Sahitya Akademi.

Raghavan, V. (1980b). 'The Ramayana in Sanskrit literature.' In Raghavan, ed., *The Ramayana tradition in Asia*, pp. 1–19.

Raghavan, V. (1980c). 'The Raghuvaṃśa of Kālidāsa.' In V. Raghavan, *On Kālidāsa: twelve essays*. Mysore: Kavyalaya Publishers.

Raghavan, V. (1980d). *Abhinavagupta and his works*. Chaukhambha Oriental Research Studies, 20. Varanasi: Chaukhambha Orientalia.

Raghavan, V. (1991). 'Music in the Adbhuta Rāmāyaṇa.' In S. S. Janaki, N. Gangadharan and R. S. Bhattacharya, eds, *Dr. V. Raghavan commemoration volume: selected articles of the late Dr. V. Raghavan on the epics and purāṇas*, pp. 489–97. Varanasi: All-India Kashiraj Trust.

Raghavan, V. (1998). *Sanskrit Rāmāyaṇas other than Vālmīki's: the Adbhuta, Adhyātma, and Ānanda Rāmāyaṇas*. Chennai: Dr. V. Raghavan Centre for Performing Arts.

Raghuvaṃśa. See Devadhar and Suru (1934) and Karmakar (1954).

Rahula, Walpola (1967). *What the Buddha taught*, second edition. Reprint, London: Gordon Fraser, 1978.

Rajshekar, V. T. (1995). *Dalit: the black untouchables of India*. With a foreword by Y. N. Kly, an essay by Runoko Rashidi, and an appendix by Laxmi Berwa. Originally published in India as *Apartheid in India* (1979). Third edition, Atlanta, Georgia: Clarity Press.

Ramanujan, A. K. (1973). *Speaking of Śiva*. Harmondsworth: Penguin.

Ramanujan, A. K. (1991). 'Three hundred *Rāmāyaṇas*: five examples and three thoughts on translation.' In Richman, ed., *Many Rāmāyaṇas*, pp. 22–49.

Rāmāyaṇa. See *Adhyātma Rāmāyaṇa*, *Ānanda Rāmāyaṇa*, *Bhuśuṇḍi Rāmāyaṇa*, *Rāmcaritmānas*, *Vālmīki Rāmāyaṇa*.

Rāmcaritmānas of Tulsīdās. *Gosvāmī tulasīdāsakṛta śrīrāmacaritamānasa*, ed. R. C. Prasad, with Hindi and English translations, compact edition. Delhi: Motilal Banarsidass, 1990.

Ranade, Ramchandra Dattatreya (1983). *Mysticism in India: the poet-saints of Maharashtra*. Reprint, Albany: State University of New York Press.

Report of the Bhagavan Valmiki Action Committee (2000). Typescript compiled and edited by Lekh Raj Manjdadria, convenor of the Bhagavan Valmiki Action Committee, 24 March.

Reynolds, Frank E. (1991). '*Rāmāyaṇa*, *Rāma Jātaka*, and *Ramakien*: a comparative study of Hindu and Buddhist traditions.' In Richman, ed., *Many Rāmāyaṇas*, pp. 50–63.

Ṛgveda. *Ṛgveda-Saṃhitā with the commentary of Sāyaṇācārya*, vol. 1, second edition. Poona: Vaidika Saṃśodhana Maṇḍala, 1972.

Richman, Paula, ed. (1991). *Many Rāmāyaṇas: the diversity of a narrative tradition in South Asia*. Berkeley: University of California Press.

Richman, Paula, (1999). 'A diaspora Ramayana in Southall, Greater London.' *Journal of the American Academy of Religion*, 67, 33–57.

Richman, Paula, ed. (2000). *Questioning Rāmāyaṇas: a South Asian Tradition*. Reprint, Berkeley: University of California Press, 2001.

Risley, Herbert H. (1908). *The people of India*. Calcutta: Thacker, Spink & Co.

Robb, Peter, ed. (1993). *Dalit movements and the meanings of labour in India*. SOAS Studies in South Asia series. Delhi: Oxford University Press.

Rocher, Ludo (1986). *The Purāṇas*. A History of Indian Literature, ed. Jan Gonda, 2 (3). Wiesbaden: Harrassowitz.

Roy Burman, B. K. (1994). *Tribes in perspective*. Encyclopaedia on Scheduled Tribes, Scheduled Castes and Disadvantaged People, 1. Delhi: Mittal Publications.

Rushdie, Salman (1988). *The Satanic verses*. London: Viking.

Saberwal, Satish (1990). *Mobile men: limits to social change in urban Punjab*. First edition, Shimla: The Institute of Advanced Study, 1976. Second revised edition, Delhi: Manohar Publications.

Sachchidananda (1977). *The Harijan elite*. Fridabad: Thompson Press.

Sachchidananda, and R. R. Prasad, eds (1996). *Encyclopaedic profile of Indian tribes*, 4 vols. Delhi: Discovery Publishing House.

Sahai, Sachchidanand (1993–4). 'Vālmīki: his authorship, date and personality as gleaned from Indochinese sources.' Proceedings of the Ninth International Rāmāyaṇa Conference, Torino, April 1992. *Indologica Taurinensia*, 19–20, 285–93.

Sahdev, Manjula (1980). *Maharṣi Vālmīki: ek samīkṣātmak adhyayan*. Patiala: Punjabi University Press.

Sahdev, Manjula (1983). 'The contribution of Panjab to Ramayana literature.' *The Panjab Past and Present*, 17 (1), April, 84–90. Patiala: Department of Punjab Historical Studies, Punjabi University.

Sahdev, Manjula (1986). 'Adi Kavi Valmiki, or The first classical Sanskrit poet: Valmiki.' *The Divine Life: Monthly Journal of the Divine Life Society*, 48 (1), January, 12–16.

Sahdev, Manjula (1997). *Vālmīki: rāmāyaṇa men chanda-viśleṣaṇa (Metrical analysis of Vālmīki-Rāmāyaṇa)*. Delhi: Nag Prakash.

Saheb, Shaik Abdul Azeez (1996). 'Valmiki.' In Sachchidananda and R. R. Prasad, eds, *Encyclopaedic profile of Indian tribes*, 4, 1030–3.

SAHMAT [Safdar Hashmi Memorial Trust], October 1993, New Delhi. Extracts entitled 'SAHMAT performance and exhibit for cultural understanding results in criminal charges: a selection of accounts', in *Bulletin of Concerned Asian Scholars*, 25 (4), October–December, 69–71.

Saifullah Khan, Verity (1977). 'The Pakistanis: Mirpuri villagers at home and in Bradford.' In Watson, ed., *Between two cultures*, pp. 57–89.

Salomon, Richard (1995). 'On the origin of the early Indian Scripts: a review article.' *Journal of the American Oriental Society*, 115 (2), 271–9.

Sandesara, Upendraray J. (1959). 'A note on the article "About Vālmīki".' *Journal of the Oriental Institute, Baroda*, 8 (3), March, 350.

Sarkar, H. B. (1985). *Cultural relations between India and southeast Asian countries*. Delhi: Indian Council for Cultural Relations and Motilal Banarsidass.

Sarma, C. R. (1994). *The Ramayana in Telugu and Tamil: a comparative study*, second edition. Madurai: Lakshminarayan Granthamala.

Sarma, Sreeramula Rajeswara (1997). 'Review article: the metres of the Rāmāyaṇa.' *The Journal of Religious Studies*, 28 (2), autumn, 77–85. Patiala: Guru Gobind Singh Department of Religious Studies, Punjabi University.

Sattar, Arshia, tr. (1996). *The Rāmāyaṇa, Vālmīki, abridged and translated*. Delhi: Penguin Books India.

Scharfe, Hartmut (1977). *Grammatical literature*. A History of Indian Literature, ed. Jan Gonda, 5 (2). Wiesbaden: Otto Harrassowitz.

Schomer, Karine, and W. H. McLeod, eds (1987). *The sants: studies in a devotional tradition of India*. Berkeley Religious Studies series. Delhi: Motilal Banarsidass.

Searle-Chatterjee, Mary (1981). *Reversible sex roles: the special case of Benares sweepers*. Oxford: Pergamon Press.

Searle-Chatterjee, Mary, and Ursula Sharma, eds (1994). *Contextualising caste: post-Dumontian approaches*. Oxford: Blackwell.

Sen, Makhanlal, tr. (1965). *From the original Valmiki Ramayana*. Reprint, Bombay: Rupa & Co., 1989.

Shackle, Christopher (1983). *An introduction to the sacred language of the Sikhs*. London: School of Oriental and African Studies.

Shackle, Christopher, Gurharpal Singh and Arvind-pal Singh Mandair, eds (2001). *Sikh religion, culture and ethnicity*. London: Curzon Press.

Shah, Priyabala, ed. (1958). *Viṣṇudharmottara-Purāṇa, third khaṇḍa: vol. 1, text, critical notes etc.* Gaekwad's Oriental Series, 130 (general editor, B. J. Sandesara). Baroda: Oriental Institute.

Shah, U. P., ed. (1975). *The Vālmīki-Rāmāyaṇa: critical edition*; vol. 7, *The Uttarakāṇḍa*. Baroda: Oriental Institute.

Sharma, M. P. (1983). *The concept of equality in the Indian Constitution*. Aligarh: Aman Publications.

Sharma, Ram Sharan (1990). *Śūdras in ancient India: a social history of the lower order down to circa A.D. 600*. First edition, 1958. Third revised edition, Delhi: Motilal Banarsidass.

Shastri, Hari Prasad, tr. (1937). *The world within the mind (Yoga-Vasishtha): extracts from the discourses of the sage Vasishtha to his pupil, Prince Rama, and the story of Queen Chudala, translated from the Sanskrit of Valmiki*, sixth edition. London: Shanti Sadan.

Shastri, Hari Prasad, tr. (1962, 1969, 1976). *The Ramayana of Valmiki*, vols 1 (second edition), 2 (second edition), and 3 (third edition). London: Shanti Sadan.

Shastri, J. L., ed. (1970). *The Śiva-Purāṇa*, translated by a board of scholars, parts 1–3. Ancient Indian Tradition and Mythology, 1–3. Delhi: Motilal Banarsidass.

Shastri, Satya Vrat (1997). 'Personality of Maharṣi Vālmīki as the *Rāmāyaṇa* reveals it.' In Manjula Sahdev, ed., *Maharṣi vālmīki vyaktiva evaṃ kṛtitva*, pp. 27–35. Patiala: Punjabi University Press.

Shaw, Alison (1991). 'The making of a Pakistani community leader.' In Vertovec, ed., *Aspects of the South Asian diaspora*, pp. 112–31.

Shaw, Alison (1994). 'The Pakistani community in Oxford.' In Ballard, ed., *Desh pardesh*, pp. 35–57.

Shee, Monika (1986). *Tapas und tapasvin in den erzählenden Partien des Mahābhārata*. Studien zur Indologie und Iranistik, 1. Reinbek: Dr. Inge Wezler.

Shende, N. J. (1943a). 'The authorship of the Mahābhārata.' *Annals of the Bhandarkar Oriental Research Institute*, 24, 67–82.

Shende, N. J. (1943b). 'The authorship of the Rāmāyaṇa.' *Journal of the University of Bombay (n. s.)*, 12, 19–24.

Sher-E-Punjab, weekly newspaper in Panjabi and English. 'Bhagwan Valmik Ji Maharaj', in Diwali issue, 1987, p. 9.

Sheth, Noel (1984). *The divinity of Krishna*. With a foreword by Daniel H. H. Ingalls. Delhi: Munshiram Manoharlal.

Shukra, A. (pseudonym) (1994). 'Caste: a personal perspective.' In Mary Searle-Chatterjee and Ursula Sharma, eds, *Contextualising caste: post-Dumontian approaches*, pp. 169–78.

Shulman, David (1979). 'Sītā and Śatakaṇṭharāvaṇa in a Tamil folk narrative.' *Journal of the Institute of Asian Studies*, 10 (2), 1–26.

Shulman, David (2000). 'Bhavabhūti on cruelty and compassion.' In Richman, ed., *Questioning Rāmāyaṇas*, pp. 49–82.

Siddhantaratna, Nagendranath (1935). 'Introduction.' In *Adhyātmarāmāyaṇam* with the commentaries of Narottama, Ramavarman and Gopala Chakravarti, vol. 1, pp. 1–78. Calcutta Sanskrit Series, 11. Calcutta: Metropolitan Printing and Publishing House.

Sims-Williams, Nicholas, and Joe Cribb (1996). 'A new Bactrian inscription of Kanishka the Great.' *Silk Road Art and Archaeology*, 4, 75–142.

Singh, Amarjit (1982–3). 'From Das(s)a to Dalit Panther: a historical survey on caste system.' *The Service*, 1 (2) [pages not known]; 1 (3), 22–3; 1 (4), 22–3; 1 (5), 21–3; 1 (8), 10–12, 23; 1 (10), 13–15.

Singh, Bhagwati Prasad (1980). '*Bhuśuṇḍi Rāmāyaṇa* and its influence on the mediaeval *Rāmāyaṇa* literature.' In V. Raghavan, ed., *The Ramayana tradition in Asia*, pp. 475–504.

Singh, Gurcharan, Saran Singh and Ravinder Kaur, eds (1983). *Panjabi–English Dictionary*, fourth edition. Amritsar: Singh Brothers.

Singh, K. S. (1993). *The Scheduled Castes*. People of India, National Series vol. II. Anthropological Survey of India. Delhi: Oxford University Press.

Singh, K. S. (1994). *The Scheduled Tribes*. People of India, National Series vol. III. Anthropological Survey of India. Delhi: Oxford University Press.

Singh, K. S. (1998). *India's communities, A–G*. People of India, National Series vol. IV. Anthropological Survey of India. Delhi: Oxford University Press.

Singh, Pashaura (1998). 'Recent trends and prospects in Sikh studies.' *Studies in Religion*, 27, 407–25.

Singh, Pashaura (2000). *The Guru Granth Sahib: canon, meaning and authority*. Delhi: Oxford University Press.

Singh, Piar (1996). *Gatha Sri Adi Granth and the controversy*. Michigan: Anant Education and Rural Development Foundation.

Skanda Purāṇa. *Śrī-Skāndaṃ Mahāpurāṇam*, 7 volumes in folio format, with illustrations, ed. Khemrāj Śrīkṛṣṇa. Bombay: Śrī Veṅkaṭeśvara Steam Press, 1910. Reprint, Delhi: Nag Publishers, 1986, second edition 1995.

Skanda Purāṇa. *Skandapurāṇam*, 7 volumes, ed. Pañcānana Tarkaratna. Sanskrit text in Bengali script. Bombay: Vaṅgavāsī Electro Machine Press, 1911.

Skanda Purāṇa. *Skandapurāṇasya Ambikākāṇḍaḥ*, ed. Kṛṣṇaprasāda Bhaṭṭarāī. Mahendraratnagranthamālā, 2. Kathmandu, 1988.

Skanda Purāṇa. See also R. Adriaensen, H. T. Bakker and H. Isaacson (1998).

Slaje, Walter (1990). 'A guide to the philosophical and religious terms in the *(Laghu-) Yogavāsiṣṭha*.' *Wiener Zeitschrift für die Kunde Südasiens*, 34, 147–79.

Slaje, Walter, ed. (1993). *Bhāskarakaṇṭhas Mokṣopāya-ṭīkā: ein Kommentar in der Tradition der kaschmirischen Yogavāsiṣṭha-Überlieferung. 2. Prakaraṇa (mumukṣuvyavahāra)*. Materialen für eine kritische Ausgabe des Mokṣopāya, 1. Graz: Leykam.

Slaje, Walter (1994). *Vom Mokṣopāya-Śāstra zum Yogavāsiṣṭha-Mahārāmāyaṇa:* philologische Untersuchungen zur Entwicklungs- und Überlieferungsgeschichte eines indischen Lehrwerks mit Anspruch auf Heilsrelevanz. Österreichische Akademie der Wissenschaften, Philosophisch-historische Klasse Sitzungsberichte, 609. Wien: Verlag der Österreichischen Akademie der Wissenschaften.

Slaje, Walter, ed. (1995). *Bhāskarakaṇṭhas Mokṣopāya-ṭīkā: ein Kommentar in der Tradition der kaschmirischen Yogavāsiṣṭha-Überlieferung. Die Fragmente des 3. (Utpatti-)Prakaraṇa.* Materialen für eine kritische Ausgabe des Mokṣopāya, 2. Graz: EWS-Fachverlag.

Slaje, Walter, ed. (1996a). *Bhāskarakaṇṭhas Mokṣopāya-ṭīkā: ein Kommentar in der Tradition der kaschmirischen Yogavāsiṣṭha-Überlieferung. 1. (Vairāgya-) Prakaraṇa*, in collaboration with Jutta Valent. Materialen für eine kritische Ausgabe des Mokṣopāya, 3. Graz: EWS-Fachverlag.

Slaje, Walter (1996b). 'The Mokṣopāya project.' *Annals of the Bhandarkar Oriental Research Institute*, 77, 209–21.

Slaje, Walter (2000a). 'Liberation from intentionality and involvement: on the concept of *jīvanmukti* according to the Mokṣopāya.' *Journal of Indian Philosophy*, 28, 171–94.

Slaje, Walter (2000b). 'Towards a history of the *jīvanmukti* concept: the Mokṣadharma in the *Mahābhārata*.' In Tsuchida and Wezler, eds, *Harānandalaharī*, pp. 325–48.

Slaje, Walter (2001a). 'The *Yogavāsiṣṭha* and the *Mokṣopāya*: current research.' Print-out of lecture delivered to the Department of the Study of Religions, School of Oriental and African Studies, University of London, 26 April, pp. 1–25.

Slaje, Walter (2001b). 'Water and salt (I): Yājñavalkya's *saindhava dṛṣṭānta* (BĀU II.4, 12).' *Indo-Iranian Journal*, 44 (1), 25–57.

Slaje, Walter (2001c). 'Water and salt (II): "material" causality and hylozoic thought in the Yājñavalkya-Maitreyī dialogue?' *Indo-Iranian Journal*, 44 (4), 299–327.

Słuszkiewicz, Eugeniusz (1925). 'Notes sur le Campūrāmāyaṇa de Bhōja.' *Rocznik Orientalistyczny*, 3, 107–32.

Słuszkiewicz, Eugeniusz (1957). 'Bhāsa et le Rāmāyaṇa.' *Rocznik Orientalistyczny*, 21, 409–21.

Smith, Brian K. (1994). *Classifying the universe: the ancient Indian varṇa system and the origins of caste*. New York: Oxford University Press.

Smith, John D. (1990). 'Worlds apart: orality, literacy and the Rajasthani folk-*Mahābhārata*.' *Oral Tradition*, 5 (1), 3–19.

Smith, John D. (1991). *The epic of Pābūjī: a study, transcription and translation*, with epic narration by Parbū Bhopo and illustrations by Śrīlāl Jośī. Cambridge: Cambridge University Press.

Smith, Wilfred Cantwell (1993). *What is scripture? A comparative approach.* London: SCM Press.

Smith, William L. (1981). 'Kīrttibās and the pandits: the revision of the Bengali Rāmāyaṇa.' In Asko Parpola, ed., *Proceedings of the Nordic South Asia Conference held in Helsinki, June 10–12, 1980*, pp. 229–40. Studia Orientalia, 50. Helsinki: The Finnish Oriental Society.

Smith, William L. (1988). *Rāmāyaṇa traditions in eastern India: Assam, Bengal, Orissa.* Stockholm Studies in Indian Languages and Culture, 2. Stockholm: Department of Indology, University of Stockholm.

Smith, William L. (1994). 'The saint and the bandit.' In Alan W. Entwistle and Françoise Mallison, eds, *Studies in South Asian devotional literature: research papers 1988–1991 presented at the Fifth Conference on Devotional Literature in New Indo-Aryan Languages (1991), held at Paris-École Française d'Extrême-Orient*, pp. 363–70. New Delhi: Manohar and Paris: École Française d'Extrême-Orient.

Smith, William L. (2000). *Patterns in north Indian hagiography*. Stockholm Studies in Indian Languages and Culture, 3. Stockholm: Department of Indology, University of Stockholm.

Soba, Pyara Lal, ed. (undated). *From the Yogavāsiṣṭha of Vālmīki: the concept of marriage, a study*. Southall: Shri Guru Valmik Sabha.

Sontheimer, Günther-Dietz (1989). *Pastoral deities in western India*. Translated by Anne Feldhaus from the original German version entitled, *Birobā, Mhaskobā und Khaṇḍobā: Ursprung, Geschichte und Umwelt von pastoralen Gottheiten in Mahārāṣṭra* (1976). Reprint, Delhi: Oxford University Press, 1993.

Sontheimer, Günther-Dietz (1991). 'The *Rāmāyaṇa* in contemporary folk traditions of Maharashtra.' In Thiel-Horstmann, *Rāmāyaṇa and Rāmāyaṇas*, pp. 115–37.

Sontheimer, Günther-Dietz (1997). 'King Khaṇḍobā's hunt and his encounter with Bāṇāī, the Shepherdess.' In Anne Feldhaus, Aditya Malik and Heidrun Brückner, eds, *King of hunters, warriors and shepherds: essays on Khaṇḍobā by Günther-Dietz Sontheimer*, pp. 278–322. New Delhi: Indira Gandhi National Centre for the Arts/Manohar.

Sörensen, S. (1904). *An index to the names in the Mahābhārata, with short explanations and a concordance to the Bombay and Calcutta editions and P. C. Roy's translation*. Reprint, Delhi: Motilal Banarsidass, 1978.

Southworth, William (2001). 'The origins of Campā in central Vietnam: a preliminary review.' Unpublished PhD thesis, School of Oriental and African Studies, University of London.

Srinivas, M. N. (1952). *Religion and society among the Coorgs of south India.* Oxford: Clarendon Press.

Srinivasan, K. S. (1978). 'Kamban.' In Raghavan, ed., *Rāmāyaṇa, Mahābhārata and Bhāgavata writers*, pp. 1–13.

Srinivasan, K. S. (1994). *Rāmāyaṇam as told by Vālmīki and Kamban*. Delhi: Abhinav Publications.

Steiner, Karin, tr. (1997). *Anargharāghava: das Schauspiel vom kostbaren Raghusproß*. Drama und Theater in Südasien, 1, ed. Heidrun Brückner. Wiesbaden: Harrassowitz.

Stewart, Tony K., and Edward C. Dimock (2000). 'Kṛttibāsa's apophatic critique of Rāma's kingship.' In Richman, ed., *Questioning Rāmāyaṇas*, pp. 243–64.

Stoler Miller, Barbara (1984). 'Kālidāsa's world and his plays'. In Barbara Stoler Miller, ed., *Theater of memory: the plays of Kālidāsa*, pp. 3–41. New York: Columbia University Press.

Strohl, Ralph, tr. (1990). 'The story of Bharata and Bāhubali.' In Phyllis Granoff, ed., *The clever adulteress and other stories: a treasury of Jain literature*, pp. 208–44. Oakville, New York and London: Mosaic Press.

Sukthankar, Vishnu Sitaram (1933–66). See *Mahābhārata*.

Sukthankar, Vishnu Sitaram (1936–7). 'Epic studies 6. The Bhṛgus and the Bhārata: a text-historical study.' *Annals of the Bhandarkar Oriental Research Institute*, 18, 1–76. Reprinted in P. K. Gode, ed., *Sukthankar memorial edition, vol. 1: critical studies in the Mahābhārata*, pp. 278–337. Bombay: Karnatak Publishing House, 1944.

Sukthankar, Vishnu Sitaram (1956). *The Indian heritage*. Bangalore: Indian Institute of World Culture.

Suru, N. G. (1960). Introduction to *Karpūra-Mañjarī by kavirāja Rājaśekhara, with an introduction, Prakrit text with chhāyā, English translation, exhaustive notes, appendices, glossary and Marathi translation*. Bombay: Aryabhushan Press.

Sweeney, Amin (1980). 'The Malaysian Rāmāyaṇa.' In V. Raghavan, ed., *The Rāmāyaṇa tradition in Asia*, pp. 122–41.

Tagare, Ganesh Vasudeo, tr. (1976). *The Bhāgavata Purāṇa*, part 3. Ancient Indian Tradition and Mythology, 9. Delhi: Motilal Banarsidass.

Tagare, Ganesh Vasudeo, tr. (1983). *The Brahmāṇḍa Purāṇa*. Ancient Indian Tradition and Mythology, 22–26. Delhi: Motilal Banarsidass.

Tagare, Ganesh Vasudeo, tr. (1988). *The Vāyu Purāṇa*, part 2. Ancient Indian Tradition and Mythology, 38. Delhi: Motilal Banarsidass.

Tagare, Ganesh Vasudeo, tr. (1992, 1995, 1997). *The Skanda Purāṇa*, parts 1, 7, 12. Ancient Indian Tradition and Mythology, 49, 55, 60. Delhi: Motilal Banarsidass.

Taittirīya Prātiśākhya. The Tâittirîya-Prâtiçâkhya, with its commentary, the Tribhâshyaratna: text, translation, and notes, ed. William D. Whitney. *Journal of the American Oriental Society*, 9 (1871), 1–469.

Taittirīya Saṃhitā. Die Taittirîya-Saṃhitâ, 2 vols, ed. Albrecht Weber. Leipzig: F. A. Brockhaus, 1871, 1872.

Tannen, Deborah (2001). *I only say this because I love you: How the way we talk can make or break family relationships throughout our lives*. London: Virago Press.

Temple, Richard Carnac (1884). 'The genealogies of Lâl Beg, as recorded in the private Gurmukhî MSS., kept for their own information by various Scavengers of the Ambâlâ and Karnâl Districts.' In *The legends of the Panjâb*, 1, 529–46. Reprint, New York: Arno Press Inc, 1977.

Thampi, P. Padmanabhan (1996). *Ramayanas of Kampan and Eluttacchan*. Thuckalay, South India: O. Padmakumari.

The Service. A monthly community newsletter in Panjabi and English, ed. Gardash Bharty. 1 (1), October 1982; 1 (3), December 1982; 1 (4), January

1983; 1 (5), February 1983; 1 (6), March 1983; 1 (7), April–May 1983; 1 (8), June–July 1983; 1 (9), August 1983; 1 (10), September–October 1983. Birmingham: Asian Post Fortnightly.

Thiel-Horstmann, Monika (1983). *Crossing the ocean of existence: Brah Bhāṣā religious poetry from Rajasthan: a reader*. Wiesbaden: Harrassowitz.

Thiel-Horstmann, Monika, ed. (1991). *Rāmāyaṇa and Rāmāyaṇas*. Wiesbaden: Harrassowitz.

Thomas, D. A. T., and P. A. S. Ghuman (1976). *A survey of social and religious attitudes among Sikhs in Cardiff*. Cardiff: The Open University in Wales.

Thomas, Lynn (1991). 'The identity of the destroyer in the *Mahābhārata*.' *Numen*, 41, 255–72.

Thomas, Lynn (1996). 'Paraśurāma and time.' In Leslie, ed., *Myth and mythmaking*, pp. 63–86.

Thomi, Peter (1983). 'The Yogavāsiṣṭha in its longer and shorter version.' *Journal of Indian Philosophy*, 11, 107–16.

Thompson, George (1998). 'On truth acts in Vedic.' *Indo-Iranian Journal*, 41 (2), April, 125–53.

Titze, Kurt (1998). *Jainism: a pictorial guide to the religion of non-violence*, with contributions from Klaus Bruhn, Joyoti Prasad Jain, Noel Q. King, and Vilas A. Sangave. Delhi: Motilal Banarsidass.

Trautmann, Thomas R. (1997). *Aryans and British India*. Berkeley: University of California Press.

Tripathi, Salil, with N. K. Singh, Dilip Awasthi and Nandita Sardana (1988). 'Ramayana, epic spin-offs: businessmen cash in on the public's fervour.' *India Today*, 15 July, pp. 72–3.

Tsuchida, Ryutaro, and Albrecht Wezler, eds (2000). *Harānandalaharī: volume in honour of Professor Minoru Hara on his seventieth birthday*. Reinbek: Dr Inge Wezler/Verlag für Orientalistische Fachpublikationen.

Tubb, Gary A. (1996). 'The dice-game episode in Rājaśekhara's Bālabhārata.' *Journal of Vaiṣṇava Studies*, 4 (3), 85–108.

Turner, R. L. (1966). *A comparative dictionary of the Indo-Aryan languages*. London: Oxford University Press.

Upadhyay, H. C. (1990). *Harijans of Himalaya, with special reference to the Harijans of Kumaun Hills*. Nainital: Gyanodaya Prakashan.

Upaniṣads. Eighteen principal Upaniṣads, vol. 1, critical edition by V.P. Limaye and R. D. Vadekar. Gandhi Memorial Edition. Poona: Vaidika Saṃśodhana Maṇḍala, 1958.

Uttararāmacarita. See Kale (1934).

Valmik Jagriti, 1 [undated]; 2 [undated]; 3, 25 March 1998. Southall: Shri Guru Valmik Sabha.

Valmik Yog Vasistha. Undated booklet produced to commemorate the re-release of the Panjabi edition of the *Yogavāsiṣṭha* in Jalandhar on 7 October 2001 and in Southall on 11 November 2001, second edition. Southall: Shri Guru Valmik Sabha and Jalandhar: Shri Guru Valmik Sabha International.

Vālmīki Rāmāyaṇa. The Vālmīki-Rāmāyaṇa: critical edition. 7 vols, ed. G. H. Bhatt and U. P. Shah. Baroda: Oriental Institute, 1958–75.

Valmikism. Undated booklet produced by WAVE, the Wolverhampton Association for Valmiki Education, in collaboration with the Wolverhampton Valmik Sabha, and printed in Nakodar, India.

van Buitenen, J. A. B., tr. (1973–78). *The Mahābhārata*. Vol. 1, *The book of the beginning* (1973). Vol. 2, *The book of the assembly hall, The book of the forest* (1975). Vol. 3, *The book of Virāṭa, The book of the effort* (1978). Chicago and London: University of Chicago Press.

van der Veer, Peter (1994). *Religious nationalism: Hindus and Muslims in India*. Berkeley: University of California Press.

van Nooten, B. A. (1976). 'Introduction.' In William Buck, tr., *Ramayana: King Rama's way*, illustrated by Shirley Triest, pp. xiii–xxii. Berkeley: University of California Press.

Vasiṣṭha Dharmasūtra. Sanskrit text ed. A. A. Führer. Bombay: Department of Public Instruction, 1883. Third edition, Poona, 1930.

Vaudeville, Charlotte (1955). *Étude sur les sources et la composition du Rāmāyaṇa de Tulsī-Dās*. Paris: Librairie d'Amérique et d'Orient.

Vaudeville, Charlotte (1993). *A weaver named Kabir: selected verses with a detailed biographical and historical introduction*. French Studies in South Asian Culture and Society, 6. Oxford: Oxford University Press. Oxford India Paperbacks.

Venkatesananda, Swami (1984). *The concise Yoga Vāsiṣṭha*, with an introduction and bibliography by Christopher Chapple. Albany: State University of New York Press.

Venkatesananda, Swami (1993). *The supreme Yoga: a new translation of the Yoga Vasiṣṭha*, third edition. Garhwal: The Divine Life Society.

Vertovec, Steven, ed. (1991). *Aspects of the South Asian diaspora*. Oxford University Papers on India, 2 (2). Delhi: Oxford University Press.

Vertovec, Steven (1994). 'Caught in an ethnic quandary: Indo-Caribbean Hindus in London.' In Ballard, ed., *Desh pardesh*, pp. 272–90.

Vinayapatrikā of Tulsīdās. See Allchin (1966).

Viramma, Josiane Racine and Jean-Luc Racine (1997). *Viramma: life of an untouchable*. Originally published as *Une vie paria: le rire des asservis, Inde du Sud* (1995). Translated from the French by Will Hobson. London: Verso.

Viṣnudharmottara. *Viṣṇudharmottara-purāṇe tṛtīya-khaṇḍaḥ*, ed. Priyabala Shah. Gaekwad's Oriental Series, general ed. B. J. Sandesara, 130. Baroda: Oriental Institute, 1958.

Vogel, Jean Philippe (1926). *Indian serpent-lore, or The nāgas in Hindu legend and art*. London: Arthur Probsthain.

Vogel, Jean Philippe (1962). *The goose in Indian literature and art*. Memoirs of the Kern Institute, no. 2. Leiden: E. J. Brill.

Voice of Dalit International (2000). *Dalits in the new millennium: report of the proceedings of [the first] international conference on dalit human rights, 16–17 September 2000*. London: Vod International.

Voice of Dalit International Newsletter, 1, January 2001; 2, December 2001; 3, February 2002; and 4, in press.

von Führer-Haimendorf, Christoph (1982). *Tribes of India: the struggle for survival*. With contributions by Michael Yorke and Jayaprakash Rao. Berkeley: University of California Press.

von Glasenapp, Helmuth (1954). 'Die Yoga-Lehren des Vāsishtha.' *Schopenhauer-Jahrbuch*, 35, 1953–54, 34–43.

von Stietencron, Heinrich (1983). 'Die Göttin Durgā Mahiṣāsuramardinī: Mythos, Darstellung und geschichtliche Rolle bei der Hinduisierung Indiens.' *Visible Religion*, 2, 118–66.

Vyas, Lallan Prasad, ed. (1992). *Ramayana: its universal appeal and global role*. Delhi: Har-Anand Publications.

Vyas, N. N., and R. S. Mann, eds (1980). *Indian tribes in transition*. Delhi: Rawat Publications.

Warrier, Shrikala (1994). 'Gujarati Prajapatis in London: family roles and sociability networks.' In Ballard, ed., *Desh pardesh*, pp. 191–212.

Watson, James, ed. (1977). *Between two cultures: migrants and minorities in Britain*. Oxford: Basil Blackwell.

Weber, Albrecht (1858). 'Das Vâjasaneyi-Prâtiçâkhyam.' *Indische Studien: Beiträge für die Kunde des indischen Alterthums*, 4, 65–171.

Weber, Max (1958). *The religion of India: the sociology of Hinduism and Buddhism*, translated from the German and edited by Hans H. Gerth and Don Martindale. New York: The Free Press.

Wezler, Albrecht (1979). 'Śamīka und Śṛṅgin: zum Verständnis einer askesekritischen Erzählung aus dem Mahābhārata.' *Wiener Zeitschrift für die Kunde Südasiens*, 23, 29–60.

White, David Gordon (1991). *Myths of the dog-man*. Chicago and London: University of Chicago Press.

Whitney, William D., ed., tr. (1871). *The Tâittirîya-Prâtiçâkhya, with its commentary, the Tribhâshyaratna: text, translation, and notes. Journal of the American Oriental Society*, 9, 1–469.

Wilhelm, Friedrich (1991). 'Hunting and the concept of *dharma*.' In Julia Leslie, ed., *Rules and remedies in classical Indian law*, pp. 7–16. Panels of the VIIth World Sanskrit Conference (1987), general ed. Johannes Bronkhorst, 9. Leiden: E. J. Brill.

Williams, Joanna (1996). *The two-headed deer: illustrations of the Rāmāyaṇa in Orissa*. Berkeley: University of California Press.

Wilson, Horace Hayman (1961). *The Vishńu Puráńa: a system of Hindu mythology and tradition, translated from the original Sanskrit and illustrated by notes derived chiefly from other Purāṇas*, third edition. Reprint, Calcutta: Punthi Pustak, 1972.

Wilson, Horace Hayman, V. Raghavan, K. R. Pisharoti and Amulya Charan Vidyabhusan (1955). *The theatre of the Hindus*. Calcutta: Susil Gupta Limited. Contains material from *Select specimens of the theatre of the Hindus* (first published 1827).

Witzel, Michael (1987). 'On the origin of the literary device of the "frame story" in old Indian literature.' In Harry Falk, ed., *Hinduismus und Buddhismus: Festschrift für Ulrich Schneider*, pp. 380–414. Freiburg: Hedwig Falk.

Wujastyk, Dominik (1984). 'The spikes in the ears of the ascetic: an illustrated tale in Buddhism and Jainism.' *Oriental Art (n. s.)*, 30 (2), 189–94.

Wujastyk, Dominik (2001). *The roots of āyurveda*, second edition. Delhi: Penguin Books India.

www.dalitstan.org/journal/buddhism.

www.indiatogether.org/dalit.

www.indology.org.uk. This website includes the archives of the Indology discussion list (currently, *indology@liverpool.ac.uk*), founded in 1990.

www.indologie.uni-halle.de/forschung/Moksopaya. See Mokṣopāya Project.

www.positivenegatives.co.uk. See Dixie (2001).

www.radioauthority.org.uk. See *Radio Authority* (2000, 2001b).

Yardi, M. R. (1994). *The Rāmāyaṇa, its origin and growth: a statistical study.* Bhandarkar Oriental Series, 26. Poona: Bhandarkar Oriental Research Institute.

Yogavāsiṣṭha. Ādikavi-śrīvālmīkimunipraṇītam yogavāsiṣṭhamahārāmāyaṇam hindīvyākhyopetam, Sanskrit text with Hindi commenatry, 2 vols, ed. Thakur Prasad Dwivedi. Delhi: Chaukhamba Sanskrit Pratishthan, 1988.

Yokochi, Yuko (1999). Mahiṣāsuramardinī myth and icon: studies in the *Skandapurāṇa*, II.' *Studies in the History of Indian Thought (Indo-Shisōshi Kenkyū)*, Journal of the Department of Indian Philosophy, Kyoto University, 11, May, 65–103.

Yokochi, Yuko (2000). 'The story of the seven brahmans in the *Harivaṃśa*: studies in the *Skandapurāṇa*, IV.' In Tsuchida and Wezler, eds, *Harānandalaharī*, pp. 525–52.

Youngson, J. W. (1906). 'The Chuhras.' *Indian Antiquary: A Journal of Oriental Research*, 35, March, 82–96; November, 302–10; December, 337–56.

Youngson, J. W. (1907). 'The Chuhras.' *Indian Antiquary: A Journal of Oriental Research*, 36, January, 19–31; March, 71–83; April, 106–16; May, 135–48.

Zaehner, R. C., tr. (1969). *The Bhagavad-Gītā, with a commentary based on the original sources.* Reprint, Oxford: Oxford University Press, 1972.

Zelliot, Eleanor (1996). *From Untouchable to Dalit: essays on the Ambedkar movement*, second revised edition. Delhi: Manohar.

Zelliot, Eleanor, and Maxine Berntsen, eds (1988). *The experience of Hinduism: essays on religion in Maharashtra.* Reprint, Delhi: Sri Satguru Publications, 1992.

Zene, Cosimo (2000). '"We too are humans (*Amrao je manus*)!": the Rishis' struggle for a "religious/human" identity.' SOAS Working Papers in the Study of Religions (December), pp. 69–97. London: The School of Oriental and African Studies, University of London.

Zene, Cosimo (2002). *The Rishi of Bangladesh: a history of Christian dialogues.* London: RoutledgeCurzon.

Zinkin, Taya (1962). *Caste today.* Institute of Race Relations, London: Oxford University Press.

Zvelebil, Kamil V. (1975). *Tamil literature.* Handbuch der Orientalistik, II.II.1. Leiden and Köln: E. J. Brill.

Zvelebil, Kamil V., tr. (1987). *Two Tamil folktales.* UNESCO Collection of Representative Works, Indian Series. Delhi: Motilal Banarsidass.

Zvelebil, Kamil V. (1988). 'Rāvaṇa the great in modern Tamil fiction.' *Journal of the Royal Asiatic Society*, pp. 126–34.

Index